Ethnicity, Pluralism, and

the State in the Middle East

15.95
70   604

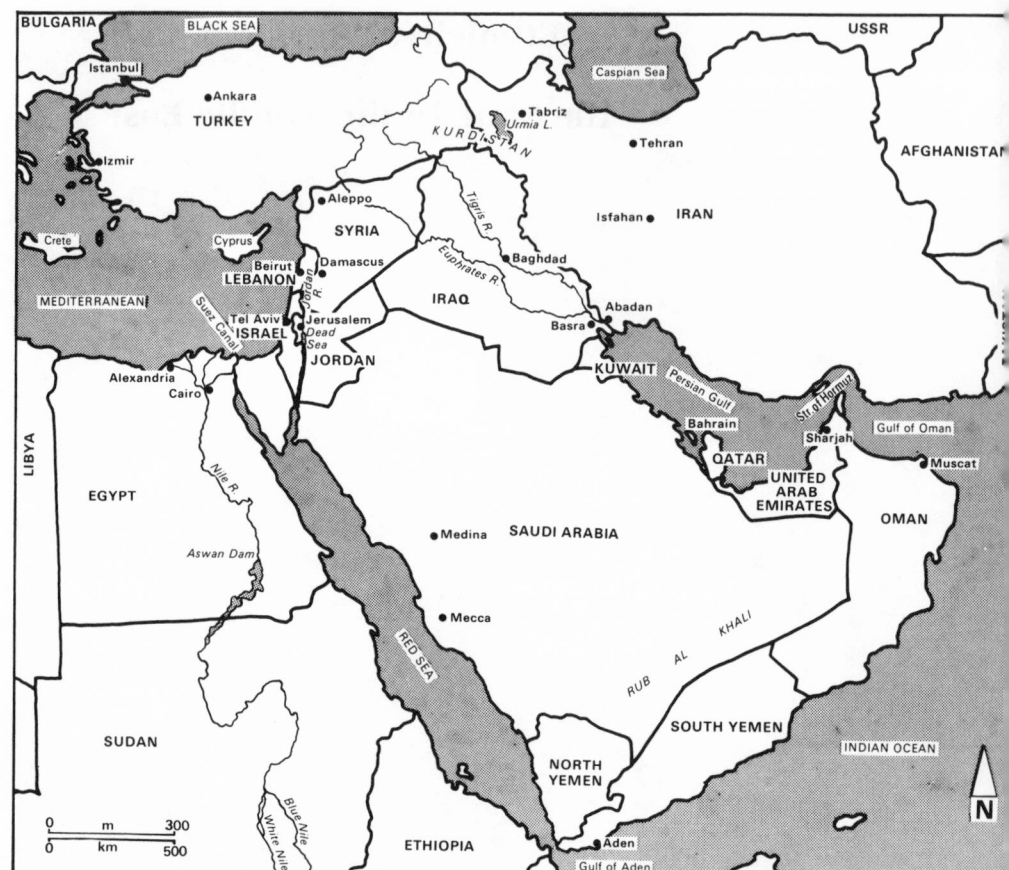

Political map of the Middle East. From *Maps on File* (0.008). Copyright © 1986 by Martin Greenwald Associates. Reprinted with permission of Facts On File, Inc., New York.

Ethnicity, Pluralism, and the State in the Middle East

EDITED BY

MILTON J. ESMAN AND

ITAMAR RABINOVICH

Published in Cooperation with the Dayan Center for
Middle Eastern and African Studies at Tel Aviv University

CORNELL UNIVERSITY PRESS

Ithaca and London

First published 1988 by Cornell University Press.
First printing, Cornell Paperbacks, 1988.
Second printing 1991.

International Standard Book Number (cloth) 0-8014-2001-6
International Standard Book Number (paper) 0-8014-9502-4
Library of Congress Catalog Card Number 87-47866
Printed in the United States of America
Librarians: Library of Congress cataloging information
appears on the last page of the book.

Contents

Preface

This volume is the product of several forms of academic cooperation. It originated in discussions between a social scientist and a student of Middle Eastern history on the merits and deficiencies of their respective disciplines and on the prospective benefits of a joint effort to examine so critical an issue as ethnicity from both a regional and a comparative perspective. The discussions led to the convening of a conference, at Tel Aviv University in May 1984, at which historians, political scientists, sociologists, and anthropologists addressed the ethnopolitics of the Middle East from a variety of vantage points. Their contributions constitute this volume. The conference can also be seen as part of what has now become a tradition of cooperation in the area of Middle Eastern studies between Cornell University and Tel Aviv University. From this point of view, it is most appropriate that the volume is published by Cornell University Press.

The structure of the book reflects the original point of departure as mitigated by reality. Part I ("Nationalism and Ethnicity") and the Conclusion, and to an extent some of the case studies, seek to provide comparative and methodological dimensions. Part II ("Legacies of the Past") examines the historical roots of the structures and ideas that shape the current ethnopolitics of the Middle East. The other four parts contain clusters of case studies that illustrate the diversity of the region as well as the complex interactions between the ethnic factor and other determinants of social and political behavior.

It is our pleasant duty to thank all those who made this project possible: The Bronfman Program for the Study of Arab-Jewish Relations, The Walter and Elise Haas Fund, The Barclay Trust, and the USIA Office at the American Embassy in Tel Aviv. We are both grateful to our respective institutions,

Tel Aviv University's Dayan Center for Middle Eastern and African Studies and the Government Department at Cornell University. The Fulbright Program made it possible for Professor Esman to spend the academic year 1983–84 with the Political Science Department of the Hebrew University of Jerusalem. At the Dayan Center, Amira Margalith, Edna Liftman, and Lydia Gareh were particularly helpful in organizing the 1984 conference and putting together the manuscript and typing it. We are grateful to Michael Busch and Arline Blaker at Cornell for their skillful assistance with the manuscript.

MILTON J. ESMAN
ITAMAR RABINOVICH

Ithaca, New York, and
Tel Aviv, Israel

PART I

NATIONALISM AND ETHNICITY

1

The Study of Ethnic Politics in the Middle East

Milton J. Esman and Itamar Rabinovich

In any particular place, ethnic groups may be majorities or minorities, dominant or subordinate, and their membership may overlap the boundaries of territorial states. Some may be long-standing inhabitants of their territory, others may be recent immigrants. Most ethnic groups are not monolithic. They are divided internally, and some of these divisions may have an ethnic quality. They are bound together by a sense of peoplehood or shared destiny, which is frequently reinforced by external pressures from hostile neighbors or from governments. For the purpose of this book, we define ethnicity in its broadest meaning—collective identity and solidarity based on such ascriptive factors as imputed common descent, language, customs, belief systems and practices (religion), and in some cases race or color.

The institutional framework for the promotion and defense of ethnic group interests in the Middle East, as elsewhere in the modern world, is the territorial state. In the contemporary Middle East—from Iran in the east through Turkey, the Fertile Crescent, and the Arabian Peninsula, to Egypt in the west and the Sudan in the south—there are now more than twenty states that claim exclusive sovereignty over all their inhabitants. The modern state in the Middle East has unprecedented power and control of resources, especially when compared with the weak polities of the immediate postindependence period. Middle Eastern societies, however, are quite pluralistic, several ethnic groups coexisting within the boundaries of a single state. Conditions that give rise to ethnic politics are (1) control by the modern state of political and economic resources that are vital to the security and well-being of its inhabitants and (2) tensions between the pluralism of society and the claims of the state to regulate the lives of all who live

3

within its territorial boundaries. Though external influences may at times be significant, the arena for ethnic conflict—for the political expression of ascriptive pluralism—is the modern state.

This has not always been the case. Except for Iran and the southern Sudan, the Middle East was ruled for four centuries or more by the Ottoman Empire until World War I. Though the Ottoman Turks were the hegemonic people and Sunni Islam was the state religion, ethnic communities were tolerated and even protected as long as they complied with the authority of the state. It was the successors to the fragmented Ottoman polity who adopted the European model of the sovereign state and the European ideology of nationalism—that the state should be the homeland and incorporate the aspirations of a single people or nation. This was the threat to minorities, and in some cases to majorities, that exacerbated tensions among the various ethnic communities in the Middle East and between those communities and the new states.

Ethnic pluralism has been an important dimension of politics in the Middle East during most of the twentieth century. While it has not been entirely neglected by scholars who specialize in Middle Eastern affairs, it has not benefited from scholarly attention in proportion to its importance. In other words, ethnic conflict can explain more of politics in the Middle East than is reflected in academic writing. We shall attempt to account for this neglect later in this chapter, but here we briefly state that we believe we can attribute it to two factors. The first factor is the intellectual positions of American and European scholars, committed as many have been to modernization and Marxist paradigms, both of which denigrate the importance of ethnic solidarity as an explanation for social behavior. The second factor is that scholars of Middle Eastern origin are not inclined to attach importance to a phenomenon they consider "backward," one that might also imply unwelcome disunity in their societies.

The chapters in this volume were originally commissioned for an international symposium at the Dayan Center at Tel Aviv University in May 1984. The purpose of the symposium was to promote the more systematic treatment of ethnic politics in scholarship on the Middle East by bringing together the knowledge in depth of Middle East specialists and the more theoretical concerns of social scientists. The comparativists and social scientists who aspire to general explanations would be required to confront the concrete realities and complexities of Middle Eastern societies and governments, while area specialists would be encouraged to reach out for more powerful explanations from concepts and propositions that have been developed and refined, for the most part, in other world areas. Theory might illuminate the experiences of the Middle East, while data from the region could test and enrich general propositions. To enhance this creative tension, we commissioned theory-based essays by Milton J. Esman and Elie Kedourie;

papers providing region-wide perspectives by Kermal Karpat, P. J. Vatikiotis, and Gabriel Ben-Dor; a set of essays dealing with Israel and the Palestinians by Hanna Herzog, Elie Rekhess, and Aziz Haidar; two papers by David Menashri and Farhad Kazemi on Iran; another set on Syria and Lebanon by Kais Firro, Theodor Hanf, and Itamar Rabinovich; and case studies on the Sudan and the Kurds by Haim Shaked and Yehudit Ronen, and by Charles G. MacDonald, respectively. We believe these essays are a fair reflection of the current state of scholarship on this subject.

To introduce the reader to this set of essays, we believe it would be useful to review two streams of scholarship that are relevant to the eventual integration of area specialization and theory-based social science as they relate to the ethnic dimension of Middle East politics. The first is the treatment of ethnic politics in previous scholarship; the second is an outline of major themes that have informed the theoretical treatment of ethnic politics—themes that may have explanatory relevance for the Middle East.

The Ethnic Factor in Middle Eastern Politics: An Overview

In tracing the profound changes that have taken place in the ethnic politics of the Middle East and in the literature on this subject during the past sixty years, it may be useful first to distinguish between four principal phases.

Phase One. World War I brought about the end of a traditional order. During the four previous centuries, most of the region was ruled by the Ottoman Empire. The Ottomans drew on both Islamic and Byzantine legacies in order to develop the *millet* system, described and analyzed in Kamal Karpat's chapter. The *millet* system was the chief mechanism for regulating the relationship between the Ottoman state and the diverse groups that constituted its governed majority. The Ottoman Empire was a Muslim state, successor to the tradition of the great Muslim empires, and membership in its ruling class was open to Sunni Muslims who possessed the "Ottoman way"—its Ottoman-Turkish culture. The large non-Muslim groups—Greek Orthodox and Armenian Christians, as well as Jews—were organized in formal *millet*s. These offered a considerable degree of autonomy, which compensated for the absence of political rights and equal status. Other groups, such as heterodox Muslims, were not formally recognized as *millet*s but in practice lived under similar conditions.

In this polity, informed by religious affiliation and solidarity, ethnic identity played a marginal role. Well into the nineteenth century, the terms "Arab" and "Turk" designated in most cases nomads—Bedouin or Turkoman—in contrast with the sedentary population. It was only then, and even more so during the decade preceding World War I, that ethnic solidarity and differences became an important factor in the political life of the Ottoman Empire, and nationalism, or at least proto-nationalism—Turkish, Arab, and across the border, Iranian—appeared on the scene. But until the dismemberment of the empire (and in some cases not even then) most Arabs continued to view the Ottoman Sultan as their legitimate Muslim ruler.

It is difficult to point to a linear, let alone uniform, progression in the Middle East from a "traditional" political community predicated on religion to "modern" communities based on nationalism. This becomes apparent when the nineteenth-century antecedents of Arab nationalism, the dominant political creed in the post–World War I Middle East, are examined. A secular streak and an Arab "ethnic" resentment of Turkish preeminence can be discerned among the early proponents of Arab nationalism, but soon thereafter Arab nationalism acquired a distinct Sunni Muslim quality.

Furthermore, close examination of the particular evolution of the region's different parts reveals a confounding variety. In Egypt, Egyptian nationalism after 1882 developed to a considerable degree as a reaction to British occupation and consequently had strong Muslim and pro-Ottoman components. In the Lebanese Emirate, religion had played a relatively minor role in the political institutions of earlier centuries, and Muslim-Christian animosity became an important factor only in the middle of the nineteenth century. Then the violence and bloodshed of the years 1840–1860 led different Lebanese to seek a solution in radically different ways—Christian-Lebanese nationalism, secular Arab or Syrian nationalism, and Ottoman pluralism. Several of the important ideological trends in the twentieth-century Arab world can be traced back to that period.

Phase Two. In the interwar period the destruction of the Ottoman Empire and the settlement made by the victorious Powers laid the foundations of a new state system in the region, which is described in Gabriel Ben-Dor's chapter. At an early stage, Turkey and Iran appeared to be on their way to becoming nation-states, though later events were to show how difficult it was to fashion Turkish or Iranian territorial nationalisms, free from Islam, and how significant the minority problems were in both countries.

In the Arab world, Egypt is closest to the West European model of a nation-state, but in the interwar period it too went through a process that has been aptly defined as a "search of political community." Was Egypt a nation unto itself with pre-Islamic roots and a Mediterranean "face," or was it part of the Arab and Muslim worlds? This was not the crux of the issue, but the answer to this question was to have important ramifications for the positions of the relatively small but significant Coptic minority in the Egyptian state.

The equivalent developments in the Fertile Crescent were far more complex. Unlike the well-defined Egyptian entity, the new states of the Fertile Crescent, while anchored in some historical tradition, were carved up by the British and the French rather arbitrarily. The final borders of the new states in the Fertile Crescent, as well as the relationship between geographic entity, state, and political community, had to be defined and settled.

For a number of reasons, problems of ethnicity played a crucial and prominent role in this process. The population of these new states was fragmented and divided. The sway held by the doctrine of Arab nationalism pitted the Arab Sunni establishment against the other communities, and the policies of Great Britain and France, by design or unintended consequences, tended to exacerbate intercommunal relations.

These problems can be stated in terms that apply to the whole region. They can also be seen in their specificity—the development of the confessional system in Lebanon, the Arab-Jewish national conflict in Palestine, the Shi'ite and Kurdish problems in Iraq, and the relationship between the Arab Sunni majority and the various minorities in Syria.

Phase Three. In the late 1940s a new phase began in which there was a decline in the relative importance of ethnic issues and conflict. The British and French departed, most of the states in the region became independent, and a territorial status quo was consolidated.

In Turkey and Iran, conflicts over the direction of public and political life continued, but the patterns established in the 1920s were not seriously challenged. Minority problems, which had been highlighted by the circumstances of World War II—Soviet encouragement of Azeri and Kurdish separatism in Iran, and the pressure exerted on non-Muslims and on the large Kurdish minority in Turkey—resumed their normal place as one of the many issues that made up the political complexion of the two countries.

In this respect, the situation in the Arab part of the Middle East in the 1950s and 1960s was quite similar. That was a period of intense conflicts and radical and profound changes. Ethnic issues provided part of the political spectrum—the Kurdish rebellion in Iraq, the Lebanese civil war of 1958, southern secessionism in the Sudan, the elimination of the vestiges of Druze and Alawi autonomy in Syria—but their relative importance declined, and they were overshadowed by the greater issues of the day: the Soviet-American rivalry, the political, social, and economic revolutions in several Arab countries, the quest for unity, and the conflict with Israel.

Furthermore, Arab nationalism in its Nasserite and Ba'thi versions appeared to be dominant. Egypt's conversion to Arabism, and the Arabian Peninsula's fuller participation in the region's politics, seemed to have dwarfed the minority problems of the Fertile Crescent that had loomed much larger in the smaller Arab world of earlier decades.

Phase Four. In the 1970s, the perspective changed once again as problems of ethnicity acquired new importance and saliency and came to affect almost all the states in the region. In some cases the problem was at the very core of a country's political life—for example, the collapse of the confessional system in Lebanon, the Sunni revolt against Alawi domination in Syria, Jewish-Arab relations and Sephardi-Ashkenazi tensions in Israel, the relationship between East Bankers and Palestinians in Jordan, and the challenge to Arab-Sunni ascendancy in Iraq. In other cases—tensions between Copts and Muslims in Egypt, Alawi discontent in Turkey, fear of Shi'ite and Iranian effervescence in the Arabian Peninsula—ethnic issues remained marginal to the core problem of these states.

These changes derived from diverse sources. Some were regional in nature (the revived political role of religion—most importantly Islam—and the related decline of overlapping or competing ideologies, such as pan-Arab nationalism and socialism). Others were specific to a country or a subregion, such as the evolution of the Israeli-Palestinian conflict after 1967, the erosion of the foundations of the Lebanese state, and the extraordinary process that brought members of the Alawi minority to power in Syria.

The role of the ethnic factor in Middle Eastern politics during the past decade or so should also be seen in the context of the dichotomy between formal continuity and underlying unrest that has characterized most states in the region in this period. As a rule, the weak regimes of the 1950s and 1960s were replaced by more powerful regimes that have survived challenges and crises through coercion and dexterity. (Lebanon and the Shah's Iran are the two obvious exceptions.) This has enabled minority groups in Syria and Iraq to use the state for their purposes and to stifle the discontent of the majority. In other countries, minority groups encountered state power that had been conspicuously absent twenty years earlier.

The Ethnic Dimension in Middle Eastern Scholarship

Serious systematic study of the ethnopolitics of the Middle East (the term itself is anachronistic) began in the aftermath of World War II as part of a larger effort to build a scholarly academic approach to the study of contemporary social and political developments in the region. An impressive body of academic literature had been published earlier—dealing with individual communities, sects, and minorities, with Islam's attitude to members and other religions, and with other related topics—but this literature did not necessarily have a contemporary focus, nor did it as a rule address the problem from a regional perspective.

The new focus and perspective became apparent with the publication of such works as Albert Hourani's *Minorities in the Arab World*[1] and his later essays entitled "Race, Religion, and Nation-State in the Near East" and "The Regulative Principle." Several of Elie Kedourie's essays, such as "Minorities" and "Religion and Politics," or J. C. Hurewitz's chapter entitled "The Minorities in the Political Process" in S. V. Fisher's *Social Forces in the Middle East*,[2] and Gabriel Baer's chapter "Religious and Ethnic Communities" in his *Population and Society in the Arab East*,[3] provided fresh, authoritative data on communities, sects, and minorities in the Arab world and placed the issue in its broader social context. Bernard Lewis's *The Middle East and the West*[4] did not address the issue of ethnicity as such, but it did illuminate such pertinent issues as the relationship between religion and politics or the concept of nationhood. The Turkish, Iranian, and Jewish components were also brought into the picture.

It is a curious and significant fact that the first major efforts of American social scientists to apply their discipline to the study of Middle Eastern politics failed to recognize the central role of ethnicity. This is true of Daniel Lerner's *Passing of Traditional Society*,[5] Manfred Halpern's *Politics of Social Change in the Middle East and North Africa*,[6] and even of Carleton Coon's perceptive anthropological study, *Caravan: The Story of the Middle East*.[7] The chapter entitled "Social Groups: Economic, Religious, and National" in Morroe Berger's sociological survey *The Arab World Today*[8] is a brief exception to this rule.

Several factors seem to account for this difference between the historians and the social scientists. The latter tended to view the region through conceptual lenses—modernization, empathy, the rise of a new middle class—which, while affirming important new insights, served to conceal part of the social and political reality. Some social scientists, working through questionnaires and research assistants, lost or failed to acquire contact with that reality. They were influenced in part by the apparent decline—referred to above—of the ethnic factor in the 1950s. They may also have been influenced by the manifest reluctance of Middle Easterners, particularly intellectuals, to admit the lingering importance of traditional (not to say archaic) loyalties that modernity should have swept aside. To date, there appears to be a tendency among Middle Easterners to view any study of cleavages in their society as a hostile attempt to foster division and combat integration and unity.

[1] London: Oxford University Press, 1947.
[2] Ithaca, N.Y.: Cornell University Press, 1955.
[3] New York: Praeger, 1964.
[4] Bloomington: Indiana University Press, 1964.
[5] Glencoe, Ill.: Free Press, 1958.
[6] Princeton: Princeton University Press, 1963.
[7] New York: Holt, 1958.
[8] Garden City, N.Y.: Doubleday, 1962.

The dichotomy between historians and social scientists faded gradually in the 1960s and 1970s as works published by social scientists tended increasingly to address the region's social and political realities more squarely. The change seems to have come under the combined impact of intellectual developments within the pertinent fields of study and actual developments in the Arab world itself. For a student of Syrian and Iraqi politics of the middle and late 1960s, it was clearly easier to recognize the importance of ethnicity than it had been a decade earlier.

Leonard Binder's *Ideological Revolution in the Middle East*[9] is a good starting point. It is a work by a prominent social scientist in which the role of religion and confessionalism is recognized and analyzed astutely, as are the relationships between the state and the political community. Two years later, Binder published an edited volume, *Politics in Lebanon*,[10] which drew on the proceedings of an international conference held in Chicago. From our vantage point, that book is important because it places the study of Lebanon's confessional system within the mainstream of Middle East studies. Previously, it had been difficult to avoid the feeling that there was something archaic, quaint, and slightly amusing about Lebanon and its communities that separated them from the main course of events in the rest of the region.[11]

This shift was reinforced in the late 1960s and still more in the 1970s by a body of literature that brought out the importance of ethnopolitics in the rest of the Fertile Crescent by unearthing the social basis of Syrian, Iraqi, and Palestinian politics. Nor was Israel an exception. The exacerbation of Jewish-Arab and Sephardi-Ashkenazi tensions in Israeli society generated academic interest and writing in which some fundamental assumptions of Israeli sociology were questioned (see the chapter in this volume by Hanna Herzog).

By the late 1970s—following the Lebanese civil war, the Sunni revolt against the Alawis in Syria, and the conspicuous Shi'ite-Sunni and Muslim-Christian tensions in the region—further changes in scholarly writing on the ethnopolitics of the Middle East became apparent. The literature became more voluminous. In addition to a large number of essays and papers, edited volumes seeking to replace Hourani's long-outdated book appeared. R. D. McLaurin's *Political Role of Minority Groups in the Middle East*[12] is representative of this trend.

Still more important is the recognition extended to the ethnic dimension

---

[9]New York: Wiley, 1964.

[10]New York: Wiley, 1966.

[11]See the comments by William Zartman, "Political Science," in *The Study of the Middle East*, ed. L. Binder (New York: Wiley, 1973), esp. pp. 271–276.

[12]New York: Praeger, 1979.

in general works on the region. Occasionally an interpretation was still offered in which the ethnic factor had almost no role to play,[13] but this was not a mainstream approach. The change that took place in the 1970s is clearly manifested through two textbooks on Middle Eastern politics. In 1974 James Bill and Carl Leiden first published a popular text, *The Middle East: Politics and Power*,[14] in which ethnicity is assigned a minor role. Michael Hudson's *Arab Politics: The Quest for Legitimacy*,[15] which appeared a few years later, has an entirely different focus. The difference can be explained in part by the different perspectives acquired in previous works on Iran and on the Fertile Crescent, but it seems also to reflect the political developments of the 1970s.

Recognition of the ethnic factor was followed by recognition first of the phenomenon and then of its complexity and nuances. In Hudson's *Arab Politics*, the ethnic dimension does not provide the cutting edge of the analysis of Syrian or Iraqi politics. A similar tendency can be noticed in Hanna Batatu's *Old Social Classes and the Revolutionary Movements in Iraq*.[16] Despite its title, the book's scope extends well beyond Iraqi politics— it is full of intriguing information about the ethnic composition of Iraqi and other political parties. But in the final analysis it is social class, and not ethnic community, which Batatu sees as the important determinant. In this respect, his interpretation of Iraqi modern history and politics is markedly different from the interpretations offered by Elie Kedourie (in his essay "The Kingdom of Iraq: A Retrospect") and Abbas Kelidar (in his book *The Integration of Modern Iraq*[17] and in his essays "Religion and Politics in Syria" and "The Shi'i Imami Community and Politics in the Arab East"). It should, from a different perspective, be juxtaposed also with that of Fouad Ajami, who in *The Arab Predicament*[18] and other works introduces his readers to the powerful emotional dimension of ethnic affiliation and alienation in the Arab world. It should, however, be added that Batatu's work on Syrian politics, mentioned below in the essay on Arab ideological parties, does ascribe a significant role to sectarian solidarity and rivalry.

---

[13]See Malcolm H. Kerr and El-Sayed Yassin, eds., *Rich and Poor Nations in the Middle East* (Boulder, Colo.: Westview, 1982), esp. the essay in that volume by Egyptian sociologist Saad Eddin Ibrahim, "Oil, Migration and the New Arab Social Order." The same applies to Ibrahim's *Al-Nizam al-Arabi al-Ijtima'i al-Jadid* (New Arab social order) (Beirut, 1982). In both it is the stimulating and dislocating impact of huge oil revenues that is to be the prime shaper of the social and political organization of the Arab world. The oil-producing states and Egypt are portrayed as the two chief poles of Arab life, and the Fertile Crescent and its peculiar problems are relegated to a secondary place.

[14]Boston: Allyn & Bacon, 1974.

[15]New Haven: Yale University Press, 1977.

[16]Princeton: Princeton University Press, 1978.

[17]New York: St. Martin's, 1979.

[18]New York: Cambridge University Press, 1981.

Concepts and Issues in Ethnic Politics

At the present state of the art, there is no unified theory that empirical investigation can use as a guide. Instead there is a variety of often competing perspectives and partial theories that purport to explain the genesis and the dynamics of contemporary ethnic conflict.[19] On some of the basics, however, most scholars are in agreement: that ethnic and religious conflict is primarily a political problem, that the relevant contemporary context is the territorial state, and that what is to be explained are the relationships and terms of coexistence among two or more ascriptive solidarity groups, and between them and the agencies of the state. At stake are such fundamental values as relative power, wealth, security, and status.

At the outset, one might expect that certain features of Middle Eastern pluralism would be especially significant. These include the relative weakness of the state in relation to the societies over which they claim jurisdiction, the limited legitimacy these states enjoy among significant minorities, the tight boundaries, deep cleavages, and often intense hostilities among the component communities, and the high levels of coercive control that characterize conflict regulation. This suggests that, for the Middle East, models of society and politics whose point of departure is conflict rather than integration are likely to have greater explanatory value.[20] We now move directly to the elements of theory.

Primordialism vs. Instrumentalism

One of the more intriguing controversies in current theoretical debate is between the "primordialists" and the "instrumentalists."[21] The primordialists argue that ethnic and religious solidarities are deeply rooted in historical experience and in the socialization of individuals. The cultures, and the social structures they encompass and the loyalties they evoke, should therefore be regarded as stable continuing realities. So profound are the sentiments of peoplehood, so securely are identities and loyalties transferred between generations, that even when they appear to subside they can readily be reignited. To the primordialists, communal solidarities represent his-

---

[19]For a good summary and evaluation of the state of theory on this subject, see Joseph Rothschild, *Ethnopolitics: A Conceptual Framework* (New York: Columbia University Press, 1981).

[20]On the difference between the integrationist and conflict approaches to ethnic pluralism, see R. A. Schermerhorn, *Comparative Ethnic Relations* (New York: Random House, 1970).

[21]This debate is summarized by James McKay, "An Exploratory Synthesis of Primordial and Mobilizational Approaches to Ethnic Phenomena," *Ethnic and Race Relations* 5 (October 1982): 395–420.

torical continuity and should be considered objective "givens" for purposes of social and political analysis.

The instrumentalists, on the other hand, emphasize the adaptive and opportunistic quality of communal identities and solidarities. Not only can their boundaries and even their designations be modified as circumstances require, but the very content of their culture can be adapted to environmental pressures. Outsiders can be incorporated, and insiders may pass out of the community. Ethnic solidarities can be adjusted to meet the material, security, and status needs of their members. When other collective identities (e.g., class, occupation) better serve practical needs, ethnic solidarity may atrophy or disappear.[22] To the more extreme instrumentalists, ethnic and confessional solidarities survive only as long as they pay—as long as they provide more security, status, and material rewards than do available alternatives. Some argue that Jewish solidarity survived in the Middle Ages because the occupational specialization of the Jews yielded higher incomes than would have been available had they chosen to assimilate, as many in fact did.[23]

What does evidence from the Middle East suggest about this controversy? Are the solidarities of ascriptive groups likely to be eroded by economic and status opportunities for individual advancement outside the group? Are such opportunities for passing likely to be available in the Middle East? Or do communal loyalties and solidarities persist independently and in defiance of such opportunities? Do groups successfully maintain their boundaries, membership, and social control even when their cultural markers, such as language, must be sacrificed?[24] Are there differences in the staying power of ethnic and of religious communities? Does the combination of ethnic and religious distinctiveness (Jews, Greeks) provide especially powerful and persistent primordial solidarity?

Integration vs. Conflict Models

How can pluralism most usefully be conceptualized and analyzed? As an inherently conflictual relationship, characterized by the competitive struggle for power, prestige, and material resources, in which order is maintained by coercive domination? Or as patterns of interdependence

[22]On the variety of choices among collective identities, see *The Mobilization of Collective Identities: Comparative Perspectives*, ed. J. Ross (Washington, D.C.: University Press of America, 1981), chap. 1, pp. 1–30.

[23]Orlando Patterson, *Ethnic Chauvinism: The Reactionary Impulse* (New York: Stein & Day, 1977).

[24]On boundary maintenance, see Fredrik Barth, ed., *Ethnic Groups and Boundaries* (Boston: Little, Brown, 1969).

sustained in large measure by consensus, each group making its contribution to the maintenance of the system and deriving significant if not
equivalent benefits? Which general model is more useful may depend on
whether the analyst is a functionalist—emphasizing value consensus, in-
terdependency, and system maintenance—or a structuralist, emphasizing
struggle, conflict, and hierarchy. Most functionalists agree that, up to a
certain point, conflict is useful for system maintenance, or actually fosters
integration. Conflict theorists concede that some cooperation and interdependence are essential to the functioning of any society and polity, even if
it is based on domination and oppression.[25] Are the ethnically and confes-
sionally divided societies in the Middle East held together primarily by
coercion or primarily by consensus? What is their relative weight?

Do national, sectarian, and racial solidarities represent differences in
kind, or only in the degree of pluralism? Can the same models be used to
analyze and explain differences among Ashkenazic and Sephardic Jews as
between Jews and Arabs in Israel? Or does the choice depend on how the
parties themselves and the authoritative structures of society define their
position in the polity and their relations with one another? Are religious
solidarities likely to be especially intractable and uncompromising, and
thus to generate and sustain intense conflict? Is the cumulation of group
cleavages—ethnicity and religion, Greek-Christian, Turkish-Muslim—more
likely to provoke and sustain conflict and make integration or peaceful
coexistence more problematic than the existence of only a single line of
cleavage? If the cleavages are cross-cutting, if some Greeks and Turks were
both Muslim and Christian, would that mitigate conflict? Has the fact that
Kurds are Sunni Muslims affected the character of their relations with Sunni
Iraq and Shi'ite Iran?

The Effects of Modernization

There has been a sharp debate about the effects of modernization on
communal conflict.

Modernization theorists argue that industrialization, urbanization, and
secularization are transforming phenomena that break down traditional
loyalties and solidarities and confront the individual with new requirements
and opportunities that depend on individual achievement according to universal criteria. As people come to desire the same goals and rewards, they
become more similar.[26] Occupational and class differences become the

---

[25]See Schermerhorn, *Comparative Ethnic Relations*.

[26]For the modernization perspective on politics, see Karl Deutsch, *Nationalism and Social Communication* (Cambridge: MIT Press, 1953).

salient social differentiators, displacing traditional solidarities that lose their utility and are reduced to innocuous cultural vestiges; loyalties are transferred from parochial to more encompassing national symbols produced by powerful and irreversible nation-building processes. The individual is incorporated into the communications networks and institutions of the modern economy, society, and state. In brief, modernization erodes and eventually destroys traditional, parochial solidarities, attenuates ethnic and confessional conflict, and gradually eliminates ascriptively based pluralism. The persistence of "traditional" ethnic solidarities is an indicator of political underdevelopment traceable to the colonial legacy. This was the dominant paradigm of the 1950s and the 1960s among Western social scientists.

More recent scholarship has challenged this paradigm and made the opposite claim—that modernization intensifies communal conflict.[27] The expansion of markets and improved communications increases contact and generates competition among communal groups. As people aspire to the same social and economic rewards, competition intensifies and communal solidarities become an important—often the most important—vehicle for mutual support and promotion, especially in urban areas. The expanding role of the state invites and even requires groups to mobilize for collective action to struggle for their share of the benefits available from government and for political access, cultural rights, and economic opportunities. These tend to be allocated to individuals primarily through group membership.

The competition resulting from modernization produces both winners and losers. Groups that begin with educational, occupational, status, or political disadvantages soon convert their sense of deprivation into protest. Individuals feel discriminated against in their capacity as group members; feeling deprived as a group, they mobilize along ethnic lines for political action. Their mobilization, in turn, provokes countermobilization by advantaged ethnic groups to resist the threat to their acquired positions. The competition generated by economic development thus politicizes ethnic pluralism and makes it even more salient than in earlier periods. According to this perspective, modernization does not erode communal solidarities; it modernizes them and converts them into more-effective instruments of group defense, promotion, and combat. The individual cannot melt into an undifferentiated mass. He finds his needs for security and advancement in a competitive environment served at least in part by familiar communal associations. Politics and government become arenas of conflict between ascriptively organized political movements that, according to modernization theories, were expected to disappear.

---

[27]Robert Melson and Howard Wolpe, "Modernization and the Politics of Communalism: A Perspective," *American Political Science Review* 64 (December 1970): 1112–1130.

The Role of the Territorial State

The territorial state, which claims sovereignty over all its inhabitants and demands their political loyalty, is the institutional context in which most contemporary communal conflict occurs. Colonial regimes maintained coercive control over competitive and often hostile communal groups. When the colonial powers departed, successor regimes were usually weak, yet forced to deal with the naked reality of competitive pluralism.

Two types of state structures emerged.[28] The first were those, such as Israel and Turkey, that explicitly incorporated the aspirations of a dominant ethnic group. Nonmembers were expected to accept a different relationship to the state than members of the dominant group. They might enjoy explicit and recognized minority rights, they might be encouraged to assimilate as individuals, or they might be culturally repressed, economically subordinated, and in some cases encouraged to emigrate. Other combinations are possible, the main point being that the state is regarded as the instrument of a single ethnic group; other groups must accommodate themselves to the terms of coexistence determined by the dominant group. The state may attempt to co-opt and absorb minorities as individuals with the objective of eliminating pluralism (Turkish efforts to absorb the Kurdish minority), or it may recognize the pluralism as inevitable (the Arabs in Israel). To reduce the costs of control, the state may accord specific rights to minorities (as in southern Sudan), or it may consign them de facto or de jure to subordinate status, with inferior economic roles and limited participation in the polity. When this occurs, the state, which demands the loyalty of all its subjects, lacks legitimacy among its minorities and must rely on coercive measures of control. Is the Ottoman *millet* system, or a modernized version of it, a means by which the state can successfully appease subordinate minorities with cultural autonomy?

The alternative is a state that maintains sufficient freedom of action to avoid capture by any of its component ethnic communities. In this case, the state is not the agent of a dominant sector—as some theorists claim the state must always be—but a more or less neutral manager attempting to reconcile differences and regulate conflict. The state may be juridically and symbolically independent of its ethnic constituents, or it may incorporate them on a consociational basis, attempting at the same time to represent and to mediate among them. Scholars are not agreed on whether a consociational structure—based on such practices as elite bargaining, proportionality, mutual veto, and internal autonomy—can survive the com-

---

[28]For a good treatment of different roles for the state in postcolonial politics, see *State versus Ethnic Claims: African Policy Dilemmas*, ed. D. Rothchild and V. A. Olorunsola (Boulder, Colo.: Westview, 1983). See also Paul Brass, "Ethnic Groups and the State," in his edited volume *Ethnic Groups and the State* (New York: Barnes & Noble, 1985).

petitiveness of its components, or whether it is doomed to break down in conflict, to fragment, or to fall under the sway of one of its components.[29]

Ethnicity and Class

Marxist perspectives are currently prominent and influential among intellectuals and social scientists. This applies to the interpretation of ethnic and other ascriptive phenomena. In the Marxist Weltanschauung, class—defined as the position of the individual in the structures of economic production and control—is the main objective indicator of interests and of cleavage. Other solidarities are the vestiges of earlier historical periods or manifestations of "false consciousness" by which the ruling class attempts to mystify and split the proletariat. Marxists are likely to find that what appears to be ethnic is only the outward platonic shadow of the deeper phenomenon of class. Ethnic groups are subordinated in order to provide cheap labor, whose surplus can be appropriated by the dominant capitalist class. When workers from the dominant ethnic group refuse to support workers from subordinate ethnic groups, it is because the former have been manipulated and bought off by their own ruling class. Under socialism, antagonistic class differences (contradictions) will be eliminated, and ethnic differences will eventually be reduced to vestigial folk memories because the economic basis for ethnic conflict and for meaningful ethnic differences will have come to an end.

While some Marxist scholars have departed from these fundamentalist premises, the persistence of communal identities and solidarities remains an unresolved and perhaps insoluble dilemma for Marxist theory.[30] Eighty years ago Austrian socialists Otto Bauer and Karl Renner recognized national and cultural solidarities as permanent phenomena and attempted to reconcile cultural autonomy with socialist development. Their views were rejected by Lenin and Stalin, who were nevertheless compelled to make explicit concessions to the claims of national minorities in Imperial and Soviet Russia and to recognize most colonial and anti-imperialist national movements as "progressive" forces.[31] Marxist theory cannot, however, abandon the primacy of class or class conflict. It blames capitalism for racial and ethnic conflict, and it seeks class-based explanations for communal

---

[29]For an authoritative statement of consociational theory, see Arend Lijphart, *Democracy in Plural Societies: A Comparative Exploration* (New Haven: Yale University Press, 1978). For an anticonsociational perspective, see Alvin Rabushka and Kenneth Shepsle, *Politics in Plural Societies: A Theory of Democratic Instability* (Columbus, Ohio: Merrill, 1972).

[30]See Walker Connor, *The National Question in Marxist-Leninist Theory and Strategy* (Princeton: Princeton University Press, 1984).

[31]Joseph Stalin, *Marxism and the National Question* (1913; Moscow, 1950).

solidarities, for communal conflict, and for the communal division of labor. Thus, the main purpose of Israel's occupation of the West Bank, aside from its service to American imperialism, is to provide a reservoir of cheap labor for Israel's capitalist economy.

Non-Marxist scholars also deal with class, but not merely as an expression of capitalist exploitation. Analysts of plural societies identify some ethnically divided societies as segmented; ethnic groups coexist with parallel sets of institutions and include members of all economic classes. Other ethnically divided societies are said to be stratified—one communal group being politically and economically dominant—while other groups are subordinated in the distribution of power, status, wealth, and income. In the latter case, some ethnic groups may also be classes, "ethnoclasses," or "ethclasses"; those at the bottom are deprived both culturally and economically. There are many combinations and degrees of segmentation and stratification, usually the outcome of historical experience. Culturally based solidarities, however, are authentic realities that may exist and function independently of class relationships. Conflict among them is not necessarily the product of capitalist exploitation. Relative power determines relationships among competing communal groups. The specific configurations are empirical questions that depend on the economic, technological, organizational, and political resources they command and on their cohesion and skill in using these resources. Such conflicts have existed during all historical periods and persist within socialist societies. They cannot be explained by Marxist class categories or by the logic of capitalist exploitation.[32]

Class analysis does sensitize the observer to the importance of divisions and of politics *within* communal groups. Such groups are seldom monolithic; competitors are likely to vie for power and influence within the group. Differences may be based on class interest, but they may be intersected along ideological, kinship, or factional lines within and even across communal boundaries. The current situation in Lebanon illustrates the complexity of communal politics and the importance of recognizing cleavages within as well as among communal groups.

Mobilization

Communal groups may exist as culturally differentiated collectivities, but until they mobilize and organize to define, promote, and defend their collective interests, they cannot be politically significant. Communal groups tend to mobilize at different times—often the consequence of earlier ex-

---

[32]For a plural society perspective, see *Pluralism in Africa*, ed. L. Kuper and M. G. Smith (Berkeley: University of California Press, 1969).

posure to modern commerce or Western education. The earlier mobilizers tend to gain access to economic opportunities, cultural privileges, or political power, often at the expense of later mobilizers. Whatever the sequence, competitive mobilization and the generation of competing, irreconcilable demands on the state and on other ethnic groups often become occasions for communal conflict.[33]

What precipitates communal mobilization? The most common factor seems to be the emergence of a collective and ethnically defined sense of absolute or relative deprivation compared with the position of significant others. Other causes may be perceived threats or challenges to the established cultural, economic, or political interests of the group, or the demonstration effect of successful challenges to the status quo by other similarly situated communities. Who are the mobilizers, and what are the main sources of leadership? It appears that a necessary condition for mobilization is leadership provided by people who have sufficient education to articulate grievances and demands in language that reaches both the masses of their own community and significant outsiders. Among the latter are the governing elites, who must react to the challenges posed by fresh demands. Contemporary theory assigns a major role to intellectuals, who are acculturated at least in part to the dominant society, as the original mobilizers of communal self-awareness and as spokespersons for its grievances and demands.[34] Sources of leadership, tactics, and demands may depend on whether the mobilizing community is an immigrant group or a collectivity that can claim special, even national, status in its ancestral homeland.[35]

What of their demands? Usually they begin modestly and tend to escalate as the group gains confidence and as competitors emerge to challenge and outbid the original mobilizers. The challengers usually claim that the demands and style of the existing leadership are too modest and insufficiently militant. The dynamic quality of communal demands is a function both of competition within the group and of responses on the part of the state authorities. There are three main classes of demands: (1) demands for hegemony, control of the state on behalf of repressed majorities; (2) demands for group autonomy in the form of secession and independence, of territorial control (federalism) within the original political system, or of institutional distinctiveness (e.g., education) controlled by the group but recognized and financed, at least in part, by the state, and (3) demands for nondiscriminatory inclusion and access to economic opportunities, po-

---

[33]On the effects of different rates of mobilization, see R. S. Milne, *Politics in Ethnically Bipolar States* (Vancouver: University of British Columbia Press, 1981), pp. 83–105.

[34]On the role of the intellectuals, see Anthony D. Smith, *The Ethnic Revival in the Modern World* (New York: Cambridge University Press, 1981).

[35]Milton J. Esman, "Two Dimensions of Ethnic Politics: Defense of Homelands, Immigrant Rights," *Ethnic and Racial Studies* (July 1985): 438–440.

litical participation, or cultural status (e.g., language recognition), either on an individual basis or through some pattern of group proportionality. There are many variations and combinations of such claims—for example, institutional autonomy plus participation in government decision-making and a fair share of the state's resources and services. Intragroup conflict may revolve around the kinds of demands the group should express, who should be the group's interlocutors to outsiders, and what tactics should be pursued.

The tactics employed by ethnic groups vary from working within the rules of the political system—through negotiation, bargaining, and intergroup pressures—to the use of violence, terrorism, and revolutionary warfare. To those who employ economic models of rationality to analyze political behavior, ethnic groups will use the tactics that represent the least cost to them in security and material terms. When political channels of expression, influence, and participation are available, these will be employed; when they are not available or are unavailing, ethnic activists will resort to direct action (demonstrations, strikes) and eventually to acts of violence or civil war. The majority of scholars, however, have less confidence in models of calculating rationality to explain either the goals or the tactics of activists and their adversaries.

Cleavages within the ethnic community are likely to be exhibited when it comes to questions of tactics. Those with property or official connections are likely to counsel more patient tactics, extracting what is possible within the rules of even an inequitable system. Those with less to lose, especially students and youth, are more likely to gravitate to direct action and the use of violence and even terror. As levels of violence escalate, moderate leadership tends to be displaced by the militants; those with weapons begin to intimidate the advocates and practitioners of more moderate tactics. As the community becomes radicalized and the authorities respond to violence with violence, even moderates begin to sympathize with the terrorists (freedom-fighters)—respecting their sincerity and courage, if not their prudence, in the face of oppressive and unresponsive authorities who are presumed to be acting on behalf of the ethnic enemy.

The choices of tactics by ethnic minorities are directly conditioned by the policies and the actions of the regime. The demands of dissatisfied ethnic groups must be dealt with by the managers of the state in what can be regarded as a classical action/reaction or challenge/response process. We turn to the practices by which those who control the state attempt to manage or regulate the demands of ethnic communities.

Conflict Management

The state, as we have previously indicated, can be regarded either as the neutral manager of public affairs, as in American pluralist doctrine, or as the instrument of a dominant group, as in Marxist and structuralist paradigms. In pluralistic theory, ethnic groups, like other organized interests, have access to government to promote their demands. Governments attempt both to enforce the rules of the polity impartially and to accommodate competing demands from society. Because they enjoy access, ethnic groups are likely to use political means to impress their needs on the agencies of government; governments, in turn, emphasize measures of accommodation and expedient concessions, employing coercive measures only as a last resort.[36]

Where divisions are deep, the polity may be organized along corporatist or consociational lines, as indicated earlier. Ethnic or confessional groups are explicitly recognized as legitimate political actors and incorporated into the structures of decision-making. They may be granted considerable autonomy in the management of their separate institutions; they may have the power to veto or at least delay measures they consider detrimental to their vital interests, while access to resources and positions of influence may be governed by formulas of parity or proportionality. Before 1975, Lebanon was an example of a relatively stable and highly institutionalized consociational order.

When the state represents and acts in the interests of a hegemonic ethnic or confessional community, it may employ a large arsenal of measures to enforce that hegemony. It may promote assimilation of individuals into the dominant community while denying recognition to minorities as a group, with the objective of weakening minorities as communities and eventually eliminating them. This may involve nonrecognition or discrimination against subordinate groups as entities but not necessarily against individuals, as long as they are willing to acculturate and be absorbed into the majority.

In contrast to assimilation, the state may enforce patterns of discrimination or exclusion against minorities, denying their members equal access to economic opportunities and public services and consigning them to inferior social, cultural, and political status. There are numerous combinations of neglect, harassment, and institutionalized discrimination by which states deprive and repress members of subordinate communities. Inferior status may be combined with substantial cultural autonomy, as in the Ottoman *millets* and the South African homelands. The state may cultivate and exploit divisions within subordinate communities along kinship, sectarian, urban/rural, or class lines, in order to weaken them, or it may co-opt compliant individuals and make them dependent on minor but selective handouts from government. Such draconian measures as enslavement, gen-

---

[36]Donald Horowitz, *Ethnic Groups in Conflict* (Berkeley: University of California Press, 1985), esp. pp. 563–684.

ocide, and expulsion have been practiced by governments against conquered or subordinate ethnic and confessional communities.

States that enforce hegemonial control on behalf of one ethnic group are inclined to employ repressive measures against challenges to the ethnic status quo or to specific practices. Such challenges are regarded as subversive to the regime. Because peaceful political challenges are proscribed, there is no outlet for grievances except civil disobedience or violence. In order to reduce the costs to the regime, governments may combine expedient accommodation with repression, and the accommodative measures may be acceptable to some elements among the ethnic minority. Seldom will a government make concessions that fundamentally affect the structure of the regime unless the costs of maintaining the status quo become unbearable, as in the Sudan in 1972. Even when alienated ethnic groups resort to sustained violence, most contemporary states have the capacity to contain the challenge. When they lose that capacity, as in Lebanon after 1975, the state disintegrates, and its component communities are forced to look after their own security and to provide for their collective needs outside the framework of the state.

It is an article of conventional wisdom that economic growth and prosperity provide the ideal context for the management of ethnic conflict, since increments of growth can be used to pacify ethnic discontent at no absolute cost to advantaged groups or to the regime. There are two contrary hypotheses. The first holds that during periods of rapid growth subordinate groups develop high expectations, and that failure to realize these expectations (despite real economic improvement) produces frustration, relative deprivation, militancy, and heightened conflict. The counterhypothesis argues that because most communal grievances are not economically grounded, they are unaffected by economic growth. Moreover, even if growth could attenuate conflict, the critical question is how the regime distributes the surplus; the regime may be under much more significant pressures from the dominant group to channel incremental resources to their needs. A number of Middle Eastern countries have experienced significant and sustained economic growth during the past two decades. What have been the effects of such growth on patterns of ethnic coexistence and conflict? Have the conflicts been mitigated, exacerbated, or simply not affected by economic growth?

External Factors

Ethnic conflict may be generated and sustained by external as well as internal influences. In no part of the world is this more true than in the Middle East. The Jewish diaspora was instrumental in creating a Jewish society in Palestine, in establishing a Jewish state, and in sustaining Israel economically, diplomatically, and militarily. The Palestinian national movement has been sustained, and at the same time constrained, by the interventions of Arab states. The collapse of Lebanon into conflicting confessional communities has attracted the intervention of regional powers—Syria, Israel, Saudi Arabia—as well as the superpowers and produced strange, if transitory, alliances of local, regional, and external actors.

Contending ethnic and confessional communities seek help from sympathetic outsiders, who may be willing or even eager to intervene in pursuit of their strategic or ideological goals. Ethnic conflict may be played out far from the region, as with the Armenian terrorist attacks on Turkish diplomats in Europe. The outsiders may be governments, or they may be diasporas of the contending ethnic or confessional parties. Their differing motives and capabilities affect their tactics. The Jewish diaspora stands by Israel, but the Shah of Iran, after patronizing the Kurds, abandoned them straightaway when he struck a deal in 1975 with Iraq.

The literature has begun to sort out the conditions under which external parties with varying interests and capabilities intervene in domestic ethnic or confessional conflicts.[37] Where state boundaries are so porous, as in much of the Middle East, and where ethnic and confessional communities straddle the borders of two or more states, distinctions between internal and external parties to conflict often become blurred. At the current state of theory, it is easier to identify and describe transnational and international interventions in individual cases, and to explain specific motives, tactics, and consequences, than to relate outside intervention to any body of general theory.

Varieties of Experience in the Middle East

The Middle East is a congeries of ethnic communities, most of which are fated to coexist with others under the same political authority within the boundaries of the same territorial state. Most of these communities have existed as self-defined collectives for long periods of time. A few, like the Palestinians, have achieved their sense of collective identity only recently. All of them have mobilized for political combat—to promote and defend their group interests—as a consequence of the creation of new political structures following the dismemberment of the Ottoman Empire and the withdrawal of European colonial power.

The goals of these ethnic communities have differed, depending on the

---

[37]Gabriel Sheffer, ed., *Modern Diasporas in International Politics* (London: Croom-Helm, 1985); see esp. Esman's summary essay, "Diasporas and International Relations," pp. 333–349.

objective circumstances they encountered and the ideologies and assessments of their often competing aspirants for leadership. Some, such as the Kurds and the blacks in Sudan, have sought independence and separate statehood; some, such as the Maronites in Lebanon and the Sunnis in Iraq, struggle to maintain their threatened hegemony. Others—for example, the Palestinians—are committed to achieving domination in a new state, and some seek greater autonomy, recognition, and protection of minority rights, including the Copts in Egypt and the Druze in Israel and Syria. A few, such as the Sephardim in Israel, seek full nondiscriminatory inclusion in the polity—the Middle Eastern version of civil rights. These goals and strategies may change with changing circumstances—note the increasing militancy of the Shi'ites following the collapse of the consociational system in Lebanon and the ascendancy of Khomeini in Iran. The methods used to implement ethnic demands range from the civil to the very violent, as do the responses by state authorities.

We offer no single theory or explanation to account for the varieties of ethnic pluralism and conflict in the Middle East. We doubt that this variety will ever yield to single explanations of their causes, dynamics, or outcomes. We are satisfied, however, that ethnically defined collectivities must be accepted and accounted for on their own terms as legitimate political actors. They are not the deformed manifestations of "deeper" realities such as class—though the collective interests they pursue may well be economic as well as cultural. Nor are they destined necessarily to dissolve into individualism or to wither away in the inexorable processes of modernization and nation-building. Though their contours, their tactics, and even their boundaries may change, ethnic solidarities are likely to be around for a very long time in this part of the world, to influence and in many cases to determine the course of events.

An important challenge to Middle East scholars is to strengthen their sensitivities and their skills in recognizing, analyzing, and explaining ethnic realities in the affairs of the region. It is our hope that this volume will help them to meet this challenge.

2

Ethnicity, Majority, and Minority in the Middle East

Elie Kedourie

The term "ethnicity" was, according to the *Oxford English Dictionary* obsolete and rare and meant heathendom or heathen superstition. This was the usage when the *Dictionary* was being compiled at the end of the last century. The situation is quite different now. The Supplement to the *O.E.D.* published in 1972 now recorded "ethnicity" as meaning ethnic character or peculiarity, and the adjective "ethnic" itself is also now recorded as meaning (which it did not mean when the *O.E.D.* was published) that which pertains to or has common racial, cultural, religious or linguistic characteristics, especially—the Supplement adds—designating a racial or other group within a large system.

This last explanation perhaps gives a clue to the reason both for the change in the meaning of the word, and its currency in modern social and political discourse. The words "ethnicity" and "ethnic" appear to be chosen to denote the specific and peculiar characteristics of particular groups living in so-called plural societies—groups which are different in culture, language, or physical characteristics from other, usually majority or dominant, groups in such societies. The United States is a plural society, and it is there, following the rise of Black Power and similar ideologies in the 1960s, that writers came to be preoccupied with ethnicity and its problems. The need, however, for these terms stems from the enhanced value which the specific and peculiar characteristics have come to possess for those who happen to have them—hence, for example, the great success of a work like *Roots* and similar compositions, and the popularity of so-called ethnic dress, ethnic jewelry, and ethnic hair styles. But the reasons such great value is set on

An earlier version of this article appeared in *Archives européennes de sociologie* 25 (1984): 276–82 and is here adapted by permission of the publisher.

ethnicity and on the ethnic are exactly the same reasons why, ever since the nineteenth century, nationalist theory has held the nation—as defined by the theory—and its cultural manifestations to be the supreme political value. Ethnicity and nationality share exactly the same doctrinal justification.

Ethnicity like nationality, then, sprang from a doctrine; it is not something immutable which has existed time out of mind. Thus, before the Muslim conquest of the Levant, Egypt, and North Africa, these regions had seemed profoundly and immutably Christian, just as *romanitas* and Hellenism had defined their ethos and governed their attitudes for so many centuries before the coming of Christianity. The revolutions these regions experienced when classical culture was supplanted by Christianity and when Christianity in turn was replaced by Islam were so far-reaching that, even though we assume biological continuity, yet to all intents and purposes here were entirely distinct groups which recognized no kinship, no affinity, no continuity with their putative ancestors. Human groups thus do change, and will continue to do so, sometimes quite radically, in their own estimation. A group, again, defines itself by contrast or opposition to other groups with which it is in contact, and here too change is, so to speak, a permanent condition. Great fluidity, thus, obtains in the makeup of human groups and in their view of themselves, and there is no purely definitional way of distinguishing ethnicity from other types of identity. But, to go further, ethnicity itself and ethnic identities share in this fluidity. What, for instance, are Egyptians? For millennia the inhabitants of the country of the Nile were the dumb and downtrodden subjects of the pharaohs, the Ptolemies, and the Romans. They then became and looked on themselves as members of the Muslim *umma* ruled successively by Fatimids, Ayyubids, Mamluks, and Ottomans. An ambitious Ottoman governor, Muhammad Ali, carved out for himself an autonomous province, the inhabitants of which gradually came to look on themselves as Egyptian. But even so the notion of an Egyptian remains unstable to this day. Territorial limits apart, was Egypt, as a country of the spirit, a part of Europe, as Khedive Isma'il wished to see it; or an entity with its own distinctive past and its own highly individual personality, as Egyptian thinkers between the wars believed; or part of the Arab nation, as both Faruk and Nasser urgently wanted it to be? Nor is the matter resolved to this day. What is true of Egypt is mutatis mutandis true of the French, the Spanish, the Persian, and so many other nations or ethnic groups.

The doctrine which, so to speak, conjures up nationalities and ethnic groups and endows them with supreme value is a modern Western doctrine. According to this doctrine, the only proper and genuine body politic is the nation, or ethnic group, which is a natural entity, the historical and linguistic character of which is stamped on every member of the nation. This doctrine, as is well known, spread in the Middle East in the nineteenth and twentieth centuries. But it did not come on its own; it came in a cluster with other Western political doctrines which were equally powerful in their appeal. One of these was that sovereignty was derived from the people and was not the possession or appanage of a monarch. In this view, legitimacy is conferred on a government by popular suffrage. Every citizen is a member of the body politic, which alone is the source of authority and legitimacy. These ideas came to an area which was religiously and ethnically hetero-geneous in the extreme and in which authority to rule was traditionally derived from conquest, traditional prescription, and religious warrant. Numbers of votes were not thought to have any bearing on government and its legitimacy. The heterogeneous character of the area was recognized through what is called the *millet* system, whereby those who did not belong to the dominant religion of Islam were allowed to administer their com-munal affairs under the authority of their ecclesiastical or religious heads. Once this changed—as in the course of time it did—and popular suffrage was deemed the basis of authority, given the heterogeneous character of the population, those who had been considered *millets*, with a well-defined and recognized subordinate status in the Muslim body politic, were now suddenly transformed into "minorities."

The notion of "minority"—and of course its correlative, "majority"—is part of the cluster of political ideas which, along with "nationality" and "popular sovereignty," were taken over by the Middle East from the West. The notion of minority and majority has indeed for a long time now formed part of the Western political vocabulary. How did this happen? It is a natural question, because neither the Latin words from which they are derived— that is, *minor* and *maior*—nor their derivations in various European lan-guages originally had a political bearing or implication. In English (and French), for instance, "minority" and "majority" indicated simply the age of a person with regard to issues of legal competence. A minor could not act in his own behalf, but in due course the minor will be able so to act, and we then say he has attained his "majority."

How then have these two terms come to be endowed with political meaning? The answer lies in the political institutions and concepts evolved in the medieval West to cope with new needs and situations. To do this, Western medieval lawyers naturally drew on concepts they found in Roman law and adapted to their own purposes. Thus canon lawyers found the Roman notion of a corporation to be useful in defining the arrangements and the workings of ecclesiastical organizations. A corporation in Roman law is a partnership (usually commercial) in which the partners formed a body with a legal personality that is distinct from the personality of those who set it up. A corporation was a *persona ficta*, which as such could assume legal rights and obligations. If ecclesiastical organizations could be looked on as corporations, they could then be deemed able to hold property, enter into obligations, engage in litigation, and so forth. The question then arose as to who had the right to act on behalf of the corporation. The answer, in the case of a cathedral, for instance, was that it was the dean and chapter who in their *collective capacity* would make decisions and empower someone to represent them and act on their behalf in matters affecting the cathedral. Cities, and municipalities too, came to be looked on as corporations ruled and represented by a mayor and alderman.

The idea of a corporation is, thus far, simply a legal notion. But it came to have political connotations in medieval European history. In the course of dispute and controversy about church government, particularly in the fourteenth and fifteenth centuries at the time of the conciliar movement, it became common to view the Church as a whole as a corporation, and the question arose as to who had the authority to act on its behalf. For the Papalist party the answer was that only the Pope possessed this authority. The Conciliar party, on the other hand, argued that the Council of the Church, composed of representatives of different parts of the Church, represented the Church as a whole and was above the Pope. This is a political dispute, not simply a legal one. It had far-reaching implications, not only in church government but also in secular government, which did not take long to manifest themselves.

The concept of the corporation thus came to involve two other notions: the notion of representation and the notion of a council. Both these ideas have become fundamental political notions which have spread from the West to the rest of the world.

Another Western medieval institution is feudalism. Feudalism can be looked on as a network of legal rights and obligations holding together suzerains and vassals. In the feudal arrangement, vassals had the duty and the right to offer counsel and consent. The question—which had substantial implications—therefore arose whether anyone was bound by a decision he disagreed with or did not take part in. The view of the jurists was that "what touches all must be approved by all." This principle has survived in the *liberum veto* in the Diet of pre-partition Poland, and in a way in the veto power belonging to the five permanent members of the United Nations Security Council.

The maxim "What touches all must be approved by all" appeared to be unworkable when kings began to summon parliaments in which representatives of various territorial and municipal interests sat, for in due course that maxim was replaced by another—that the larger part, the *maior pars*, was the wiser or better part, the *sanior pars*. In other words, the majority in a council or representative assembly represents the general interest or the consensus. From this it followed that the decision of a majority was binding not only on itself but also on the minority. This idea is similar to the Muslim notion of *ijma'*, or consensus, and to the Tradition attributed to the Prophet that the Muslim community will not agree on a heresy—in other words, that the *maior pars* must be the *sanior pars*.

At this point the notion of minority and majority becomes a political notion. The notion is Western in origin and is inseparable from the allied notions of conciliar and representative government. But the substitution of popular sovereignty for monarchical sovereignty had far-reaching, not to say radical, consequences for the notion of majority and minority and for its political significance. Popular sovereignty makes it impossible to maintain the maxim that "what touches all must be approved by all." The body politic is bound and its government is constituted by a majority of the popular vote. This idea can work in practice on two assumptions: one, that a majority and a minority share a common interest in the maintenance of the body politic of which they are members; and two, that a majority and a minority do not constitute a fixed and permanent quantity.

These assumptions are overturned by the idea of nationalism. If political legitimacy is conferred by the suffrage of the citizens, and if the majority of the citizens in a state are members of one "nation" among two or more inhabiting the state, the majority becomes a national majority—that is, a permanent and fixed quantity—which is pitted against other, smaller, permanent, and fixed quantities, namely of national minorities. Nationalism, then, radically changes the concept of majority and minority. This is not only because majority and minority become permanent and fixed quantities, but also because the notion of consensus, without which the *maior pars* cannot be accepted as the *sanior pars*, is subverted and in the end destroyed. With the nationalist idea of the nation, and the existence of a permanent majority, majority comes simply to mean force, the force of numbers, and force gives no legitimacy. Because they believed that kings were not appointed by God and that force was no warrant, thinkers like Rousseau concluded that the only legitimate government was one which issued from popular consent. The transformation of majority and minority into national majority and national minority is fatal to the idea of government by consent. It is transformed in this way, and divorced from its conciliar and representative matrix—as a free-floating idea endowed with great dynamism— that the notion of majority and minority came to the Middle East.

Under these conditions, given popular sovereignty and the supreme value of nationality as the foundation and cement of the body politic, *millet*s now became minorities. Such "minorities" could not claim special privileges or status since the logic of popular government required the equality of all citizens. But they could not enjoy actual equality because their "minority" status was fixed and permanent. On the one hand, this transformation was detrimental to the *millet*s and to their members. But on the other hand, the new Middle Eastern states erected on the nationality principle lacked the cohesiveness and unity which this principle is supposed to provide. Heterogeneity in polities which aspire to be nation-states is a source of great weakness. It leads to the politicization of various aspects of social life hitherto considered unpolitical and to the exacerbation of political conflicts.

Suspicion and fear increased between groups which in the past had led a more-or-less self-contained life within a state where the ruler, not the people, was the source of power and the final arbiter.

The Ottoman Empire in the nineteenth century provides an example of the steady transformation of a traditional regime into a modern polity and of *millets* into "minorities." Here, as it happened, nationalist ideology first spread among the non-Muslim *millets*, but once it began to spread among them it also had to spread to the ruling Muslim group. If the Rum *millet* now looked on itself as the Greek nation, sooner or later other Ottomans would look on themselves as Turks. Since there was no way the various groups in Ottoman society could be split into tidy, self-contained territorial units, "national minorities" came into existence, and hence the phenomenon of ethnic mobilization. Greeks, Serbians, Armenians, and Kurds would feel the pull of national unity and aspire or be urged to separate themselves from states which embodied alien and hence offensive national values. This difficult, uneasy, and potentially dangerous and disruptive situation continued after the downfall of the Ottoman Empire and of other traditional regimes and institutions.

Thus, in the Republic of Turkey all citizens are Turks, *ex definitione*. But the idea that a non-Muslim or a non-Sunni native of Turkey is a Turk in the same way as a Sunni Muslim is somewhat artificial. A "Greek Turk," an "Armenian Turk," and so on, may be legally intelligible concepts, but they are empty of political substance. Mutatis mutandis, the same is true for Iraq, Syria, or Israel, but in the case of Iraq we must notice a further complication. The largest groups of inhabitants in Iraq, and perhaps the majority, are Shi'ite Muslim. They are of course Arabic-speaking, but because Shi'ism is the religion of the Persian state with whom the Ottomans were at odds for centuries, the Shi'ites of Mesopotamia have been held at arm's length for centuries and kept in an inferior position. They had no share in government, and their religious courts were not even officially recognized. The situation did not change much when the state of Iraq was set up. Iraq is an Arab state, and the Shi'ites of Iraq are undoubtedly Arab, but their position of inferiority remained by and large unchanged. The Arab nationalism which the Iraqi state promotes has remained for the Shi'ites a more-or-less alien cause, the synonym of domination by the Sunni Arabs, who are a numerical minority in Iraq. By the logic of Arab nationalism, the Shi'ites, an actual majority in Iraq, are reduced to a minority. Shi'ites find themselves in a similar situation in Kuwait, in Bahrain (where they are a majority), and in Saudi Arabia, where they predominate in the oil-bearing province of Hasa. Their disaffection toward the regimes under which they live, and their sympathy and sometimes enthusiasm for the Shi'ite cause now upheld by the Islamic Republic of Iran, cannot literally be called a case of ethnic mobilization, but it is basically indistinguishable from ethnic mobilization. Mobilization is a term of warfare, and under these conditions politics is warfare by another name.

We now bring to attention two attempts to prevent or neutralize ethnic mobilization by means of political arrangements. The first is Cyprus, where a constitution was set up in 1960, a main purpose of which was to calm the mutual fears of the Turkish Cypriots (who constituted about 20 percent of the population) and the Greek Cypriots. The first were afraid of being swamped by the majority, the second were afraid of intervention by Turkey in support of fellow-Turks. The constitution included elaborate devices containing nearly four hundred clauses, whose purpose was to obviate the danger of a permanent majority perpetually tyrannizing a permanent minority. These devices quickly proved unworkable, and by 1963 the constitution had broken down and there was a de facto separation between the two communities. This separation was confirmed and perhaps made irrevocable by the Turkish military intervention in 1974. Cyprus thus provides the most striking case of ethnic mobilization.

The second case is that of Lebanon. As it emerged into independence at the end of World War II, Lebanon included areas in the north, south, and east which had been joined to Mount Lebanon by the French Mandatory in 1920 in order to form Greater Lebanon—le Grand Liban. These areas included large numbers of Sunni and Shi'ite Muslims who felt no particular attachment to the Lebanese state. To hold all these heterogeneous elements, the Lebanese constitution of 1926 included elaborate provisions to ensure the parliamentary representation of all groups and their proportional participation in political office and in bureaucracy. This was the so-called confessional system. But after independence the system broke down quickly. In 1958, and more seriously after 1975, civil war dealt a powerful and perhaps mortal blow to the confessional system. And there can be no doubt that mobilization of the Sunni and the Shi'ite citizens of Lebanon by outside powers—the United Arab Republic, Syria, and latterly the Islamic Republic of Iran—was the main cause of the Lebanese civil war. The Lebanese Sunnis, in particular, hankered after a pan-Arab nationalism that was incompatible with confessionalism and, as it turned out, destroyed the balance of communities in Lebanon.

Thus, both in Cyprus and in Lebanon the European vocabulary of politics and the modern European concepts of the state have visibly led not to greater welfare and security but to insecurity and destruction for the inhabitants of the two countries.

PART II

LEGACIES OF

THE PAST

3

The Ottoman Ethnic and Confessional Legacy in the Middle East

Kemal Karpat

The political system of the Middle Eastern countries is built on the concept of the territorial "state" borrowed from the West and on an idea of "nation" that derives from the area's own ethnoreligious communal system of organization. However, both the concept of the territorial state and that of the nation-state as the West understands it, despite their apparently successful adaptation, remain alien to the area's historical experience, its political culture, and its idea of community. Whatever their modern appearance, the surviving powerful traditional concepts of sociopolitical organization are part of the Ottoman legacy in the Middle East.

This chapter considers religion and ethnicity to be the source of individual and group identity, and the term "community," as used herein, represents the concrete organizational expression of ethnoreligious identity and solidarity. The territory is important, but not essential, for the existence of a Middle Eastern community, which is regarded both as an association and as an organization. A community may become an "organization," or a unit within a larger administrative or political entity, without losing its character as an "association," but it may change or disappear entirely when confronted with larger associations of its kind. The concept of "nation" is essentially that of a communal type of association rather than an organization.

Ottoman principles of social and political organization were diametrically opposed to the ideas of territorial state and ethnic nationality. In fact, as is now well known, the downfall of the Ottoman state was caused at least in part by its inability to accept, reconcile, and assimilate the principles of ethnic nationality and territorial statehood with its own traditional principles of social organization based on the combination of the two key

35

elements of community and faith. Nevertheless, the Ottoman state succeeded in using the European notions of nationality and statehood to transform the traditional *umma* within its territory into a Muslim nation with a national ideology rooted in a politicized notion of faith. To put it another way, Islamism (inaccurately denoted "pan-Islamism"), which developed in the 1860s, gradually raised the Muslims' sense of communal-religious identity to the level of a political identity. In contrast to the Muslims, the Orthodox Christians, especially in the Balkans, absorbed the idea of ethnic nationality, even though they also were ill prepared to do so, and their acceptance of ethnicity as a principle of political organization led to the disintegration of the Orthodox Christian *millet* in the Balkans and the Middle East. The dissolution of this *millet* in turn profoundly affected the entire Ottoman political order, for the patriarchate and the sultanate were mutually dependent upon each other. Although nationalist-minded scholars may see the Ottoman government and the Greek Orthodox patriarchate as perennial antagonists, they were actually partners in the administration of the ethnocommunal system.[1] (The power of the Armenian patriarchate was considerably less than that of the Greek, as its followers were much fewer in number, and its control over the old Eastern churches it represented was very limited.)

The Ottoman religious-social-political system evolved over a long period of time in three distinct phases. The first was a lengthy period of growth and development during which the constitutional framework was established and the state subjected the ethnic and religious communities under its jurisdiction to a basic and lasting reorganization.[2] This phase lasted roughly from 1413 to 1839. The Ottoman approach was realistic and in many ways modern for its time. Instead of tampering with the sense of group identity and solidarity based on community of faith that prevailed in Middle Eastern society, the Ottoman rulers maintained and bolstered this loose system, giving the religious communities organization and an avenue for group political expression that had not previously existed. Having made the principles of ethnoreligious identity and community the foundation of the political organization, the sultans employed the powerful central bureaucracy to enforce these principles. This conscious use of an

---

[1] This is of paramount importance for any study of communal coexistence and ethnicity, especially in the Middle East. At a conference, or Muslim-Christian dialogue, held at Hellenic College and Holy Cross Greek Orthodox Seminary in Brookline, Massachusetts, in March 1985, the phenomenon was discussed at length. The papers delivered at the conference, including this author's contribution, "The Ottoman Views and Policies toward the Orthodox Christian Church," are published in the *Greek Orthodox Theological Review* 31, nos. 1 and 2 (1986).

[2] A recent account of this development, including references to previously published works, is found in *Christians and Jews in the Ottoman Empire: The Functioning of a Plural Society*, ed. B. Braude and B. Lewis (New York: Holmes & Meier, 1982). See also F. W. Hasluck, *Christianity and Islam under the Sultans*, ed. M. M. Hasluck, 2 vols. (Oxford: Clarendon, 1929).

existing social-religious structure as the constitutional foundation for a state political system was unique.

During the second phase of development—the period from 1839 to 1865—in response to force exerted by the European powers and to internal pressures generated by structural changes within the society, the Ottoman government attempted a reorganization of the religious-ethnic communities.

The final phase was one of national transformation, encompassed most obviously in the years from 1865 until World War I. It was a period during which nationalism arose in strength and the territorial states were established on Ottoman lands.[3] In a broad sense this third phase—the national transformation of the Ottoman state—continues to the present day in Turkey and in the countries of the Middle East.[4]

The main contention of this chapter is that the sense of identity and solidarity in all the Middle Eastern "national" states derives to a large extent from their sense of religious identity and communality instead of from feelings of ethnic and/or linguistic group solidarity. The aggregation of these distinct religious communities in a political imperial system produced a sort of "national unity" that was the foundation and enduring strength of the Ottoman state. Although ultimately the state was broken into many pieces, that foundation has remained solid even though new political entities have arisen in the territory. Regardless of the different ethnopolitical labels under which these "national states" are presented today, the citizens' sense of identity is nurtured psychologically, largely by the old communal identities.

Community and the Faith: Their Effect on Religious Groups of the Empire

The idea of community was pervasive in Ottoman thought, and even the various social classes and groups were conceived of as "communities." The origins of this concept were rooted in the Turks' tribal and nomadic past. The strong kinship ties, the Shamanist faith, the geographic and economic conditions in Central Asia, and the life-style that was partly settled and partly nomadic combined to produce a sense of identity embodied in the concept of *soy* (i.e., lineage) that was very like ethnicity. *Soy* became the basic qualification for recruitment to leadership and was the concept em-

---

[3]See, e.g., Roderic Davison, *Reform in the Ottoman Empire, 1856–1876* (Princeton: Princeton University Press, 1963).

[4]For an account of the social bases of these developments, see Kemal H. Karpat, *An Inquiry into the Social Foundations of Nationalism in the Ottoman State: From Social Estates to Classes, from Millets to Nations*, Princeton University Center of International Studies, Research Monograph no. 39 (Princeton, N.J., 1973).

ployed to promote group solidarity and the establishment of ties and allegiances that were communal rather than personal. Indeed, although the term, used widely by the Turks in referring to kinship groups, may be taken to mean strictly "lineage" or "race," in everyday usage *soy* came to be the word for a group of people bound together by strong ties based on kinship and family relationships but actually superseding them. Thus it meant simultaneously the blood relationship and the relationship to the larger family and the community. With the conversion of the Turkish tribes and tribal states to Islam, over the period from the eighth through the tenth century, an allegiance and sense of identity stemming from Islam superseded in one way the old, nonreligious communal-ethnic identity. At the same time, however, the traditional sense of identification was strengthened by the addition of the nonmaterial dimension of a universal monotheistic religion to the existing elements of solidarity.

The concept of the supranational or supratribal state as created by the Seljukis, and subsequently by the Ottomans in the Anatolian peninsula, was the legacy of Genghis Khan and his heirs. During the twelfth and thirteenth centuries, nearly all the Turkic tribes and states of central Asia and eastern Europe were brought under Mongol rule and consolidated under one political system as an empire-state. This created a sense of universal statehood and loyalty to a central political entity without destroying the Turks' Islamic and traditional communal identities, which continued to coexist harmoniously under the new system. Many of Genghis' descendants ruling on the western fringes of his empire accepted Islam and were assimilated into Turkic groups. This conversion of the Mongol elites to Islam helped maintain and perpetuate the imperial political tradition, making it acceptable to the masses and guaranteeing that the sense of universal statehood and loyalty would survive the demise of Genghis's original empire. Thus, when the Seljuk Empire and later the Ottoman Empire were established (largely under Mongol pressure and partly under their suzerainty), their elites were well grounded in the principles of statecraft and had as their model a political system that could accommodate the ties of faith and ethnicity that existed among its citizens alongside their broader ties to the state.[5]

Relatively weak genealogical traditions seemingly made the Turkish tribal society able to adapt itself readily to a complex nontribal political organization and prone to easy acceptance of political identity above tribal loyalty. Because the Ottoman state, unlike the Iranian monarchy (after the sixteenth century) and the Arab dynasties, was not hampered by tribal ties, the rulers were free to act in the best interests of the dynasty and of the

---

[5]See René Grousset, *The Empire of Steppes: A History of Central Asia* (New Brunswick: Rutgers University Press, 1970), part 2, and endnotes for references.

state.[6] Islam unified those Turkish tribes that had the proper sort of political organization and converted their sense of ethnicity to a new religious identity, with the old ethnic ties as a secondary element of the group solidarity. David Urquhart was correct when he said that for the Turks the community was the basis of the social organization and that the community was essentially a religious one.[7] However, the Ottomans' basic view of the community was secular; they sought to subordinate the smaller community— be it tribe or ethnic group—to the larger religious-confessional community, which was then made the basic unit of the administration, subordinate always to the political system. The principle was preserved in the administration of the very small social-civic units, such as the villages and town quarters. Represented by its head man, a village as a whole, rather than its individual citizens, would be made responsible to the state.

Although ostensibly dedicated to the promotion of the faith, the ruling elites in reality used the faith to legitimize the authority of the state, which engaged mainly in the promotion of the secular political goals of the rulers.[8] Nevertheless, in their effort to consolidate the community the Ottomans stressed its religious rather than its ethnic basis in the belief that religion generated stronger feelings of solidarity than blood and kinship. This approach was consistent with the pre-Ottoman pattern of organization in the Middle East, where the religious-ethnic community was in fact the basic unit of the political organization but was not formally recognized as such within a constitutional framework.

Islam produced profound changes in every aspect of Turkish life and identity, bringing the Turks into the universal Muslim community and eventually turning them into fierce champions of the faith. Yet the Turks, including the Ottoman Turks, preserved a number of their pre-Islamic concepts of organization and leadership and also some of their ethnic memories. This was especially true among villagers and tribesmen. A cursory comparison of the Ottoman Islamic society with other Muslim societies reveals remarkable differences in matters ranging from architectural style to social attitudes and behavior.

The Ottomans' intentional promotion of the community, notably the religious community, as the unit of the administrative organization had not begun during the period of growth in the thirteenth and fourteenth centuries, when the Ottoman state was predominantly an ethnic Turkish

[6]See Rudi Paul Lindner, *Nomads and Ottomans in Medieval Anatolia* (Bloomington: Indiana University Press, 1983), for a summary, with a new interpretation, of the role of the tribes in the origin of the Ottoman Empire.

[7]David Urquhart, *Turkey and Its Resources: Its Municipal Organization and Free Trade* (London: Sanders & Otley, 1833).

[8]See Halil Inalcik, *The Ottoman Empire: The Classical Age, 1300–1600*, trans. N. Itzkowitz and C. Imber (London: Weidenfeld & Nicolson, 1973), and Stanford J. Shaw, *History of the Ottoman Empire and Modern Turkey*, vol. 1 (Cambridge: Cambridge University Press, 1976).

entity. The policy was generated in the fifteenth century, when the inclusion of large non-Turkic and non-Muslim groups turned the state into an empire in which groups of different religious persuasions were the main divisions. The *millet* system evolved over the second half of the fifteenth century, during which the Christian Orthodox *millet* (under the Greek Orthodox patriarch), the Armenian *millet* (which included all the non-Orthodox Eastern Christians), and, finally, the Jewish *millet* were successively established. The institutionalization, of the existing religious communities, with formal recognition of their legal status, marked the transformation of the early Ottoman state into an imperial entity.

The *millet* system had its origin in the basic Islamic concept of *dhimmi* (or *zimmi*)—that is, the recognition accorded Jews and Christians as the "Peoples of the Book."[9] The Muslim states had a strong religious mandate to protect non-Muslim citizens by subjecting the relations between them and the predominantly Muslim society in which they resided to government control. Thus a strong, well-organized, and law-abiding Muslim government was the best guarantee of the rights of non-Muslims. (The Christian states, on the other hand, were bound by no biblical reference to Muslims to offer them protection or ensure any rights for them. Because there was therefore no room for non-Christians in the new Christian-dominated territorial states, Muslim communities in the Balkans were destroyed even after the Berlin Treaty of 1878 articulated the principle of minority rights.[10])

The Ottoman state carried out the mandate to provide a place for non-Muslims with a high degree of sophistication. It concentrated its organizational efforts on the three broad categories of non-Muslim religious faith, but it did not try to eliminate all the interfaith divisions stemming from the different ethnic characteristics of various groups so long as those ethnic characteristics were useful in consolidating the community and especially the state. In practice there was considerable diversity within the apparently homogeneous religious groups. The Orthodox and Armenian *millet*s were officially presided over by their respective patriarchs and synods, but they had subdivisions—bishoprics and parishes—that followed ethnic and linguistic lines. For example, during the reign of Suleyman the Magnificent the Serbians, officially part of the Orthodox *millet*, were permitted to reopen their own church, apparently through the intercession of the grand vizier, Mehmet Sokollu (Sokolovich). The Serbian church was closed in the eighteenth century under the pressure of the Greek patriarchate's neo-Byzantine

---

[9]C. E. Bosworth, "The Concept of *Dhimma* in Early Islam," in *Christians and Jews*, ed. Braude and Lewis, pp. 37–51.

[10]Kemal H. Karpat, "The Social and Political Foundations of Nationalism in Southeast Europe after 1878: A Reinterpretation," in *Der Berliner Kongress von 1878: Die Politik der Grossmachte und die Probleme der Modernisierung in Sudosteuropa in der zweiten Hälfte des 19. Jahrhunderts* (Wiesbaden: Steiner, 1982), pp. 385–410.

nationalism; however, in the countryside the Orthodox church continued to function, divided as always into parishes in which the language was Bulgarian, Serbian, Vlah, and so on, according to the prevailing ethnolinguistic characteristics of the inhabitants of the various areas. The Greek patriarchate sought to hellenize the Slavs, but the effort was thwarted not only by the resistance of the non-Greek-speakers but also because the community, in addition to being a religious ward, was an administrative unit tied to the Ottoman government. The government's reliance on the religious communal organizations of the various ethnic groups helped maintain cohesion within these groups and strengthened the hands of the local leaders among the Bulgarians, Serbians, Albanians, Romanians, and so forth, who were opposed to being hellenized. After 1850, village heads were officially recognized as representatives of the central government, which gave them greater power to oppose effectively the Greek patriarchate's designs.

The subdivision of the Christian *millet*s into religious ethnic communities was even more pronounced in the Middle Eastern territory than in the Balkans. With the advent of Muslim rule there in the seventh century, the domination of the Greco-Roman church was ended and the various ethnic groups were allowed to reassert their identities and reestablish the separate churches that had been created as each group initially accepted Christianity. Under Ottoman rule, the Orthodox patriarchate was allowed to reestablish its religious hegemony over Orthodox Christians, but it was not permitted to curtail the freedom of the older churches that had emerged after the schism between Rome and Constantinople in the ninth century. Thus Ottoman rule in the Middle East preserved the ethnic and religious integrity and continuity of the Eastern churches, despite the special status accorded the Orthodox patriarchate, notably in the Holy Land.

The outstanding characteristic of the Christian groups in the Middle East was the strong coincidence of ethnicity and, sometimes, language—either spoken at home or used purely liturgically—with the faith. This was much less pronounced among Balkan Christians, whose religion stemmed mainly from the patriarchate in Constantinople and whose non-Greek ethnic identity had therefore been partially submerged. In contrast, the Middle Eastern Christian groups were like mini-nations. They were tightly controlled by their community leaders (unlike the Muslims, who could more easily bypass their local representatives to deal directly with the government). The *batras* (patriarchs) and *mutans* (archbishops) of the Armenians, Georgians, Assyrians, and so on, were official religious-communal heads with extensive authority over their co-religionists, whose allegiance to the Armenian patriarchate was nominal (unlike the case in the Balkans, where the Orthodox patriarchate ruled supreme). Although formally appointed by the *qadi*, these local officials were selected mainly on the advice of the notables of their respective groups. This pattern of strong and continuous communal leadership played a major role in preserving the religious-ethnic integrity of these groups and their sense of unique identity. Even in the payment of the *jiziya*—the head tax levied on adult males—and other taxes, many of the ethnoreligious communities of the Middle East insisted on being regarded as separate from other Christian groups, particularly the Orthodox Christians. (Again the case was different in the Balkans, where ethnic differences were not as a rule observed in the collection of taxes among the Orthodox.)

Scholars argue that this tight adherence of Christians to their ethnic-religious identities and communities strengthened their resistance to Ottoman rule and, incidentally, to conversion and assimilation into the Muslim society. The opposite was true with regard to their relationship with the Ottoman government, for that government assured the survival of their communities as separate ethnoreligious entities; the rights of local self-government and cultural-religious autonomy were not special—perhaps transitory—privileges granted these particular groups, but were Ottoman constitutional principles. The government lost the allegiance of these smaller groups only when it failed to restrain the larger groups from actions that threatened their ethnic integrity and autonomy. Even in the Balkans, where the sense of ethnicity was less strong, the effort of the Greek church to hellenize the Slavs stirred up reactions. The Serbian revolt, coming as early as 1804, and especially the Bulgarian national movement of 1850–1870.[11] were major examples of actions taken in opposition to hellenization. The Ottoman government failed actively to uphold its own principles and did not try to stop the Greek patriarchate's assimilation efforts until it was too late, thus losing credibility with the ethnic groups. In the Middle East as early as the seventeenth century the Melkite union with Rome—spurred partly by France, which had penetrated Syria—was a reaction to failure of the Ottoman government to guarantee the status quo of the local Orthodox community against the growing effort of the Istanbul patriarchate to centralize its authority. (It may even have been a particularly shrewd move on the part of the Syrian Orthodox leaders to head off individual conversion of its members to outright Catholicism, which made them fully subject to the jurisdiction of Rome and thus separated them completely from their community.) By 1712 the pope and patriarch of Antioch, Cyril al-Zaim, had also made obeisance to Rome (again in large part to thwart the Istanbul Phanariots in their attempt to dominate the hierarchy of the Eastern Orthodox church). Preservation of the integrity of the ethnic-religious com-

[11]G. D. Todorov and N. Zecev, "Documents ayant trait aux cultes des Bulgares pour une église et des écoles nationales en Macedonie vers le milieu du XIX siècle," *Études Historiques* 3 (1966): 173–239; see also Richard J. Crampton, *Bulgaria, 1878–1918: A History*, East European Monographs (Boulder, Colo., 1983).

munity was clearly a key consideration in the politics of the Christian groups of the Middle East.

It was a key consideration also for the Ottoman government, despite lapses in enforcement of the principle. To the Ottomans, government was the art of ruling the unruly, reconciling the irreconcilable, and creating harmony out of ethnoreligious discord. The method it selected to accomplish these ends was that of reinforcing the religious and social differences among its subjects, with clearly defined boundaries designed to minimize trespass and the resulting intergroup strife, while assuring each group its place in the administrative structure and guaranteeing its communal rights, so that these groups would not feel oppressed either by the central government or by other groups. As long as the government was free to act out of its own wisdom, it was in the main successful. For example, the regime established in the Lebanon after 1861 endured, despite changed conditions, until our time, when ethnic nationalism destroyed the ethnoreligious communal system of organization.[12]

In sum, the establishment of religion as the chief identifying characteristic of both Muslims and non-Muslims, through official promotion of religious symbols and the authority given the church hierarchies of the Christians, and the relegation of the ethnic sense of identity to a position of secondary importance did not destroy the ethnic sense but in fact strengthened it as well as the religious identity, from which it became inseparable. Moreover, the groups were not constrained from emphasizing whichever of these identities seemed the more important under various circumstances. Thus, in the nineteenth and twentieth centuries, under European influence, the ethnoreligious identity metamorphosed into a "national" identity, and ethnicity acquired parity with—and even greater importance than—the religious identity in the perception of the Christian groups.

The Jewish community presented the least difficulty to the Ottomans in their reorganization of the non-Muslim religious groups because, among the Jews, ethnicity, religion, and community coincided. Thus the *millet* was established with its own *hahambashi* (chief rabbi) continuing in authority, an arrangement that seems to have been highly unusual and must have come about because the Jewish community posed virtually no problems as far as its internal organization and relations with the state were concerned. In fact, one may argue that the Jewish community was from the start close to the apparent Ottoman ideal of the synthesis of ethnicity, religion, and community that was to be the building material of its political edifice. The various divisions in the Jewish community—Sephardi, Ashkenazi, Romaniote, and Qara'im—were not ethnic or religious in origin, but arose from

[12]John P. Spagnolo, *France and Ottoman Lebanon, 1861–1914*, St. Antony's Middle East Monographs no. 7 (London: Ithaca, 1977).

the influence of the various regions and the dominant cultures under which they had lived. The Qara'im, who probably represented the most important ethnic and doctrinal challenge to the uniformity of the Jewish *millet*, never became a real threat, partly at least because they seem to have been left outside the *millet* ruled by the rabbis. The main problem faced by the Jewish community in the Ottoman state was maintaing Jewish law and identity in the face of Muslim law and customs enforced by the state.[13]

The situation of the Muslim community was different from that of the non-Muslims. The Muslims were not officially recognized as a separate *millet*, although certain organizational features, such as the recognition accorded Seyhulislam as the head of the Muslim community, were similar to those of the *millets*. However, the administrative prerogatives of the chief *mufti* were rendered insignificant, his duties related to the administration of the Muslim community being assumed directly by the government. The much discussed notion that the Muslims were the ruling—and oppressive—group with exclusive control of power in the Ottoman state is a fictitious one, deriving in part from Western ignorance of the Ottoman government system and in even greater part from Christian misrepresentations designed to excite the sympathy of the Europeans. While the Ottoman government took its legitimacy from Islam and enforced, to the extent possible, Islamic legislation, it did not identify itself politically and ideologically with the Muslim community until the nineteenth century.[14] As a ruling group the Ottoman elites had as little to do with ordinary Muslims as with the non-Muslims. True, government power was the exclusive preserve of the Muslims, but it was available only to those Muslims—some of whom were converts—who first accepted everything the ruling order stood for. By entering government service, a Muslim—convert or otherwise—committed himself to accept a code of behavior and values and a way of life that the Anatolian Turkish peasant specifically termed *Osmanli*, referring to the governing class as *Osmanli paşalari* (Ottoman generals).[15] The Muslim's

---

[13]This issue is treated at length in Aryeh Schmuelevitz, *The Jews of the Ottoman Empire in the Late 15th and 16th Centuries* (Leiden: Brill, 1984), pp. 41–80.

[14]The political changes that necessitated ideological identification of the ruling elite with Islam are discussed in Kemal H. Karpat, "The Muslim Hijra from Russia, the Balkans, and India: The Process of Self-definition in the Ottoman State (1850–1917) and the Subcontinent" (Paper delivered at the Conference on the Process of Identity Change and Self-definition among Muslims, organized by the Social Sciences Research Council, New York City, April 1986). Interesting suggestions about the structural changes preceding and accompanying this identity change are in *Land Tenure and Social Transformation: Proceedings of a Conference Held at the American University at Beirut, February 1983*, ed. T. Khalidi (Beirut, 1983).

[15]The following anecdote, with basis in fact, surfaced during the early phase of party activity in Turkey in 1946. The late Celal Bayar (d. August 1986), head of the opposition Democratic Party, was invariably addressed by the villagers with whom he came in contact as *passam* (literally "my general," although the title *passa* has wider social and political connotations too), even though he held no military rank. Asked why they addressed him thus, the villagers

sense of religious identity deepened and came to supersede all other group and subgroup identities under the program to develop the enthnoreligious community as the basic unit of the constitutional system. The average Muslim knew that he lived under the authority of an Islamic government, but he knew too that he had little power in it. Only in the nineteenth century did he consciously begin to consider the government and the state "his." At that time, under the pressure of Western imperialism, the state-Islam relationship was politicized and popularized and thus became the basis of a new national-Islamic identity.

The Muslim community encompassed a great number of ethnic and linguistic groups. Before it became a predominantly imperial entity, the early Ottoman state recognized these ethnic divisions. Islamic doctrine explicitly recognizes ethnic and tribal differences (in the famous sura 49:13), but it forbids the use of tribal and national affiliation to achieve domination over other Muslims. The *berats* (appointment letter) given to the Kurdish lords and Turkmen chiefs as *boz millet* and *kara millet* (gray nation and black nation) respectively, and the *Ulah kanunnamesi* (Law of the Wallachians), for example, were forms of recognition of ethnolinguistic differences; they were without political significance, however. The Bosnians and the Albanians nonetheless continued to preserve their separate ethnic-linguistic identity despite dedication to their new Muslim identity. The imperial policy of Mehmed II and the pressure to follow a more Orthodox Islamic line after the conquest of Syria and Egypt in 1516–1517 combined to relegate ethnic and linguistic differences among Muslims to a very subordinate position as identifying characteristics. Although in practice various groups, especially in the countryside, did maintain ethnic and/or linguistic distinctiveness, the emphasis on religion as the foundation of the community, and the co-opting into the ruling system of the Muslim tribal chiefs, heads of prominent families, and communal leaders, reduced the bases of the appeal of ethnic and linguistic consciousness.

The above statements are clearly supported by Ottoman government census documents. In the early censuses, beginning in the fifteenth and sixteenth centuries, the non-Muslim citizens were classified as Christian, Armenian, and Jewish (with, oddly enough, a separate classification for Kipti—i.e., gypsies). In the second half of the nineteenth century the Christians began to be classified into ethnoconfessional categories—for example, Bulgarians, Maronites, Syriacs. However, throughout the existence of the Ottoman state, in all its censuses, the Muslims were listed as one group and never categorized according to ethnic or linguistic differences.

---

replied that anyone daring to criticize the government must be a *passa*—the higher military being traditionally the only group that could challenge the rulers.

The Transformation of the Ethnoreligious Community

The nineteenth century brought change in the traditional Ottoman political system based on the ethnoreligious community and also in the entire range of group-identity symbols and priorities. Indeed, the transformation of the ethnoreligious identities among Christians into "national" identities with ethnicity as the basis of the new "nationality" occurred chiefly within the nineteenth century. I have dealt elsewhere in detail with the forces that brought about the transformation of the classical Ottoman *millets*.[16] Suffice it to say that the changes in the Ottoman social structure and the weakening of the central authority encouraged the rise of local ethnic and particularist tendencies in the form of a movement toward decentralization. The increased trade with Europe, and the economic, political, and military supremacy of the West, led to the rise of new merchant and intellectual classes among the non-Muslims. This change, in turn, caused a drastic transformation in the structure, philosophy, and identity of the non-Muslim *millets*, especially the Christians, who broke up into smaller groups in which ethnic and linguistic affinity became outwardly the basis of identity (although this new "secular" identity remained anchored in religion). The Greek revolt of 1821, which undermined the authority of the patriarch as the leader of the Orthodox community, was the turning point for both the *millets* and the Ottoman government. After that uprising the government's view of its Christian subjects was altered, and there was a pronounced change of consciousness in the *millets*.

The original three *millets* underwent a reorganization in the period 1862–1866. Under the new system the patriarch and the synods of the Orthodox and Armenian *millets* were elected by the community, and the synod now came to include a number of merchants and craftsmen, whereas in the past all had been members of the clergy. The synod, staffed now by laymen, became the ruling council of the *millet*, while the patriarch's duties remained confined to strictly religious affairs. A sort of representative regime was thus established. The Jewish *millet* underwent only a cosmetic leadership change, because there the differences between the laymen and the leaders of the community were insignificant. Meanwhile, several new religious *millets*—there were nine by the end of the century—were recognized. The term *millet* (nation) denoted now mainly a narrow confessional group, in which ethnicity was given added weight, rather than a broad communal entity in which religion and ethnicity were amalgamated, but with religion having the greatest weight and being determinative of identity.[17] (Today

---

[16]See footnotes 4, 10, and 14.

[17]In the Balkans, until our own times, when asked to identify himself the Christian peasant would say he was Orthodox, while the educated Christian preferred to use the ethnic-national

the term *millet* is used by Europeans primarily in this narrow sense. Among the Muslims, especially the Turks, it still is defined as "nation"—equivalent to the Arabic *qawm*, the ethnic connotation of both *millet* and *qawm* being strong in modern usage.)

There was fragmentation among the Balkan constituents of the Orthodox *millet*. The Serbians, Bulgarians, and Romanians established themselves as separate "nations" with their own national churches. Greece too, in the period 1821–1829, established a national church, that was totally independent of the Istanbul patriarchate (although later, for political reasons, it sought to link the Greek national church with the patriarchate). In the end the Orthodox patriarch's rule had diminished to include only a handful of Orthodox Christians in the Middle East, the islands, and the Americas.

Middle Eastern Christians also became divided into a variety of ethnoconfessional subgroups, but that division was largely a reconfirmation of the old identities that had been preserved under the Ottomans. There were the Melkites, who were Greek Orthodox turned Catholic (Greek Catholic); there were the Greek Orthodox proper, who continued as Orthodox but adopted Arabic as their language; there were the Syrian Orthodox (Jacobites) and the Nestorians, who retained Syriac as a liturgical language. (The Jacobites, who were part of the Armenian *millet*, had fought hard to maintain their group integrity against the assimilation efforts of the Armenian patriarchate; they were recognized as a separate *millet* in 1882 and had their own representative in Istanbul.[18]) It is interesting to note that by 1882 the Ottoman government was listing separately its various ethnoreligious groups, and by the census of 1906–1907, for example, it listed as new *millets* (in addition to the Bulgarians, Protestants, and the Greek and Armenian Catholics) the old ethnoreligious groups, such as the Maronites, the Suryani (Syriac), the Chaldeans, the Jacobites, and even the Samaritans; but the Greek Orthodox, Armenian, and Jewish *millets* still occupied the prime rank.[19]

This fragmentation of the Greek and Armenian *millets* cannot be attributed to secular nationalism, for none of the small groups that broke away from the two umbrella communities had any real secular sense of nationhood or territorial aspiration beyond the village or local area. It was simply the case that the old religious identities—with ethnic characteristics, real or manufactured, prominently displayed—acquired special political significance during the nineteenth century. Language affinity was a reinforcing

---

label. Even today, the Muslims respond that they are Muslims (or "Turks," which in the Balkan world came to be synonymous with "Muslim").

[18]Sir Henry Charles Joseph Luke, *The Old Turkey and the New: From Byzantium to Ankara*, 2d ed. (London: Bles, 1955).

[19]For the classifications and numbers, see Kemal H. Karpat, *The Ottoman Population, 1830–1914: Demographic and Social Characteristics* (Madison: University of Wisconsin Press, 1985).

element of some of these freshly defined political identities, but was not indispensable or even basic.

The example of Lebanon is instructive. The Maronite Christians, who had been part of the Armenian *millet*, were granted a degree of autonomy in Mount Lebanon in 1860–1861. For generations this group had oscillated between the Arab Middle East and the Christian West. Language—Arabic or French as the situation demanded—was often the *symbol* of the orientation of the moment, but it played no part in the *choice* of orientation. Similarly, the fictitious Maronite claims of descent from either the early Phoenician inhabitants of the area or the French crusaders of Christian Europe are clearly designed to establish the legitimacy of their assertion of hegemony over the Lebanon and their identification with the West, rather than true statements of ethnic origin. Which of these two claims of descent is put forward depends on the audience.[20] Both are fictitious. Basically the source of Maronite identity is embodied in their religious community, yet the Maronites were the only Christian group in the Middle East actually to have any sort of basis upon which to lay claim to "nationhood" in the Western sense. They had been dwelling in the mountains for centuries (having taken refuge there after the Constantinople Council of A.D. 680 banned Monophysitic Christianity) and were closely associated with that limited territory in much the same way as the Serbians, the Albanians, and so forth, were associated with particular areas of Europe. It is significant that the geographical designation of their territory became the national name of the state in which they were then the clearly dominant group. All the new European territorial nations that emerged during the decline of the Ottoman Empire were named for the dominant ethnic group of the area. On the other hand, none of the Muslim states created on the Ottoman Asian lands—with the exception of Turkey itself—took an ethnic name, although several Arab states belatedly added the term "Arab" to the original name that denoted geography rather than ethnicity.

Conclusions

The Muslims in the Ottoman state in the nineteenth century followed a course that was similar to that of the other ethnoreligious groups, but the

---

[20]The problem of Lebanon has been much discussed lately and does not require lengthy analysis here. In brief, the conflict stems from the efforts of one group—the Maronites—to create a national state and an identity that is in accord with its own image of what these should be, an image that fails to take into account the existing ethno-communal-religious elements of the society or the facts of history. See K. S. Salibi, *The Modern History of Lebanon* (New York: Praeger, 1965), and esp. Michael Hudson, *The Precarious Republic: Political Modernization in Lebanon* (New York: Random House, 1968).

end was different. Islam was not employed to reinforce ethnic or tribal identity (as happened among some Muslim groups in Russia; for example, Islam was strongly associated with the ethnic identity of the Khazan Muslims and became their medium of cultural preservation and opposition to Russification). The Ottomans used Islam to develop a culturally homogeneous Muslim community with a sense of religious identity that superseded the purely ethnic and linguistic attachments and loyalties. This promotion of the religious identity was successful, partly because, with the exception of the Arabs, the Muslim groups under Ottoman rule did not have historical memories of national grandeur, literary achievement, or the like to generate opposition to the prospect of being submerged in a larger Islamic identity. This was true for the Turks, whose pre-Islamic past seemed pale when compared with their position and achievements after conversion (although some historical background was later "rediscovered" in the Republic as nationalistic fervor grew). However, political and social changes in the Ottoman state in the second half of the nineteenth century drastically changed the situation of the Muslim segment of the society.

The mass immigration that began in the 1860s and reached a peak in 1878 turned the Ottoman state into a predominantly Muslim entity. In addition, the same structural, administrative, political, and demographic changes that culminated in the establishment of new nations in the Balkans produced also the necessary class conditions for the transformation of the traditional Muslim community into an Ottoman Muslim nation. The disintegration of the traditional social and occupational structure; the demographic changes resulting from the massive immigrations, the settlement of nomadic tribes, and an internal migration from rural to urban areas; the introduction of a capitalistic economic system; the changes made in the administrative and political systems—all these combined to turn the Ottoman state into a different sociopolitical entity, a territorial state that was still Muslim in character. Although it had all the characteristics of a modern nation, it was basically a politicized and enlarged community united by bonds of Islamic solidarity. The individual allegiance and loyalty of the citizens were transferred from the sultan to the impersonal national Muslim state. The ideological force that triggered this development at the grass-roots level was a form of fundamentalist-populist Islam that drew its strength from various heterogeneous *sufi tariqats*, including the Naqshibandis, whose membership consisted of both immigrants and locals. In light of these developments it is clear that the position of the non-Muslims had to be redefined. Thus they became "minority groups" rather than autonomous communities of faith.

The policies of the central government in education, administration, fund allocation, and ideological leadership followed a course that paralleled these "national-Islamic" developments. The Islamic policy adopted by Sultan Abdulhamid II centered around his position as caliph, which he used to master, contain, control, and coordinate fundamentalism with the more orthodox Islamic ideology of the elites in order to achieve internal cohesion. Eventually this policy achieved also the ideological and cultural amalgamation of the immigrants and large segments of the Muslim middle and upper classes, including the Arabs of the urban areas of Syria and northern Iraq, into a relatively cohesive political-social unit that outwardly appeared as the new Ottoman Muslim nation.

The individual Muslim citizens gradually came to identify themselves with this new entity, formed of different tribes and ethnic groups but having Islam as its binding ideology and Turkish as its official language. This was the territorial state, the motherland, the *vatan*, to which, ideally, all the Muslims would pledge allegiance and loyalty. Implicit in the development of a supreme *vatan* was that its survival and welfare took precedence over the rule of the sultan, who could be challenged and deposed when his presence and policies became detrimental to the interests of the nation and *vatan*. Moreover, the idea that certain conditions within the motherland could be improved so as to strengthen the nation and make life better for the Muslims gained acceptance. Thus, the Muslim looked now on the *vatan* not only as an arena in which to cultivate virtue and prepare himself for the next world, but also as a place in which to fulfill worldly aspirations. The idea of active participation in world affairs espoused by the Naqshibandis was an outgrowth of this new outlook. This acceptance of change and material improvement in one's existence—or "modernization," as it was often called—was implicit in Abdulhamid II's Islamist policy.

Abdulhamid II played a vital role, using his policy of "Islamism" to shape the identity of the emerging Muslim nation. His task was basically a secular undertaking, but he approached it in purely religious terms and relied on absolutist power to carry out his policies. Thus he alienated the liberal intelligentsia (i.e., most of the modern literati) and even some of his own religious followers. He confused the conscious use of religion and of religious identity to create a new and possibly secular nation with piety and religious observance. Abdulhamid II did not have the intellectual capacity, or especially the courage (even though he appeared aware of what was happening), to acknowledge that he was seeking to build a modern Muslim nation with the Ottoman building blocks. Nor was he prepared to accept the economic and social conditions for modern statehood, which might call for his dismissal as an absolute ruler.

The political identity of the individual Muslim living in this transformed Ottoman state was strikingly different from that of his predecessors. The transformation had been precipitated by Europe, and the political reorganization undertaken in defense against European designs resulted in creation of an entity that resembled formally the European counterpart.

However, the new nation was distinguished from both European and older Islamic states, including the Ottoman state of the pre–1850s, by various new Islamic characteristics. Furthermore, the language of the new state was Turkish, which had been merely the language of administration, rather than that of a politically and culturally dominant group, until the Young Turks sought to make language the basis of national identity. The Young Turks tried to transform this Islamic nation, in which the Turks and Arabs were the main actors, into an ethnic Turkish state on the basis of the European ethnic-national model. The early secularism of the new rulers, which aimed essentially at liquidating the clerics' influence in the government, and their positivism were viewed by both Arab and non-Arab Muslims as directed at the essence of the newly emerging Muslim-Ottoman nation. By the time the Union and Progress Party realized that it had made a fatal mistake by adopting secular nationalism as state policy other forces had entered the fray, and, consequently, the effort to rectify the error was futile. The unity was broken as Arabs and Turks went their separate ways to build nation states confined to precisely defined boundaries. (The issue is far from settled among Arabs who claim to be one single nation but continue to live in separate territorial states that determine their loyalties, interests, and political identities.)

The period after the two world wars witnessed the emergence of a series of territorial states in the Middle East. Turkey was the first Muslim state to declare itself a national state. Theoretically, it was a secular nation, and the republican leaders made frantic efforts to find roots for their national identity in such nonreligious sources as language, folklore, and the pre-Islamic traditions of the ancient Turks, some of which had survived. These efforts were to a great extent fruitless because the so-called secular elements of the national culture either remained unaccepted except by a small minority or acquired religious dimensions once they found their way into the popular ethos. The very concept of nationhood in Turkey was communal in character: the basic characteristics of a modern nation as defined by Turks correspond perfectly to the characteristics of a community—and the only community the Turks knew was the historical religious community (though it had strong lay foundations). The cohesion and solidarity of this community were based on cultural similarities with roots in history and/or faith. Ziya Gökalp, the ideologue of the Turkish nationhood, based his theory of nationality and nationalism on precisely these characteristics.[21] A student

---

[21]The basic writings of Ziya Gökalp have been translated into English by Niyazi Berkes (although I contend that the introduction gives a totally false picture of Gökalp and his ideas): Ziya Gökalp, *Turkish Nationalism and Western Civilization*, trans. and intro. by Niyazi Berkes (New York: Columbia University Press, 1959); see also *Essays on Islam and Western Civilization Presented to Niyazi Berkes*, ed. P. Little (Leiden: Brill, 1976), and Niyazi Berkes, *The Development of Secularism in Turkey* (Montreal: McGill University Press, 1964).

of contemporary Turkish culture and society is bound to conclude that the Turkish nation is in some ways an extension of the Muslim nation that emerged out of the Muslim *millet* in the nineteenth century. The same can be said for the Arab states of the Middle East. Indeed, any Muslim state that emerges in the Middle East is likely to share to some extent the common national characteristics exhibited by all the others. To put it more bluntly, the Muslim segment of the defunct Ottoman state, although now divided into a number of territorial states, preserves characteristics of an Islamic-Ottoman nation as developed in the late nineteenth and early twentieth centuries. (Time and space does not permit development of this theme, which is an independent project in itself. While I contend that there is today an ideological Islamic continuity among the Muslim states of the Middle East, I recognize the extraordinary impact of the territorial statehood and national interest on the common ideological characteristics inherited from the past.)

"Secularism" had its place in these developments, but in meaning and scope that term, as defined by its advocates and practitioners in the area, cannot be equated with the European concept of secularism. In this new age of nationhood-territorial statehood, into which the Muslims have been dragged willy-nilly, the element of secularism will continue to be important. It will, however, continue to be Muslim-style secularism, confined to the conduct of government affairs and having little impact on the common view of the "nation." This is not to say that ethnic, linguistic, and cultural differences do not exist or that they have no impact on Middle Eastern Muslims. Many of the differences extant during the Ottoman era still survive, but they do not provide solid foundation material for the nationhood of Muslim states. I do not minimize the ability of governments to structure their territories in ways of life and patterns of collective behavior totally different from that in neighboring countries, as is actually happening in the Middle East today. The question is whether these artificially created nations can survive in the long run unless they find a way to develop a theoretical foundation and to organize themselves so that the similarities and differences between them all are acknowledged and allowed to coexist.

I cannot assert that the cultural-religious affinity between these Muslim states, despite considerable talk, is a basis that will lead to unity between them. "Pan-Arabism" and "pan-Turkism" have been shown by experience to be concepts that do not have much chance of prevailing, at least in the foreseeable future. Muslim political leaders have not in the past united for common Islamic causes, and I do not expect that they will do so unless forced by the pressure of Islamic fundamentalism. (The outcome of the war between Iran and Iraq may be decisive.) Yet, national statehood has not been a satisfactory experience in the Muslim Middle East. Opulence, efficiency, and ego satisfaction are not necessarily the only, or even the major, goals to which humanity ought—or does in fact—aspire. Peace, contentment, and the satisfaction derived from living in a congenial cultural and religious environment in harmony with other human beings in their own chosen environments are alternative goals. Although the nation-state may well be the most efficient form of political organization known to mankind, few national states have thus far been able to come close to achieving these latter goals for their citizens. In fact, the era of establishment of national entities has brought calamity on the Middle East, accounting for losses of human life and livelihood that far surpass those incurred during the four hundred years of Ottoman rule. The religious-ethnic communities that continued to exist and thrive throughout the Ottoman era are today threatened with assimilation or even outright destruction by ruling majorities, despite legal safeguards designed to protect them.

Although the Ottoman Empire is destroyed and cannot be reconstructed, there still exists throughout the area one legacy of the Ottomans: the memory of peaceful religious and ethnic coexistence on the basis of mutual recognition and acceptance. This legacy is a valuable one that should be appreciated and preserved, and this memory of the days of peaceful coexistence should be converted into a present-day reality in the Middle East.

4

Non-Muslims in Muslim Society:
A Preliminary Consideration of the
Problem on the Basis of Recent
Published Works by Muslim Authors

P. J. Vatikiotis

The title of this chapter is deliberately taken from the title of a recent book by Yusuf al-Qardawi.[1] The fact that the publisher is Maktabat Wahba in Cairo leads one to suspect that the author is either a member or a sympathizer of the Muslim Brotherhood in Egypt. Nevertheless, al-Qardawi, a prolific contemporary writer on Islamic themes,[2] is considered to be an *alim* and a *faqih*—that is, someone well versed in the study of Islam, Islamic law, and jurisprudence. What is interesting is that in the same year, 1977, a book by Jamal Badawi on the communal disturbances in Egypt appeared.[3] Only a year before that, William Sulayman, a Copt, published his *Dialogue between Religions*.[4] Tariq al-Bishri's series of articles in *Al-Tali'a*, entitled "Misr bayna Ahmad wa al-Mashi" (Egypt between Ahmad and the Messiah), was published in the 1970s and culminated in his book *Al-Muslimun wa al-Aqbat fi itar al-Jam'a al-wataniyya* (Muslims and Copts in the na-

---

A slightly modified version of this essay appears as a chapter entitled "The Obstacles to Plural Politics and a Pluralist Polity in Islam" in my book *Islam and the State* (London, 1987).

[1]Yusuf al-Qardawi, *Ghayr al-muslimin fi al-mujtama al-islami* (Non-Muslims in Muslim society) (Cairo, 1977).

[2]E.g., *Al-halal wa al-haram fi al-islam* (The permitted and the proscribed in Islam), eleven printings; *Al-hall al-islami, farida wa durura* (The Islamic solution, a precept and a necessity), two printings; and *Al-iman wa al-hayat* (Faith and life), five editions.

[3]Jamal Badawi, *Al-fitna al-ta'ifiyya fi misr: Judhuruha wa asbabuha* (The sectarian conflict in Egypt: Its origins ["seeds"] and causes) (Cairo, 1977).

[4]William Sulayman, *Al-hiwar bayna al-adyan* (The debate between religions) (Cairo, 1976).

tional community).[5] The public debate between Tawfiq al-Hakim and Louis Awad, representing secular Egyptian nationalism on one side, and their pro-Arab nationalism detractors and interlocutors on the other side, was published in Cairo in 1981 under the title *Al-In'izaliyyun fi Misr* (The isolationists in Egypt). The writings of a leading Azharite and Muslim Brotherhood sympathizer, Muhammad al-Bahiy, on Islamic thought and contemporary society of the mid–1960s, were reprinted in new editions.[6] A thesis at Cairo University by Muhammad Shawqi Zaki, published in 1980, was given wide publicity.[7] In the same year, the Copt Milad Hanna's *Naam Aqbat Lakin Misziyyun (Copts yes, but nonetheless Egyptians)*, was given equally great publicity.[8] Similarly, the works of Abd al-Hamid Mutawalli on the crisis of Islamic political thought throughout the 1970s were widely read.[9] And this is only a small sample of the proliferation of the more sophisticated and detailed works on Islam and society. But there is also the unending stream of popular booklets and tracts on Islam that litter sidewalk newsstands and bookstalls in the major cities and towns of Egypt.

These writings of the 1970s and early 1980s are an attempt to gloss and build on their earlier writings of the "masters," such as Hasan al-Banna, Sayyid Qutb, Muhammad al-Ghazali, Abd al-Qadir Awda, and other leading personages of the Muslim Brotherhood. In arguing the case and calling for the building of an Islamic society and political order, guided by the word of God and governed by his revealed law, all these writers, without exception, oppose secular political orders (*ilmaniyya*) as belonging to the "age of ignorance" (*jahiliyya*) and as having an infidel provenance from the West and East alike. They all argue that secular political orders are unacceptable because a Muslim can lead a believer's life only in an Islamic state and society and because he must not obey any other man-made law or those who legislate and enforce such laws.[10] The separation between the true

[5]Cairo, 1980.

[6]Muhammad al-Bahiy, *Al-fikr al-islami wa al-mujtama al-mu'asir: mushkilat al-hukm wa al-tawjih* (Islamic thought and contemporary society: The problem of rule) (Cairo: 1st ed., 1965; 2d ed. [1975]; 3d ed. [1982]). See also the companion volume, *Mushkilat al-usra wa al-takaful* (The problem of the family and cooperation) (Cairo: 1st ed., 1967; 3d ed., 1982).

[7]Muhammad Shawqi Zaki, *Al-ikhwan al-muslimum wa al-mujtama al-misri* (The Muslim Brothers and Egyptian society), 2d. ed. (Cairo, 1980).

[8]Milad Hanna, *Aqbat na'am . . . wa lakinna misriyyin* (Yes, Copts, but nevertheless Egyptians) (Cairo, 1980).

[9]See Abd al-Hamid Mutawalli, *Azamat al-fikr al-siyasi al-islami* (The crisis of Islamic political thought) (Alexandria, 1970). See also his several works on administrative and constitutional law (1936–1952) and his later *Masadir al-ahkam al-dusturiyya fi al-shari'a al-islamiyya* (Sources of constitutional rules in the Shari'a) (Cairo, 1963); "Al-islam wa mushkilat al-siyada fi al-dawla" ("Islam and the problem of sovereignty in the state"), *Majallat al-huquq* 1 and 2 (1964–65); and "Mabadi nizam al-hukm fi al-islam" ("The principles of government in Islam") and "Al-islam wa hal huwa din wa dawla" ("Islam: Is it religion and state?"), *Majallat al-qanun wa al-iqtisad* (Cairo University) 4 (1964) and 5 (1965).

[10]E.g., al-Qardawi describes an Islamic society as "a society that has accepted Islam as the

believer and such "materialist," transient orders is complete and unbridge-able. At the same time, all these writers feel constrained to touch on the subject of non-Muslims, the so-called *ahl al-dhimma*, in an Islamic political order. They invariably defend the doctrinal—that is, Qur'anic—revelations about this matter, ignore the record of historical experience, and assert that the true condition and correct position of non-Muslims in Muslim society are reflected in these revealed instructions and the administrative record of the first four Orthodox caliphs. This, they contend further, is ample evidence and guarantee of the possibility of pluralism in an Islamic order. Therefore, later in this chapter we shall survey the stated position regarding this matter as formulated, argued, and presented by some of these writers, before we comment on basic principles that can be derived from such exposition.

Although Hamilton Gibb and Harold Bowen concluded the two parts of their study *Islamic Society and the West*[11] with a long chapter on *dhimmis*—the recognized and tolerated religious and ethnic minorities in the Ottoman Empire—they only touch on the doctrinal position. Their work dealt mainly with the corporate nature of the *millet* in the Ottoman state and the history of the relations between these communities, or minorities, and the Ottoman government. The only monographic study in English of the relationship between non-Muslim subjects and their Muslim rulers is the one by A. S. Tritton published almost sixty years ago. After careful consideration of original sources, beginning with Caliph Umar's "covenant," Tritton concluded:

> This study of the relations between the government and its subjects who did not profess Islam can only produce confusion in the mind. At one moment the

---

basis of its life and conduct, a constitution for its government, and a source for its legislation and the direction (instruction and guidance) for all matters of life, individual and social, material and moral, local and international" (al-Qardawi, *Ghayr al-muslimin*, p. 5). Abd al-Qadir Awda states: "Islamic rule is the best the world has known" (*Al-islam wa awda'una al-siyasiyya* [Cairo, 1978], p. 8). He refers to sura 3:85: "And whoso seeketh as religion other than the Surrender [to Allah: i.e., Islam] it will not be accepted from him, and he will be a loser in the Hereafter." (All Qur'anic suras and verses quoted in English are from M. Pickthall, *The Glorious Koran* [New York: New American Library, Mentor, 1954].) According to Awda, the Muslim has no choice because "it becometh not a believing man or a believing woman when Allah and His Messenger have decided an affair [for them], that they should [after that] claim any say in their affair; and whoso is rebellious to Allah and His Messenger, he verily goeth astray in error manifest" (sura 33:36). Moreover, all these writers depend on the revelation "Whoso judgeth not by that which Allah hath revealed: such are disbelievers" (sura 5:44; repeated in verse 47). In asserting that Islamic society is the only one in which faith is the bond of political association, Sayyid Qutb (*Ma'alim fi al-tariq* [Cairo, 1964], p. 146), refers repeatedly to these revelations: "So judge between them by that which Allah hath revealed" (sura 5:49); "Ye are the best community that hath been raised up for mankind.... And if the People of the Scripture had believed, it had been better for them. Some of them are believers; but most of them are evil-livers" (sura 3:110).

[11]Vol. 1, Parts 1 and 2 (London: Oxford University Press, 1950, 1957).

dhimmi appears as a persecuted worm who is entirely negligible, and the next complaint is made of his pernicious influence on the Muslims round him. . . . There is no constitutional growth, events move in irregular curves, not in a straight line. . . . The rule of Islam was often burdensome, the revolts in Egypt prove it. . . . Restrictions were placed on their dress, and the attempt to oust them from official posts began.

Recognizing that individual Christians and Jews were often close to the ruler and sometimes held the highest posts, Tritton went on to say: "Though *dhimmis* might enjoy great prosperity, yet always they lived on sufferance, exposed to the caprices of the rulers and the passions of the mob." On the eventual spiritual isolation of Islam, he noted, "The world was divided into two classes, Muslims and others, and only Islam counted."[12]

In 1947 Albert Hourani published his *Minorities in the Arab World*[13] under the auspices of the Royal Institute of International Affairs. It dealt mainly with Egypt and the Fertile Crescent, the latter comprising relatively recent states under British and French mandates. But these states were also encumbered by a high proportion of minorities, reflecting ethnic and sectarian diversity. After considering the status and condition of these minorities in each country, guarantees for their protection and their freedom of religious practice, and the impact of nationalism in both its secular Arab and Islamic varieties, as well as the historical tradition of fear, suspicion, and resentment among the various communities, Hourani concluded that the majority and the minorities did not fully constitute a national community in any of these countries. In enumerating problems of intermarriage, conversion, and civil and political equality, he wondered whether secular nationalism was sufficient basis for a national community and stable government. Moreover, neither assimilation nor autonomy seemed to him to constitute permanent solutions to the problem. In examining the historical, religious, and demographic reasons for the presence of so many minorities, he observed that non-Muslims (Christians and Jews) did not form part of the community of the state—that is, the body politic. He also noted that these were closed communities, "all marginal, shut out from power and historic decision."[14]

Later in 1950, Gibb and Bowen defined a *dhimmi* as a non-Muslim subject of a Muslim ruler. Relations with the ruler are regulated by contract once the non-Muslim community is incorporated in the Domain of Islam. Under certain conditions the contract provides for toleration of the infidel *dhimmi*

---

[12]A. S. Tritton, *Non-Muslim Subjects of Muslim Rulers* (Cambridge: Cambridge University Press, 1930), pp. 229–232; Arabic translation, *Al-Islam wa ahl al-dhimma*, by Hasan Habashi (Cairo, n.d.), and Abd al-Karim Zaydan, *Ahkam al-dhimmiyyin wa al-musta'minin fi dar al-Islam* (Cairo, 1947).

[13]London: Oxford University Press, 1947.

[14]Ibid., p. 22.

and allows him to practice his religion. They emphasize, therefore, the division between believers and infidels, both in Islamic society and in the world. But even under this contract what is offered the non-Muslim is in return for payment of a special poll tax (*jizya*, abolished in the Ottoman Empire in 1855 and in Egypt in 1856) and an agreement to be subject to certain restrictions. The term *dhimmi* refers to the member of a caste inferior to fellow Muslim subjects. The *dhimmi* is at a legal disadvantage, is at times subject to laws regarding distinctive clothing, and must refrain from building new places of worship unless certain specific regulations are complied with.[15] In such a political order, *dhimmis* are dealt with by the government not as individual citizens or subjects of the state but as members of a distinct and separate community. Therefore the status, rights, and duties of the *dhimmi* derive exclusively from membership in a protected community. The *millet* idea was not an original invention of the Muslims or the Ottomans. Romans and Byzantines practiced such discrimination between the *homoioi* and the other, especially by the Byzantines with regard to the Jews.

After a lengthy discussion of the history of these minorities and how they fared in their relations with the state, Gibb and Bowen conclude that the *dhimmi* status is one of inferiority. They further enumerate certain consequences of the classification in Islam of *dhimmis* by religion—for example, it affected adversely the solidarity of the Ottoman society and discouraged primary loyalty to the Sultan, because such political loyalty was subordinated to the primordial attachment to the religious or ethnic community. Although in the rural areas the distinction between *dhimmi* and Muslim tended to fade away, in the urban centers the distinction and separation were pronounced. Consequently, integration was difficult and not encouraged by either the Muslim ruler or the leaders of the various non-Muslim communities, for economic and other reasons. Finally, while the Shari'a enjoins the toleration of scriptural infidels, it insists on their inferiority.[16]

These studies show, first, that the relationship between non-Muslim subjects and Muslim rulers was originally contractual and, second, that there was no systematic legal development either to regulate this relationship or to integrate the non-Muslims into the Islamic polity. The nearest thing to a regularized system was the Ottoman *millet*, which if anything consecrated and institutionalized the separateness of the *dhimmi* from the larger society

---

[15]It should be noted that the communal trouble in Khanka in Egypt in 1972 involved the use of the premises of a Coptic lay society for church or divine services without a permit from the Ministry of the Interior. See Jamal Badawi, *Al-fitna al-ta'ifiyya fi misr* (Cairo, 1977).

[16]Sura 9:29: "Fight against such of those who have been given the Scripture as believe not in Allah nor in the Last Day, and forbid not that which Allah hath forbidden by His messenger, and follow not the religion of truth until they pay the tribute readily, *being brought low*" (italics added).

and political order. Third, much of the status and condition of this relationship depended in the final analysis on the individual ruler.

Until the mid–1960s the question of non-Muslims in Muslim society did not attract the attention or engage the energies of Arab Muslim writers, apart from the known tracts of the leaders of the Ikhwan.[17] This may have been partly because of the Arab nationalist and generally radical euphoria of the 1950s and early 1960s under the leadership of Nasser in Egypt and the Ba'th in the Fertile Crescent. As already indicated, more-recent literature suggests that now that secular political ideas in the Middle East have been devalued and are in retreat, and their proponents are on the defensive—some of these writers, in fact, anticipate a rout of secularism—the only possible alternative is restoration of an Islamic political order throughout the region.

My purpose in this chapter is not to comment on specific instances of the history of minorities in Islamic countries or to define and analyze the phenomenon of ethnic diversity in this part of the world. Instead, I want to highlight the doctrinal basis and confusion of religious pluralism and its political negation—that is, the failure to accommodate it politically. In doing so, I shall refer only in passing to the difference between an asserted support and protection of pluralism on the basis of the scriptures, on the one hand, and its indifferent fate in actual practice—or at least historical experience—on the other hand. In short, I propose to help define the religious-social-political environment and the shaky foundation upon which such religio-political pluralism exists and the extent to which it is only a putative political pluralism.

By ethnicity I assume we mean a diversity of ethnic groups or "nations" within the territorial boundaries of a state. This is not to preclude the existence of the same ethnic group across state boundaries, as in the case of the Kurds, for instance, but I shall not deal with that phenomenon. Pluralism, on the other hand, I take to mean religious and cultural diversity within and across state boundaries, but in Western political usage it refers to the private and public acceptance of opposing political views, promoted by freely organized voluntary associations, interest groups, and political parties and the toleration of alternative governments or regimes. There are a few regimes today, mostly in the West, that subscribe to values that uphold a plural political system. Many others, especially in the Middle East, do not subscribe to plural political systems, or at least are unable to construct them, even though the society in them is characterized by ethnic diversity and religious pluralism. They simply have been unable to accommodate this diversity politically.[18]

[17]I am using Ikhwan interchangeably with Muslim Brotherhood.
[18]Syria, Iraq, Iran, and even Egypt—the official religion of the state in all of these is Islam.

One of these systems, Lebanon, which constructed its political system on a confessional basis, has recently disintegrated.[19] That particular crisis has been a manifestation of a wider, more general, political problem in the Middle East, where religion is a potent ideological force that challenges territorial rule. The religion-based identity of the people of the Middle East has resisted the secular integration of nationalism, and politics itself has been understood and regarded as a variant of religion. What Carleton Coon called the religious and ethnic mosaic of the Middle East has tended to ignore—and in certain cases even reject—the national boundaries so recently imposed on it. Movements of religious reform, imported ideas, and institutions of nationalism and constitutionalism were used to reconcile the belief system, cultural perceptions, and traditional institutions of an earlier age to the requirements of the modern Western state system without much success. Unfortunately, there was no philosophical commitment to secularism and its values of skepticism, experimentation, and tolerance so essential to pluralistic politics. With one or two exceptions, states have arisen in the Middle East that are not nation-states. As a political concept, the nation-state is characterized by an authority that is territory-based, not by universalist, extraterritorial conceptions of it.

The term nation-state is therefore misleading when applied to the several countries in the Middle East, because in most of them the nation is considered in religious terms to encompass those beyond and across the territorial boundaries of the individual states. There is a constant clash between the exigencies of the modern territorial state and the wider nation or community of believers, which until the recent past was governed by reference to religious precepts and what was believed to be God's revealed pattern for the universe.

Caught between the burden of tradition, with its insistence on the supremacy of the nation of Islam, and the requirements of the modern/territorial secular state, temporal governments in the Middle East found themselves set on a dangerous course. Lebanon and Iran, two recent examples, foundered. Failing to construct regimes outside religion, one collapsed into chaos, the other succumbed to the tyranny of a near-medieval fundamentalism. In Lebanon territorial jurisdiction gave way to sectarian jurisdiction and nationality. In Iran, the dominant Shi'a community of

---

Neither radical nationalism and socialism led by Egypt in the 1950s and 1960s nor Ba'thism in the Fertile Crescent succeeded in separating religion from the state. See my "Authoritarianism and Autocracy in the Middle East," in my *Arab and Regional Politics in the Middle East* (London: Croom Helm; New York: St. Martin's Press, 1984), pp. 135–151.

[19]The remainder of this paragraph and the next two paragraphs were previously published in a slightly different version in "Crisis in Lebanon: A Local Historical Perspective," *The World Today*, March 1984, pp. 85–92, of which see esp. p. 92. On Carlton Coon, see *Caravan: The Story of the Middle East* (New York: Holt, Reinhart and Winston, 1958).

believers ignores territorial boundaries and seeks to extend its "universal truth" among fellow believers across boundaries. Such notions of power and authority based on religion and ideology suggest that throughout the Middle East the legitimization of power is still widely contested and that authority is tenuous.

More than a decade ago, Elie Kedourie underlined the clash between nationalism in which the "primordial value is the nation, not, say, class or religion" and other ideological conceptions of the nation.[20] When Islam became the experession of Arab national genius and was thus inexorably linked to Arabism, the secular trend of the nineteenth and early twentieth centuries was abandoned in favor of an older dichotomy—the one between the solidarity of a superior Islamic nation and all other political systems. This suggests that the more rigid the ideological definition of a nation or political order is, the more difficult it is to accommodate ethnic and religious diversity within its territorial boundaries. As for political pluralism, it is rejected outright by such a total ideological order, because the political system separates the non-Muslim body politic by merely tolerating *dhimmi*s as members of a separate community.[21]

I assume that one reason we are looking at ethnicity and pluralism is to ascertain how Islam and the Muslims perceive them. Another is to consider in what kind of political order they can be accommodated and, more specifically, whether the Muslim doctrinal provisions and historical perceptions render such accommodation easy, difficult, or impossible. Thus, if Islam and those who claim to represent it and want to implement its law and rule over man, society, and the polity reject all other human forms of law and rule and insist on the necessity of a total—that is, all-embracing—ideological purity and uniformity, then there is an unbridgeable gap between them and all other social and political arrangements. In practice, this has taken the form of a conflict between those who want to adapt secular temporal political arrangements and the champions of the rule of God on earth, between those who contend that a Muslim can be a believer, a member of the *umma*, and a carrier of Islamic culture, and still organize his life on earth on the basis of man-made law, on the one hand, and those who insist that a person is not a Muslim by any definition unless he establishes the law

[20]Elie Kedourie, "Religion and Secular Nationalism in the Arab World," in *The Middle East: Oil, Conflict, and Hope,* ed. A. L. Udovitch (Lexington, Mass.: Heath, 1976), pp. 181–194.

[21]The writings of the Muslim Brotherhood until today provide ample evidence of this requirement. See esp. Hasan al-Banna, *Majmu'at rasa'il* (Cairo, n.d.); Awda, *Al-islam wa awda'una al-siyasiyya* (n. 10, above); Sayyid Qutb, *Nahwa mujtama islami* (Amman, 1969) and *Ma'alim fi al-tariq* (Cairo, 1964).

of God as the only regulator of his earthly life, on the other hand. Theoretically at least, the former, accepts the integration of a national
community and body politic that includes non-Muslims as full members. Public affairs are regulated by a uniform law of the land; authority and power are territory-based. Because the latter recognizes no
territorial boundaries, only the bond of faith, he rejects all of this outright and refers to divine dispensation regarding non-Muslims in the
umma. Any society that is governed by and governs according to anything other than God's law is an infidel society. No one can really lead
the life of a true Muslim except in such an Islamic state.[22]

This is the main thrust and argument of the proponents of the Islamic
state and rule up to the present, and it is within this context that they deal
with, or ignore, the question of non-Muslims. Yet it is interesting to note
that their argument begins with the issue of power on the basis of the
Qur'an:

> They say: Surely, if we return to al-Madina the mightier will soon drive out
> the weaker; when might belongeth to Allah and to His Messenger and the
> believers, but the hypocrites know not; . . . and Allah will not give the disbe-
> lievers any way of success against the believers; And fight them until persecution
> is no more, and religion is all for Allah.[23]

In fact, Hasan al-Banna proclaimed, "We demand power for all of us"[24]
until the Muslims raise the "banner of the Qur'an everywhere."[25] People
are clearly divided over this power between believers and unbelievers. In
the end, though, "God must inherit the earth" so that, while protecting
non-Muslims, the believer must not cease to call on them to embrace the
true faith and submit to God's perfect law.[26] Because Islam is there and
available, no other order on earth will do. After all, power is the symbol
of Islam, and earthly government is one of its pillars. Therefore, the first
requirement in the establishment of such an order is the transformation
of society from a powerless Islamic society to a society in which power is
monopolized by the Muslims in it.[27]

Qardawi states that the legal position of non-Muslims in Muslim society
is that they have the same rights and duties as the Muslims except in certain

---

[22]See note 10, above.

[23]Sura 64:8, 4:141, 8:7, 39.

[24]*Majmu'at rasa'il*, p. 19.

[25]Ibid., pp. 20, 180–184.

[26]He uses sura 9:32: "Fain would they put out the light of Allah with their mouths, but
Allah disdaineth (aught) save that He shall perfect His light, however much the disbelievers
are averse."

[27]Sayyid Qutb, in his *Ma'alim*, is particularly adamant on this point, and so are all the other
Muslim Brothers. See esp. Zaynab al-Ghazali, *Ayyam min hayati* (Cairo and Beirut, 1982).

clearly defined exceptional cases. Their special position, as *dhimmi*s, is based on revelation that provides a covenant from God, the Prophet, and the community (*umma*) which guarantees protection and security for them. They are granted citizenship on certain conditions: payment of the *jizya* and observance of the Shari'a in all matters other than religion. Otherwise, they are members of the Domain of Islam (Dar al-Islam). While they have the right to protection against external enemies and internal oppression, security, freedom of worship, freedom to work and make a profit (but not from *riba*, usury and interest), the right to hold official state posts other than religious ones (these are enumerated as the *imama*, head of state, leadership of the armed forces, judicial posts entailing adjudication between Muslims, and the administration of *waqf*s), they must respect Islam and the religious feelings of Muslims by not displaying their own religious symbols prominently and not erecting churches or synagogues in places where they had none before.[28] The difficulty arises over the guarantees for these rights of non-Muslims. The Shari'a enjoins believers to respect these rights, and the Imam and the *umma* must observe the law. Yet in the end the only guarantee is that of the Muslim's conscience.

A legitimate point made by Qardawi and many others is that as citizens of an Islamic state non-Muslims must observe all the laws that do not affect their religious belief and freedom of worship—civil, criminal, and commercial. But non-Muslims cannot preach beliefs that are contrary to Islam, the religion of the state—that is, they cannot hold, entertain, or publish opposing or differing views and beliefs. This position is common to all other writers on the subject too. Despite the historical record, they readily admit, they all extol the unique tolerance of non-Muslims by Islam, in doctrine and in practice, in sharp contrast to the persecution of religious minorities, especially the Jews, in Christian Europe. This can be attributed partly to their perception of the Islamic state as being similar to the state in existence at the time of the Prophet and the Four Orthodox Caliphs. But Qardawi complains, "It is not part of forgiveness to ask of the Muslim to forgo and freeze his religious rules and the law of God . . . the destruction of his religious guide to life for the sake of non-Muslim minorities so as not to cause them anxiety or hurt their feelings."[29] If the rules of his faith bring the Muslim closer to his God, non-Muslims must accept them as the law of the land and obey the state order that is accepted by the majority.[30] It is not toleration to substitute nationalism for these rules, because nationalism is contrary to Islam and to Christianity.[31] Islamic society is based on a belief

[28]Al-Qardawi, Ghayr Al-Muslimin, p. 20.
[29]Ibid., p. 82.
[30]Ibid.
[31]Ibid., p. 83.

and an ideology from which flow ethics and rules of conduct.[32] God prohibits the Muslim from governing by or obeying any law except God's own law. No other social and political "bond" (e.g., nationalism) is permissible or can replace that of religion. The Muslim cannot allow or live under an administration or political order controlled by non-Muslims.[33]

It is on the basis of the above notions that most of these writers try to explain away, albeit unconvincingly, the occasional special laws applied to *dhimmis* for purposes of social distinction and the periodic hostility of Muslims to *dhimmis*, as well as the uprisings against them. They justify their hostility to a secular order by saying that secularism has been "the octopus which destroyed Islamic society and its values."[34] At the same time, they link their insistence on an Islamic political order with independence from an infidel world and liberation from its harmful ideas. They also cite their right to an Islamic state based on impressive potential power. There are some thirty-seven to forty independent Islamic countries, occupying very strategic locations in the world—the Suez Canal, the Dardanelles, the Red Sea, and the Persian Gulf. These countries control more than 60 percent of proven oil reserves, 70 percent of rubber, and 50 percent of jute. Some 60 percent of Mediterraneans are Muslim. One-fifth of the world's population is Muslim. Of about forty-one African states, twenty-three are Muslim, and nearly 60 percent of the continent's population are Muslim. In other words, the feeling of growing and potential power encourages the demand for an Islamic order.

Abd al-Hamid Mutawalli, a prolific contemporary writer who supports the idea of an Islamic order, nevertheless recognizes the crisis in Islamic political thought arising from the abject emulation by Muslims of the West in the conduct of their public affairs and the tyranny of despotic rule in Islamic countries.[35] But despite his attempt at a liberal interpretation of doctrine and law, he rejects the notions of popular sovereignty and elections as non-Islamic concepts. Political choice in this order will be denied to non-Muslims; they will remain outside the body politic.

The Islamic order, with its doctrinal provisions for non-Muslims, is also viewed by many of these writers as necessary in order to combat alien, infidel ideologies—that is, it is an aspect of the ideological and political separation between what is Muslim and what is non-Muslim. God made the Muslims, not anyone else, his vice-regents on earth to rule and govern. After all, Allah's religion is Islam[36] and nothing else will do.[37] Rule belongs

---

[32]See esp. Qutb, *Ma'alim*, and *Al-islam wa awda'una al-siyasiyya*.

[33]Note the adamance of al-Ghazali in *Ayyam min hayati*; she repeatedly appeals to sura 3:28.

[34]Ahmad al-Bahiy, *Al-fikr al-islami wa al-mujtama al-mu'asir: mushkilat al-hukm wa al-tawjih* (1982 ed.), p. 371.

[35]Abd al-Hamid Mutawalli, *Azamat al-fikr al-siyasi fi al-Islam* (Alexandria, 1970).

[36]Sura 3:19: "Lo! religion with Allah [is] The Surrender."

[37]Sura 3:85 (quoted in note 10, above).

to God; all other rule is infidel and must be rejected. The constitution of the Shari'a is universal, good for the whole world. Islamic rule is legitimate, all other rule is tyranny and despotism. Unbelief (*kufr*) is synonymous with tyranny (*zulm*).[38] It is in the nature of Islam to be superior and dominate all else.[39] Islamic precepts are implemented not by individuals, but by states and governments.[40]

Although Abd al-Qadir Awda, for instance, utters the usual pious formulas about the equality between Muslims and *dhimmis*, he suggests that a civil society in Islam is not possible, that there can be only a religious-ideological society. And while for him and others like him the *Shari'a* has universal applicability, its actual implementation is possible only where Muslims hold power—that is, in the Domain of Islam (Dar-al-Islam). In the meantime, circumstances have rendered the Shari'a's sway (or domain) regional rather than universal. The citizens of Dar al-Islam are of two categories: those who embrace Islam the faith, and those who abide by its rules without embracing the faith—that is, the *dhimmis*.

It cannot be emphasized enough that the Islamic order is being put forth as the imperative total alternative to a pluralistic system. This may be the reason that non-Muslim minorities remain anxious and apprehensive. In addition, because temporal regimes have failed to construct political orders wholly detached from religion (that is, provide a distinct alternative to Islam as *din wa dawla*), pluralism has suffered even more and the feeling of political separation on the part of minorities has persisted. The pronounced trend to take the side of an Islamic order over a pluralistic system is exemplified best in the writings of the late Sayyid Qutb of the Ikhwan throughout the 1950s and 1960s until his execution. For him, Islam is the only liberating force remaining in a perverted, corrupt world, and the political future belongs to it. He emphasizes the collective total society offered by Islam in contrast to the extreme individualism of Christianity and the exclusiveness of Judaism.[41] He even gives credit to Islam for inspiring the European movements of humanism and the Renaissance—unaware of the Greco-Roman roots of these movements. The failure of the actual historical experience and practice of Islam to attain the ideal Islamic order is, for Qutb, merely a transient aberration and deviation. While it is true, as Qutb contends, that Christianity is not a social theory and cannot be the basis for a social and political system, whereas Islam is, he ignores the more permanent ethical and metaphysical principles that influenced, or at

[38]Awda, *Al-islam wa awda'una al-siyasiyya*, using sura 31:13 ("Ascribe no partners unto Allah. Lo! to ascribe partners [unto Him] is a tremendous wrong") and sura 2:254 ("The disbelievers, they are the wrongdoers"). See also Qutb, *Ma'alim*, pp. 200–202.

[39]See Awda, *Al-islam wa awda'una al-siyasiyya*, p. 65.

[40]Ibid., pp. 70–75.

[41]On Judaism and the Jews especially, see Ali Husni al-Kharbutli, *Al-arab wa al-yahud fi al-asr al-islami* (Cairo, [n.d.]), and *Al-ilaqat al-siyasiyya bayna al-arab wa al-yahud* (Cairo, 1969).

least informed, the evolving order in Europe. He also denies that human beings have any choice in devising a temporal order, since the Islamic social system is original, created by revelation as a "godly order." The historical forms that Islamic society has so far taken do not, according to Qutb, define, limit, or exhaust all other possible forms of this society for every generation. It is a unique system because it was founded not by humans but by God's revealed law (nizam kulli da'im).[42]

Qutb makes the usual statements about non-Muslims, but he admits to religious fanaticism (ta'assub).[43] He goes further than other writers when he suggests that non-Muslims in Muslim society can submit to the general ethic (manhaj) based on the worship of God alone even though they are not Muslim.[44] At the same time, he is more Manichean in his sharp distinction between good (Islam) and evil (all else), and the two cannot coexist. There is only one world, that of Islam, and for a Muslim there is no nation or country except one in which God's Shari'a reigns supreme.[45] The Domain of Islam is where everyone, including dhimmis, accepts the Shari'a as the regulator of private and public life. All lands where Islam is not in control of the public order constitute the World of War, which Muslims are to oppose and fight against.[46] Qutb's dialectic, or dynamic, of constant struggle between Muslim and non-Muslim is interesting because the latter also includes Muslims who refuse to set up a truly Islamic order on earth. There can be no compromise. Truth is absolute and indivisible.[47] The duty and role of Islam and of the Muslim is to divest the world of jahiliyya-type leadership. There is one choice only—between unbelief (kufr) and belief (iman), tyranny and faith.[48]

Needless to say, Qutb's well-known tract Ma'alim fi al-tariq (Signposts on the way) was a stirring call to action. Boldly explicit in its demand for power to be placed in the hands of a leader who is committed to the establishment of the Islamic order and state, as well as in his attack on the then regime in Egypt, it is no wonder he was arrested and executed. He was openly proclaiming his, and all true Muslims', disobedience of constituted authority and defying the power of the state.[49]

Despite all the difficulties, non-Muslims have survived in Muslim societies, states, and empires for the last fourteen hundred years. However, they did so mainly, and for most of that period, as separate, corporate communities

---

[42]Qutb, Nahwa mujtama islami, p. 53.
[43]Ibid., pp. 110, 130.
[44]Ibid., pp. 87–131, and Qutb, Ma'alim, pp. 86–89.
[45]Qutb, Nahwa mujtama islami, pp. 184–185.
[46]Qutb, Ma'alim, pp. 192–193, 198.
[47]Ibid., pp. 200–202.
[48]Ibid., pp. 202–208.
[49]See al-Ghazali, Ayyam min hayati.

in a special relationship with their Muslim rulers. On the unofficial, private level, many non-Muslims have coexisted as infidel minorities relatively peacefully with the Muslim majority. A very small elite among them even reached high positions of state in the courts of Muslim rulers. But to some extent, from the sixteenth century to World War II, many of these communities enjoyed the protection of their more powerful co-religionists from Europe under special arrangements. In the interwar period, and more recently at the height of nationalist fervor, several of them experienced the restrictions imposed on ethnic and/or religious minorities in Turkey, Iraq, and elsewhere. The trend, though, was for newly established national governments to adopt secular forms, and at least effect the integration of all their inhabitant subjects as citizens of a territorial nation-state. The attempt was confused, indeterminate, and weakened by society's deep attachment to tradition. The lingering influence of European power acted for a while as some kind of guarantee against blatantly violent conflict between the majority and the minorities.

Egyptians, for example, proudly refer to their own efforts to construct a clearly secular national community, allowing for both ethnicity and pluralism, especially under the leadership of the Wafd. Yet even this singular and brief attempt was flawed because it was marred by vacillation between desiring the returns in power and popularity that a less-secular stand would bring and fearing the unknowns involved in establishing a secular order. The clearly weak and hesitating champions of a secular public order, who were marked by a measure of political pluralism, were soon defeated by the return of traditional despotism alongside a growing movement for an Islamic order. In fact, many erstwhile secularists had already succumbed to such an ethic. But secularism of the sword remained, and indeed prospered. Secularism associated with the rule of a law that was not of divine provenance atrophied and collapsed. Greater deference to the Islamic ethos was demanded, and given.[50]

In these conditions of failure, confusion, and in some respects despair, the sharpened and violent clash between the champions of a uniform and total Islamic order and the secular state (now no longer controlled by those who were initially willing to permit at least formal pluralism, but by powerful military and other autocrats) has been revived. The failure of the nation-state in Lebanon is a matter of record, as is the persecution of religious minorities and opposition political groups by a proclaimed Islamic order in Iran. The fear and insecurity of the Coptic minority in Egypt during the last thirty years led to an open confrontation between its leadership and the state in 1972, requiring the promulgation of the Law for the Pro-

---

[50]Here I refer to developments in Egypt, Syria, and the Sudan at least since the 1930s.

tection of National Unity in August 1972.[51] Some Coptic writers frantically argued for a secular order in which a plural society could flourish and in which the essence of citizenship was allegiance to the nation, not to a religion. They called for an allegiance based on territory, language, a common life, and shared historical experience.[52]

All this suggests that, despite Islamic protestations to the contrary, minorities remain anxious and apprehensive, and sectarian conflict persists. If an Islamic order is, as defined by its proponents, a total system, it cannot entertain political pluralism, only political separatism. No wonder non-Muslims were attracted in the past to secular solutions for the national community. Today, however, as a result of Islamic militancy and the demise of orders that at least theoretically allow pluralism, they are willing to consider for themselves a guaranteed separate status.

Muslim writers point to the awful persecution of minorities, especially the Jews, in Europe. Yet in the liberal democracies the decision was made more than 150 years ago to emancipate such minorities and treat them as full members of the body politic under a secular law of the land. Their rights and duties no longer derive from their separate status. Such a step is not one that the proponents of the Islamic state propose to take. On the contrary, they simply wish to revert to the doctrinal provisions of the faith insofar as non-Muslims are concerned. In fact, according to these proponents, only the law of God can prevail; all other sources of authority in society must be rejected. They insist on a "godly community" and a "righteous political leadership" as the minimum requirement for a true Muslim religious and political life. Uniformity of conduct under the Shari'a must prevail over any national integration based on political accommodation of ethnicity and pluralism. There must be one cultural tradition, the Islamic tradition, to guide and inspire the citizens of the Islamic state.[53]

There are also those who argue that the imposition of the righteous view of the public order insisted on by some Muslims is simply a stage in the historical evolution of the societies—akin to, for example, the Cromwell and Puritan episode in seventeenth-century England—and that it is not a view or position that is peculiar to Islam. The analogy, in my view, is false. The Cromwellian revolution ended with the legislative ascendancy of Parliament, the restoration of the monarchy, and the supremacy of civil law and was soon followed by religious toleration and later gradual political

---

[51]See Badawi, *Al-fitna al-ta'ifyya fi misr*, for details, esp. pp. 9–17.

[52]See al-Ghazali, *Ayyam min hayati*; al-Bahiy, *Al-fikr al-islami wa al-mujtama al-mu'asir* (n. 34, above).

[53]See the interesting argument by Tariq al-Bishri, *Al-aqbat wa al-muslimin fi itar al-jam'a al-wataniyya* (Cairo, 1980), pp. 679–750.

emancipation—to pluralism. Human values once more became the measure of a public order. The fact that Christianity does not provide in its doctrine any legal or juridical schemes for regulation of the temporal relations between human beings, or the conduct of their earthly affairs, was an advantage. What is interesting is that Muslim writers recognize this and argue from it that, except in matters of faith and religious practice, non-Muslims in an Islamic order must come under the jurisdiction of the Shari'a.[54] This theoretically plausible proposition is one that non-Muslims may have to consider a serious possibility in the future. On the other hand, when the same writers insist there are no human—only divine—values,[55] the possibility of pluralism becomes remote, because divine values are eternal, immutable, and final.

The essence of secularism—apart from the separation between religion and state—is acceptance of the propositions that no one person or group has exclusive possession of absolute and indivisible truth and that no single form is final. A corollary of this is the recognition that there are alternative notions about humanity and the world and, what is more significant, the toleration of these alternative views. This implies skepticism, not certitude, toward absolutist assertions, and experimentation with alternative forms. If this is a fair distinction between secularism and a total, ideological-divine order, then the essence of the problem of ethnicity and pluralism remains

---

[54]Awda, *Al-islam wa awda'una al-siyasiyya*, pp. 90–92.

[55]Salim Azzam, secretary-general of the Islamic Council, recently sent me a copy of "A Model of an Islamic Constitution." Two suras introduce the publication: 4:105, "We have revealed to you the Book with the truth so that you may judge between people by that which Allah has shown you; so do not plead for the treacherous," and 5:44, "Those who do not judge in accordance with what Allah has revealed are the unbelievers." The introduction states: "The contemporary Islamic world is passing through a period of creative tension; 'tension' because the real state of affairs, at individual, collective, and state levels, is generally at variance with the ideals and norms of Islam; 'creative' because this tension has released forces positive and powerful enough to bring about an upsurge in the Muslim world directed toward making Islam the guiding light in the reconstruction of individual and social life." It also records Muslims' "disillusionment with secular ideologies and their firm resolve to build their society on the foundations of Islam.... The Qur'an has enunciated not only moral norms for the individual, and rules and regulations for family and social life, but also a number of civil, commercial, criminal, constitutional, and international laws and principles of judicial conduct. Unless there is an Islamic state, parts of the Shari'a will remain in suspension." Article 14, Chapter 2, "Obligations and Rights" reads in part: "Every Muslim has a right to seek citizenship of the State...." There is no explicit statement regarding citizenship for non-Muslims. Article 16(c), regarding non-Muslims, reads: "In matters of personal law the minorities shall be governed by their own laws and traditions, except if they themselves opt to be governed by the Shari'a. In case of conflict between parties, the Shari'a shall apply." Article 18(a) states: Citizens have a right to assemble and to form groups, organizations, and associations—political, cultural, scientific, social, and other—as long as their programs and activities are consistent with the provisions of the Shari'ah." Finally, articles 24 and 26 suggest that non-Muslims may not hold elected office.

its political accommodation—or nonaccommodation—in the state, and to-day in the territorially defined nation-state.

The problems of ethnicity and pluralism are not confined to the Middle East or to Muslim societies. The peculiarity of the conflict-generating history of the Middle East may derive only in part from Islamic exclusiveness—the insistence on implementing God's law on earth, and the sharp distinction between what is Muslim and what is not. The distinction is nevertheless endemic to the conjoining of a universal religious message or truth with a particular community and social order on earth. In short, it follows from the sanctification of temporal power. To this extent, the problem is not one of historical development or evolution, simply because European, or non-Muslim, societies have gone through it. Rather, it is peculiar to an ideological faith that is tied to temporal power that cannot be shared with others who are not of the same faith.

All the same, one must consider the logical argument that once the Shari'a becomes the sole basis of public order in these societies, non-Muslims must accept it as the law of the land, along with whatever restrictions it may impose upon them. In this case, pluralism is not an option or a possibility. Whether such an order can be constructed (or restored) in any of these societies is another matter, and largely one of speculation. In the one instance where it has—Iran—it required no further comment.

It is also fair to point to the relentless struggle between governments in the Middle East—for example, in Egypt—and those who call for their overthrow as usurpers, tyrants, and infidels. In Egypt the conflict is between a basically secular state authority and those who deny its legitimacy because it refuses to establish a purely Islamic order. Yet the conflict is characterized by the hesitation of state authority to impose a functioning, institutionalized secular system. This hesitation accentuates the problems of ethnicity and pluralism. Moreover, the state itself has tended to impose a political uniformity of its own that is in effect a practical denial of pluralism. So long as advocates of Islam insist that there is a specific Islamic political order, they will always challenge the authority of any order not based on the tenets of the faith.

Finally, the so-called Balkanization of the region on the basis of ethnic-sectarian autonomy is impractical and bloody. The only two alternatives are for political accommodation of ethnicity in integrated secular political orders or acceptance by minorities of tolerated and protected status in mainly Islamic societies under the rule of the Shari'a.

5

Ethnopolitics and the
Middle Eastern State

Gabriel Ben-Dor

"Considered as societies, . . . new states are abnormally susceptible to serious disaffection based on primordial attachments."[1] The political arena of the Middle East is an extraordinary example of this statement by Edward Shils. If the central problem in contemporary Middle Eastern politics today is the building and maintenance of legitimate territorial states,[2] then Joseph Rothschild's thesis that "though several new 'issues' have arisen in the twentieth century, ethnic nationalism—or politicized ethnicity—remains the world's major ideological legitimator and delegitimator of states, regimes and governments" looms large. In fact, Rothschild argues that all around the world "politicized ethnic assertiveness is . . . a valid but not exhaustive explanation of the contemporary state's renewed crisis of legitimacy."[3] In an effort to gain insight into the nature of the political process in the Middle East, we shall look at ethnopolitics in relation to the Middle Eastern state.

The basis of ethnopolitics appears to be what Clifford Geertz terms "primordial attachments":

[1] Edward Shils, "Primordial, Personal, Sacred, and Civil Ties," *British Journal of Sociology*, quoted in Clifford Geertz, "The Integrative Revolution: Primordial Sentiments and Civil Politics in the New States," in *Political Development and Social Change*, ed. J. L. Finkle and R. W. Gable, 2d ed. (New York: Wiley, 1971), p. 656.

[2] See Gabriel Ben-Dor, *State and Conflict in the Middle East* (New York: Praeger, 1983). The ideas and formulations related to the state in this chapter draw heavily on this book. See also Gabriel Ben-Dor, "Stateness and Ideology in Contemporary Egyptian Politics," in *Islam, Nationalism, and Radicalism in Egypt and in the Sudan*, ed. G. R. Warburg and U. M. Kupferschmidt (New York: Praeger, 1983), pp. 73–96.

[3] Joseph Rothschild, *Ethnopolitics: A Conceptual Framework* (New York: Columbia University Press, 1981), pp. 14, 19. This book contains a lengthy bibliography related to ethnopolitics (the term is also borrowed from it).

By a primordial attachment is meant one that stems from the "givens"—or more precisely, as culture is inevitably involved in such matters, the assumed "givens"—of social existence: immediate contiguity and kin connection mainly, but beyond them the givenness that stems from being born into a particular religious community speaking a particular language, or even a dialect of a language, and following particular social practices. These congruities of blood, speech, custom and so on, are seen to have an ineffable, and at times over-powering, coerciveness in and of themselves.[4]

What later came to be called ethnopolitics, the politics of primordialism, has a dimension that is qualitatively different from other attributes of political conflict:

Economics or class or intellectual disaffection threaten revolution, but disaffection based on race, language or culture threatens partition, irredentism or merger, a redrawing of the very limits of the state, a new definition of its domain. Civil discontent finds its natural outlet in the seizing, legally or illegally, of the state apparatus. Primordial discontent strives more deeply and is satisfied less easily.[5]

Thus, a coupling of weak states and strong primordial sentiments would be a debilitating liability in an attempt to maintain a legitimate political community, yet in many parts of the Middle East this is more or less the case.

What exactly is ethnopolitics? Beyond the politicization of primordialism, the answer is not clear, but the notion of primordialism is sufficiently powerful to capture the substance and essence of the phenomenon:

Politicized ethnicity, ethno-politics, ethno-nationalism, ethno-regionalism, ethno-secessionism, and so on, are all terms used . . . in analyzing what happens when such entities bring their social, cultural, and economic interests, grievances, claims, anxieties and aspirations into the political area—the intrastate and/or the interstate arena. Nor would it be helpful, or even possible, to separate out the idea of ethnic consciousness, solidarity and assertiveness from religious, linguistic, racial and other so-called primordial foci of consciousness, solidarity and assertiveness. . . . Suffice it to state . . . that the terms ethnicity and ethnic . . . are used generally . . . to refer to the political activities of complex collective groups whose membership is largely determined by real or putative ancestral inherited ties, and who perceive these ties as systematically affecting their place and fate in the political and socio-economic structures of their state and society.[6]

---

[4]Geertz, "Integrative Revolution," p. 656.
[5]Ibid., p. 651.
[6]Rothschild, Ethnopolitics, pp. 8–9 (italics in the original).

Geertz describes six possible foci of primordialism, which are *not* mutually exclusive: assumed blood ties, race, language, region, religion, and custom.[7] To this Rothschild adds, somewhat surprisingly, a seventh:

A population's political experience within political institutions, eventually creating a politically derived sense of ethnonationalism, initially unbuttressed, or only minimally buttressed, by racial, kinship, religious, linguistic or other prepolitical, primordial marker-distinctions. In other words, whereas it is conventional to say that ethnonations create or strive to create states of their own, it is also the case that states may create ethnonations out of the demographic raw material, so to speak, of their population.[8]

Here Rothschild nudges the notion of ethnopolitics beyond the realm of primordialism, but the result is a certain difficulty on the conceptual level— that is, it is quite difficult to analyze the "givens" of social and cultural life and political experience leading to a common consciousness on the same analytical level. Nevertheless, such processes do exist in the empirical world, and it is well to bear in mind the duality of the process, just as it is well to recall that in ethnic politics "tradition" and "modernity" are not mutually exclusive notions.[9]

Beyond the general identification of primordial foci, Geertz is much more concerned with the construction of some basic typology "of the concrete patterns of primordial diversity that are found within the various states" (the Middle East obviously included).[10] A simple typology yields five categories, or patterns, in Geertz's terminology. The first pattern is a single dominant and usually (though not inevitably) larger group set over against a single strong and chronically troublesome minority (e.g., in the Middle East, Jordan). The second pattern is one central group, geographically *or* politically, and several medium-large and at least somewhat opposed peripheral groups (e.g., Morocco and Iran). The third pattern is a bipolar pattern of two nearly evenly balanced groups (e.g., Sunnis and Shi'ites in Iraq; Christians and Muslims in Lebanon; "Cyrenica" [*sic*] and Tripolitania in Libya); the fourth pattern is of relatively even gradation of groups in importance, with no clearly dominant groups and no sharp cutoff points (no examples of this in the Middle East); finally, there is simple ethnic fragmentation with multiple small groups (no examples of this in the Middle East).[11]

[7]Geertz, "Integrative Revolution," pp. 651–659, elaborated in Rothschild, *Ethnopolitics*, pp. 86–83.

[8]Rothschild, *Ethnopolitics*, p. 94.

[9]Lloyd I. Rudolph, "The Modernity of Tradition: The Democratic Incarnation of Caste in India," *American Political Science Review* 59 (December 1965): 975–989.

[10]Geertz, "Integrative Revolution," p. 660.

[11]Ibid., pp. 660–661.

Thus we have in the Middle East three basic patterns: majority vs. minority, central group vs. peripheral groups, and a complex case of evenly matched groups. All three tend to exacerbate political conflict over the assets of the state. The two patterns missing in the Middle East seem better designed to diffuse such political struggles to a certain extent.[12]

Of course, the primordial "givens" are theoretically latent phenomena and need not become manifestly political. Whether they do or not is an empirical question of concrete political experience, and as such it depends to a large extent on the management of leaders and elites, who at times are adept in manipulating dormant primordial resentments into synthetic neo-particularism. Such leaders must formulate goals or strategies that are appropriate for the political context.

According to Rothschild, such potential goals and strategies can be divided into five major categories.[13] The first is multidimensional integration to the point of full assimilation. This is an unlikely possibility, but such things have been known to happen—especially in times when strongly attractive pan-ethnic ideological movements dominate the political scene. The second is intended to accomplish the pluralistic goal of full political and "life-chances" integration combined with publicly guaranteed and officially protected cultural autonomy. The third strategy is intended to overcome the precariousness of cultural autonomy by developing a system of

---

[12]Although a voluminous literature exists, alternative basic formulations are not easy to find. See the bibliography in Rothschild, *Ethnopolitics*, and in Gabriel Ben-Dor, *The Druzes in Israel, a Political Study: Political Innovation and Integration in a Middle Eastern Minority* (Boulder, Colo.: Westview, 1979). For representative articles, see Ian Lustick, "Stability in Deeply Divided Societies: Consociationalism versus Control," *World Politics* 31 (April 1979), 324–344; Nelson Kasfir, "Explaining Ethnic Political Participation," *World Politics* 31 (April 1979):365–388; Astri Shurke, Lela Gerner Noble, and Robert L. Beckman, "Ethnic Conflict and International Regulations," *Plural Societies* 9 (Winter 1978): 3–22; Akber Aghajanian, "Ethnic Inequality in Iran: An Overview," *International Journal of Middle East Studies* 15 (1983):211–224; Jeffrey A. Ross, "A Text of Ethnicity and Economics as Contrasting Explanations of Collective Political Behavior," *Plural Societies* 9 (Winter 1978):69–82; Alastair Drysdale, "The Syrian Political Elite, 1965–1978: A Spatial and Social Analysis," *Middle Eastern Studies* 17 (January 1981):3–30; Cynthia A. Enloe, "The Issue Saliency of the Military-Ethnic Connection," *Comparative Politics* 10 (January 1978):267–285; D. J. Grove, "Ethnic Socio-Economic Redistribution: A Cross-Cultural Study," *Comparative Politics* 12 (October 1979):87–98; P. C. Salzman, "The Study of 'Complex Society' in the Middle East: A Review Essay," *International Journal of Middle East Studies* 9 (1978):539–557. See also Cynthia A. Enloe, *Ethnic Conflict and Political Development* (Boston: Little, Brown, 1973); Nathan Glazer and Daniel P. Moynihan, *Ethnicity, Theory, and Experience* (Cambridge: Harvard University Press, 1975); S. Excel, ed., *The Ethnic Dimension* (Sydney: Allen & Unwin, 1981); Stanislaw Ehrlich and Graham Woolton, *Three Faces of Pluralism* (Westmead, U.K.: Gower, 1980); William C. McCready, ed., *Culture, Ethnicity, and Identity: Current Issues in Research* (New York: Academic Press, 1983); A. C. Herburn, *Minorities in History* (New York: St. Martin's Press, 1979); Crawford Young, *The Politics of Cultural Pluralism* (Madison: University of Wisconsin Press, 1976); R. D. McLaurin, ed., *The Political Roles of Minority Groups in the Middle East* (New York: Praeger, 1979). In addition, two special issues of the *Middle East Review*, vol. 4, nos. 1 and 2 (1976–1977) are devoted to ethnic and religious minorities in the Middle East.

[13]Rothschild, *Ethnopolitics*, pp. 150–152.

political territorial autonomy, such as federalization along ethnic lines, ethnohistorical devolution, or "cantonization." These forms are frequently used in reference to conflict resolution in Lebanon and the Sudan, but the experience with such strategies in the Middle East has generally not been happy, and somehow the Arab cases demonstrate the inherent difficulty of implementing a concept of "nonterritorialized political autonomy," which is often considered as a derogation of sovereignty.[14] The fourth strategy is secession to full political independence. In the Middle East, in the age when the territorial status quo enjoys a virtual regional political sanctity, that is hardly realistic, but this does not mean it does not exist as an aspiration. The fifth and last goal or strategy is domination, or reversing the power relations within the existent state. Rothschild argues that "the ethnic dominants usually but not always resist these two radical subordinate strategies."[15]

One might add again that in some ways the categories relevant to the Middle East seem to have a radical dimension. The most extreme cases are clearly the assimilatory pressures, which are characteristic of Arab nationalism, and the strategies of domination or its reversal, as in the case of Lebanon to a certain extent, or even in Syria. One could hypothesize that such strategies are less conducive to an accommodating posture in politics than at least two of the three categories in between the two extremes. (To a certain extent this is true even with regard to secession, although less so than in the other cases.)

As Rothschild points out, these are normally the strategies of the subordinate ethnic groups. If the multiethnic character of the state is not quite acceptable to the dominant elite, any one of the extreme and coercive policies may result[16]—for example, genocide, expulsion, compulsory assimilation, other forms of acculturation, divide-and-rule-like manipulations, and belittlement of "backward" ethnic cultures. Because these are unilateral strategies, they do not entail processes of bargaining, compromise, or accommodation. In this case, the leaders of the state as well as those of the ethnic group are likely to find it necessary to develop or adopt one or more of the available regulatory political mechanisms and techniques in order to contain ethnic conflict within tolerable limits and to diffuse its potential volatility to the greatest possible extent. The ability to deal successfully with these conflict-containing techniques and mechanisms is a most important trait of political elites in multiethnic states. The mechanisms and procedures are as follows:[17]

[14]Ibid., p. 152. See also Gabriel Ben-Dor, "Federalism in the Arab World," in *Federalism and Political Integration*, ed. D. J. Elazar (Ramat Gan, Israel, 1979), pp. 191–214.

[15]Rothschild, *Ethnopolitics*, p. 153.

[16]Ibid., pp. 155–158.

[17]Ibid., pp. 162–167.

1. "The deliberate depoliticization of issues that could, if they were politicized, take on an ethnically divisive cutting edge. This is how Israeli leaders try to handle the current socio-economic life-chances gap between Ashkenazim and Sephardim, as they simultaneously work to narrow the gap."

2. "Constitutional or institutional arrangements designed to keep potentially disruptive or divisive ethnic issues off the central government's political agenda and resolve them at other decision-making levels. . . . In Lebanon . . . analogous arrangements, albeit explicitly federalistic, functioned reasonably well until that country's domestic political system was overloaded and overwhelmed by the external intrusion of the Palestine problem."

3. "Advance agreement by the several ethnic leaderships to persist within coalition governments no matter what the outcome of elections or oscillation of public moods." (A form of consociationalism?)

4. The mutual veto, more or less in line with Calhoun's doctrine of the "concurrent majority." This assures that the leaders of important—even if relatively small—ethnic groups will not be relegated to political impotence. They are issued a virtual right (sometimes even in formalized, structured procedures) to veto policies genuinely perceived to be endangering the vital interests of the ethnic groups.

5. and 6. "Proportional representation as a mechanism and prudential self-restraint as a technique are similarly intended to assuage the anxieties of the leaders of smaller, weaker or subordinate ethnic groups and politically integrate them into the state's macro-system. Pre-civil war Lebanon and contemporary Czechoslovakia may serve as respective examples of these two devices."

7. "Wrapping several controversial issues and recalcitrant problems together into a single package of reciprocal trade-offs, such that 'everybody gets something, nobody gets everything, nobody gets nothing' (in the rhetoric of the operational code of Chicago's Daley machine)."

Examples in the Middle East do not abound in this formulation. Israel is cited once, in a way that a fair number of experts would dispute. Lebanon is cited twice, but a former success in the proverbial status quo ante bellum only to collapse in the tide of never-ending civil war. In terms of conflict regulation and containment, the regional record appears very poor indeed. One reason may be that "all these conflict-containing mechanisms and procedures secure ethnic leaders and brokers, immune to being outbid by more militant challenges or ousted by grassroots revulsion against the compromise that these devices necessarily entail."[18] But such political conditions have not prevailed in the Middle East for quite some time—on the contrary, the radical style of mass politics was the order of the day at least until the 1970s, and even since then the secure conditions allowing political elites room to maneuver hardly existed. The other obvious reason is that "the several itemized (and other) conflict-management mechanisms and tech-

[18]Ibid., p. 164.

niques are also elitist in the more diluted sense that they require astute timing in their institutionalization. If a suitable opportunity to implement one or several of them is allowed to slip away, history may not give the leaders another chance, because the situation context will not stand still."[19]

In other words, the ability to regulate ethnic conflict depends on the capacity to institutionalize a variety of techniques, mechanisms, and procedures. By definition, therefore, ethnic conflict will be most difficult to contain in societies that have a low level of institutionalization, which is precisely a salient feature of political culture in the Middle East.[20] Institutionalization is "the process by which organizations and procedures acquire value and stability."[21] Ethnic conflict and ethnic loyalties hinder the development of the four components-criteria of institutionalization. "The level of institutionalization of any political system can be defined by the adaptability, complexity, autonomy and coherence of its organizations and procedures."[22] Strong primordial ties do not really allow strong structures and procedures that are not imbedded in ethnicity mechanisms to develop for ethnic conflict-reduction, and we are witnessing a true which-comes-first situation. Most students of Middle Eastern politics would surely identify the "amoral ethnicity" implied in Samuel Huntington's argument:

> Political institutions have moral as well as structural dimensions. A society with weak political institutions lacks the ability to curb the excesses of personal and parochial desires. Politics is a Hobbesian world of unrelenting competition among social forces—between man and man, family and family, clan and clan, region and region, class and class—a competition ameliorated by more comprehensive organizations. The "amoral familism" of Banfield's backward society has its counterparts in amoral clanism, amoral groupism, amoral classism.[23]

And, one might well add, amoral ethnicism.

How can this vicious cycle be broken? How can the political arena acquire a level of institutionalization that will enable it to develop a set of relatively autonomous organizations and mechanisms (manned and steered by a relatively autonomous elite) that might give it some capacity to contain ethnic conflict within tolerable limits? Historical experience suggests that

[19]Ibid., pp. 165–166.
[20]This point is argued and demonstrated in detail in Gabriel Ben-Dor, "Political Culture Approach to Middle East Politics," *International Journal of Middle East Studies* 8, 1 (1977): 43–63.
[21]Samuel P. Huntington, *Political Order in Changing Societies* (New Haven: Yale University Press, 1968), p. 12.
[22]Ibid. See also Gabriel Ben-Dor, "Institutionalization and Political Development: A Conceptual and Theoretical Analysis," *Comparative Studies in Society and History* 17 (July 1975): 309–325.
[23]Huntington, *Political Order*, p. 24.

the key to understanding this problem is the real target of ethnic conflict, as well as almost every other political conflict—the state. A well-known basic textbook on ethnic conflict concludes:

> The fact that the struggle to establish new boundaries for meaningful political action is going on in countries at several different stages of modernization warns against relying on the inevitability of the nation-state or assuming that political development leads to modernity. The mobilization of ethnic groups may reflect the traumas of casting off tradition, but it may also portend innovative political forms for the future, beyond modernity.[24]

Clearly we do not yet know just what lies beyond modernity. We do not know what modernity is. We do know that in the Middle East, as elsewhere, the profoundly meaningful target of ethnopolitical activity is the territorial (not the "national") state.[25] It is the ultimate prize, as it is also the ultimate enemy, the ultimate resource base, and the ultimate umpire of ethnic conflict—if any real umpiring is to be done.

Yet a good deal of respectable research on stresses and strains (such as ethnic conflict) in Middle East politics has focused on ideology in an effort to understand manifold political change in the regional system. Such change in several key countries in the region has been of immense magnitude. No wonder students of ideological transformation in politics have a virtual "field day" attempting to explain the puzzle of the Middle East, mostly (though not exclusively) within the paradigms of two major theoretical orientations: a Marxist (or neo-Marxist) school, on the one hand, and a systemic-functionalist school feeding on the Weberian heritage, on the other hand. However, both suffer from at least one conspicuous liability: they lack an adequate theory of the postimperial and postcolonial state. Yet such a theory is the only one that helps make sense of the vicissitudes of Middle Eastern politics in our time.[26]

Can the puzzle really be explained primarily in ideological terms? Probably not if we accept Karl Mannheim's skeptical definition of ideologies as "more or less conscious disguises of the real nature of the situation."[27] Perhaps yes if we follow the influential formulation of Geertz:

> Ideology is a response to strain . . . . It is a loss of orientation that most directly gives rise to ideological activity, an inability for lack of useable models, to comprehend the universe of civic rights and responsibilities in which one finds

[24]Enloe, *Ethnic Conflict*, p. 274.

[25]See Ben-Dor, *State and Conflict*, and idem, "Stateness and Ideology," on which this formulation draws heavily.

[26]For the detailed argument, see Ben-Dor, *State and Conflict*, chap. 1: "The Post-Colonial State and the Study of Middle East Politics."

[27]Karl Mannheim, *Ideology and Utopia* (New York: Harcourt Brace, 1954), p. 49.

oneself located. It is . . . the attempt of ideologies to render otherwise incomprehensible social situations meaningful. . . . Ideology . . . provides . . . novel symbolic forms against which to match the myriad "unfamiliar somethings," that like a journey to a strange country are produced by a transformation of political life. Whatever else ideologies may be . . . they are, most distinctively, maps of problematic social reality, and matrices for the collective conscience.[28]

This conception of "response to strain" has been most influential in the attempts to come to terms with the volatile nature of ideological change in the Middle East in general and Egypt in particular. The nature of the "strain" or stress in question is normally identified as the "dialectics of modernization." Thus, James Bill and Carl Leiden argue:

The dialectical relationship that prevails between the intertwined processes of modernization and political development is a central issue in the contemporary Middle East. Modernization acts as a catalytic process, stimulating demands that must be confronted by the various political systems. At the same time, the political elites must make most of the key decisions that promote and shape patterns of modernization. The circular and reciprocal interaction between these two dynamic processes is riddled with uncertainty. Many of the fundamental problems that now confront the Middle Eastern people emanate from this situation.[29]

It is within the discussion of these "fundamental problems"—the ideological strain of modernization—that Islam is referred to as the *other* component of political ideologies. "Religion and politics . . . are often critically intertwined. It is not an exaggeration to say that no understanding of the complex political patterns of the area can be attempted without giving prior attention to its religious characteristics."[30]

The resulting political flux and instability are described well by Michael Hudson. Hudson relates radical socialist and nationalist ideologies to the problem of legitimacy, which in turn is generated by the difficulties of "social mobilization," his preferred term for rapid modernization and accelerated political participation. His conversations with politicians and government officials throughout the Arab world uncovered "a sense of frustration": "They find themselves caught between ideology and political-administrative realities." In addition to frustration, "Arab politicians are

---

[28]Clifford Geertz, "Ideology as a Cultural System," in *Ideology and Discontent*, ed. D. E. Apter (New York: Free Press, 1964), p. 64.

[29]James A. Bill and Carl Leiden, *The Middle East: Politics and Power* (Boston: Allyn & Bacon, 1974), p. 22. This formulation draws heavily on the deservedly influential work by Manfred Halpern, *The Politics of Social Change in the Middle East and North Africa* (Princeton: Princeton University Press, 1963), and later studies by Halpern that further evolve the ideas there presented.

[30]Bill and Leiden, *Middle East*, p. 25.

beset by insecurity and fear of the unknown." No wonder "Arab politics today are not just unstable ... [but] also unpredictable to participants and observers alike."[31]

Hudson claims that the reasons for the seeming unpredictability of Arab political systems can be discovered by analyzing the ideological consequences of the political debilitation caused by rapid social mobilization. True to the Weberian-functionalist heritage, he anchors the argument in the variable of legitimacy: "The central problem of government in the Arab world today is political legitimacy. The shortage of this indispensable political resource largely accounts for the volatile nature of Arab politics and the autocratic, unstable character of all the present Arab governments."[32]

This type of thinking—concerned with ideological change as a response to problems of legitimacy generated by the process of modernization—dominated political analysis of the Middle Eastern scene for almost a generation and somewhat paralleled the virtual obsession of the politicians of the region with related ideological themes. Only recently has the inadequacy of an approach that unquestionably followed the intellectual-ideological fashions of the day, and that invariably failed to make adequate distinctions between the countries of the region (when the differences between them are all too obvious to ignore), become clear, and only recently, too, has a "new" trend gained momentum. This new trend may be labeled a neo-classical approach (for the lack of a better term). The "neo-classic" label is justified because the subject matter is classical but the approach is new. The subject matter, which has been ignored for too long, is the *state*, which has emerged as the most comprehensive and important political structure in the Middle East.[33]

To a large extent, intellectual preferences and vogues are the reason the state has been almost ignored for so long. Among political scientists, fascination with "systems" and "superstructures" (and related variables *like* legitimacy) replaced the almost exclusive preoccupation with the state as a legal-formal phenomenon.[34] And yet in the real world of politics it is precisely that ancient concept— the state—that has again come to dominate the political consciousness of the relevant elites. Far from "withering away," the state in the Middle East today is stronger than ever. In this respect, intellectual fashions must either change or become even more irrelevant to praxis. This simple but persuasive argument was made emphatically by

---

[31]Michael G. Hudson, *Arab Politics: The Search for Legitimacy* (New Haven: Yale University Press, 1977), pp. 2–3 (italics added).

[32]Ibid.

[33]After all, this is the structure that should concern us in terms of legitimacy. Governments and elites constitute a level of analysis that may be too low; "political systems" may be too high and abstract. In principle, illegitimacy of *governments* is not all that difficult to overcome, but illegitimacy of *states* is always a devastating political problem.

[34]See the recent special issue of *Daedalus*, vol. 108 (Fall 1979), devoted to this question.

the late British political sociologist J. P. Nettl: "The concept of the state is not much in vogue in the social sciences right now. Yet it retains a skeletal, ghostly existence largely because, for all the changes in emphasis and interest in research, *the thing exists and no amount of conceptual restructuring can dissolve it.*"[35]

But the revival of the state does not necessarily have to do with political sociology. In the past decade there has been renewed interest in the lessons of the extension of the European state system around the world[36] and among historians as well. And in attempting to sketch the political agenda for the Middle East in the 1980s, Bernard Lewis, a well-known historian of the region, argues:

> A remarkable feature of the modern age and of the changes that modernization has brought to Islam has been the strengthening, not the weakening, of the state as a focus of activity . . . . With the process of modernization in the Islamic world, . . . intermediate powers have one by one been weakened or abolished, leaving the state with a far greater degree of autocratic control over its subjects than it ever enjoyed in traditional Islamic societies. And whereas the limiting powers have dwindled or disappeared, the state itself now has at its disposal the whole modern apparatus of surveillance and repression. The result is that the modern states in the Islamic world, even those claiming to be progressive and democratic, are—in their domestic affairs at least—vastly stronger than the so-called tyrannies of the past.

Then Lewis points emphatically to the "somewhat surprising phenomenon of the recent and current Middle Eastern world—the extraordinary persistence of states once created." The facts here speak louder than all ideologies:

> As a result of two world wars and of the extension and withdrawal of European imperial power, a whole series of new states were set up, with frontiers, and even identities, largely devised by colonial administration and imperial diplomacy. Some of these rested on genuine historical entities; some were entirely artificial. Nevertheless, in spite of the very strong ideological urge toward unification arising from pan-Arabism, not a single one of these Arab states has disappeared. On the contrary, they have shown—even the most improbable of them—an extraordinary capacity for survival and for self-preservation, often in very adverse circumstances. The barriers to greater Arab unity arise within

---

[35]J. P. Nettl, "The State as a Conceptual Variable," *World Politics* 20 (July 1968): 559 (italics added). Nettl's brilliant effort here is worthy of greater attention.

[36]See, e.g., Charles Tilly, ed., *The Formation of National States in Eastern Europe* (Princeton: Princeton University Press, 1975).

the Arab world and the failure of the mergers testifies to the remarkable persistence and growing power of the state itself as a political factor.[37]

Egyptian diplomat-intellectual Tahsin Bashir echoes: "The trend that I see is that the 1960s and 1970s witnessed the *strength* of the state. The state became the strongest dominant shadow over the lives of the individual and society."[38]

The emergence of the state at the expense of radical social and nationalist ideologies is demonstrated by the small amount of evidence we have from empirical research. Based on a study at Kuwait University, Fuad Ajami argues: "The vacuum left behind as a result of the demise of pan-Arabism is being fulfilled by religious belief on one level and by *loyalty to the state* on another." His data led him to conclude that the discussions of "one Arab nation" and "Arab brotherhood" are myths and exhausted slogans.[39]

Ajami soberly concludes that, while loyalty to the state is more or less "practical ideology,"[40] "Muslim universalism is a safer doctrine than the geographically more limited but politically more troublesome idea of pan-Arabism; the 48 Muslim countries and 700 million Muslims is a safe and distant symbol, giving a semblance of 'super-legitimacy' without posing a threat to the reason of state." As for the domestic problems involved in the rise of militant, popular Islam, it is "at least in the Arab context . . . a different problem from the disruptive doctrine of pan-Arabism, for it is a *challenge contained within the boundaries of the state.*"[41]

The turbulence in inter-Arab relations continues today, but the decades of high ideological tensions, heated rhetoric, and serious quarrels have created an extremely skeptical political climate in the Arab world. This is partly demonstrated by the data gathered recently by the Center for Research on Arab Unity (CRAU), located in Amman and Beirut, as published in the March–May (1981) edition of CRAU's Beirut monthly, *Al-Mustaqbal al-Arabi* (The Arab future):

> The coordinator of the research concludes that the romantic support to Arab unity is gone; that supporters of Arab unity prefer—in the short run—a partial unity; that there is a surprising lack of enthusiasm for unity among the high level professionals, media people and university educators; and that there is

[37]Lewis quotations are from Bernard Lewis, "Loyalties to Community, Nation, and State," in *Middle East Perspectives: The Next Twenty Years*, ed. G. S. Wise and C. Issawi (Princeton: Darwin, 1980), pp. 13–33.

[38]Tahsin Bashir, "Intellectual and Cultural Trends," in ibid., pp. 83–84.

[39]Fuad Ajami, "The End of Pan-Arabism," *Foreign Affairs*, Winter 1978–1979, p. 364 (italics added).

[40]The term is borrowed from Clement Henry Moore, "On Theory and Practice among Arabs," *World Politics* 24 (October 1971): 106–126.

[41]Ajami, "End of Pan-Arabism," p. 364 (italics added).

the danger that the clash between religious and secular unity will further undermine any Arab unification attempts.[42]

These conclusions strengthen the Ajami argument that Arabism is losing ground to the state, on the one hand, and to Islam, on the other.[43] By necessity, an honest and penetrating analysis[44] leads to an image that appears to be much closer to capturing the reality of the present Middle Eastern scene than does the mainstream of the earlier "conventional" literature. This should justify a detailed application of the notion of "stateness" to some key aspects of Middle Eastern politics, in the hope that such application will yield useful theoretical and analytical insights. In the Middle East it is states that make war and peace, states that people rebel and revolt against, and states that allocate resources—therefore, more than any other factor, it is the state that permeates phenomena that are of interest to the political scientist. These considerations are important in their own right, but what should interest us most at this stage is the extent to which we can utilize the variable "stateness" to learn something about such considerations of explanatory and/or predictive value that may otherwise have been overlooked.

The variable of "stateness," however, is a necessary improvement of modern political sociology on the classical school of studying the state. Functionalist approaches, such as "the state is the institutionalization of authority," are far too abstract and vague. The classical approaches are too formal, legalistic, and rigid.[45] In all these conceptions, there appears to be a profound problem—a false dichotomy. A political system is either a state or it is not. If it is, it has certain specified attributes, formal-legal or functional-structural. But in the real world of politics, this either-or approach yields but meager results. Is Lebanon a state in the strict sense of the term? If not, what is it? Is Syria a state in the strict sense of the term? Was it a state two decades ago? If it was not a state then, but it appears to be more a state now, how do we account for the dynamics of the process?

What we need is a more discriminating theory of the state, one that treats politics not as either states or nonstates but as merely more or less statelike—in other words, in which the question is not "to be [a state] or not to be," but to have more (of "stateness") or less of a certain political structure and concomitant logic of political behavior. The closest thing to such a theory of the state at our disposal from "neo-classicist" or "revisionist" sources is still Nettl's 1968 effort, "The State as a Conceptual Variable." Nettl does

[42]Al-Mustaqbal al-Arabi (The Arab Future) (CRAU's Beirut monthly), March–May 1981, p. 3; quoted in Weekly Media Abstracts, March 11, 1981.
[43]Ajami, "End of Pan-Arabism," p. 264.
[44]The composite picture of Lewis, Basheer, Ajami, Farah, the CRAU, and others.
[45]See Harry Eckstein, "On the 'Science' of the State," Daedalus 108 (Fall 1979): 1–20.

not treat the state as a given generic phenomenon—that is, he believes that the state's importance does not lie in its being the ubiquitous unit of analysis (as was assumed in an earlier age) sure to be found in the real world of politics. Quite the contrary, he believes that its importance lies in our ability to ask significant, researchable questions about its existence (and degree thereof) in any given particular case: "This argument suggests that the concept of the state is and ought to be treated as a variable in social science, as a reflection of the varying empirical reality with which social science concerns itself."[46]

Nettl suggests that first several definitional and conceptual problems must be addressed in order to engender the possibility of rigorous comparative analysis, for which we need reasonably well defined dimensions of variance. Four of these, which are included in the very definition of the state, are "the variable qualities of statehood or stateness."[47] Briefly, these are: (1) the state as "a collective that summates a set of functions and structures in order to generalize their applicability"; (2) the state as "the basic, irreducible unit" in the field of international relations; (3) the state as the representation of "an autonomous collective, as well as a summating concept of high societal generality" ("It is thus in a functional sense a distinct *sector* or arena in society"); (4) the state as an "essentially socio-cultural phenomenon."[48]

Of these variable qualities of statehood (hence the term "stateness"), the fourth is by far the most intriguing, challenging, and interesting to the scholar of Middle Eastern politics. It is also the major departure from all other approaches. Indeed, on this dimension Nettl points to researchable questions on the macro-societal level:

What is being argued here is that the identification of state with nation— indeed, the more general recognition of the state as a significant factor in political and social life—depends not only on empirical problems relating to the activity and structure of a particular state but on the existence of a cultural disposition to allot recognition to the conceptual existence of a state at all. This disposition can be isolated in various ways. One is *historical*: Is there a primacy, autonomy, and sovereignty of a state? Another is *intellectual*: Do the political ideas and theories of the society past or present incorporate a notion of state, and what role do they assign to it? Yet another approach is *cultural*: To what extent have individuals generalized the concept and cognition of state in their perceptions and actions, and to what extent are such cognitions salient? This last is perhaps the most important of the approaches, since it appears to be the only one that makes possible any kind of systematic ordering in what must

[46]Nettl, "State as Conceptual Variable," p. 562.
[47]Ibid., p. 566.
[48]Ibid., pp. 563, 564 (italics in the original), 565.

otherwise seem to be a random proliferation of quantitatively as well as qual-itatively distinct phenomena captured by the all too general notion of state.[49]

In principle, at least, these questions are eminently researchable in a variety of disciplines, notwithstanding the serious methodological problems that have been left unresolved.[50] Such research seems eminently suitable to "analytical history" and "soft" social science.

Historical, intellectual, and cultural research should help establish the saliency of the state as a sociocultural notion (as well as a concrete socio-political structure). This saliency is the crucial determinant of the notion of "stateness," the central concept of this entire neo-classical school of thought. One should hasten to add that the utility of this concept is enhanced by its applicability even to societies where an absence of the state does not absolutely preclude stateness, because the functions of the state are still performed. There are five such functions: the process of administration, the institutionalization of sovereignty, sectoral autonomy, law enforcement, and social goal attainment and representation.[51]

Stateness in the Middle East, though, is an exceedingly complex phenom-enon. Indeed, one can speak of the dialectics of postcolonial stateness in that part of the world. The essence of this dialectic lies in the tensions and contradictions between state and nation. Through both direct rule *and* indirect cultural penetration, the European colonial powers exported to the Middle East the most advanced governmental technology available in the form of the state apparatus. This governmental technology has a logic of its own, which, however, is not easily exportable. The Europeans exported, instead, the logic of nationalism, taken from their own radical style of politics, which was soon to pass its peak (though not before it had created one of the greatest devastations in the history of humankind). Therefore, the people of the Middle East (chiefly the Arabs) inherited the *structure* of the state and the *idea* of the nation. This is the heritage that generated the "dialectics of postcolonial stateness" and the ensuing grim struggle between the two poles.

It is not surprising that the ruling elites of the Arab countries were quick to grasp the immense potential inherent in the power of the state (the most powerful, and thus most attractive, modern structure) and to take advan-tage of the fact that the *structure* of the state is a transferable commodity. But stateness is more than a structure; it has behavioral and attitudinal attributes, and these are *not* easily transferred or exported. Thus the Arab world ended up with the powerful instrument of the state, but instead of tempering this instrument by its own logic, it was inflamed with the passion

---

[49]Ibid., p. 566 (italics added).
[50]These are specified and discussed in the first chapter of Ben-Dor, *State and Conflict*.
[51]Nettl, "State as Conceptual Variable," pp. 579–581.

of nationalism, which was itself reinforced by social radicalism and revolutionary ideals derived from totalistic (though not necessarily totalitarian) religious-cultural systems. This contradiction has had to be worked out gradually, slowly, and progressively, and the ensuing process has been grim, painful, and violent. The chances of resolving this contradiction in the Arab world are proportional to the level of stateness. This is why Egypt is a paragraph ahead, so to speak, of the other Arab countries.

Egypt is indeed the most statelike Arab country. Lewis puts it in a historical perspective:

> Before the First World War there were in effect only two—or, we might say, two-and-a-half—states in the Middle East. The two were the surviving monarchies of Turkey and Iran . . . .The half is Egypt, which although under external suzerainty or domination, first Ottoman, then British, nevertheless retained a very large measure of autonomy in its internal affairs. There was an Egyptian government, an Egyptian administration running Egypt, under fairly remote Ottoman or somewhat less remote British control. In this sense, Egypt has functioned as a political entity for a very long time, even if not as an independent state.

On the other hand, the rest of the Arab world, by and large, "has had no experience of separate statehood or the exercise of political sovereignty for a very long time . . . .Their very names and boundaries were subject to frequent change and—with the exception of Egypt—they had little historical or even geographical significance."[52] Even if the contrast may appear to be somewhat overstated (half-stateness vs. nonstateness, so to speak), the fundamental truth of the analysis is correct: a single Arab country—Egypt—has possessed historically a qualitatively higher level of stateness than all the other Arab "states," a fact that is reinforced by geographic, demographic, and economic factors that make Egypt a more controllable, centralized, and homogeneous entity than the rest of the Arab world.

A complex *problem*, plaguing Arab nationalism, resulted, inherent in its very duality as expressed in the uneasy coexistence of *qawmiyya* and *wataniyya*. This duality has had both a destabilizing and a paralyzing effect on modern Arab politics. Other than the immense hold of Islam, Arab nationalism completely dominated the center for decades and left almost no room for anything else. But the supreme irony (as in many other dialectical processes or movements) in Arab nationalism was that while the appeal of *qawmiyya* was strong enough to destablize all competing or alternative political structures, it was not strong enough as a "practical ideology." Ajami quotes Haykal as having once

---

[52]"Loyalties," pp. 15–17.

made the distinction between Egypt as a state and Egypt as a revolution, and [defending] the right of the "Arab revolution" to interfere in the internal affairs of Arab countries . . . .He told Mr. Kissinger that Egypt was not merely a state on the banks of the Nile, but the embodiment of "an idea, a tide, a historical movement." To this Mr. Kissinger is reported to have said that he himself could not deal with latent tangible forces, or negotiate with an idea.[53]

Kissinger's reply contained a profound truth. The political impossibility of the idea was not only its unsuitability as a negotiating partner, but also its unsuitability as a practical ideology. It could destroy but not build, it could create internal conflict but not resolve it, it could prevent peace with Israel but not create an Arab policy vis-à-vis the Israeli problem; it could captivate the Palestinians in the "dialectics of dependence" but not settle the Palestine issue. In short, either the idea had to triumph so thoroughly as to make it an overwhelming political reality (which did not and could not happen) or it had to be abandoned de facto. The transitory situation between these two poles debilitated and "de-normalized" Arab politics for more than a generation.

Of course, the old order never passes away easily. Much of the nationalist turbulence in the Arab world continues. Nevertheless, a *qualitative* change seems to have taken place in several key Arab countires, and above all Egypt. A more "normal" system of states (motivated—like all state-like structures—more and more by *raison d'état*) emerged, with enormous implications for inter-Arab as well as Arab-Israeli relations—or, as Ajami put it picturesquely in 1979: "*Raison d'état*, once an alien and illegitimate doctrine, is gaining ground. Slowly and grimly, with a great deal of anguish and of outright violence, a 'normal' state system is becoming a fact of life."[54] This is even more visible as the 1980s unfold. It is only this evolution that has enabled such statements as "whether Egypt makes peace or war is primarily its own affair" to become facts of life, whereas until a short time ago they were tantamount to treason. Paraphrasing the greatest Islamic political thinker, Ibn Khaldun, we might say that the logic of the *mulk* (the imperfect, but real power-state) has triumphed over the logic of the ideal but only imaginary *caliphate*. The *mulk* is tempered by Islamic ethics, and its cultural attributes (in this case, its Arabness) will have inevitable consequences. In political terms, however, it is responsible and accountable only to its own constituency. Thus, "Whether Sadat's diplomacy stands or falls, it will do so on its own merit, judged in terms of what it will or will not do for Egypt; charges of treason or tribunals against Sadat by Iraq or

[53]Ajami, "End of Pan-Arabism," p. 356.
[54]Ibid.

Libya will be to no avail."[55] It is important to emphasize that stateness in Egypt does not and cannot preempt other ideologies. A more state-like Egypt may have already outgrown the shallow slogans of radical socialism or pan-state nationalism, but it may be particularly vulnerable to radical Islam.

The nagging questions about Islam often arise precisely at the point where the state is so strong that it is almost beyond challenge. Popular, militant Islam does not challenge the state machinery. It wants to *use* it in order to implement a set of policies intended to create a social order (usually only vaguely defined) different from the one offered by the incumbents. In some ways, then, we witness yet again the intriguing relationship between Islam and the state: as it is likely to have created a sort of ideological vacuum via the centrality of nationalism, it is the strong state that has already outgrown the stage of searching for identity via nationalism that is most vulnerable to the Islamic wave. Once a reasonably strong state is institutionalized on the basis of an established sense of identity, it is unable to supply answers to the policy-oriented questions of the day insofar as those relate to priorities in distribution and social justice.

Is Egypt, then, likely to be the next target of Islamic fundamentalism? This may seem paradoxical, but Lewis correctly observed in January 1976 that *"as regimes come closer to the populace*, even if their verbiage is left-wing and ideological, *they become more Islamic."*[56] In a way, they also become more ethnic, for the very same reason—namely, authenticity. Nationalism and socialism may or may not be authentic concepts generating real political communications, but Islam and ethnicity certainly are. Moreover, Islam and ethnicity— along with social radicalism, the three authentic forces confronting the state—are not mutually exclusive or even contradictory. Islam has been known to be tolerant, pluralistic, and integrative; it has lived reasonably well with ethnic conflict, as well as with others. Indeed, in many cases in the Middle East the ethnic and Islamic foci of identity are quite similar in that they both produce charismatic communities. In some of these cases, Islam, the *umma*, is the ultimate community, the charismatic community of communities. But this does not necessarily undermine the possibility of other communities existing on other levels, feeding on other sources of charisma. Therefore, Islamic resurgence and ethnic reassertion are not at odds, as nationalism and ethnicity are, at least on the abstract level.

In many parts of the Middle East, the question is complicated by the presence of "compact minorities,"[57] territorially concentrated and often

[55]Ibid., p. 370. Ajami's ideas are further elaborated in his *Arab Predicament: Arab Political Thought and Practice since 1967* (Cambridge: Cambridge Unversity Press, 1981).

[56]Lewis, "The Return of Islam," *Commentary* 61 (January 1976): 148 (italics added).

[57]This term was coined by P. Rondot and made current by A. M. Hourani; see Itamar

occupying geostrategically easily defensible areas. In such areas—for instance, in Syria—it would not be realistic to expect anything less than intense ethnic competition for the resources of the state. Indeed, the very potency of the modern state often serves as an added element in producing a strengthened ethnic consciousness. The Syrian state is a more attractive prize for the Alawis than any alternative potential asset. In the case of the Lebanese Shi'a community, the resources that the state can *potentially* mobilize are perceived to be essential for producing and maintaining the minimal level of well-being acceptable to the community. In earlier times Arab nationalism helped mobilize and politicize such communities, and its partial decline left something of an ideological vacuum. Islamic sentiments and communal loyalties came to replace to a large extent the nationalist revolution that had devoured its own sons. The ethnic elites, in turn, manipulate nationalist and other radical slogans, but underneath the thin veil of ritual ethnopolitics they are there for all to see.

Nationalism also created, by way of generative tension, added impetus to the strengthening of ethnic consciousness in competitive (bipolar) situations, and this in turn may have contributed to the strengthening of the orientation *toward* the state, *away* from pan-state foci of identity. An example is the Sudan, where initial pan-Arab tendencies (accompanied by Islamic motifs) assured vociferous opposition from the ethnic groups of the non-Arab and non-Muslim South. The strength of that opposition, in turn, was a factor of considerable importance in holding the leadership in Khartoum back from inter-Arab commitments in the 1970s, when the Sudan was considered an important potential partner in Arab federal schemes.[58] In this case, ethnicity worked to strengthen the state and perpetuate its structure. On the other hand, the quasi-federal schemes of devolution and autonomy have not yet been shown conclusively to be working, even though they may well signify the correct frame of reference in terms of thinking about the future of a viable Sudanese state.

Ethnic facts of political life have also been manipulated for interstate purposes. A conspicuous Middle Eastern example is that of the Kurds, who probably have as many attributes of ethnopolitics as any group in the Middle East. Yet they are unable to secede, or break away, from the state structure either in Iraq or Iran, much less elsewhere. Nor are they able to compete effectively for capturing the state machinery, as they have no access to the central elites in the relevant countries. On the other hand, the Druze have adopted differing political strategies in Syria, Lebanon, and Israel, emphasizing and demonstrating the diversity of political resources available to

---

Rabinovich, "The Compact Minorities and the Syrian State," *Journal of Contemporary History* 14 (1979): 693–712.

[58]See Ben-Dor, "Federalism."

"compact minorities" in the Middle East.[59] In Syria the Alawis have had considerable success in capturing and maintaining the heart of the state machinery. In Iraq, an elite drawn from the Sunni urban public dominates a majority of rural Shi'ites. In Iran the dominant central group of Persians faces numerous peripheries of centrifugal minorities. In Jordan, by all counts, the Palestinians have become a majority, yet it appears that the Bedouin military elite is still firmly in control. Lebanon exhibits all the horrors of ethnic havoc—which is but one cost of a *very* low level of stateness. Perhaps most noteworthy is the curious case of Egypt, where disengagement from the turmoil of Arab nationalism, and the twin trends of state-consciousness and Islamic flavor, have provoked a surprisingly strong activistic reaction from the Coptic minority, which has not been politically very militant—all this precisely after Egypt's inter-Arab ideological excitement has virtually subsided.

The territorial state has by and large survived, and so have ethnic polities. The two can perhaps coexist, but they have not yet been fused. Neo- "ethnonationalism" (the state creating *its* nation) is not yet evident in the Middle East. Almost *all* the patterns of ethnopolitics identified by the theoretical literature exist in the region. Primordialism is widespread, and primordial ties tend to be multiple and mutually reinforcing. In the case of the Kurds, for instance, language, custom, region, and "race" (i.e., assumed ancestry coupled with characteristic features) all combine to strengthen "ethnic" uniqueness. In most other cases the combination is perhaps less formidable, yet it exists in a potent dosage. The Islamic element is not sufficient as a unifying force. In itself it may even at times serve the opposite purpose, for Islam itself is split into numerous sects, which are as strong an element of ethnicity as any. Moreover, Islam can contain and perhaps *to an extent* supersede ethnic loyalties, but it cannot replace them. In Ibn Khaldun's terms, neither Islam nor the territorial state has generated *asabiyya* (group solidarity) comparable to the genuine article found in ethnopolitics.

However, the Middle Eastern state is a new historical phenomenon. Its recent history has been one of fragility and vulnerability. Its greatest accomplishment so far has been its very survival, notwithstanding great odds in a harsh environment. It withstood even the greatest assault of nationalism, in particular the Arab variety. "The incongruence between nation loyalty and all-Arab care concerns, on the one hand, and specific state loyalty and state interests, on the other, adds additional disarray to the Arab political scene. Arabism is not intense or exclusive enough to eradicate—at least for the foreseeable future—the state political systems that

---

[59]See Ben-Dor, *Druzes*, chapter entitled "Toward a Comparative Study of Druze Political Behavior."

have developed since World War I."[60] That this is becoming a political fact of life gains increased articulation in Arab political circles:

> The boundaries of Arab states have been around now for nearly six decades. It is not their existence which is novel, but their power and legitimacy—the power (as much as that power exists in the modern state system) to keep pan-Arab claims at bay and effectively claim the loyalty of those within. They are no longer as "illusory and permeable" as they used to be. The states that lie within them are less "shy" about asserting their rights, more normal in the claims they make.[61]

Albert Hourani argues that there is a new Arab political elite and a shift in its ideology. "The need to carry out economic and social development rapidly and by direct intervention of the state, and the concentration of effective force in the hands of the army, will tend towards the formation of governments of military politicians assisted by technocrats, which at least hold out the promise of strong executive power." In terms of ideology, "there has emerged a wide consensus in favour of a cautious, mixed, empirical type of policy less exposed to the winds of ideology; secularist without a radical break with religion, Arab but not to the extent of sacrificing sovereignty or local interests."[62] When established, the emerging new state will have to adopt at least one major characteristic of the Islamic legacy it tends to lack: "Traditional Islam survived for more than a millennium in a harsh and uncertain environment because it was capable of converting constant tension and conflict into a force for constant political renewal and social survival."[63] However abstractly put, this was the secret of the historical coexistence of Islam and ethnicity.

As we have seen, several patterns of relationship between primordial groups persist in the contemporary Middle Eastern state, but they tend to be less accommodating than the average patterns elucidated in the theoretical literature. Hence there is the added necessity of creating manifold mechanisms of tension management and conflict containment. But it is precisely the fragility of these mechanisms that stands out in the weakly institutionalized Middle Eastern state. The combination of such feeble mechanisms in a weak state, coupled with exacerbated ethnic tensions, has extracted a human and political cost in Lebanon that only monstrous oppression would have otherwise imposed. Ethnic havoc encouraged by weak stateness (also penetrated by stronger neighbors!) may be no less horrible than strong stateness coupled with repression.

[60]Hudson, *Arab Politics*, p. 55.
[61]Ajami, "End of Pan-Arabism," p. 365.
[62]Albert Hourani, "Lebanon, Syria, Jordan, and Iraq," in *The Middle East: Oil, Conflict, and Hope*, ed. A. L. Udovitch (Lexington, Mass.: Heath, 1976), pp. 289–290.
[63]Halpern, *Politics of Social Change*, p. 10.

The emerging strength of the state should ensure its survival in the foreseeable future. The question increasingly becomes one of the *nature* of this future state that will constitute the characteristic future structure of regional politics.[64] The state will have to confront a plethora of identities, attempting to harness at least some of them in its own increasingly pragmatic purposes. Yet to be even potentially successful its pragmatism must be in tune with the politically relevant sectors of the people: it must be comprehensible and acceptable to them. The need is for the politics of authenticity, rather than for the politics of identity dictated by pan-state ideological obsessions. This is where the twin pillars of Islam and ethnopolitics can serve as solid foundations in a strong state with strong institutions, or as battering rams against political order in a weak state with weak institutions.

In terms of formal logic, several patterns of ethnopolitics may be eminently suitable to conflict management on the Middle Eastern scene, perhaps none more than the devolutionary-federal model, which in a region of "compact minorities" may well be the best model for the Sudan, Iraq, Lebanon, and perhaps others as well.[65] Federal thinking, however, is geared toward the sharing of sovereignty by states and other political forces in an institutionalized structural arrangement. It is the devolution of some state power to political subcommunities. But state power, in order to be *devolved*, is first to be *had*—and it is not yet available in the necessary quantity—or quality. For the sharing of sovereignty between the state and the subcommunities, the state must first acquire sufficient institutionalized strength to be able to deal with sovereignty in the first place, and such strength is still in short supply (though it has recently been growing). If some other regions of the world have fared better in dealing with ethnic problems, it is not because they have had easier problems but because they have had stronger solutions, or at least frameworks for solutions. The trouble in the relationship between ethnopolitics and the Middle Eastern state is not too much ethnicity, but too little stateness.

---

[64]See the last chapter in Ben-Dor, *State and Conflict*, "Stateness and the Future of Middle East Politics," which deals with various dimensions of this problem, and in particular the question of the "state with a human face."

[65]See Ben-Dor, "Federalism."

PART III

THE ISRAELI SCENE
AND THE PALESTINIANS

6

The Different Levels of Palestinian Ethnicity

Aziz Haidar

Following the 1948 War and the establishment of the State of Israel, the Palestinians were dispersed across different geographical areas in neighboring Arab countries. Different groups of Palestinians have undergone different experiences, besides their shared experience as minorities.

The discussion that follows will examine the effects of these shared and differing experiences on the consolidation of ethnic and national identity by the different Palestinian groups. This discussion includes two sections. The first one deals with the relations between the Palestinians and the Arab host countries and includes four main topics: the civil rights granted to the Palestinians, the degree to which they enjoyed freedom of economic activity, the right to organize and act politically, and the nature of the relations that developed between them and their host populations at both group and individual levels. The second section deals with the relations between different Palestinian groups, paying special attention to relations between the Palestinians in Israel and the rest of the Palestinian groups, in particular after the June 1967 War. In addition we shall discuss the interaction between inter-group relations and in-group relations, as well as the interaction between the nation-building process and the development of ethnic relations.

The Borders of National and Ethnic Identity

In this chapter an ethnic group or community is a group or community whose members are aware that certain characteristics set them apart from other groups or communities—for instance, language, religion, culture, or historical experience.[1] The group members' consciousness of these characteristics is an important element in their definition as an ethnic group. In connection with the Middle East, Carleton Coon emphasizes the ethnic division of labor during the period up to the end of the last century,[2] providing another way to distinguish ethnic groups. To this we can also add the geographical dimension. In the Middle East, different ethnic groups inhabited different geographical regions. Moreover, although these groups were all ruled by a single governing authority, whether in the Ottoman Empire or the Persian Empire, they maintained clear differences in their social and political forms of organization.[3]

These distinct characteristics and qualities in a group did not determine its definition as an ethnic group. Rather, the consciousness of the group members regarding their ethnic identity defined the group itself. Ethnic consciousness rose and crystallized within various groups in the Middle East following the rapid development of transportation and communication. Even though this development blurred some of the distinguishing characteristics of various groups, it also gave rise to ethnic-based conflicts.

The case of the Palestinians is different. Until 1948 they did not constitute a group that had any sort of crystallized ethnic identity—cultural, religious, or based on community, life-style, or language. Instead, they were an inseparable part of the Middle Eastern Arab population. Actually, the differences between the Palestinians and the bordering peoples of the region were less obvious than the differences within the Palestinian population itself—even though from World War I onward certain indications of a separate political identity began to be obvious, based on the Palestinians' own historical experience of their struggle against the British Mandate, on the one hand, and the Zionist movement on the other.

Pre-1948 Palestinian society was divided both horizontally and vertically. It was characterized by noticeable regional differences that distinguished northerner from southerner, hill-dweller from valley-dweller, nomad from permanent settler, urban-dweller from villager, and Christian from Muslim.[4] These divisions significantly affected the 1948 war moves and their consequences, and the resulting developments within Palestinian society.

Following the mass flight of the Palestinians and the establishment of

---

[1]Albert H. Hourani, *A Vision of History: Near Eastern and Other Essays* (Beirut: Khayats, 1961), p. 723.

[2]Carleton S. Coon, *Caravan: The Story of the Middle East* (New York: Holt, Rinehart & Winston, 1964), p. 3.

[3]Iliya F. Harik, "The Ethnic Revolution and Political Integration in the Middle East," *International Journal of Middle East Studies* 3 (July 1972): 303–323, 307.

[4]Don Peretz, "Palestinian Social Stratification: The Political Implications," *Journal of Palestine Studies* 7, no. 1 (1977): 48–74; see also Salim Tamari, "Factionalism and Class Formation in Recent Palestinian History," in *Studies in Economic and Social History of Palestine in the 19th and 20th Centuries*, ed. Roger Owen (London: Macmillan, 1982), pp. 177–202.

the State of Israel within the borders of the Green Line, four main segments were created within Palestinian society: (1) The 160,000 Palestinians who remained within the State of Israel, (2) the 350,000 residents of the West Bank, who remained under Jordanian rule and were annexed to that country two years later, (3) the 70,000–100,000 residents of the Gaza Strip, who were under Egyptian rule, and (4) the 750,000 Palestinian refugees who were dispersed among the three regions mentioned above as well as in Jordan, Lebanon, Syria, and Iraq. These various Palestinian groups underwent more-or-less similar experiences. Besides their shared experiences, however, each different geographic concentration was subjected to different experiences. Therefore, certain characteristics and qualities that were similar and sometimes even identical were preserved or created, while others were created and consolidated according to the specific historical experiences of each individual group.

The discussion that follows will examine the effects of these shared or different experiences on the consolidation of ethnic and national identity by the different Palestinian groups.

The Palestinians in Their Arab Host Countries

The status of the Palestinians in their Arab host countries was not in the past, and is not today, influenced by their numbers, their professional and economic integration, or their educational level. Although objectively the Palestinians did not constitute a defined ethnic group, they were treated as an identifiable minority. On many levels the host country restricted their movements and prevented their integration.

Civil Rights

This limitation was particularly true in the area of civil rights. Only one Arab country, Jordan, granted full civil rights to individuals, but not to Palestinians collectively. There were attempts to draw them into the life of the country as individuals.

In the remaining Arab host countries, particularly Lebanon, Kuwait, and Saudi Arabia, the Palestinians were treated as foreigners. In Iraq and Syria their situation was not much different, although officially there was no discrimination against them. It was only in the Gaza Strip that the Egyptian authorities considered the Palestinians a clearly defined political group. There the laws of the British Mandate were preserved, and the Palestinians as a group were granted the right to organize. Two Arab countries, Jordan and Kuwait, allowed the Palestinians to enter the government administration, including senior positions. In Syria the Palestinians worked in important government and political positions, though in very small numbers and with far less impact than in Jordan and Kuwait. Their situation in Lebanon was particularly difficult because of that sectarian country's distribution of positions and power foci. There, the Palestinians' entry into government posts would have shaken the sectarian criteria that ruled the delicate balance among the various communities.

Freedom of Economic Activity

Jordan and Syria were the only two Arab states to grant Palestinians full rights of property ownership. Kuwait, Lebanon, and Iraq considered Palestinians foreigners and therefore denied them these rights. In three Arab countries, Jordan, Lebanon, and Kuwait, the Palestinians were able to improve their economic situation.

In Jordan they spearheaded economic development in both the public sector and the private sector and thus constituted the great majority of the middle class in that country.[5] In Lebanon wealthy and experienced Palestinians made use of the open economic structure. The generally encouraging environment enabled them to make a significant contribution to the capitalistic development of the economy. Their role in the economic sphere far exceeded their weight in the population,[6] but unlike the situation in Jordan, here their activities were restricted to the private sector. In Kuwait the Palestinians played a determining role in the modernization of the state. Middle-class Palestinians still comprise the largest group within this class. It is estimated that 35 percent of the Palestinians in Kuwait belong to the middle class. In addition, 5 percent are counted among the country's top entrepreneurs.[7] In Syria the Palestinians played only a limited economic role because of the restrictions imposed by the government on economic activity by both Syrians and foreigners.[8]

The first Palestinians to arrive in Iraq (in 1948) were penniless villagers who were housed in "shelters" in the three big cities. Both their own limited abilities and resources, and Iraqi government policies, prevented them from participating in any intensive economic endeavor.[9] It was only at the end

---

[5]Naseer Aruri and Samih Farsoun, "Palestinian Communities and Arab Host Countries," in *The Sociology of the Palestinians*, ed. Khalil Nakhleh and Elia Zureik (London: Croom-Helm, 1980), pp. 112–146, 117.

[6]Yosef A. Sayigh, "Toward a Theory of Entrepreneurship for the Arab East," *Explorations in Entrepreneurial History* 10, nos. 2–4 (1958): 125.

[7]Aruri and Farsoun, "Palestinian Communities," p. 135.

[8]Peretz, "Palestinian Social Stratification," p. 62.

[9]Isam Sakhnini, "Al-Filistiniyyon fi al-Iraq" (The Palestinians in Iraq), *Shu'un filistiniyya* 13 (September 1972): 90–116.

of the 1950s that relatively highly skilled Palestinians began to arrive in Iraq, and these integrated smoothly into the economic structure as merchants, civil servants, and free professionals.

In the Gaza Strip the Palestinians were granted total freedom in the economic sphere, but in practice the refugees suffered from a high unemployment rate and were exploited by the local population, which paid them extremely low wages.[10] Then too they were not included in the Egyptian government's plans for economic development on the pretext that theirs was a temporary problem.[11]

The Freedom to Act Politically

The Arab host countries did not allow the Palestinians to organize politically. In Jordan, Palestinians were subjected to a government policy that discriminated between the residents of the East Bank and the West Bank. Attempts to influence the political situation were cruelly crushed by the government. Force was used against any political party or political or military movement, as the events of 1957 and 1971 proved. In Syria the Palestinians were allowed to participate in political activities but not in independent frameworks. Later the government permitted some Palestinian organizations to establish military training camps and to mobilize the refugee camp residents on a political basis (but under the state's control). Kuwait was the only Arab country to allow the Palestinians independent political activity. This right was granted in particular to the Palestine Liberation Organization, which could even collect taxes from Palestinians and maintain an independent educational system.

In Lebanon the situation of the Palestinians was complicated. Still, their vital economic contribution in the private sector and the general liberal atmosphere enabled Palestinians to become involved in political and intellectual life. They participated in the pan-Arab nationalist political parties and movements. The special situation that existed in Lebanon between 1967 and 1978 while its society was undergoing a transformation allowed the Palestinians there freedom of activity. The rise of the nationalist Palestinian movement in Lebanon occurred simultaneously with the exacerbation of the sociopolitical crisis that caused the split in Lebanese society. This movement became an integral part of the Lebanese imbroglio and a side in the struggle between the warring camps. From the beginning of the 1970s, the Palestinians underwent political and military mobilization in

---

[10]James Baster, "Economic Problems in the Gaza Strip," *Middle East Journal* 9 (Summer 1955): 323–327.

[11]Mohammad A. Khalousi, *Attanmiya al-Iqtisadiyya fi Qitaa Gaza 1948–1962* (Economic Development in Gaza) (Cairo, 1967).

cooperation with the forces of the Left and on the basis of an understanding of mutual support. As a result, the Palestinian problem and its solution became closely tied to the Lebanese crisis and its solution.[12]

This survey of the Arab countries' policy toward the Palestinians in the spheres of civil rights, freedom of economic activity, and the freedom to act politically reveals that officially Palestinians were discriminated against, to varying degrees and in different areas of activity. Even when the claims and excuses for the discriminatory policies were the "preservation" of Palestinian identity, the results were no different. Moreover, even the countries that did grant Palestinians a degree of freedom to act independently did so because of the Palestinians' economic power and their ability to organize and influence, their vital role in the building and development of the particular country (e.g., in Kuwait), or the weakness of the central government and the splits that characterized the society (in Lebanon).

The official government policy of the Arab host countries affected the Palestinians' chances of integrating socially within those societies. This important factor is only one of many that determined the attitude of the host societies to the Palestinians and the type of relations that were established between the two groups.

Relations between the Palestinians and the Host Populations

It is always difficult to adjust to new social groups, and it is not always easy to establish ties with a host society. Prior to 1948 the Palestinians did not constitute a defined ethnic group in the Middle East, so they should have easily become assimilated into social groups in the host countries. But what happened was the opposite. The longer the Palestinians were in Arab countries, the more difficult their absorption and adjustment became. They eventually became a separate group with its own characteristics. Certain factors and processes were responsible for the development of a distinct ethnic identity.

First, after 1948 the Palestinians were for the most part penniless refugees, dependent for their existence and livelihood on the United Nations Relief and Works Agency (UNRWA). They lacked the crucial criterion for respect and status in Arab society—ownership of land. The host peoples viewed and related to them as "inferiors." Sharing the same social values, the Palestinians saw themselves in the same light, and therefore social meeting and exchange were both difficult and painful for them.

Second, at least two-thirds of the refugees were of fellahin-village origins, but most now found themselves in the host countries' most modern cities,

---

[12]Aruri and Farsoun, "Palestinian Communities," p. 133.

usually the capital and its environs.[13] Their rural origin was a decisive factor in their inability to be absorbed into the labor market. Because they were unskilled, their integration into the work structure of the host countries was difficult.[14] Dwelling in the midst of relatively developed urban populations, they were treated as inferiors because of their subhuman living conditions and their rural origins. The attitude was so demeaning that, for example, the residents of Sidon in Southern Lebanon termed the Ayn al-Hilwa refugee camp "a zoo." In Lebanon there were many stories of children who asked their parents to buy them "a Palestinian" (as a pet).[15] Even the Palestinian refugees of fellahin origin living in rural fellahin areas had a difficult time establishing ties because of religious barriers. The refugees were for the most part Sunni Muslims, while the Lebanese fellahin were Shi'ites, Druze, and Christians.

A third factor was that Palestinian refugees were isolated both spatially and socially. They were housed in refugee camps or in shelters (as in Iraq), and later waves of refugees were housed in the same quarters. This isolation greatly reduced the opportunity to establish ties with the surrounding population. Moreover, the host populations labeled residents of refugee camps "inferiors." Even within the Palestinian population of the West Bank and the Gaza Strip, residence in the refugee camps was a sign of lowly status. A common insult was "He looks like a refugee."

The social structure of each refugee camp effectively shut residents off from the outside world. Because the residents of each camp usually gathered on the basis of family ties and shared origins, according to village and region, the seclusion and social isolation increased and acted to preserve some of the characteristics the refugees brought with them from their villages of origin, thus isolating them even more. The situation in the Lebanese refugee camps has been described as follows:

From the social point of view they [the Lebanese refugee camps] are unlike the slum areas of large western cities and much closer to the village type in social organization. In fact, the inhabitants of the camps are grouped around the Palestinian villages from which they originated and the extended family units are still the basis of social life.... The camps, in fact, grew up in spontaneous formations rather than in accordance with some U.N. refugee relief plan.... This pattern thus meant the transfer of whole Palestinian villages, districts, or larger kin groupings more or less to the same residential areas in exile. This fact helped them retain their Palestinian dia-

[13]Rosemary Sayigh, "The Palestinian Experience: Integration in the Arab Ghourba," *Arab Studies Quarterly* 1 (Spring 1979): 96–110, 99.

[14]Halim Barakat, "The Palestinian Refugees: An Uprooted Community Seeking Repatriation," *International Migration Review* 7 (Summer 1973): 160.

[15]Sayigh, "Palestinian Experience."

lects, social customs, even their distinctive folklore. Significantly, Palestinians typically intermarried with one another and not with the Arabs of the host countries.[16]

The customs, foods, costumes, and dialect that the Palestinians took with them from their villages of origin, reflecting cultural differences between them and the host societies, became far more significant and loomed much larger than their actual importance warranted, because of the refugees' miserable circumstances.

In addition, the host societies did not help the Palestinian refugees to rehabilitate themselves and were even hostile to them. At the group level, the Palestinians were accused of eating the bread of the host countries, of betraying their country, of spying for Israel, and of being responsible for their downfall and their fate.[17] On the individual level the Palestinian was treated with contempt and was teased and accused of weakness, cowardice, and lack of self-respect: "For a long time the host societies provoked Palestinians with accusations of moral disintegration. For example, they would call someone a zombie, or taunt him with being a despicable creature with no backbone and lacking in manliness. They would sneer at him, saying he had sold his homeland and then gone to weep like a woman or a child. They compared him with his Algerian brothers, using this analogy as proof of the Palestinian's inferiority and the Algerian's courage."[18]

All these factors, in conjunction with the official policy of the Arab governments, placed heavy obstacles in the way of Palestinian integration within the host societies. Although some Palestinians escaped from their appalling situation and left the camps, as a result of either education or economic activity, and even made significant contributions to the economic development of certain countries, the group as a whole stood out as a "lowly" minority in each country.

The Palestinians' Reactions

A small number of Palestinians who succeeded in extricating themselves from their financial distress and who improved their status sought to as-

[16]Basim Sirhan, "Palestinian Refugee Camp Life in Lebanon," *Journal of Palestine Studies* 4, no. 2 (1975): 91–107.

[17]Anis Al-Qassim, *Men a-Sahra'a ila al-Quds* (From the desert to Jerusalem) (Tripoli: Dar a-Nashr al-Libiyya, 1965).

[18]Niqula Ad-Dur, *Hakaza daat wa hakaza taod: Dawr a-naft wa al-Madfaa fi tahreer Filasteen* (So it has been lost and so it could be returned: The role of oil and artillery in the liberation of Palestine) (Cairo: Dar Al-Maarifa, 1964).

similate within the Arab host societies.[19] The more common trend, however, was to take action to preserve Palestinian identity.[20] In general, the Palestinians objected to assimilation within the host societies and worked at maintaining their social, cultural, and political identities, while at the same time expecting the goodwill and understanding of the host countries.[21] The host countries did not meet these expectations, and the result was disappointment both on the part of the governments and on the part of the peoples of those countries.

In reaction, the Palestinians developed a sense of nonbelonging and alienation.[22] Hostility and hatred crept into their feelings toward the Arab governments and people, a hostility even greater than the hatred they felt toward the Israelis.[23] The sense of alienation was especially strong in the West Bank and the Gaza Strip. Because these two regions are part of Palestine, the Palestinians believed that the populace in those areas would be even more supportive.

Another Palestinian reaction was preservation of their cultural-social distinctiveness. Until the mid-1960s, however, there were no attempts to establish separate political institutions. On the contrary, the Palestinians were active in parties and governments that stressed pan-Arab nationalism. Because they believed that unification of the Arab peoples was their only guarantee of liberation and return to the land of their birth they were the Arab world's strongest proponents of unification.[24] "I live my life with a belief in the broad meaning of the word 'Arab and Arabism.' I was born in Jerusalem, I worked in Amman, I studied in Beirut, married a Lebanese woman, lived in Cairo. For me, my citizenship is that of the homeland, and my homeland extends from the Ocean to the Gulf."[25]

During the first period, until the beginning of the 1960s, it was the Palestinians who were interested in blurring the differences and stressing the similarities with the host societies and in becoming as much like them as possible (although without assimilating), all in the spirit of pan-Arab nationalism. But the Arab governments and peoples stressed the dividing factors, "in order to preserve Palestinian identity and the Palestinian prob-

[19]Husam Al-Khatib, "Athawra al-Filistiniyya ila ayn" (Whither the Palestinian Revolution), *Shu'un filistiniyya* 4 (September 1971): 5–31.

[20]Arnold Hottinger, *The Arabs* (London: Thames & Hudson, 1963), p. 246.

[21]Ingrid Galtung and Johan Galtung, *A Pilot Project from Gaza* (Oslo: Institute for Social Research, 1964), p. 19; Fawaz Turki, *The Disinherited: Journal of a Palestinian Exile* (New York and London: Monthly Review Press, 1972), p. 54.

[22]A. L. Tibowi, "Visions of the Return: The Palestine Refugee in Arabic Poetry and Art," *Middle East Journal* 17 (Late Autumn 1963): 507–526; see also Turki, *The Disinherited*.

[23]Turki, *The Disinherited*, p. 53.

[24]Anis Sayigh, *Falasteen wa al-Qawmiyya al-Arabia* (Palestine and Arab Nationalism) (Beirut: Markiz al-Abhath al-Filistini, 1966).

[25]Nasir-Adeen Nashashibi, *Safeer mutajawwil* (A Wandering Ambassador) (Beirut: Dar Al-Itihad, 1970), pp. 14–15.

lem." They isolated the Palestinians in every way and at all levels and so helped to maintain their sociocultural distinctiveness. In the mid-1960s, however, the Palestinians realized that the pan-Arab frameworks had failed. Palestinian national institutions were established because of changes that improved circumstances within the Palestinian population. Palestinians who acquired education and skills were able to get out of the camps and integrate themselves into the economies of the Arab countries, particularly the oil-producing countries. The enthusiasm for study was one reaction to the attitude of the Arab societies.[26] It reached a point at which the Palestinian student was ashamed if he did not outdo his fellow Arab students.[27]

As a result of the relatively high standards of education and their contribution to the development of the Arab countries, which became noticeable in the 1960s, the Palestinians began to see themselves in a new light. They began to see themselves as the "chosen" among the Arabs; they became aware of the important contribution they had made to the advancements taking place in the Arab world. This new perception had in it a recognition of the pride resulting from the demand of the oil-producing countries for skilled Palestinian labor, the large number of educated people within their ranks, and the important strides made by Palestinians in the academic and commercial worlds.[28]

The June 1967 war contributed much to these changes and feelings. The failure of the "revolutionary" Arab governments led the Palestinians to stress their social-cultural-political exclusiveness more and more, and they pointed out that Palestinians were not responsible for the outcome of this war. The Arab countries, for their part, supported the Palestinian political and military frameworks and praised the Palestinians in their struggle for liberation.

From this point on, distinctive Palestinian identity in the social, cultural, national, and political sense became an accomplished fact for the Arab peoples as a whole and for the Palestinians in particular. Their self-image was now the antithesis of what it had been when they first made contact with the host countries.[29] The host countries also altered their image of the

---

[26]Nabil Badran, "The Means of Survival: Education and the Palestinian Community, 1948–1967," *Journal of Palestine Studies* 4, no. 4 (1980): 44–74.

[27]Lutuf Gentus, "A-tarkeeb A-tabaqi Fi Al-Qadiyya Al-Filisteeniyya" (The influence of status composition on Palestinian problems), *Dirasat Arabiyya*, November–December 1965; Al-Qassim, *Men a-Sahraa ila al-Quds*; Turki, *The Disinherited*.

[28]Al-Qassim, *Men a-Sahraa ila al-Quds*, p. 21; Mohammad Abu-Shilbaya, *A-Tariq ila al-Khalass, al-hurriyya wa a-ssalam* (The path to salvation, freedom, and peace) (Jerusalem: n.d.).

[29]Ahmad J. Dhaher, "Changing Cultural Perspectives of the Palestinians," *Journal of South Asian and Middle Eastern Studies* 4 (Spring 1981): 38–64. Dhaher reports on sociocultural changes in the exiled Palestinian population and stresses that they ceased to define themselves as "refugees," while expressing their pride when defining themselves as "Palestinians."

Palestinians, so that the latter began to establish ties with the local populations on a basis of equality and mutual respect.

In-Group Relations among the Palestinians

The social-cultural-political changes, the change in the Palestinian self-image, and the change in Arab perceptions of the Palestinians affected in-group relationships too. The June 1967 war also had far-reaching effects on relationships among the Palestinian groups, particularly with regard to relations between the Palestinians in the Arab countries and the territories and those in Israel. The Palestinians, and the Arabs in general, suddenly "discovered" that there were hundreds of thousands of Arabs living within the borders of Israel. This discovery was accompanied by a substantive change in the attitudes of Palestinians and Arabs in general toward the Palestinians in Israel. This frame of mind was quite influential in defining the Israeli Palestinians' national, ethnic, and political identity; moreover, it affected their self-image and their relationships with the other Palestinians and with the Arabs. Relations between Israeli and other Palestinians progressed through three main stages.

Stage 1 (1947–1967): Toward Pan-Arabism

A small Arab minority of some 160,000 persons remained in Israel. Most of them (75 percent) lived in small villages in two areas: the Galilee in the north and the "Little Triangle," in the central part of the country. A minority lived in mixed cities, such as Haifa, Jaffa, Acre, Lydda, and Ramla. The Bedouins were established in the Negev.

Relations between the Jewish majority represented by the Israeli government and the Arab minority in Israel defined the borders of Arab identity in all its aspects, especially the ethnic aspect. Government policy contributed to the separation of the two populations and to a constantly growing sense of alienation among the Arabs. It was expressed by (1) expropriation of economic resources owned by the Arabs and redistribution of those resources to serve Jewish national needs;[30] (2) discrimination against the Arab sector in the distribution of economic resources for development purposes;[31] (3) keeping Arabs out of important decision-making political and economic

---

[30]Simcha Flapan, "Planning Arab Agriculture," *New Outlook* 6, no. 9 (1963): 65–73; Yitzhak Oded, "Land Losses among Israeli Arabs Villagers," *New Outlook* 7, no. 7 (1964): 10–25; Ran Kislev, "Land Expropriations: A History of Oppression," *New Outlook* 19, no. 6 (1976): 23–32.

[31]Yosef Waschitz, "Commuters and Entrepreneurs," *New Outlook* 18, no. 7 (1975): 48–53.

positions;[32] (4) institutionalization of the unequal relations between the two populations and of control of the Arab minority by the Jewish majority in all spheres of life (the Arab minority was denied the right to accumulate resources, which might have served as a basis for change in its situation);[33] (5) institutionalization of a negative majority attitude toward the minority because of the constantly widening gap between the two.

Relations between the two sectors were and continue to be characterized by increasing tension, which encompasses all aspects of life. This tension was exacerbated by various political and military events, particularly after the 1967 and 1973 wars. There has been no agreement between the two sectors about shared life-styles. The Jewish majority has not considered the Arab minority to be part of Israeli society and has expressed dissatisfaction with the very presence of this minority in its midst.[34] The majority has therefore chosen to maintain its distance from the minority in all spheres.[35] This gap was perpetuated and even intensified by institutionalized differentiation on the social and cultural levels. Both sides have legitimized this separation based on the ethnic factors of exclusive fundamental cultural values (origin, language, nationality, religion), important judicial distinctions (the Law of Return, the Law of Religious Communities, the Education Law), and separate institutions (schools, media, voluntary organizations).[36] This trend has been encouraged further by the geographical isolation of the two sectors, which in turn gave each sector the feeling that it constituted a separate social entity. Moreover, during the first seventeen years of the state of Israel's existence, a military government was imposed upon the Arab population, which further alienated the two sectors from each other.

This pattern of separation and the institutionalization of the gaps between the two sectors has been reflected in the day-to-day contacts between individuals and groups. During work hours, Arab employees are in contact with the Jewish worker or employer and with institutions of Jewish society. Shared public services also provide opportunities for chance meetings. These contacts are not egalitarian. The Arab is in a position of inferiority vis-à-vis the Jew, who has traditionally been the employer, manager, official,

---

[32]Ian Lustick, *Arabs in the Jewish State* (Austin: University of Texas Press, 1980), p. 186; Sammy Smooha, "Arabim viyihudim bi-Yisrael: Yachasay mioot-rov" (Arabs and Jews in Israel: Minority-majority relations), *Megamot* 22, no. 4 (1976): 397–423, and "Midinioot kayyemet omidiniot alternatevit klappay ha-Arabim bi-Yisrael" (Existing and alternative policy toward the Arabs in Israel), *Megamot* 26, no. 1 (1980): 7–36.

[33]Smooha, "Midinioot kayyemet omidinioot alternatevit."

[34]P. Adi and D. Freulich, *Hayachas le noseem poleetyem ochivratiyeem* (The attitude to political and social issues), Publication no. 11, Ministry of Education (Jerusalem, 1970, mimeo.).

[35]Ilyaho L. Cuttman and Shulamet Levi, *Aravim ViAmadoot shil HaNoar Halomed Bi-Yisrael* (Arabs and the attitudes of the learning youth in Israel), Publication no. 581 (Jerusalem, 1976).

[36]Smooha, "Arabim and Yihudim," p. 418.

teacher, police officer, or provider of services. There are few neighborly and friendly contacts, and mixed marriages are rare and considered deviant.[37]

The social and political barriers and geographical isolation have resulted in prejudices on both sides. For the Jewish majority, the prevalent stereotype of the Arab has been of a primitive, inferior, hostile, Jew-hating person.[38] The Arab minority has perceived the Jew as arrogant, materialistic, and lacking in positive personal qualities. All this, in addition to the status gap between the two populations, has increased the sense of alienation that Israeli Arabs have and has lowered their expectations for achieving their ambitions and reaching equality with the Jewish majority.[39] The relations that have crystallized between the two populations in Israel deepened the gaps and sharpened the ethnic differences. In this way they strongly influenced the attitude of Israeli Arabs toward Palestinian groups outside Israel and the way they defined their national, political, and ethnic identity.

During the period under discussion, the Israeli Arab population was almost totally cut off from the external Arab world. It is significant that Palestinians shared with the Arab world all its cultural symbols.[40] Very little information about the actual living conditions of Israeli Arabs reached outside. The Israeli media and Christian pilgrims gave the impression that the Israeli Arabs were completely integrated and enjoying a high standard of living. The pilgrims, however, bought all kinds of goods for themselves, and some also bought in order to import to Israel because of the difference in prices. Moreover, they refrained from political discussions because they were afraid of being followed by Israeli intelligence services. They also left the impression that the Arabs in Israel were fully integrated and unconcerned about the nationalist problem.

Some of the Christian pilgrims who were permitted to cross the border honestly believed that the situation of the Israeli Arabs was very good. They also gave the impression in Israel, perhaps unintentionally, that the economic situation in the Arab countries was better than in Israel, because of the quantities of goods the pilgrims imported from across the border at such low prices. The Arab media also projected a similar impression. All this contributed to the Israeli Arabs' sense of alienation. They believed that "redemption" from Zionist rule was not far away. Actually, at this stage the Israeli Arabs perceived themselves as Arabs (and were treated as such by the government), not as a separate identifiable group. This also did not

[37]Ibid., p. 404.

[38]Yochanan Peres, "Ethnic Relations in Israel," *American Journal of Sociology* 76, no. 6 (1971): 1021–1047.

[39]John E. Hofman, *Identity and Intergroup Perception in Israel* (Haifa: Jewish-Arab Center 1976, mimeo.).

[40]Khalil Nakhleh, "Cultural Determinants of Palestinian Collective Identity: The Case of the Arabs in Israel," *New Outlook* (1975): 31–40.

distinguish between Palestinian and Arab, and they generally used the term "Arab" rather than "Palestinian."

Their experiences with the Israeli government were similar to those of the Palestinian refugees in the Arab countries; they did not know that their refugee brethren were in similar circumstances. They thought the Palestinians had been received with sympathy and understanding and that they were being treated even better than the native citizens. This feeling was enhanced by the rise of revolutionary and pseudo-revolutionary regimes in certain Arab countries. Like their counterparts in the Arab countries, they believed in the unity of all the Arab peoples as the best guarantee of liberation and gave their wholehearted support to the pan-Arab national movements and particularly to President Nasser of Egypt, as leader of all the Arabs.

At this stage their social, economic, and educational level prevented them from exhibiting symbols of a collective Palestinian identity. Because of the pressure exerted by the military government, they actually displayed an opposite behavior pattern, which Yinger described: "Pressure against a weak group demoralizes the members, heightens intragroup conflict, accentuates the tendencies toward self-hatred and programs of escape."[41] Few Israeli Arabs defined themselves publicly as Palestinian Arabs or just as Palestinians. Among those who did, the trend was most noticeable in the works of writers and poets who "saw themselves as Palestinians and whose Palestinian identity was a far more powerful force than their Israeli citizenship."[42]

Stage 2 (1967–1976): Abandonment of Pan-Arabism in Favor of Palestinianism

After the June 1967 war the illusions of the Israeli Arabs were destroyed, but their greatest surprise was the fate of their fellow refugees outside Israel and in the West Bank and the Gaza Strip. The war only increased emotional tension and confusion among Palestinians. Therefore the period that began with the war's end could be labeled a period of shock. The immediate reaction of many Israeli Arabs was a denial of pan-Arab nationalism and the concept of Arab unity. They began to search for a new identity that would emphasize their "differentness" from the other Arabs; some even began to stress their Israeliness. Other Palestinians still hoped Nasser would achieve pan-Arabism. Shortly after the war this group looked for proof that

[41]J. Milton Yinger, "Social Forces Involved in Group Identification or Withdrawal," *Daedalus* 90 (Spring 1961): 247–262, 254.

[42]*Haaretz* (daily Hebrew newspaper), November 2, 1914.

he was not responsible for the outcome. They were shocked by his resignation in September 1970.

These shocks overshadowed the first contacts between the Israeli Arabs and the West Bank and Gaza Strip residents, which left negative impressions: the waves of beggars who arrived in the Arab villages of Galilee and the Triangle; the wealthy merchants from the West Bank and the Gaza Strip who were indistinguishable from the beggars and who came to sell their wares in the Arab villages; the unskilled Arab workers from the territories who agreed to accept any work at any pay; and various negative phenomena encountered by the Galilee and Triangle Arabs in their visits to the West Bank and the Gaza Strip, such as the merchants' bargaining system, the lack of fixed prices, with each potential buyer being presented a different price, and the exploitation of opportunities. In addition, Druze and Bedouin soldiers serving in the occupied territories told of cooperation between Palestinians in these territories and the Israeli authorities and as these stories passed from person to person with subsequent embellishments, they constituted a type of indirect contact that only confirmed the already present negative impressions.

Moreover, the Israeli Arabs were often disappointed in their own relatives, who visited them from the Arab countries, Lebanon in particular. Many of the visitors complained about their poor financial situation and appeared to be miserable and destitute. Their Israeli family members gave them money and asked members of the hamula and other village residents to help the destitute relatives. These donations were considered obligatory for all. In many cases the Israeli branch of the family borrowed money from the bank, and some even sold property and goods, to help these relatives. But the Israeli Arabs began to discover that much of what they had heard from their relatives was untrue, that they had been cheated and exploited. In fact, some of the "poor" relatives were much better off than their Israeli Arab families. Then there were relatives from the Arab countries who, not satisfied with the financial assistance they were offered, demanded their share of properties not expropriated by the Israeli authorities. The negative feelings engendered by this kind of cheating caused the Israeli Arabs to refuse to arrange visas for return visits to Israel by their families abroad.

Nevertheless, certain contacts did lead to the accumulation of positive impressions. In this situation of renewed contact, the Palestinians from the Arab territories bore a distinct national identity of Arabs living under Arab rule. In contrast, the Israeli Arabs projected the image of citizens living under military government for 17 years. The Palestinian sense of superiority was expressed in the meetings between the intelligentsia from both sides of the Green Line. These meetings deepened the frustration of the Arab intellectuals.

The resistance, particularly on the military level, to Israeli rule by the Palestinians in the occupied territories, and other forms of protest, as well as reports of heavy punishments meted out to young people there, increased the respect the young Israeli Arabs had for their counterparts on the other side of the Green Line. Their feelings of inferiority were heightened. In addition, the educational level in the occupied territories was relatively higher than that of the Israeli Arabs. Visitors from Arab countries told of Palestinians who had succeeded in the economic and scientific spheres in the oil-producing countries, the United States, and other places.

These positive impressions contradicted the negatives and enhanced the self-image and identity of some of the Israeli Arabs. These people began to differentiate between the negative and positive levels of contact with the "other" Palestinians, and they started to identify more strongly with them in the national and political sense, which was a positive level of contact. As the same time, the Israeli Arabs felt inferior on the socio-cultural level.

The process of "Palestinization" among the Israeli Arabs was accelerated by certain factors. First, the Palestine Liberation Organization (PLO) had successfully consolidated its international and pan-Arab status up to the mid-1970s. The legitimization that the United Nations granted the PLO, and the Rabat Arab Summit Conference in 1974, were important in this development. Second, the reports about the policy of the Arab countries toward the Palestinians, the Jordanian massacre of the PLO during Black September 1970 in particular, and Palestinians' success in the economic and educational spheres convinced them of and further entrenched their belief in the superiority of the Palestinians compared with the other Arabs. This assured the Israeli Arabs that the Palestinians were not responsible for the outcome of the June 1967 war.

A third factor was the Palestinian Covenant, which had already to all intents and purposes defined the Israeli Arabs as Palestinians: "The Palestinians are those Arab citizens who were living normally in Palestine up to 1947, whether they remained or were expelled. Every child who was born to a Palestinian parent after this date whether in Palestine or outside is a Palestinian" (article 6). After the war the Arab media praised the Israeli Arabs for resisting Israeli rule and preserving their culture and identity. Especially outstanding was the positive attitude of the media toward the Israeli Arab writers and poets. Literary criticism in the Arab countries described the difficult conditions under which the "resistance" writers were living in Israel and pointed out that these young people had established an entire network of cultural creation based on resistance.

A fourth factor was the October 1973 war, which deeply affected the Israeli Arabs by increasing their sense of national identity and encouraging them to change their attitude toward the State of Israel. It fortified their self-confidence and their belief in the Arabs' ability in general. The expression "Our Arab honor is restored" became a standard phrase.[43]

Contacts that developed between the Israeli Arabs and political and community elements in the West Bank and the Gaza Strip were another factor that encouraged many Israeli Arabs to believe that there were also "other" Palestinians, not only those who had left such a bad impression. While the Israeli Arabs did not forget their negative impressions, the positive impressions of the Palestinians living in the territories also received great support, and it is the latter that determined the consolidation of the Israeli Arabs' national identity as Palestinians. This increased the tendency to distinguish between different levels of activity in dealings with other Palestinians and resulted in the belief that even though they were Palestinians on the nationalist level, they were a different breed on social and cultural levels.

The Palestinians living within the Green Line also left certain impressions on their brethren in the territories and elsewhere. The huge quantities of merchandise purchased by the Israeli Palestinians on their shopping trips to the West Bank and the Gaza Strip led the merchants to believe that the Israeli Arabs were fully integrated into Israeli society and enjoying a comfortable standard of living. This impression was further strengthened by their use of Hebrew, in which the young Arabs were fluent. Some even used Hebrew to accentuate their differentness; others spoke Hebrew because they believed it was the way to get things they might otherwise not achieve. Some Arabs even came to the markets accompanied by Jews.

The Israeli Arabs were more experienced in the Israeli labor market than their counterparts from the territories. Because they often spoke Hebrew well, they flaunted their superiority by their use of Hebrew in contacts with their colleagues from the territories. They emphasized their ability to get along while accusing the other Palestinians of being ignorant. Moreover, some were managers for their employers. Workers from the territories perceived these people as collaborators with the Zionist conquerors against their own people. These workers were perhaps treated unfairly by the Israeli Arabs. In addition, at least during the first stage of the encounter, there were discussions in which the level of Israel's development was compared with that of the Arab countries, leaving a negative impression among the workers from the territories. Some of the Israeli Arabs stressed Israeli superiority.

Ra'ises (middlemen in the enlistment of workers) took advantage of the opportunity offered by the war to recruit and supply workers for Israeli industry from unskilled West Bank labor. They exploited the workers' ignorance and lack of experience in the Israeli job market and their desperate need to find work at any cost, and since these *ra'ises* made fortunes at the

---

[43]*Al-Hamishmar* (daily Hebrew newspaper), December 6, 1974.

expense of this cheap labor, they left a bad impression, which the workers from the territories extended to include all Israeli Arabs, to whom they referred as "collaborators with the Jews."

Most of the territories residents' contacts were with Israeli Arabs, who had little education, particularly in their places of work. This instilled in them a sense of "educational superiority," and they deduced that the Israeli Arabs preferred to send their children to work in order to make money instead of sending them to learn. And because most of the contacts with the Israeli army authorities were through the medium of Arabic-speaking police and soldiers of the Druze and Bedouin communities, they concluded that the Israeli Arabs were actively enlisting and fighting in the Israeli army against their own brethren.

The Israeli media used to, and still does, give the impression in the territories that the Israeli Arabs have been integrated into Israeli society, that they are uninterested in politics, and that the Palestinian problem does not concern them. Personal discussions and arguments in which the territories' residents displayed a much wider knowledge than the Israeli Arabs of Arab history and the Palestinian problem only deepened this impression. To this we add that in comparisons of the two sides, as presented in various forums, the territories' residents came out on top with regard to their active resistance to Israeli rule.

The types of contact mentioned above left the territories' residents with a very negative opinion of the Israeli Arabs and emphasized negative feelings between the two groups. But certain levels of contact left the Palestinians in the occupied territories with a much more positive feeling about their Israeli counterparts.

Family visits to Israeli Arabs in some cases left the impression that the latter had guarded their identity, language, customs, and social relationships. In addition, the literature of the resistance writers within the Green Line had an important function; it satisfied the need of the Palestinians in the occupied territories and beyond to convince themselves and the rest of the Arabs that the Palestinians had accepted a leadership role and that there was still hope they would free themselves from the distress that resulted from the military defeat and disappointment of the 1967 war.

When it came to resistance to Israeli rule, the Palestinians in the occupied territories became aware of the existence of even a limited amount of cooperation between the young people of the territories and those living within the Green Line. Intense political activity followed on the part of groups and leaders within the Green Line who define the Israeli Arabs as part of the Palestinian people; some tied the fortunes of the Israeli Arabs to those of the other Palestinians. The results of the municipal elections in Nazareth in 1975, and the many activities of the Arab students in the Israeli universities, were especially significant in this regard.

For many Palestinians in the occupied territories and further afield, these positive impressions took precedence over the negative ones and shaped their conception of the Israeli Arabs at this stage. They based their image on the national-political, rather than sociocultural, aspects. From this point on, the tendency was to differentiate among the various spheres of activity, to stress the unifying factors shared by all the Palestinian groups, and to blur or ignore the differences and the rifts. We shall see that this tendency was intensified even more during the next stage.

The social-cultural-economic-political developments and changes that took place up to the mid-1970s prepared the background for a new stage in the relations between the Israeli Palestinians and the Israeli authorities and society, as well as between them and the other Palestinians in the territories and elsewhere. They also helped shape the Palestinians' self-image and the definitions of the boundaries of their affiliation frameworks.

Stage 3: Land Day 1976 and Its Aftermath

Land Day, March 30, 1976, was not a chance event. It symbolized the changes that had accumulated through the years in the life of the Israeli Arabs and heralded the advent of a new stage in the relations between the Arabs and the Israeli authorities, and Israeli society in general, as well as a change in the Arabs' self-image and attitude toward the other Palestinians.

As the culmination of all that had taken place until the mid-1970s, Land Day drastically altered the negative attitude of the Palestinians in the territories and elsewhere toward Israeli Arabs. It signaled the beginning of a new kind of relationship between the two sides. After 1948 it was the first event in which a deep sense of shared fate developed between the Palestinians on both sides of the Green Line. Each felt closer to the other than ever before. When the Israeli Arabs declared a general strike, Palestinians in the territories and elsewhere supported them in force. The Israeli authorities' reaction convinced everyone, particularly the Arabs within the Green Line, that they were all being subjected to the same treatment.

The developments presented here, which occurred in Israel, in the territories, and throughout the Middle East, brought the Palestinians from both sides of the Green Line closer together in their definition of national identity. Within the Green LIne the percentage of Arabs who defined themselves as Palestinians was growing as the number of those who termed themselves simply Arabs or Israelis decreased.[44] Today they comprise the majority of the Palestinians in Israel.

[44]Mark A. Tessler, "Israel's Arabs and the Palestinian Problem," *Middle East Journal* 31 (Summer 1977): 313–329, 328.

The definition of national identity has a cumulative influence on social relations with people of other national groups.[45] Of course, national identity also influences the individual's relationships within the national group with which he affiliates himself. The Arab living within the Green Line who defines himself as a Palestinian begins to minimize the divisions in the group and focuses on the Palestinian aspects of his identity. One characteristic of the Palestinian definition of national identity is an increasing acceptance of the cultural differences that exist between the groups on either side of the Green Line.

A study conducted by Sharif Kanaana shows that each of the two groups studied—the Palestinians in Israel and the Palestinians of the West Bank—perceives itself as a separate and distinct entity.[46] The West Bank residents speak of the Israeli Arabs as "Arabs of Israel," "the Arabs inside," and "the 1948 Arabs." The two latter titles evolved later and are in common use today, symbolizing the inclusion of the Palestinians in Israel within the framework of the Palestinian people. At the same time, however, these titles indicate a need to distinguish between the Palestinians in Israel and other groups within the same nation on the sociocultural level. The Israeli Arabs refer to the West Bank residents as "the Arabs of the West Bank" or "the 1967 Arabs." They have no parallel for the term "Arabs of Israel," such as "Arabs of Jordan" or, in the case of the Gaza Strip, "Arabs of Egypt." This may reflect the fact that no one within the Green Line doubts the national identity of the West Bank and Gaza Strip residents, although the latter do question that of the Israeli Arabs. The same study reveals that both groups perceive each other both positively and negatively.[47] In addition, they seem to have crystallized similar images with regard to the members of the other group, and there appears to be a distinction between impressions on the national level and on the sociocultural level.

Basically the Palestinians on both sides of the Green Line are agreed about the boundaries of Palestinian nationalism. While it includes both groups politically, it does not preclude the existence of negative images on the sociocultural level. This agreement does not encompass all the Palestinians beyond the Green Line, some of whom do not differentiate between the aspects of national and sociocultural identity. It does question Israeli-Arab affiliation with Israel. On the other hand, from the start the process of crystallization of Palestinian national identity among the Israeli Arabs was accompanied by a growing recognition of the sociocultural pluralism that existed within the one people.

[45]Ibid.

[46]Sharif Kanaana, *A-ttaghayyor wa-al-istimrariyya: Dirasat fi taatheer al-Ichtilal ala al-mojtamaa al-Arabi al-Filistini* (Change and Continuity: Studies on the effect of the occupation on Arab Palestinian society) (Jerusalem: Arab Studies Society 1983).

[47]Ibid., pp. 86–90.

The development of this trend was probably influenced by the following factors. First, the Israeli example, with its two main and distinct ethnic groupings—Ashkenazi and Sephardi—and the other communities of various origins, was familiar to the Israeli Arabs. The influence of the Israeli example of an ethnic-based split was associated with a recognition of Israel's strength and superiority compared with the other Middle Eastern countries, particularly in the military sphere. The Israeli Arabs internalized the idea that ethnic-based differences would not necessarily weaken a society. Of course, internalization of this idea was based on an awareness that various subcultures existed within the Palestinian people too.

A second factor was that Palestinian society was already split both lengthwise and breadthwise even before 1948. Most of the Arab population that remained in Israel was concentrated in the Galilee so that cultural differences existed between them and the West Bank and Gaza Strip populations even before the borders separated them. In addition, the majority of refugees from the Galilee reached Lebanon and Syria, while those who came to the West Bank and the Gaza Strip were from the more southern regions. This meant that the geographical distance that separated the two sides remained intact. Then again there was a total disruption of social and political contact after 1948, and no communication between refugees from the Galilee and the local residents and refugees of the West Bank and the Gaza Strip. Moreover, each group had different experiences and underwent its own sociocultural changes.

The attitude of the "original" inhabitants of the West Bank and the Gaza Strip toward the Palestinian refugees gathered in the refugee camps was no different from that of the other Middle East countries, and this might also have been a factor in the development of a Palestinian national identity among Israeli Arabs. The camp residents constituted the weakest and most poverty-stricken level within the Palestinian populace.[48] Those who succeeded in leaving the camps and improving their lot did so on their own, unaided by their hosts. This policy strongly affected the Israeli Arabs' attitude toward the other Palestinians, not just toward the other Arab countries. None of the latter assisted the refugees, who in some cases were relatives or inhabitants of the Israeli Arabs' own villages (particularly in the area of the Triangle and the cities of Jaffa, Ramla, Lydda, for example).

It must also be mentioned that the stratification of Israeli Arab society underwent drastic changes. The semifeudal class disappeared from the Israeli Arab village as early as 1948, and with it all its characteristic status symbols. The gaps between the classes were greatly narrowed, and the dominant class became the proletariat, whose chief source of wealth derived

---

[48]Ahmad S. Saad and Abdulkadir Yasin, *Al-haraka al-wataniyya al-Filastiniyya, 1948–1970* (The Palestinian national movement, 1948–1970) (Jerusalem: Salah A-din 1975).

from its work as hired labor in the Jewish sector.[49] This drastic change was accompanied by profound value changes, including those of social stratification.[50] The Arabs in the West Bank and the Gaza Strip, on the other hand, preserved for the most part the pattern of social stratification, the values and behavioral norms that had characterized Palestinian society prior to 1948. The Israeli Arabs were "frightened" when they saw the huge gaps between the different classes in the territories and were shocked by the preservation of traditional status symbols. This was particularly true of young people born after the establishment of the State of Israel, who had never known traditional Palestinian society. More than any other group within the Israeli Arab populations, it was the young intellectuals who were repelled by the life- style and behavior of the upper classes in the territories, and particularly by their attitude toward the rest of the populations. These intellectuals were the group most insulted by the rejection of the bourgeois families of the West Bank and Gaza Strip cities, who still control most of the government and public institutions.

Stories and jokes about relations among the different classes in the territories are widespread among the Israeli Arabs and are told with more than a hint of scorn and much bitterness. They are used by many Israeli Arabs to emphasize the differences between the social and cultural levels, differences that gave birth to the concept of pluralism within the Palestinian people and to the distinction between the boundaries of national identity and those of sociocultural identity.

The existence of the distinctions mentioned above and the separation of the different levels of contact between the two groups is reflected in the types of contact and mutual ties that developed between them. For instance, marriages were in one direction and few in number. Some young Israeli Arabs married young West Bank women or young Palestinian women from the refugee camps in Lebanon. In the West Bank such cases are viewed as matches contracted by low-class young women who would never be able to find husbands in the West Bank and therefore look for husbands among the Israeli Arabs, which in turn is an indication of the low social status of the latter. The Israeli Arabs see the situation in an entirely different light: A young Arab living in Israel who cannot find a "high-class" woman willing to marry him can find any woman in the West Bank because there they are willing to sell their daughters to the highest bidder.

These marriages are only some of the relationships included in Kanaana's study.[51] Kanaana also points out that most of these marriages fail and

---

[49]Henry Rosenfeld, "The Class Situation of the Arab National Minority in Israel," *Comparative Studies in Society and History* 20 (July 1978): 374–406.

[50]Aziz Haidar, *A-taaleem al-mihani fi al-madaris al-Arabiyya fi Israel* (Technical education in Arab schools in Israel) (Birzeit: Birzeit University Research Center 1985).

[51]Kanaana, *A-ttaghayyor wa-al-istimrariyya*, p. 99.

thereby contribute to the institutionalization of negative images in both groups.

Another example of the types of relationships that developed between the two groups and that demonstrates again the sociocultural rifts between them is found in the city of Jerusalem. Since 1967, about seventy families from the Galilee and Triangle areas, mostly young people, have settled in Jerusalem. Most of the husbands are educated people who studied in Jerusalem and have found their place in the labor market of the Old City or the West Bank, either as free professionals or as teachers in the universities and other learning institutions in the West Bank towns. These families live in almost total isolation. They constitute a tightly knit social group, and their social and cultural life-style is very different from that of the surrounding populace. A field study reveals cultural differences between Palestinians in the territories and those from the Galilee and the Triangle, which are expressed in the forms of social organization, customs, work and administrative patterns, and even in outlook. These examples of cultural differences and others demonstrate the attempt of each group to maintain its distance from the other and to limit the forms and patterns of social contact.

The above process of sociocultural differentiation occurred simultaneously with the consolidation of national consciousness in all concentrations of the Palestinian population, which in turn was accompanied by recognition of the sociocultural pluralism existing within the total nationalistic framework of the Palestinians. This tendency was more noticeable in the Palestinian population of Israel than elsewhere, because of the Israeli Palestinians' many years of different experience and the special conditions of their life-style. A large proportion of the Israeli Palestinians distinguish between their affiliations with three different frameworks: Palestinian national identity, the Israeli political framework, and the specific "ethnic" identity, as opposed to other ethnic identities within the Israeli population, on the one hand, and the identities of cultural subgroups within Palestinian society, on the other.

In recent years many changes and developments have taken place within the Palestinian population of Israel. These indicate a process of the crystallization of very small political groups whose intention is to sever themselves from the Israeli political framework and to blur the cultural differences among the various Palestinian groups or to diminish their significance.

The final intent of these groups is the creation of a framework in which the boundaries of national identity will be identical with and parallel to those of ethnic identity. This trend is further fortified by similar processes taking place in the West Bank, the Gaza Strip, and other sectors of the Palestinian population: (1) an increasing similarity in the life-style and behavior norms of the West Bank and the Gaza Strip, because the Palestinian labor force has become a proletariat that depends on salaried jobs in Israel for its livelihood; (2) an effort by many Palestinians to be more tolerant and understanding of the Israeli Arabs, particularly since Land Day 1976 (this trend is most obvious within the Palestinian political leadership and among political groups in the territories that are sharing experiences similar to those of the Israeli Arabs), (3) in a continuation of the above-mentioned process, the attempt to push the Palestinians in Israel out of the periphery of Palestinian society and pull them more into the center, particularly of the political structure—which would give them the feeling that their place is at the hub of activity and not at its edge. The outcome of these processes and trends depends on political, economic, and social developments within the Palestinians of both Israel and the entire Middle East.

Other developments that have affected the continuing process of redefining the affiliation frameworks and attitudes of the Palestinians in Israel are the peace treaty between Egypt and Israel, and the attitude of the Arab countries, particularly Syria, during the Israeli invasion of Lebanon in 1982. These developments have led to an increasing emphasis among Palestinians in Israel on Palestinianism and disregard for pan-Arabism.

At the same time, Palestinian leaders have increased their emphasis on the centrality of the West Bank and the Gaza Strip in the process of liberation and in the resolution of the Palestinian problem. This has meant increasing support, especially financial support, to the populations of both these areas for their steadfastness and resistance to the Israeli occupation. The Palestinians in Israel, observing and contemplating these developments, have begun to feel that they are disregarded and excluded from this support and that their steadfastness is unrecognized. Furthermore, numerous stories about corruption of the Palestinian administration have spread among them, in particular the corruption of leaders in the occupied territories, to whom the Palestinian leadership and Arab regimes have funneled support.

These developments, I believe, have accelerated the feeling of "difference" among the Palestinians in Israel in recent years and have intensified their inclination to differentiate between various frameworks of affiliations and different levels of behavior. It is noteworthy that along with increasing emphasis on their Palestinian national identity, the Palestinians in Israel have enhanced their struggle to get rights in Israel that are equal to those granted to the Jewish citizens of the state.

Conclusions

The consolidation of ethnic identity within the Palestinian groups throughout the Middle East was mainly the result of their inferior economic, social, and political status in the communities with which they came in

contact, not of basic cultural differences between them and the other populations of the region. The cultural differences did not determine the boundaries of the Palestinians' ethnic identity, but they did emphasize the social
borders and status gaps that separated them from the other Middle Eastern
populations by imbuing them with a significance far beyond their actual
weight. From this we can conclude that the social border, and not the
visible differences in behavior patterns and life-styles, are the most important factor in determining a community's ethnic identity.

Differences in behavior and life-style cannot be the basis for construction
of ethnic boundaries, but cultural differences on a deeper and more basic
level could certainly serve as such a basis. Therefore only the codification
of obvious differences in complementary status systems which become the
basis for distinctions between affiliation groups, a codification supported
by differences of origin, can provide the basis for establishing ethnic boundaries.[52] The codification of cultural differences was the basis for constructing
the ethnic boundaries that separated the Palestinian communities from the
other communities in the Middle East. This process has been determined
by the minority status of Palestinian communities in the region.

No such process took place among the Palestinian communities. The
cultural distinctions among these groups were preserved and even strengthened, but they do not reflect basic cultural differences or constitute a solid
basis for establishing clearly defined ethnic boundaries. As with other
groups in the Middle East, Palestinians comprise various groups defined by
behavior patterns and life-styles, while at the same time they belong to the
same ethnic group. As various researchers report, in this region nomad,
fellah, and city-dweller can belong to the same ethnic group.[53]

The renewed contact among the Palestinian communities from either
side of the Green Line did not blur their cultural differences, just as the
contact with the Arab societies did not blur the differences between the
Palestinians and those host societies. What determined the ethnic boundaries was not the interaction but the kind of contact, the circumstances in
which the contact occurred, the status gap between the groups that came
in contact, and the self-images of the members of each group and their
attitudes toward the members of the other group. In the case of the Palestinians the contact actually helped institutionalize the existing differences
and even strengthened and accelerated the constructing of ethnic boundaries separating the Palestinian communities from the other communities.
However, for several reasons this contact did not lead to the establishment
of clear ethnic boundaries among the Palestinian groups: the status of all

[52]Jan P. Blom, "Ethnic and Cultural Differentiation," in *Ethnic Groups and Boundaries*, ed.
Fredrik Barth (London: Allen & Unwin, 1969), pp. 74–85.
[53]Fredrik Barth, "Introduction" in Barth, *Ethnic Groups*, p. 26.

the Palestinians in the Middle East and the attitudes of the various societies toward them, the military events and political processes that encouraged the tendency to blur or ignore cultural differences, and the conscious acceptance of the existence of sociocultural pluralism within the Palestinian people.

7

Jews and Arabs in the Israeli Communist Party

Elie Rekhess

The central problem faced by both Palestinian and Israeli Communists has been how to expand in a region where two national movements have been in conflict with one another for many years. Communism offered its own solution to the struggle between Arabs and Jews—a comprehensive ideological system for internationalist unity designed to bridge the differences between the two peoples. Jewish and Arab Communists genuinely believed that the Marxist socialist class-struggle system provided an appropriate political and social solution to the national conflict in Palestine. Unified in an anti-Zionist and anti-Imperialist stance, they advocated establishment of a revolutionary proletarian regime that would secure the rights of both peoples equally. The details of the plan under which the Jewish-Arab national aspirations were to be achieved had been frequently modified in accordance with the occasional changes in Soviet perception.

From the beginning, Communists' endeavors in Palestine were hindered by major obstacles. They tried to implant a theory that was quite alien to local political and social conditions and to implement a policy that primarily suited a foreign power—the Soviet Union. Over and above these difficulties, however, Communists had to contend with the national struggles in the region. The Jewish-Arab conflict was traditionally reflected in microcosm within the local Communist party, thus bringing about and perpetuating its bi-national division. Party members were torn by their contradictory loyalties to internationalist principles and to national principles. The con-

The author is grateful to the Bronfman Program for the Study of Arab-Jewish Relations for its assistance.

tinuous intensification of the Jewish-Arab conflict and the frequent political changes in the Middle East have persistently upset the party's inner cohesion as well as its ethnic balance. Factionalism and ideological differences were the predictable result. The circumstances prevailing in each of the three major periods in the party's history—the mandate years (1919–1948), the MAKI[1] era (1948–1965), and the period of RAKAH[2] (1965 to date)—have determined the extent of Jewish-Arab compatibility within the Communist Party.

Twice, in 1943 and 1965, the Communist Party split because of national-ist-ideological controversies between Jews and Arabs. Since 1965, RAKAH has established itself as the sole Communist party. Despite latent tension and occasional friction, the party has succeeded in maintaining its integrity. Officially, RAKAH has remained a Jewish-Arab organization, but the part-nership has not rested on an equal basis. While key leadership positions were given to a small Jewish minority, an increasing number of RAKAH's members, sympathizers, and voters were Arabs. After the June 1967 war, RAKAH grew even deeper roots in the Israeli-Arab community.

We shall be examining the interaction between the various conflicting forces that underlaid the unique structure of the Israeli Communist Party and survey the elaborate system of tactics and strategies that enabled the Communists to preserve their cohesion.

The Mandate Period

In the years following its establishment in 1919, the Palestine Communist Party (PCP) was predominantly Jewish in character.[3] It had no success among the Arab masses, whose attraction to Marxist ideas was virtually nil. The turning point came in 1924, when the party was accepted by the Communist International (Comintern). The Comintern believed that in an area with a clear Arab majority the PCP's future was in "territorialization",

---

[1]Hebrew acronym for Hamiflaga hakomonistit hayisraelit, the Israeli Communist Party (ICP).

[2]Hebrew acronym for Hareshima hakomonistit hahadasha, the New Communist List.

[3]On the PCP, see G. S. Yisraeli, *MPS—PKP—MAKI. Korot hamiflaga hakomonistit beyisrael* (M.O.P.S.—P.C.P.—MAKI: The history of the Communist Party in Israel, 1919–1953) (Tel Aviv, 1953); Walter Z. Laqueur, *Communism and Nationalism in the Middle East* (New York: Praeger, 1956); Yehoshua Porat, "Mahpekhanut veterorism bemediniyut hamiflaga hakomon-istit hapalestina'it" ("Revolution and terrorism in the policy of the Palestine Communist Party [PCP], 1929–1939"), *Hamizrah Hehadash*, 18, nos. 3–4 (1968): 255–267; Mario Offenberg, *Kommonismus in Palestina: Nation und Klasse in der antikolonialen Revolution* (Meisenheim an Glan, 1975); Alexander Flores, "Nationalismus und Sozialismus in arabischen Osten. Das Verhältnis der kommunistischen Partei zur arabischen Nazional-bewegung in Palestina, 1919–1948" (Ph.D. Thesis, University of Münster, 1979); and Alain Greilsammer, *Les Communistes israeliens* (Paris, 1978).

in other words, Arabization.[4] The party failed to carry out this external directive. Only a few Arabs were recruited, leaving the Jews in a dominating position.[5]

Following the violent clashes between Jews and Arabs in August 1929 the process of Arabization was accelerated.[6] The PCP's expressed sympathy for the Jewish stand provoked the Comintern to intervene. Moscow tended to side with the Arabs and criticized the position of the PCP. The Soviets attributed the party's erroneous response to the situation to the ethnic composition of the party and consequently insisted that Arabization be pursued more vigorously.[7]

The external intervention aroused Jewish protest. Some Jews were disappointed and emigrated from Palestine, others left the party. In recently published studies on the early history of the PCP, Arab scholars claim that the Jewish Communists misinterpreted the principle of Arabization.[8] Having failed to understand the true nature of the national problem in Palestine, they argue, the Jews erroneously regarded Moscow's instruction as chauvinistic or, in an oversimplification, as an administrative order to replace Jewish cadres by Arabs. Arabization, some concluded in retrospect, was a genuine political program based on the scientific principles of Marxism-Leninism and expressing a historical stage in the struggle for socialism, national liberation, and independence.

Despite Jewish opposition, several Arab Communists who were studying in Moscow at that time were ordered to return to Palestine and take over the organization of the party. In 1930, under instructions from the Comintern, party members appointed a Central Committee and a Politburo with an Arab majority.[9] Four years later an Arab member, Ridwan al-Hilu (Musa), was appointed secretary-general of the PCP, a post he held until

[4]Laqueur, *Communism and Nationalism*, p. 77. The Comintern maintained that the PCP could no longer be "a party of Jewish emigrants" and should therefore become a party of Arab laborers that would also accept Jews who had "acclimatized, grown into the Palestinian conditions, and knew Arabic" (cited by Yisraeli, *MPS*, p. 29).

[5]See Porat, "Mahpekhanut," pp. 258–259.

[6]For a detailed discussion on the 1929 riots, see Yisraeli, *MPS*, chap. 7, pp. 60–73; and Porat, "Mahpekhanut," pp. 256–258.

[7]Yisraeli, *MPS*, p. 79.

[8]Maher al-Sharif, *Al-shuyu'iyya wal-mas'ala al-qawmiyya al-'arabiyya, 1919–1948* (Communism and the Arab national question in Palestine, 1919–1948) (Beirut: 1981), pp. 57–58. For similar approaches, see Sulayman Bashir, *Al-mashriq al-'arabi fil-nazariyya wal-mumarasa al-shuyu'iyya* (The Arab mashriq in Communist theory and practice) (Jerusalem, 1977); Musa Khalil, "Al-hizb al-shuyu'i al-filastini" (The Palestine Communist Party), *Shu'un Filastiniyya* 39 (November 1974): 111–142; Samih Samara, *Al-'amal al-shuyu'i fi filastin* (Communist action in Palestine) (Beirut, 1979); Musa Budeiri, "The Palestine Communist Party: Its Arabization and the Arab-Jewish Conflict in Palestine, 1922–1948" (Ph.D. thesis, London School of Economics, 1977); Alexander Flores, "Recent Studies on the History of the PCP," *Khamsin* 7 (1980): 41–52.

[9]Porat, "Mahpekhanut" p. 259.

1943. In 1935, Palestinian delegates to the Comintern Congress could report that Arabization of their party was continuing and that only "the reliable and honest Jewish comrades in the party's ranks" were permitted to continue their participation.[10]

The sharp escalation in the Jewish-Arab conflict between 1936 and 1939 eroded Communist unity considerably. Jewish members drew closer to the Yishuv, while Arab Communists adopted a more positive attitude toward their own national movement. Shortly after the general strike was declared in April 1936, the PCP's Central Committee asserted that Arab members should actively participate in the campaign against Zionism and imperialism, while the role of the Jews was to weaken the Zionist entity from within.[11] In the initial stages of the disturbances, the party identified wholeheartedly with the national goals of the Arabs, cooperating with the Muslim Supreme Council. Two Arab Communists actually joined the headquarters of the fighting Arab units.[12]

After the first wave of terror ceased, Jewish members began to oppose the party's official line. Some withdrew, while others organized, in 1940, a separate framework known as "the Jewish Section," which for the first time admitted that there were progressive elements within the Zionist camp and that Jews too had national interests in Palestine.[13] The rift between the Jewish faction and the Arab-dominated Central Committee lasted for two years. In 1942 the rival factions became reconciled to one another, but this reconciliation lasted only briefly.

The friction between the two increasingly nationalistic groups peaked in 1943, when the PCP split into two national organizations, a pattern that was to recur in later years. The immediate cause for the cleavage was a general strike of British army camp employees, declared by the General Federation of Jewish Labor, the Histadrut.[14] The predominantly Arab Central Committee opposed the action taken by the Zionist organization, while certain leading Jewish members, mainly from Haifa and Tel Aviv, supported it. The gap between the two groups became unbridgeable. The Arabs formed the National Liberation League (Usbat al-Taharrur al-Watani), insisting that it be an Arab organization.[15] Following the policy of the Muslim

[10]Martin Ebon, "Communist Tactics in Palestine," *Middle East Journal*, 2 (July 1948): 257.

[11]Yisraeli, *MPS*, p. 120; Porat, "Mahpekhanut," pp. 263–266.

[12]Nimr Awda and Fu'ad Nassar. The latter later became secretary-general of the Jordanian Communist Party. See Laqueur, *Communism and Nationalism*, p. 97.

[13]Yisraeli, *MPS*, pp. 185–89; Yehoshua Porat, "Haliga leshikhrur leumi, usbat al-taharrur al-watani, tekumata, mahuta vehitparkuta, 1943–1948" (The National Liberation League: Its emergence, essence, and dissolution, 1943–1948), *Hamizrah Hehadash* 14, no. 4 (1964), pp. 354–355.

[14]Yisraeli, *MPS*, pp. 179–184; Porat, "Haliga," p. 356.

[15]Shortly before the split occurred, three Arab assistants to the party's secretary-general published an appeal that stated: "The truth is that the PCP is a national Arab party, though it contains individual Jews who accept its national programme." One of the signatories was

Supreme Council, the league advocated establishment of democratic government in an independent Palestine, but while the Arab national movement demanded expulsion of Jews who settled in Palestine after World War I, the Arab Communists agreed to recognize all Jewish inhabitants as citizens of the future Palestinian state. The rest of the league's political aims were identical to those of its Arab counterpart. The Jewish Communists, on the other hand, reestablished the PCP with an exclusive Jewish membership. From 1943 onward the party recognized the Jewish national aspirations in Palestine. It later supported autonomy for geographical regions populated by Jews and finally agreed to the establishment of a federal state.

Thus, for five years two different Communist organizations, each pursuing its own community's national interests, existed in Palestine. The reunification of the Communist Party became possible only after 1948, when the Soviet Union, which supported the 1947 partition plan and recognized the State of Israel, exerted pressure on the two factions, which consequently merged. The bi-national framework advocating "territorialization"—dissolved in 1943—was reconstructed.

MAKI, 1948–1965

The ratio of Jewish to Arab inhabitants of Israel has changed dramatically since the State was established. In sharp contrast to the mandatery period, the remaining Arab population became a minority in a predominantly Jewish state. The new division was immediately reflected in MAKI. During the War of Independence, many Arab Communists left Palestine, relocating in neighboring Arab countries. Many settled on the West Bank of the Jordan River, where they joined the local Communists. Most party members in Israel were Jews.[16] New recruits came mainly from the waves of *olim* (newcomers) who immigrated to Israel in the early 1950s. The Jewish element was further strengthened in 1954, when Moshe Sneh and his left Socialist Party joined MAKI. Now representing the majority, Jews dominated

---

Emil Habibi. (Cited in Laqueur, *Communism and Nationalism*, p. 110.) On the league, see also Porat, "Haliga", pp. 354–366; Maher al-Sharif, "Usbat al-taharrur al-watani wal-mas'ala al-qawmiyya al-'arabiyya fi filastin, 1919–1948" (The National Liberation League and the national Arab question in Palestine, 1943–1948), *Shu'un Filastiniyya* 108 (November 1980): 66–94.

[16]Berl Balti, a former MAKI Jewish leader estimated that in 1949 the party was composed of 68 percent Jews and 32 percent Arabs (interview by Alain Greilsammer; see Greilsammer, *Les Communistes israeliens*, p. 343). Similar figures were given by Laqueur, *Communism and Nationalism*, p. 118. In 1961 the party furnished the following official figures: 74.3 percent Jews; 25.7 percent Arabs. The Israeli Communist Party, *The Fourteenth Congress* (Tel Aviv, 1961), p. 112.

the party's central institutions.[17] Shmuel Mikunis, a Jew, was elected secretary-general. Jews also constituted the majority of MAKI's Knesset representation from 1951 onward.[18] The distribution of power within MAKI's political bodies seemingly won Moscow's approval. In contrast to their policy during the mandatory period, when the Comintern had insisted on Arabization, after 1948 the Soviets accepted the Jewish majority rule in MAKI in order to prevent a possible takeover by nationalist representatives of the Arab minority.[19]

MAKI became a legitimate party, operating legally within the Israeli political system and participating fully in the new state's parliamentary life. Votes for MAKI were mostly Jewish, but the proportion of Arab voters was not insignificant. In the 1951 Knesset elections, 32 percent of MAKI voters were Arabs; ten years later, in 1961, the figure was nearly 50 percent.[20]

During the MAKI period, just as in the days of the mandate, only a few Arab voters were attracted by Marxist-Leninist ideology. MAKI's improved standing among the Arabs had a number of different causes. First, it was the only party offering membership to Arabs on equal terms with Jews.[21] Second, party activists had organizational experience gained in the mandatory period. And finally, the Arab minority knew that Arab members of MAKI who had formerly belonged to the National League supported Arab nationalist ideas. Until the late 1950s, when the Al-Ard movement was established, the Communists faced no competition from any rival nationalist force. Its pro-Arab and unambiguously anti-Zionist attitudes expanded the party's popularity among Arab communities. MAKI became the principal champion of civil and national rights for Israeli Arabs. Instances of injustice or discrimination were constantly emphasized by the party's propaganda. In this way MAKI was successful in uniting all discontented elements in the Arab sector on the basis of a national Arab platform.[22]

MAKI's electoral support from the Arab minority was also strengthened by the political changes in the Middle East. The rise of Arab nationalism

[17]In 1957, e.g., the Central Committee consisted of fourteen Jews and six Arabs; in 1961 the Jewish proportion increased to 14:5. See M. Czudnowski and J. M. Landau, *The Israeli Communist Party and the Elections to the Fifth Knesset, 1961* (Stanford, Calif.: Hoover Institution, 1965), p. 16.

[18]In 1951, MAKI had three Jewish and two Arab Knesset deputies; in 1955 the proportion was 6:2, in 1959 it was 2:1; in 1961 it was 3:2 (Greilsammer, *Les Communistes*, p. 345).

[19]Yehuda Lahav, "Hamediniyut hasovietit bamizrakh hatichon ba'aspaklariya shel yakhas brit hamo'atsot lishnei haplagim hakomonistim beyisrael" (Soviet Policy in the Middle East as reflected in the USSR attitude to the two Communist factions in Israel), *Shvut* 8 (1981): 50.

[20]For the exact figures, see Greilsammer, *Les Communistes israeliens*, p. 345.

[21]MAPAM (Mifleget Hapoalim Hameuhedet), the United Workers Party, opened its doors to Arab members only in 1954.

[22]Laqueur, *Nationalism and Communism*, p. 115. The al-Ard group was a radical movement of Arab nationalists which operated in Israel in the early 1960s. In 1964 it was banned by the Israeli government.

following the Egyptian coup in 1952, the Soviet-Egyptian alliance after 1955, the Sinai war, and the death of forty-nine Israeli Arabs in the Kufr Qasim incident all served MAKI well, making it more attractive to the Arab masses. By its undivided support for the Arab cause and its full identification with the Soviet policy, the party's image as a symbol of Arab national aspirations in Israel was further enhanced. However, when relations between the Soviet Union and the Arab national movement underwent a crisis, MAKI suffered a significant setback in the Arab sector. In the late 1950s, rifts dividing Nasser and the Arab Communists appeared following the formation of the United Arab Republic and dividing Nasser and Qasim following the 1958 Iraqi revolution. Following the Soviet line, Arab Communists in MAKI vehemently attacked Nasser while supporting their Communist comrades in Arab states. The sudden change of policy resulted in a serious decline in popularity for MAKI, which lost 33 percent of its Arab voters in Israel's 1959 Knesset elections.

Events in 1959 highlighted MAKI's fluctuating appeal to Arab votes as well as its vulnerability to political changes in the region and to shifts in Soviet policy. The 1959 election results indicated the limited success of the Communist Party in the Arab sector as an organization advocating class struggle. Arab support for the Communists, some Jewish members realized in retrospect, depended on adoption of a conspicuous Arab nationalist policy.[23]

The call for Jewish-Arab brotherhood became one of MAKI's leading slogans.[24] Yet within the party's institutions, relations between the two ethnic groups were far from fraternal. When the two mandatory rival factions merged in 1948, former league members were compelled to denounce their "erroneous rightist deviations" over the Palestine question. The establishment of a separate national organization, they publicly admitted, created the erroneous impression that the Arabs could liberate their land independently, without participation of revolutionary Jewish forces.[25] Similarly, Arab members who had opposed the 1947 partition plan condemned their former position.[26]

Tension between Jews and Arabs continued, nevertheless, to prevail. On the organizational level, the principles of unification were not fully carried out. In 1948 Jewish leaders naively believed, as they later admitted, that in mixed localities the party's organizations would operate on a joint Jewish-

[23]See the memoirs of Nessia Shafran, *Shalom lecha komonism* (Farewell Communism) (Tel Aviv, 1983), p. 163.
[24]One interesting feature of ethnic relations inside the party was Jewish-Arab intermarriage. Several Arab Christian Communist leaders, including Emil Tuma, George Tubi, and Saliba Khamis, married Jewish women.
[25]Yaacov Silber, "25 Years after the Self-Criticism of Toubi-Habibi," *Israel at Peace* 12 (December 1973), p. 6.
[26]Among them was Emil Tuma.

Arab basis. But in mixed towns, like Haifa, cells in purely Jewish or Arab neighborhoods continued to function separately. When the matter was raised in MAKI's central bodies, Arab representatives argued that the division was maintained because of language difficulties, different working hours, and divergent patterns of daily life. Exclusively Arab cells, branches, and districts often acted independently of the party's center. The Triangle area, a district in central Israel densely populated by Arabs, operated as "a state of its own,"[27] according to a former Jewish leader.

At times, Arab leaders tailored different arguments for Arab or Jewish audiences. A Jewish member of the Central Committee who visited the village of Tayyiba in the 1960s was astonished to discover that a leading Arab member, who had frequented the local branch earlier, told his listeners that MAKI opposed the Law of Return and Jewish immigration to Israel. Both statements stood in total contrast to the party's official line.[28] From time to time, the independence of the Arabs' line became apparent in the party's Arabic press. Most Jews were unfamiliar with the Arabic language; only a few Jewish members of Iraqi origin who spoke and read Arabic noticed the discrepancies between texts published in *Al-Ittihad*, the organ in Arabic, and *Kol Ha'am*, the Hebrew organ. When they drew the attention of the central institutions, however, the party's leadership preferred to ignore the facts.[29] Party leaders did their utmost to preserve the image of Jewish-Arab Communist unity. Any piece of information indicating friction between the two groups was immediately concealed. A former MAKI member admitted years later that none of the Jewish cadres had imagined that the communism of the Arabs differed from that of the Jews.[30]

Fierce internal debates over ideological and political issues did surface occasionally, when leading Arab members criticized the party for being too moderate, especially on the Palestinian question. In 1951, for example, Emil Habibi, then representing MAKI in the Knesset, protested that the National League framework should be preserved in the Galilee because the 1947 U.N. General Assembly's partition plan had allotted that area to a future Arab Palestinian state.[31] Habibi's proposal was rejected. Shortly afterward, however, in 1952, Arab members succeeded in passing a resolution declaring MAKI's support for Israeli Arabs' right to self-determination, including the right to secede from the state. Not until 1961 were the Jews who rejected the resolution able to reverse MAKI's position.[32]

In 1958 another crisis erupted. Tawfiq Tubi, a member of the Knesset

[27]Yaacov Silber, interview with author, June 26, 1983; Shafran, *Shalom*, p. 171.

[28]Yaacov Silber, interview with author, June 26, 1983.

[29]Shafran, pp. 170–171.

[30]Ibid., p. 161.

[31]Shmuel Mikunis, in an interview with Meir Edelstein, "Likrat hapilug bemaki be–1965" (Toward the split in MAKI in 1965), *Meassef* 5 (March 1973): 166.

[32]Jacob M. Landau, *Ha'aravim biyisrael* (The Arabs in Israel) (Tel Aviv, 1971), pp. 102–113.

and a prominent Arab Communist, demanded that the party adopt the veiw that establishment of the State of Israel resulted from faulty Stalinist policy and was responsible for the consequent injustice to the Palestinian people. The Jewish majority in the Central Committee rejected Tubi's demand.[33] Shortly afterward, several Arab leaders met secretly in the Nazareth home of Habibi to discuss the possibility of setting up a separate Arab Communist Party in Israel[34] and of organizing guerrilla activities in the Galilee, according to the Algerian model. MAKI's Jewish leaders were informed of the gathering by Israel's general security services.[35] The participating Arab members denied the allegations, but even so the incident loosened the party's cohesion. The disputes between Jews and Arabs at that time laid the seeds of the party's second major split. By 1965, the contradiction that had characterized MAKI from its inception—namely, the attempt to unite Jews and Arabs in common cause in one party in spite of their different national backgrounds— became unmanageable. As before, in 1943, the party divided essentially along Jewish-Arab lines, but this time some prominent Jews attached themselves to the Arab faction.[36]

Tactically, the Jewish faction, led by Shmuel Mikunis and Moshe Sneh, tried to recruit more Jewish votes for the forthcoming November 1965 Knesset elections. The Arab-Jewish faction, headed by Meir Vilner and Tawfiq Tubi, tried to attract more votes from the Arab community. Ideologically the Vilner-Tubi group attacked what it defined as Israel's imperialist policies toward the Arab national liberation movements. While Israel was preparing wars of aggression, the leaders argued, the Arab states were advancing toward socialism. They interpreted Arab chauvinist tendencies as temporary and exceptional. In their opinion, peace would inevitably follow an about-face in Israel's policies. The Arab-Jewish faction accused their Jewish rivals of reviving the Hebrew national communism of the mandate period. In Israel's circumstances, they alleged, a Communist party with no Arabs as members was, to quote Vilner, like "a rabbi wearing a big cross over his chest."[37]

In this same way that Arab nationalism became a focus for Arab Com-

---

[33]Mikunis and Yair Tsaban (former leader of the MAKI youth organization), interview by Alain Greilsammer, "Tsiyunei derech leshivato shel Moshe Sneh latsiyonut" (Landmarks in the return of Moshe Sneh to Zionism), *Medina Umimshal Veyehasim Benleumiyim* 10 (Autumn 1977): p. 62.

[34]Shafran, *Shalom*, p. 192; Dunia Habib Nahas, *The Israeli Communist Party* (London: Croom-Helm, 1976), p. 55.

[35]Mikunis and Silber, interview by Edelstein, "Likrat hapilug," p. 166; Tsaban, interview by Greilsammer, "Tsiyonei derech," p. 62; Shafran, *Shalom*, p. 192.

[36]On the split, see the articles by Lahav (note 19) and Edelstein (note 31) and the following: Maurice Friedberg, "The Split in Israel's Communist Party," *Midstream* 12 (February 1966): 19–28; Kevin Devlin, "Communism in Israel: Anatomy of a Split," *Survey*, 62 (January 1967): 141–151; Martin Slann, "Ideology and Ethnicity in Israel's Two Communist Parties: The Conflict between MAKI and Rakah," *Studies in Comparative Communism*, Winter 1974, pp. 359–374.

[37]Israeli Communist Part, *The Fifteenth Congress* (Tel Aviv, 1968), p. 140.

Table 1 Votes for RAKAH, 1965–1981

	6th Knesset	7th Knesset	8th Knesset	9th Knesset	10th Knesset
	Nov. 2, 1965	Oct. 10, 1969	Dec. 31, 1973	May 17, 1977	June 30, 1981
Total voters	27,413	38,827	53,354	80,818	64,919
Arab voters	20,691	29,375	42,642	65,253	54,052
% of Arab voters	75.5	75.6	79.9	80.7	83.2

Source: Harari, Yehiel, *Osef netunim: 'arviye yisrael, 1981–1982. Habkhirot laknesset ha'asirit bayishuv ha'aravi* (Collection of data: Israeli Arabs 1981–1982: The elections to the 10th Knesset in the Arab sector) (Givat Haviva: Center for Arab Studies, November 1982), table 51, p. 71.

Note: The figures include votes given to RAKAH in purely Arab-inhabited localities. Because no official statistics on Arab voters in mixed Jewish-Arab towns are available, the figures understate RAKAH's strength in these areas. For example, Harari, p. 99 (see source note, above) calculated that in 1981 an additional 6,781 votes were cast for RAKAH in mixed towns, raising the percentage of Arab voters in that year to 93.7 percent.

munists, Zionism became central for Jewish Communists, who insisted that Zionism be recognized as an authentic national movement. Jewish Communists pointed out that Arab leaders in neighboring states might themselves initiate a war against Israel. Their first priority became the matter of Israel's recognition by other states in the region. MAKI's breakup reached the point of no return in August 1965, when each faction held its own congress declaring itself the only legitimate Israeli Communist Party. All subsequent attempts to reunite the party failed. Several years later, the all-Jewish MAKI disappeared from the Israeli political scene, leaving the stage to their rival, RAKAH.[38]

RAKAH, 1965–1984

The results of the elections to the Sixth Knesset, held shortly after the 1965 cleavage, left no doubt that RAKAH's support came primarily from Arabs. The party received 27,413 votes, of which more than 20,000 were cast in Arab-populated areas.[39] Since then, Arab voters have constituted between 75 percent and 85 percent of the party's electorate (see Table 1).

Most of the rank and file in RAKAH have also been Arabs. Since 1965, RAKAH has recruited only a relatively low number of Jews to its ranks. New cadres have been formed primarily in the Arab communities. Non-Communist sources had estimated that, prior to the split, MAKI had ap-

[38]On the history of MAKI since the split, see Alain Greilsammer, "Communism in Israel: Thirteen Years after the Split," *Survey* 23 (Summer 1977–1978): 172–179.

[39]In 1965, MAKI received 13,617 votes, of which only 600 were cast by Arabs.

Table 2 Jews and Arabs in RAKAH's Central Institutions, 1965–1981

Congress	Central Committee			Politburo			Central Control Committee		
	Total	Jews	Arabs	Total	Jews	Arabs	Total	Jews	Arabs
Fifteenth (1965)	19	10	9	7	4	3	5	4	1
Sixteenth (1969)	21	12	9	9	5	4	7	5	2
Seventeenth (1972)	25	13	12	9	5	4	5	3	2
Eighteenth (1976)	31	16	15	9	5	4	5	3	2
Nineteenth (1981)	35	17	18	9	5	4	7	4	3

Sources: Israeli Communist Party, *The Fifteenth Congress*, pp. 421–442; *The Sixteenth Congress*, pp. 420–421; *The Seventeenth Congress*, pp. 493–494; *The Eighteenth Congress*, pp. 181–182; *The Nineteenth Congress*, pp. 215–216.

proximately 1,700 active members, of which some 800 joined the Vilner-Tubi group. Of these, nearly 500 (69 percent) were Arabs; the remaining 250 (31 percent) were Jews.[40] It has been estimated that in the early and mid-1970s RAKAH membership numbered between 1,050 and 1,200, of which between 66 percent and 75 percent were Arabs.[41] In the late 1970s and early 1980s, there were an estimated 2,000 registered members in RAKAH, of which 80 percent were Arabs.[42]

Despite its overwhelmingly Arab membership and the fact that the Jewish public resolutely rejected RAKAH, Jews continued to control the party's central institutions.

In both the Central Committee and the Politburo, Jews had a traditional majority of one (see Table 2). Since 1965 the highest-ranking post in the party, that of secretary-general, had been kept in the hands of Meir Vilner, a Jew. Tawfiq Tubi, his Arab counterpart in the rift, was granted only the second-top party position. The chairmanship of the Control Committee was also consistently headed by a Jew.[43] (For more on Arab submission to Jewish domination, see below.)

Party spokesmen, while admitting that Jews constituted only one-third of the membership immediately after the split, have consistently claimed

[40]Moshe Meisels, *Ma'ariv*, November 8, 1965. Alain Greilsammer, *Les Communistes israeliens*, p. 315, reached similar conclusions.

[41]Dan Patir ("Turbulences Frequent RAKAH," *Davar*, February 7, 1973), gave the 1,050 figure; Moshe Meisels (*Ma'ariv*, November 5, 1975) the 1,200 figure. In 1975, Berl Balti (interview by Alain Greilsammer, in *Les Communistes israeliens*, p. 244) estimated that 75 percent of RAKAH's members were Arab.

[42]Greilsammer, *Les Communistes israeliens*, pp. 344–360; Meisels, interview with author, June 23, 1983.

[43]Since 1965, this post has been held by Ruth Luvich, later by Pninah Feinhaus, and since 1972 by Wolf Erlich. The change in the composition of the Central Committee that took place in 1981 may have reflected a strengthening of the Arab leaders' position.

that the number of Jews and Arabs has been equal since then.[44] The assessment that RAKAH's membership was equally divided has since been adopted by official Soviet publications.[45] Official party figures for RAKAH's ethnic composition have never been furnished, and party leaders have provided irrelevant explanations for the refusal to publish data on membership. For example, Tawfiq Tubi has argued that figures were concealed because of "antidemocratic processes" that the government employed against RAKAH. "Our comrades would be exposed to persecution," added Uzi Burstein, "had it become known that they belonged to RAKAH."[46] In reality, the persistent concealment seems to have stemmed from different sources. If such figures were to show that Arabs were in a majority, RAKAH's strenuous efforts to emphasize its bi-national image would be significantly weakened. Publication might also have eroded the position of the party's Jewish leaders vis-à-vis their Arab counterparts.[47]

Non-Communist observers frequently claimed that the veteran Jewish leadership often tried to decrease Arab influence in the party's organizations. Such a claim was raised in February 1972, when Habibi resigned from the Knesset and was replaced by a Jewish member, Avraham Levenbraun. Following this change, RAKAH's Knesset faction was made up of two Jewish and only one Arab member. Habibi, a talented journalist, writer, and poet, argued that he gave up his seat because of health problems and his eagerness to devote his time to writing. Nevertheless, the Israeli media speculated that the replacement was designed "to sharpen the Jewish profile of the party" and increase Jewish representation in the Knesset.[48] Party officials vehemently denied such allegations, and the fact that no similar steps were pursued in the following years lends credence to their denials.

From its inception, RAKAH had to refute charges that both ideologically and politically it was a party remote from true communism, that it was in reality nothing but a combination of Jewish nihilists and chauvinist Arab nationalists. This appraisal, voiced mainly by the rival MAKI group,[49] could hardly be applied to all the party's core leaders. Leading Jews were strongly motivated by deep ideological convictions and pure Leninist dogma that only their particular internationalist interpretation would bring about the

[44]See statement by Meir Vilner to Haviv Knaan—"57% of RAKAH's members are workers"—in *Ha'aretz*, February 21, 1969, and by Uzi Burstein to Moshe Meisels, in *Ma'ariv*, August 23, 1973.

[45]See the report on the Israeli Communist Party in *World Marxist Review* 17 (March 1974): 43–44.

[46]Haviv Knaan, "RAKAH's Kept Secret," *Ha'aretz*, December 12, 1976.

[47]Ibid.

[48]*Al-Ittihad* and *Ma'ariv*, February 15, 1972; *Ma'ariv*, February 22, 1972; *Yediot Aharonot*, February 23, 1972; and replies by Juhayna (pseudonym of Emil Habibi) in *Al-Ittihad*, February 18 and 25, 1972.

[49]See, e.g., S. Tsirolnikov, "Communism and Hypocrisy," *Kol Ha'am*, September 21, 1969.

spread of communism in the Middle East. Most Arab leaders shared their convictions, but for them the coupling of a more aggressive Arab nationalism with Marxist theory was the ideological underpinning for RAKAH. It is difficult to establish which of the two components was more influential on any individual member.

Occasionally, although infrequently, Communist authors attempted to convince Arab readers that the two ideological systems were compatible and even harmonious. Salim Jubran, a member of the Central Committee and deputy editor of *Al-Ittihad*, argued dialectically, for example, that no contradiction underlay the Marxist-nationalist synthesis.[50] It was true, he admitted, that Arabs were attracted to the party because of its nationalist character and because it represented genuine opposition to the Israeli regime. Yet after becoming acquainted with the wider scope of RAKAH's world view, they understood that the Communist Party's philosophy provided a comprehensive solution to all aspects of life. True nationalism was then consolidated into a "sincere internationalist attitude," Jubran concluded.

Nevertheless, in their appeal to the Arab electorate the Communists have consistently emphasized national aspects. As in earlier periods, revolutionary principles—such as class struggle, socialist reform, and the dictatorship of the proletariat—have been played down. In so doing, the Arab wing of RAKAH has been able to neutralize the factors commonly regarded as barriers to the expansion of communism in Arab society— namely, affinity to Islam, religiosity, individualism, and rejection of collectivist ideas.

Political developments in the Middle East since 1967 have had far-reaching repercussions on the party's character. Moscow's one-sided policy, its severing of diplomatic relations with Israel, and its fierce anti-Zionist campaign, together with its growing support for the Arab cause, combined to intensify Israeli Jews' rejection of the Communists. In contrast, the Arabs in Israel were increasingly attracted to RAKAH. For Israeli Arabs, the ascendancy of the Palestine Liberation Organization (PLO), Soviet support for Palestinian nationalism, the renewed contacts with Arabs living in the West Bank, the outcome of the October 1973 war, and their deepening alienation from Israeli Jewish society—all heightened their national feelings and encouraged political radicalization. Such developments were exploited by RAKAH, which not only continued to be the main defender of Arabs' civil rights, but also became an outspoken advocate for Palestinian national aspirations. The more pro-Arab the party has become, the more its prestige within the Arab population has grown.[51] In the 1965 elections, 22 percent

[50]"How Do People Become Communists," *Al-Ittihad*, May 9, 1975.

[51]On the national awakening of the Arab population in Israel and RAKAH's role in this process, see Elie Rekhess, *Arviye yisrael vehafka'at hakarka'ot bagalil: reka' eru'im vehashlakhot* (The Arabs of Israel and the land expropriations in the Galilee: Background, events,

of the Arab vote was cast for the Communists. In 1969 the figure rose to 30 percent, in 1973 to 27 percent, and in 1977 to 50 percent. RAKAH was nevertheless subject to several constraints in its support for the Arab cause. As one of the most orthodox Communist parties in the world, RAKAH chose to follow Moscow's policy to the letter. So, for example, the party supported a Palestinian state alongside Israel, or the U.N. Security Council Resolution 242, even though in so doing it harmed its standing within Israeli Arab nationalist circles. Whenever Soviet-Arab relations deteriorated, as happened in 1972, the party's popularity among Arabs was shaken, but this did not deter RAKAH from adopting Moscow's line. A second constraint was the leadership's concern about protecting its legal status. RAKAH leaders were always conscious that their party could be banned if it went too far and unambiguously proposed anti-Israel policies.[52]

These ideological and practical constraints meant that policies were characteristically formulated in conciliatory phrases. The party's views on sensitive national issues were worded to appeal to Arabs, but they were ambiguous enough not to be denounced as a deviation from Soviet policy or to provoke a hostile reaction from the Israeli government. This skillfully used tactic is well illustrated by the party's attitude toward PLO terrorist acts. Taking its cue from Moscow, RAKAH has ignored terrorist operations against military installations in occupied areas while denouncing similar acts against civilians, whether in Israel or abroad. To avoid offending their potential Arab voters as much as possible, the party has always distinguished its criticism of such terrorist incidents from its condemnation of Israel's official policies, which are seen as the prime cause of terrorist operations by Palestinians. The party's Arab language newspaper, *Al-Ittihad*, has often reported sympathetically on *fida'i*[53] activities. In several cases the Arab Israeli Communist press fully quoted PLO statements made in Beirut, Damascus, or Cairo. For example, on May 6, 1969, *Al-Ittihad* wrote: "Two Israeli soldiers, an officer and a sergeant, were killed, three were wounded and two *fida'iyyun* were killed in a fierce attack launched by the

---

and repercussions) (Tel Aviv, 1977); "The Politicization of Israel's Arabs," in *Every Sixth Israeli*, ed. A. Hareven (Jerusalem, 1983), pp. 135–142; "The Arabs of Israel and the Arabs of the West Bank and Gaza: Patterns of Political Attachment and National Solidarity," *Hamizrah Hehadash* (in press).

[52]Demands to outlaw RAKAH were frequently raised by Herzl Rosenblum (*Yediot Aharonot*, January 2, 1968), Amnon Linn (ibid., April 1, 1976), and Shmuel Flatto-Sharon (ibid., March 1978).

[53]Unlike the non-Communist pro-government Arab press in Israel, which refers to PLO members as *muharribun* (terrorists) or simply *musallahun* (armed elements), the Communists organs in Arabic frequently follow the PLO terminology of *fida'iyyun* (originally a religious term for the Jihad warriors willing to sacrifice their lives).

Arab *fida'iyyun* on an Israeli army post in the south of the Golan Heights. The *fida'iyyun* had waved the Palestinian flag in al-Hama for three hours. ...Fath leaders declared that the al-Hama attack indicated a new stage in the Arab *fida'i* action against Israel. The *fida'iyyun* used a new tactic: a rapid surprise attack." The Israel Defense Forces (IDF) version of events was completely ignored. Discrepancies between the Hebrew and Arabic texts of reports or commentaries have occasionally been noted. Criticism of this phenomenon, which was similar to the one that had characterized the MAKI era, was voiced in RAKAH's seventeenth congress, held in 1972. Party leader Meir Vilner sarcastically dismisssed the protesters "who walk around" comparing versions of *Al-Ittihad* and *Zo Haderech*. "What can be done?" he added. "A million things are all right and three are not. There are no special deviations in our party. At times, one [member] writes and emphasizes one aspect while another [underlines] other aspects."[54]

Party leadership also saw the need to reassure the Jewish members that RAKAH pursued the same policy in both Arab and Jewish communities. In January 1974, shortly after the elections to the Eighth Knesset, *Zo Haderech*, the party's Hebrew language organ, published a letter by a reader who questioned whether the contents of the party's platform in Hebrew was identical to the one in Arabic and whether the Arab public had been informed of RAKAH's support of Israel's sovereign existence. In reply, the paper insisted that both programs were identical.[55]

The leaders of RAKAH consistently denied that there were ideological or political differences within the party. Since the 1965 split, according to party spokesman Uzi Burstein, the vote of Central Committee or Politburo members has never been determined by ethnicity; questions of principle have never been issues of debate.[56] Nevertheless, certain Arab members, have from time to time expressed dissatisfaction with the party's official platform and have advocated a more radical, nationalist policy. Evidently disagreements revolved around such sensitive issues as Palestinian terrorism, the 1947 U.N. General Assembly partition plan, and Soviet policy in the Middle East. In October 1968 the Lebanese weekly *Al-Muharrir* quoted Samih al-Qasim, a Druze Communist poet, who stated, "Every people whose land was plundered has the right to fight, using all measures," adding that there was no escape from armed *fida'i* operations.[57] Similar support for Palestinian armed struggle in the West Bank was voiced by Habibi in a

---

[54]Meir Vilner, "Concluding Remarks," in *The Seventeenth Congress*, p. 250.

[55]See letter by B. Orly and reply by B. Avrahamit in *Zo Haderech*, January 16, 1974.

[56]Quoted by Moshe Meisels, in "The Arab Profile Is Sharpened Again in RAKAH," *Ma'ariv*, August 23, 1973.

[57]*Ha'aretz*, October 17, 1968.

closed party meeting.[58] Both Habibi and al-Qasim vehemently rejected the allegations.[59]

During the 1969 party convention, a leading Arab member, Muhammad Khass, urged the party to reconsider its policy on Israeli Arabs' right to self-determination. He also rejected the party's endorsement of U.N. Resolution 242, arguing that it did not offer a comprehensive solution to the conflict. Furthermore, he hinted that the 1947 borders might not be immutable.[60] In 1972 another crisis erupted when *Zo Haderech* favorably reported the IDF's rescue of passengers hijacked on a Sabena airliner by a Palestinian terrorist group. The item apparently angered some Arab members so much that the Politburo had to intervene. A week later the paper carried a revised report of the incident in less-approving terms.[61] Following the 1973 Nixon-Brezhnev summit talks, criticism of the Soviet Union was voiced in several RAKAH branches in the western Galilee over the omission of Security Council Resolution 242 from the Soviet-American joint communiqué, reportedly interpreted by Arab members as a sign of Soviet weakness and acquiescence to U.S. pressure.[62]

Differences between Jews and Arabs in the party surfaced again in 1976 when RAKAH set up the Democratic Front for Peace and Equality with the Black Panthers, a small pressure group claiming to represent Jews from Oriental (Middle Eastern and North African) backgrounds. For Communist Jews this development was a significant achievement because it ended their long and near total estrangement from Israeli Jewish society.[63] It also strengthened their positions within RAKAH's leadership. Until the Front's formulation, none of the attempts to make political alliance with various Israeli leftist groups had succeeded, primarily because of RAKAH's anti-Zionist and pro-Soviet views.[64] Several Arab RAKAH members appeared to be displeased about creation of the Front, fearing that it would damage

[58]Habibi's comments were quoted in 1968 by Israeli defense minister Moshe Dayan during a Knesset debate on administrative detention. Dayan also claimed that, prior to the Six Day War, Habibi expressed unequivocal support for the closing of the Straits of Tiran by President Nasser (*Ha'aretz*, November 30, 1968).

[59]Al-Qasim's denial was published only in RAKAH's Arabic organ (*Al-Ittihad*, October 25, 1968). According to *Kol Ha'am*, MAKI's Hebrew newspaper, (November 29, 1968), RAKAH decided to conceal the story from Jewish readers.

[60]For Khass' views and the reply of Secretary-General Vilner, see *The Sixteenth Congress*, pp. 149–150 and 292; and Haviv Knaan, "Identification with the Arab National Movement," *Ha'aretz*, March 16, 1969.

[61]*Zo Haderech*'s first version was published on May 10; the revised version was published on May 17, 1972. For the intervention of the Politburo, see statement by Yaacov Kujman in the general debate of the party's congress in 1972, *Seventeenth Congress*, p. 180; and *Kol Ha'am*, May 24, 1972.

[62]*Davar* and *Ma'ariv*, July 10, 1975.

[63]See Giora Goldberg, "Adaptation to Competitive Politics: The Case of Israeli Communism," *Studies in Comparative Communism* 14 (Spring 1981): 349–350.

[64]On these attempts in the early 1970s, see Daniel Dagan, "The Unknown of RAKAH: Israeli Borders," *Ma'ariv*, June 20, 1972; Uzi Burstein in the general debate, *Seventeenth Congress*, p. 207.

the party's Arab character without a compensating electoral benefit.[65] Because a majority of RAKAH's leaders refused to yield to members' pressures to disband the Front, the framework was maintained.

Disputes among ethnic groups were not confined to Jews and Arabs. There was also friction between Muslims and Christians.[66] From the 1940s onward, most of the party's Arab leaders were Christians, usually from the Greek Orthodox community.[67] Christian congregations in the Middle East were traditionally known for their advanced standard of education and higher political awareness. Christians constituted the majority of Arab representatives in the party's Central Committee and Politburo. The Christian stronghold, often referred to as "the Communist Red Cross," was also preserved because of family relations among several of the prominent leaders.[68] Overrepresentation by Christians in the central institutions stirred Muslims to object.[69] Since the early 1960s, the Communists made strenuous efforts to expand their influence within the Muslim community in Israel, especially in the Triangle area. The Muslim opposition pointed out that RAKAH's Arab voters were mostly Muslims, yet the Muslim constituency had no proper representation in the Center. This situation changed after the 1973 Knesset elections, when Tawfiq Zayyad, a prominent Muslim member in RAKAH, took a seat in the Knesset. Since then the relative proportion of Muslims in the Central Committee has gradually increased, suggesting that the party's leadership has responded to Muslim pressure, even if the veteran Christian leadership still dominates the Arabs in the party.

In the 1981 Knesset elections, RAKAH lost almost 13 percent of its Arab vote. This decline in popularity had several causes. One was that some Arabs decided to vote for the Labor Alignment, hoping to keep the Likud out of office. Another was the emergence of alternative Arab nationalist groups that were anti-Communist. The two most important organizations were the Sons of the Village and the Progressive National Movement. Since the mid-1970s, members of these groups have expressed their support for the PLO's rejectionist factions, denied Israel's right to sovereignty, and vehemently attacked RAKAH's policies as too moderate on Arab Palestinian nationalist issues.

---

[65]See, e.g., the reactions of the radical Sons of the Village movement in *Al-Jarmaq*, June 30, 1977.

[66]On the condescending attitude of Christians toward their Muslim counterparts in MAKI, see in Sammy Michael's novel *Khasut* (Refuge) (Tel Aviv, 1977): "They despise us . . . they mock us. These Christian intellectuals are similar to the Jews. They regard us as dumb villagers. They already stink of sitting with the Jews" (p. 174).

[67]Among the Christian leaders of the party were Tawfiq Tubi, Emil Habibi, Emil Tuma, Hana Naqara, Saliba Khamis, Zahi Karkabi, and Fu'ad Khuri.

[68]Tawfiq Tubi, e.g., is married to Emil Tuma's sister. He is the brother of George Tubi, while his sister is married to Zahi Karkabi.

[69]For reports on Muslim protest, see e.g., *Ma'ariv*, September 19, 1969; *Davar*, November 7, 1969; *Al-Anba'*, June 17, 1973; and *Ma'ariv*, August 21, 1973.

Another group of political activists, members of the emerging Israeli Arab intelligentsia, has also shown their opposition to RAKAH. They advocate more moderate policies than the radical nationalists, the essence of their program being similar to RAKAH's, without the Marxist dogmas.

The new nationalist trend has challenged RAKAH in much the same way that other Communist parties have been challenged in nearby Arab states. One primary weakness of Arab communism was its inability to compete with the rise of Arab nationalism. In Israel the new non-Marxist radical movement is still politically marginal, while the expanding Arab intelligentsia has not yet consolidated its political activities. But the combined effect of these two young forces has been to break RAKAH's monopolistic representation of Israel's Arab's national aspirations.

Shortly before the July 1984 elections, the Progressive Movement for Peace (PMP), a new Jewish-Arab party supporting the Palestinian cause, was established. The Jewish partners had all been members of SHELI, a former small, marginal leftist party. Arab participants were generally identified as nationalist. Best known was number one on the list, lawyer Muhammad Mi'ari, a former leader of al-Ard. The rise of the PMP presented RAKAH with a threatening challenge. The essence of the new party's program was similar to the Communist platform, though lacking the tenets of Marxist dogma. Yet RAKAH maintained one advantage—its anti-Zionist stand. Mi'ari made no public statement in support of Zionist ideals, but his cooperation with his Zionist Jewish partners, so the Communists charged, was evidence of his factual support of the Zionist state. In response, the PMP argued that their concept of Arab-Jewish partnership was more authentic than RAKAH's; unlike RAKAH, the PMP was headed by an Arab.

The PMP won no less than 18 percent of the Arab vote and two Knesset seats, a notable achievement for a new party. Nevertheless, RAKAH succeeded in maintaining its four-member Knesset representation. Approximately 33 percent of the Arab votes were cast for the Communists, which proved that their anti-Zionist policy and strong pro-Palestinian image still had considerable appeal.

Concluding Remarks

Since 1965 the Communist Party's support came primarily from the Israeli Arab sector. Arabs constituted between 75 percent and 85 percent of the party's voters in Knesset elections. Most of the rank and file in RAKAH also were Arabs. Yet, despite the Arab majority, Jewish leaders controlled most of the party's major positions of influence.

Throughout the period under review, RAKAH's internal cohesion has not been seriously threatened. Arab submission to Jewish domination appears to have resulted from several factors. Some Arab leaders were guided by genuine belief in the principles of internationalism. Others apparently adhered to the Soviet view that representatives of the majority should hold positions of power. The Arabs also seem to have understood the difficulties and dangers inherent in independent action. An all-Arab-controlled organization could easily be taken over by more-radical nationalist elements and thus lose its Marxist-Leninist character, on the one hand, and accelerate the separation of Jewish Communists, on the other hand. Such an institutionalization of "national communism" would probably not have been welcomed by Moscow and might also have provoked firm reaction from the Israeli authorities, either by outlawing the organization outright or by persecuting its members. The lesson learned after the 1943 cleavage was well remembered. As for the Jewish leadership, their interest in the RAKAH partnership system was clear. Aware of their weak standing among the Jewish public, the Jewish Communists realized that without Arab support the party would cease to exist. It was therefore a common and pragmatic interest to maintain the framework with Jewish overrepresentation.

The party's conspicuous achievement in preserving Arab-Jewish unity was the outcome of the doctrinaire belief in internationalist ideas shared by Jews and Arabs alike. These commonly held ideological convictions, in addition to practical and pragmatic considerations, enabled the Jewish and Arab factions to overcome discrepancies and political divergencies and thus maintain their joint framework.

The emergence of the PMP threatened RAKAH's hold over the Arab public. If in the future RAKAH's electoral strength declines, its leaders may then yield to possible pressures by more nationalistic Arab members to adopt a more radical position. A continued lessening of RAKAH's popularity may also encourage some Arab members to reconsider the effectiveness of joint Arab-Jewish Communist action with a view to taking independent Arab action, thereby initiating processes resembling those that caused the 1943 and 1965 splits.

8

Political Ethnicity as a
Socially Constructed Reality:
The Case of Jews in Israel

Hanna Herzog

The ethnic problem is a central problem in Israeli society. One conventional way to describe the depth of ethnic cleavage in plural societies is to indicate how it is reflected in political arenas. In this chapter we look at this issue by focusing on examples of political ethnicity.

Political Ethnicity: Theory and Measuring

The term "political ethnicity" has been applied almost exclusively to the political behavior of peoples of Asian and African origin, even though Israeli society is actually a mosaic of people from different countries—that is, of ethnic groups. In Israel the dominant groups are identified as "Israeli society" and all other groups as "ethnic." Two major factors have influenced relationships among ethnic groups in the Jewish population in Israel. One is the cultural inequality between Jews of Asian-African origin and those of European-American origin, the other is the socioeconomic stratification along ethnic lines.

The cultural issue derives from Israel's status as a society of immigrants that has adopted for a rallying cry the ideology of the melting pot (*mizug galuyot*). The melting-pot ideology has in effect meant the assimilation of all groups into the dominant culture, which was led by Eastern Europeans. In ethnic terms, this has meant that newcomers are expected to change cultural traditions and ways of life that are considered unsuitable or irrelevant to life in Israel. This social definition puts pressure on people who come from Asian or African countries to adopt Western codes of behavior.

Because cultural pluralism has not been tolerated, Asian-African immigrants and their offspring have low social esteem and status.

These immigrants, who were absorbed into Israeli society in the 1950s, have also been forced into peripheral positions and lower-paying jobs.[1] In academic work as well as in everyday life, people identify the social gap with ethnic differences. Although many studies show that the problem of class distinction does not derive directly from ethnic differences,[2] people tend to explain the socioeconomic gap in ethnic terms. Even though 60 percent of the Asian-African population in Israel are upwardly mobile and are members of the middle class,[3] speaking about ethnic stratification is both common and accepted today. In Israel, the word "Oriental" has become synonymous with "lower class." The current stereotype of a person of Asian-African origin includes characteristics of the lower class.[4]

Following Peter Berger and Thomas Luckman, I use the above description to show that there is a tendency to construe social reality in ethnic terms and to explain socioeconomic and political conflicts as ethnic conflicts.[5] This tendency is exacerbated by the lack of a pluralistic ideology. From the beginning of the Zionist movement, the ideology of ingathering the exiles has been accompanied by a melting-pot ideology—and in reality Israel is a pluralistic society.[6] Yet the pluralism among the Jews in Israel—and especially the differences among the various origin groups—has been defined as a danger to the nation's unity. Determination of policy for absorption of new immigrants is concentrated in the hands of the political center.[7] David Ben-Gurion's idea of "statehood" (*mamelachtiut*) best exemplifies the orientation toward homogeneity and uniformity. Ideologically it has been justified as the best way to realize the ideal of the melting pot. Viewing the world through the eyes of the dominant group, and lacking a sensitivity to

[1]For a sociohistorical analysis, see Sammy Smooha, *Israel: Pluralism and Conflict* (London: Routledge & Kegan Paul, 1978); and Shlomo Swirski, *Mizrakhim veashkenazim beisrael: khalukat avoda adatit* (Orientals and Ashkenazim in Israel: The ethnic division of labor) (Haifa, 1981).

[2]See Smooha, *Israel*, and Ephraim Yuchtman-Yaar and Moshe Semyonov, "Ethnic Inequality in Israeli Schools and Sports: An Expectation States Approach," *American Journal of Sociology*, no. 3 (1979): 576–590.

[3]Sammy Smooha, "Misud harivud ha'adati beisrael" (The institutionalization of ethnic stratification in Israel), Paper delivered at the Kotlar Institute for Judaism and Contemporary Thought, Twelfth International Seminar, "East and West in Israel," Bar Ilan University, Ramat Gan, and Kibutz Hafetz-Hayium Guest House, July 1–5, 1982; Ephraim Yuchtman-Yaar, "Differences in Ethnic Patterns of Socioeconomic Achievement in Israel: A Neglected Aspect of Structured Inequality," *International Review of Modern Society* (forthcoming).

[4]See Yacov Rofe and Leonar Weller, "Ethnic Groups, Prejudice, and Class in Israel," *Jewish Journal of Sociology* 23, no. 2 (1981): 101–111.

[5]See Peter Berger and Thomas Luckman, *The Social Construction of Reality* (Garden City, N.Y.: Doubleday, 1966).

[6]For the various dimensions of Israeli pluralism, see Smooha, *Israel*.

[7]See Yonathan Shapiro, *Hademokratia beisrael* (The democracy in Israel) (Ramat Gan, 1978).

the value of pluralism, the absorption policy neglected the diversity in the "Oriental" category. All the different ethnic groups included within this social category were held to be the same, and their culture was deemed irrelevant to the new, modern society in the making.

Paradoxically, two contradictory trends exist simultaneously in Israeli society. While there is a continuous classification of individuals on an ethnic basis, even when the people in question do not identity themselves on this basis, ethnicity as ideology or way of life is rejected in the name of the concept of the "ingathering of the exiles."[8] It is in the context of these contradictory trends that the forms and social meaning of ethnicity develop.

The above approach to the study of political ethnicity is based on recent research on this topic which emphasizes that ethnicity is a property that emerges, develops, and changes through interaction within and between groups. The definition and significance of social boundaries of ethnic groups are constantly and dynamically formed and altered.[9]

Ethnicity is a unique means for social organization because of its supposedly ascriptive character. By associating people with an ethnic group, one assumes multidimensional, constant, steady, and long-lasting relationships among members of the group, which bind them collectively to the past and to the future through tradition. Such social relationships awaken sentiments, making the audience more receptive to the use of symbols. As such, ethnic consciousness is an efficient and thrifty resource for social mobilization, organization, and integration. These facts explain the variation in the sources and uses of ethnicity indicated by the literature.[10] Though ethnicity would seem primordial, the uses as well as the expression and definition of ethnicity change according to the relevance and significance that individuals or groups give to this aspect of their identity.[11] Following this approach, it seems that just as ethnic origin does not by definition determine individual identity, so the significance of this aspect of identity is subject to change and continuous reinterpretation.

The question here is the extent to which an ethnic political identity in

[8]For a similar argument, see Eliezer Ben-Rafael, *The Emergence of Ethnicity: Cultural Groups and Social Conflict in Israel* (Westport, Conn.: Greenwood, 1982).

[9]See Fredrik Barth, ed., *Ethnic Groups and Boundaries: The Social Organization of Cultural Differences* (Boston: Little, Brown, 1969); Abner Cohen, *Two-Dimensional Man: An Essay on the Anthropology of Power and Symbolism in Complex Society* (Berkeley: University of California Press, 1974); and William L. Yancey, E. P. Ericksen, and R. N. Juliani, "Emergent Ethnicity: A Review and Reformation," *American Sociological Review* 41, no. 3 (1976): 391–403.

[10]For the different uses of ethnicity, see Leo Arthur Despres, ed., *Ethnicity and Resource Competition in Plural Societies* (Paris, 1975); Cohen, *Two-Dimensional Man*; Yancey et al., "Emergent Ethnicity: A Review and Reformation"; and Edna Bonacich, "Class Approaches of Ethnicity and Race," *Insurgent Sociologist* 11, no. 11 (1981): 9–23.

[11]For situational uses of ethnicity, see Shlomo Deshen, "Ethnic Boundaries and Cultural Paradigms: The Case of Southern Tunisian Immigrants in Israel," *Ethos* 4, no. 3 (1976): 271–294; and James Friders and S. Goldenberg, "Ethnic Identity: Myth and Reality in Western Canada," *International Journal of Intercultural Relations* 6, no. 2 (1982): 137–151.

Israel exists, the extent to which Israelis from Islamic countries actually exhibit a separate and unique political behavior, and the extent to which Asian-African Jews perceive their identity as ethnically oriented. Two empirical indicators are usually suggested for determining the political ethnicity of Israelis of Asian-African origin: (1) the emergence and the success of the "ethnic parties" and (2) the correlation between country of origin and political preference—or, as scholars often call it, "ethnic voting."[12] A test of these two indicators leads to contradictory conclusions about the existence of political ethnicity in Israel.

A review of the parties that have run for election, from the first Delegates Assembly (1920) up to the Eleventh Knesset (1984), reveals that parties considered to be "ethnic" participated in all the election campaigns and totaled fifty-four ethnic "lists" (parties) counting those that ran more than once separately for each election. Apparently, the increasing number of "lists" and the consistency with which they appeared are an expression of ethnic political identity.

In fact, from the standpoint of their electoral achievements, the ethnic "lists" have remained a marginal phenomenon on Israel's political landscape. This is most striking in view of the changes in the ethnic composition of the Jewish population of Israel since 1948. While in 1948 people of Asian and African origin comprised 22.5 percent of the Jewish population, since 1975 they have represented 55 percent. Although they make up more than half the Jewish population, they are not fully represented in the political sphere.[13] While there is a social disparity that is defined as an ethnic gap, and while people of Asian-African origin are the majority in the Jewish population and are defined as potential ethnic voters, the "ethnic lists" have not become a focus of political support and identification.

Though the appearance of ethnic lists has been a constant and persistent phenomenon, these lists are distinguished by organizational splits and impermanence. In sociological terms, the ethnic organizations did not become parties, but rather developed as factions—that is, conflict groups based on personal ties and loyalties between political activists of groups or pseudo-groups. The ethnic lists have been temporary and conditional alliances of political entrepreneurs.[14] All these facts lead us to conclude that according

[12]For discussion of the first, see Moshe Lissak, "Continuity and Change in the Voting Patterns of Oriental Jews," in *The Elections in Israel, 1969*, ed. A. Arian (Jerusalem, 1972), pp. 264–277. For examples of the second, see Nathan Yanai and Shlomo Aronson, "Structural and Behavioral Aspects of the 1981 Elections and Their Implications," in *The 1981 Israeli Elections*, ed. E. Gutman, D. Caspi and A. Diskin (London: Croom-Helm, 1983); and Yochanan Peres and Sara Shemer, "Hagorem haetni bebekhirot laknesset ha'asirit" (The ethnic factor in the elections to the Tenth Knesset), *Magamot* 28, no. 2–3 (1984): 316–393.

[13]See Smooha, *Israel*, pp. 151–182.

[14]For organizational analysis of the ethnic lists, see Hanna Herzog, *'Adatiut politit: dimui mul metziut* (Political ethnicity: The image and the reality) (Tel Aviv, 1986), pp. 162–169.

to the organizational as well as electoral criteria, ethnic political identity is a marginal phenomenon in Israel.

At the same time, however, analysis of voting patterns in Israel may point to the existence of political ethnicity. A recent study by Michal Shamir and Asher Arian shows that since the 1950s there has been an increasing correlation between ethnic origin and preferred party and indicates that an Oriental country of origin is the best predictor of voting for the Likud Party rather than the Labor Party.[15] The two contradictory findings must be considered and interpreted in light of the meaning that has been accorded ethnicity in Israeli society. This meaning developed largely during negotiations in the political arena. Changes in voting patterns and the chance of ethnic parties to succeed should be interpreted against the results of these social negotiations in a given period.

The following analysis is based mainly on a sociohistorical study of all the ethnic lists that took part in the elections in Israel from 1920 to 1984 inclusive. To illustrate the arguments, only selected examples are presented.[16] Data from preelection surveys and from studies of political attitudes and behavior of people of Asian-African origin are used.

The main claim is that the political behavior of people of Asian-African origin in a historical perspective is not essentially ethnic in its content and orientation, even though it is defined by others as such. This claim does not discount the ethnic factor in Israeli politics—the existence of this factor has been corroborated by many studies.[17] It differs, however, from the interpretations of these studies. The present research traces the way the political behavior of Orientals in Israeli society has been shaped.

The So-called Ethnic Parties

The label "ethnic lists" (parties) is applied in Israel to political organizations whose initiators are of Asian and African origin. The question is, Are they really ethnic lists?

The democratic principles adopted in the pre-State period encouraged every organized public group—including those organized on an ethnic basis—to participate in the organized Jewish community, "Knesset Israel." Moreover, in the effort to widen the electoral basis of the governing bodies, the leadership was even prepared to make preferential arrangements for these ethnic groups, such as providing a special voting day for citizens of Yemenite origin (1925) or permitting voting in ethnic polling stations

---

[15]The study is reported in Michal Shamir and Asher Arian, "The Ethnic Vote," in *The 1981 Israel Elections*, ed. E. Gutman, D. Caspi, and A. Diskin (London: Croom-Helm, 1983).

[16]For detailed analysis, see Hanna Herzog, *'Adatiut politit.*

[17]E.g., see Peres and Shemer, "The Ethnic Factor."

(1931). In order to mobilize political support, both the major parties and the General Federation of Labor (the Histadrut) set up special departments to deal with ethnic groups. The political parties initiated and organized the new immigrants on the basis of their origin; directly or covertly, they ofrten supported "ethnic lists."[18]

These facts indicate that on the structural-organizational level the ethnic base has been approved of and utilized as a political means in Israel. Simultaneously, on the ideological level, ethnicity as a basis for political organization has been decried. As a result of these two contradictory trends—the encouragement of ethnicity on the organizational level and its negation on the ideological level—the legitimation of ethnicity as a basis for political organization or, alternatively, its prevention, became an issue for negotiation in the political arena. Even as they made use of ethnic arrangements, the major parties tried to prevent establishment of independent organizations on an ethnic basis. They tried to define ethnic lists as representing marginal conflict groups, and organization on the basis of ethnicity as opposed to the melting-pot ideology.

The first and most salient tactic was to proclaim every list initiated by people of Asian and African origin as representing an ethnic ideology. Another tactic was to present such lists as permanently peripheral by identifying them with elements that were hostile to the state. Thus, for example, the Israeli Black Panthers were accused of being associated with hostile elements, such as the Palestine Liberation Organization. They were described as an extreme group that caused damage to the state's interests and image. The initiators of the ethnic lists were presented as ambitious careerists and power-hungry politicians, or as incapable of leadership. The leaders of the Black Panthers were branded as marginal youth, delinquents, or simply "not nice."[19] These tactics of stigmatization were part of an effort to decrease the political bargaining power of the ethnic lists. Rather than address that issue, however, the opposition tended to stress their accusation that the lists represented ethnic separation and ethnicity in itself.

The platform and election propaganda of all the ethnic lists reveal no ethnic ideology whatsoever. Ethnic organization has been used by politicians as a means for attaining or preserving power, but ethnicity was never an end in itself. The ethnic lists did not have a separatist ideology, and in most

---

[18]See Rina Zamir, "Beer-sheva 1958–1959: Tahalichim khevratiim beir pituakh (Beersheba 1958–1959: Social processes in a development town) in *Hamivneh hakhevrati shel israel* (The social structure of Israel), ed. S. N. Eisenstadt et al. (Jerusalem, 1966), pp. 335–365; Erik Cohen, Lea Shamgar, and Yael Levi, *Doch mesakem: klitat olim be'ayeret pituakh* (Summary report: Immigrant absorption in a development town) (Jerusalem, 1962); and Herzog, *'Adatiut politit.*

[19]"Not nice" was the phrase used by Golda Meir, the Israeli prime minister, to describe the Black Panthers. For the ways in which "ethnic" leaders were presented in newspapers, see *Haaretz,* June 30, 1961, June 26, 1971, April 7, 1975; and *Maariv,* August 6, 1971.

cases they did not demand the preservation of ethnic uniqueness. Like most other lists, they spoke in the name of the melting-pot ideology.

The conflict they perceived and presented represented a struggle over the reallocation of political, economic, and status resources according to criteria that had developed in Israeli society. The activists of the ethnic lists aspired to take part in the political system by adopting the rules of the game that were already accepted. They did not call for a different social order.

As a reaction to being stigmatized, they made a point of presenting ethnicity as a temporary phenomenon and the ethnic base for organization as a conditional one. Many ethnic initiators emphasized their national identity, or their representation of the masses, the workers, or the deprived, but not necessarily of Jews of Asian and African origin. They emphasized the legitimate and normative aspects of their actions. As one of the Black Panther leaders explained in referring to their chosen name: "We wanted an engaging and maybe frightening name...but, God forbid, not its ideology."[20]

Examination of the names chosen as the symbolic representation of the lists to the public reveals a growing reluctance to directly identify on an ethnic basis. For example, the names selected are Young Israel and For Justice and Fraternity. The members who split from the Black Panthers chose such names as Blue-White Panthers or Zionist Panthers. These names reflected a reaction to the efforts to drive Asian-African origin initiators out of the normative boundaries of Israeli society.

A review of the way the Tami—the "Tradition of Israeli Movement"— presented itself to the voters in the 1981 elections provides a clear illustration of the ambivalent attitudes of Jews of Asian and African origin toward ethnicity as an ideological pattern. In the first television interview of a representative of this list (May 29, 1981), the interviewer asked Eli Dayan, one of the group's activists, "Why an ethnic list?" Dayan replied, "It is not an ethnic list, it is a list of authentic leaders, a list against the system, for national social ideas, appealing to the whole nation." In the course of the interview, Dayan emphasized a number of times, "We are not ethnic, we are for the brotherhood of Israel." At the same time, the Tami's propaganda called supporters to "stand up straight," referring undoubtedly to ethnic pride. It would seem, though, that this was conditional pride—as one of the list's election posters proclaimed: "No more ethnic discrimination, no more 'quotas' according to ethnic origin, no more two nations in one country. And I, Aaron Abu-Hatzeira, hereby promise, together with my comrades, that when the day comes that these divisions do not exist anymore,

[20]See *Maariv*, June 25, 1971.

I, Aaron Abu-Hatzeira, will be the first to take down the flag I have raised today."[21]

The stigmatization of the ethnic lists, on the one hand, and their efforts to present a nonseparatist image, on the other hand, are evidence of the continuous negotiations over the meaning of ethnicity. These negotiations were carried out on the basis of a political reality in which the dominant groups saw the population of Asian-African origin as a threat, but at the same time as a source for political support.

The major parties negated ethnicity, but they also used it. The actions of politicians of Asian and African origin also reflected this duality. They used the ethnic base as a source for political mobilization, but at the same time withheld any commitment to ethnic ideas. Ethnic political identity never served as an aim; it was always a means. It was always presented as conditional and temporary. Even the changes in the last decade, when the Tami and the Shas (Sephardi Torah Guardians) passed the representation threshold, the use of ethnicity remained in the legitimized boundaries—those of religious tradition. The Tami of 1981 emphasized its orientation toward tradition and won three seats in the Knesset. The Tami of 1984 challenged the system in the name of the ethno-class ideas and lost two seats. In the same elections, the Shas raised the banner of the Torah and urged the legitimation of Sephardic tradition within the religious tradition; it won four seats in the Knesset.

So-called Ethnic Voting

The argument that there is an ethnic voting pattern in Israel is based on data that show a growing correlation between country of origin and preferred party. In the light of this statistical pattern, the question arises whether these data can be interpreted as an indication of voting on an ethnic basis, in terms of the content and significance of the behavior revealed. Some scholars answer this question positively.[22] They explain the Oriental votes for the Likud as an expression of their ethnic political identity.

In my opinion, the statistical data have been misinterpreted. I contend that the support for the Likud (the right-wing party) by people of Asian and African origin is not an expression of ethnicity, but an expression of their identification with the wider collective. There is a strong tendency among people of Asian and African origin to deny that any ethnic meaning

[21]See *Yediot Aharonot*, June 2, 1981.
[22]See Smooha, *Israel*; Swirski, *Orientals and Ashkenazim*; and Peres and Shemer, "The Ethnic Factor."

can be attached to their political behavior. Several studies of identity support this claim. They show that subjects asked about their identity and self-image indicated that the criteria of belonging most meaningful to them were the general ones—being Jewish and being Israeli. The category of Orientals is not preferred in any of the social relations that were examined—neither in neighborhood relations nor in friendships of the subjects or their children, and certainly not in marriage. According to Eliezer Ben-Rafael's findings, there is no tendency of these groups to shape group consciousness.[23] Despite the antagonisms they perceive in relations with "others," they do not become "for themselves" conflict groups. Furthermore, according to Ben-Rafael's informants, ethnic slogans in any form from outside the existing political establishment have little or no appeal for the ethnic groups. The denial of overt ethnic politics relates mainly to the group's self-definition as "temporary" and to their general belief in future integration. Sammy Smooha reports the same findings among leaders of Moroccan and Iranian origin.[24]

Investigation of junior high school students revealed similar data. Students of Asian and African origin give much significance to the identification with the Jewish people, with the nation, and with the State of Israel, and a reduced degree of ethnic-group identification has been indicated.[25] Michael Chen claims that education is the mechanism that generates internalization of social and national values of the state as well as the rules of an equitable society.[25] The achievement-oriented character of the schools makes pupils feel that their social status depends on their academic achievements and therefore decreases the weight of ascriptive factors in their feelings of deprivation. These findings point to an aspiration for integration according to accepted rules—that is, the rules of the dominant group. These aspirations prevent crystallization of ethnicity.

The above results correspond to my findings regarding "ethnic lists." Assuming that the answers subjects give reflect the way they perceive their environment and the way they want to present it to others, the picture becomes clearer. There is no tendency among Jews of Asian and African origin to construct their social world in terms of ethnic identity. On the contrary, the first and most basic element in their identities is national identity, which is corroborated by their religious tradition.

Shamir and Arian support this claim with their analysis of 1981 electoral

<hr />

[23]See Ben-Rafael, *Emergence of Ethnicity*, pp. 122–129, 150–154.

[24]Smooha, *Israel*, pp. 77–78.

[25]Michael Chen "Politica—pa'ar khevrati—khinuch: gormim hesegiim vegormim shiyuchiim beitzuv 'tkhushat kipauch' " (Politics—social gap—education: Ascriptive and achievment factors in the formation of feeling of relative deprivation," *Rivon l'mekhkar khevrati* (Social research review), no. 12–19 (1977): 149–66.

behavior.[26] They found that the statistical pattern of voting is ethnic in the sense that it overlaps country of origin, but that it has no unique cultural character, either in content or in meaning. Neither social class nor ethnic identity was found to be associated with voting for the Likud Party rather than the Labor Party. The common view that Orientals have a separate political culture, a heritage they brought from their countries of origin, has also been rejected. Their political behavior is no less Israeli than the behavior of those of European and American origin. Both groups react to the Israeli reality. It seems that the vote for the Likud was not meant as an expression of ethnic identification or as an expression of the uniqueness of the people of Asian-African origin. On the contrary, the Likud is perceived as a nationalist party, and as such, as including the "ethnic groups" as part of Israeli society.

The widening vote for the Likud has been part of a process of legitimation of that party and of the right wing, and of strengthening national and religious feelings. This process is manifested largely in the behavior of young people, both Israeli-born and of Asian and African origin, who grew up, were educated, and came to political maturity after the establishment of the State and during the fall of the hitherto dominant Labor Party. This fall was accompanied by the loss of political support from disillusioned groups and the absence of support among the new generations of voters. In addition, since the Six-Day War there has been a prevailing emphasis on national values. The voting pattern of the Jews of Asian and African origin is formed against the background of these processes, as is the voting pattern of young adults. This political behavior is not, then, ethnic in its content, but just the opposite. Because Israelis of Asian-African origin are identified with the lower class, because there is no legitimation for ethnic pluralism and ethnicity, the way to solve the problem of social marginality and to eliminate the stigma attached to being "Oriental" is to vote against the previous regime, which is apparently responsible for the present situation, and to vote for a party that declares the national ideal as its main principle.[27]

Other evidence along the same lines includes the refusal of major party activists of Asian and African origin to be identified as representatives of ethnic groups. Such identification would preclude their chances for competing for leadership of the entire society. Development town mayors of Asian or African origin who have managed to pave their road to the Knesset (e.g., David Magen or Meir Shitrit) see themselves as representative of their respective regions and of development towns, but they refuse to be labeled "professional Orientals."[28] When people of Asian and African origin were

---

[26]Shamir and Arian, "Ethnic Vote."

[27]For a similar claim, see Dan Horowitz, "Habekhirot beisrael, 1977" (The elections in Israel, 1977), *Betphutzot Hagola, 81–82* (In the Diaspora, 81–82), 18 (1977): 168–170.

[28]See *Maariv*, May 21, 1981, October 2, 1981; *Yediot Aharonot*, June 7, 1981.

asked which groups should get more representatives, the category of young people was given a much higher rate of preference than the category of "Orientals" or any other social category.[29]

Hence, the patterns of voting that have been described as ethnic, as well as the "lists" that are labeled ethnic, are not actually ethnic in their content. The greater proportion of people of Asian and African origin do not perceive their political behavior in ethnic terms, but there is a tendency among others to explain it as such. The political arena and the power conflict play an important role in the construction of reality in ethnic terms. The repeated definition of ethnic boundaries becomes the basis for social interaction in this arena. The emphasis on ethnic boundaries may generate a need to inject these boundaries with social meaning by mobilizing various symbols, either from past heritage or from present experience of socioeconomic inequality.

Conclusions

Examination of the "ethnic lists" shows that their initiators are of Asian-African origin but that their ideology is not; these lists do not claim for ethnic separatism, pluralism, or uniqueness. Analysis of patterns of voting that are considered ethnic reveals that while they may be statistically ethnic, they are not ethnic in content. The mass vote for the Likud in recent years is not an indication of the crystallization of ethnic identity, but rather an indication of the growing emphasis on identification with the collective and with the nation. The same is true of the propaganda presented by the lists comprised of people of Asian-African origin; it indicates an attempt to flee the stigma of ethnicity and the association of people of Asian and African origin in a separate and different social category.

The overlap of ethnic origin and lower social class could be a potential basis for ethno-class identity and political organizations, but the high rate of social mobility among Orientals is an obstacle. The tendency to construct reality in ethnic terms and in this way to impose ethnic boundaries could actually stimulate political ethnicity.

Stigmatization and political control were the main mechanisms used to neutralize any potential for ethnic identity. The dominant groups constructed reality in ethnic terms, but they did not allow the Orientals to fill it with a meaningful ethnic content or to translate it into organizational terms, in the cultural sphere or in the political one.

For many years the ethnic base was used by the major parties as a means for political mobilization. In internal party politics it was used for political

---

[29]For a detailed analysis, see Shamir and Arian "Ethnic Vote."

bargaining, but usually limited through controlled allocation of representation and power positions. The main problem the major parties faced, from the dominant group's point of view, was how to use ethnicity without losing control. Again, stigmatization was helpful. Many Oriental politicians in the major parties tried to burn the candle at both ends. They used ethnicity as their source of power, but at the same time tried not to be identified as Orientals only and thus stigmatized as unable to represent the wide interests of the nation.

In Israeli politics, ethnicity is a manipulative political means. While in 1981 the Likud defined ethnicity as a major problem of Israeli society, in the 1984 election campaign they claimed they had solved the ethnic problem. The Labor Party, more than the Likud, tried to handle this issue in a pragmatic way by increasing the number of Oriental candidates.

A striking phenomenon is the success of the Sephardic orthodox religious party in 1984 and the decline of the Tami. This success should be explained mainly against the background of the accepted and the legitimate distinction between Sephardic and Ashkenazic religious traditions. The partial de-stigmatization in the last decade of traditional festivals and other elements of the Oriental tradition enabled the Shas' cultural messages to overcome the usual stigma attached to ethnic parties. At the same time, the image of a radical ethno-class party that the Tami adopted in the 1984 elections suited the common accusation of "ethnic parties" and the negative meaning that is attached to ethnicity.

These findings show that the process of negotiation over the meaning of ethnicity still continues. Although the dominant trend was to deny ethnic identity, Tami's success in the 1981 elections, and the contrasting 1984 election results, might indicate the beginning of a process of change. In a situation in which the dominant groups persist in construction of reality in ethnic terms, it is useful to examine the way various groups react to it—how they use ethnicity and whether they try to formulate it with new content. As W. I. Thomas and D. S. Thomas claim, "If people define a situation as real, it is real in its consequences."[30]

[30]W. I. Thomas and D. S. Thomas, *The Child in America* (New York: Knopf, 1928), p. 572.

PART IV

THE SYRIAN-LEBANESE

COMPLEX

9

Arab Political Parties: Ideology and Ethnicity

Itamar Rabinovich

In May 1976 Karim Pakradouni, a Lebanese of Armenian extraction, a leading member of the Lebanese Kata'ib Party (the Phalanges), and a confidant of President-elect Elyas Sarkis, was sent by the latter to Damascus with a message to Syria's President Hafiz al-Asad. In the course of their lengthy discussion, al-Asad told his visitor how he had explained the complexities of Lebanese politics to an earlier visitor, Libya's prime minister, Abd al-Salam Jallud. "One should begin," al-Asad said to the prime minister, "by defining such words as 'nationalism' and 'isolationism.' If the Kata'ib are considered 'isolationists' because they want to keep the Lebanese entity outside the orbit of Arab unity, what should one call those like Kamal Junblat, who want to keep half the Lebanese isolated in Lebanon's very interior?" Al-Asad continued with an invective against Junblat, the most important leader of both the Lebanese Left and the Druze community, and leader of the Progressive Socialist Party. Al-Asad too was critical of the traditional Lebanese system and its failure to reform itself, but, he argued, "A distinction should be made ... between true national reforms and the sectarian demands of the national movement." He charged, "According to his attitude, Junblat is conducting a religious war against the Christians. In this there lies a danger for Arabism."[1]

This conversation between the disillusioned Alawi leader of the Syrian Ba'th Party and the doctrinaire Sunni prime minister of Libya, as reported to the Christian Phalangist emissary, is but one of the numerous ironies produced and insights afforded by Syria's intervention in the Lebanese civil war. It can also serve as an excellent introduction to the study of the

[1]Karim Pakradouni, *La Paix manquée*, 2d ed. (Beirut, 1984), pp. 6–8.

relationship between Arab ideological parties and the ethnic structure and problems in an important part of the Arab world.

It is difficult to speak in sweeping terms about ethnic politics in the Arab world as a whole. There is an especially marked difference between Egypt, which is closest to the West European model of a nation-state, and the states of the Fertile Crescent, where the definition of the political community is still contested and the population is divided along religious, communal, and ethnic lines. Ethnicity is a factor in Egyptian politics, but a minor one. It is a cardinal and sometimes a governing factor in the political life of Syria, Lebanon, Iraq, Jordan, and the Palestinian Arabs.

This divergence is naturally reflected in the orientation, structure, and ideology of the political movements and parties that grew up in Egypt and in the Fertile Crescent. Ethnicity played an important role in the formation and subsequent development of the Egyptian Communist Party, but not in those of the more central Wafd, Misr al-Fatat, and the Muslim Brotherhood. This is clearly not the case with a large number of parties and movements in the Fertile Crescent, five of which—the Syrian Social Nationalist Party, the Ba'th Party, the Lebanese Kata'ib Party, the Muslim Brethren in Syria, and the Communist Party we will look at below.

It is almost banal to point to the relationship between any of these parties and particular ethnic groups or problems. But other issues should be explored too. How did a party's ethnic roots or composition affect the formulation of its doctrine? How important was the ethnic factor in comparison with the other elements that shaped a movement? What relationship was there between the party and the state or states in which it operated, and between it and the community with which it has been identified or affiliated? How was the party's development affected by differences and divisions within that community? And finally, what transformations have these parties and movements undergone since they were founded in the 1920s and 1930s?

These five parties and movements were chosen for practical reasons. They offer a gamut wide enough for illustrating the complexity and richness of the subject, yet they are sufficiently circumscribed to be manageable.

The Syrian Social Nationalist Party

The Syrian Social Nationalist Party (the PPS, according to the acronym of its French name) was founded secretly in Beirut in 1932 by Antun Sa'adeh, a Greek Orthodox Lebanese who spent his formative years in Brazil and returned to Lebanon in 1929.[2] Sa'adeh formulated and expounded a doctrine of secular territorial Greater Syrian nationalism. Geographic Syria (present-day Syria, Lebanon, Israel, and Jordan, to which at a later stage Iraq and Cyprus were added) was defined as a national entity. According to Sa'adeh, nations were formed by countries, and a Syrian entity and a Syrian nation were formed in the land of Syria. But Syria and the Syrian nation were dismembered by the peace settlement of 1918–1920, and that settlement had to be undone. A Greater Syrian state, in which the Syrian nation would be reunited, should be established. The enemies of Sa'adeh's ideas and party were the defenders of the territorial status quo—France and the Lebanese state—and the other contenders for the same territory or parts of it, Arabism and Zionism.

Sa'adeh's ideas had numerous roots—secular notions of territorial nationalism that arose in Ottoman Syria and Lebanon in the late nineteenth century, Christian- and French-inspired concepts of a Syrian, non-Arab entity, and general dissatisfaction with the dismemberment that resulted from the post–World War I settlement in the Levant.[3] But Sa'adeh reflected also the dissatisfaction of the Greek Orthodox community with the Lebanese state. It was a state dominated by the Maronites and protected by the French. The Greek Orthodox, a large though diffuse group in Greater Syria, were relegated to a secondary position in Lebanon. As we shall see below, the Greek Orthodox community in the Levant has been an effervescent group, closer to Arab nationalism than other Christian communities, and active in several ideological parties. In Lebanon the PPS became the chief conduit for the community's disenchantment with the existing order and its aspirations for transforming and transcending it.

In the 1940s the party spread to Mandatory Palestine and Syria. While some of its important members were Palestinian, the PPS never became a significant actor in Palestinian politics. But its impact on Syrian politics was powerful. A number of important Syrian politicians—Akram Hourani and Adib Shishakli, to name two—received part of their political schooling in the ranks of the PPS, and it was one of the first parties in Syria to understand the importance of cultivating a following in the army's officer corps.[4] In the early 1950s the party emerged as the rear guard of the Syrian

---

[2]For the history and ideology of the PPS, see L. Z. Yamak, *The Syrian Social Nationalist Party* (Cambridge: Harvard University Press, 1966). For a portrait of Sa'adeh, see Eliahu Eylat, "Antun Sa'adeh—diokan shel mahpkhan 'aravi" in *Shivat sion ve'arav* (Antun Sa'adeh—Portrait of an Arab revolutionary" in *Zionism and the Arabs* (Tel Aviv, 1974), pp. 372–386, and Hisham Sharabi's memoirs, *Al-jamr wal-ramad* (Embers and ashes) (Beirut, 1978).

[3]A. H. Hourani, "Ideologies of the Mountain and the City," in *Essays on the Crisis in Lebanon*, ed. R. Owen (London: Ithaca, 1976), pp. 33–41.

[4]M. van Dusen, "Political Integration and Regionalism in Syria," *Middle East Journal* 9 (Spring 1972): 132–136.

Right, but it was defeated by the Ba'th and the Communists and disappeared from the scene as an effective political force.

Authoritative data are not available, but it is possible to characterize the communal appeal of the three main branches of the PPS. In Lebanon the party attracted mostly members of the Greek Orthodox community, and to a lesser extent members of other communities who were dissatisfied with the Lebanese political order—Sunnis and Druzes. In Syria the impact of Sa'adeh's personality was not so strong, and in the 1940s it was primarily the party's doctrine of secular territorial nationalism that attracted members of the minority communities—heterodox Muslims and Christians—who felt that they could not become full members in a polity defined explicitly or implicitly on the basis of Sunni Islam. The notion of secular Syrian or Arab nationalism had originally been formulated by Syrian and Lebanese Christians in the second half of the nineteenth century. For later generations in a different political configuration, the same underlying problem still presented itself. In Syria of the 1940s, the politicized youth of the "compact" heterodox Muslim communities—the Alawis and the Druzes—were added to the Christian minorities as seekers of a secular political community. Among these communities, the PPS and the Ba'th (with its doctrine of secular Arabism) were the principal competitors for the hearts and minds of the ideologically bent youth. It is in the Alawi region that this conflict has been best documented. The line would sometimes divide a single family. One telling example is the Jadid family. Two brothers, Ghassan and Fu'ad, became army officers and PPS members and were implicated in the 1955 assassination of Adnan al-Maliki, the last-ditch effort by the PPS to check the Ba'th. A third brother, Salah, was a Ba'thi officer and from 1963 to 1970 was one of the Ba'th regime's principal leaders.

Among the party's Palestinian members, communal origins appear to have been a secondary issue—the Sayyigh brothers were Christian, and Hisham Sharabi was a Muslim. Judging by Sharabi's memoirs, they were attracted by Sa'adeh's personality and by the atmosphere and the intellectual stimulation that the PPS generated in the early phases of its history. They may also have felt that the party's doctrine was a more sophisticated way of mobilizing support against the Zionists than the Arab nationalist short-lived effort in the early 1920s to define Palestine as "Southern Syria."

Since the mid-1950s, the PPS has been for all practical purposes a Lebanese party, and it was in Lebanon that the party underwent further changes and transformations. While Sa'adeh was absent from Lebanon during World War II, a pragmatic trend seeking to operate within the Lebanese state appeared, but was quashed by Sa'adeh upon his return. Following Sa'adeh's execution in 1949, the party entered a lengthy period of ideological and political confusion. Its activity as a pro-Western force in Syria of the 1950s was matched by close cooperation with President Camille Chamoun in Lebanon. An effort to mend fences with the apparently victorious doctrine of pan-Arab nationalism in 1961 was contradicted by participation in an abortive coup d'état against President Fu'ad Shihab in December of the same year.[5]

In the late 1960s the party's legacy among its former Palestinian members was manifested through the Palestine Liberation Organization's (PLO) adoption of the notion, or slogan, of "a secular democratic state" in Palestine.

In the early 1970s a new phase in the party's history in Lebanon began with consolidation of Hafiz al-Asad's Syrian Ba'th regime and the related, gradual disintegration of the Lebanese political system. The PPS became a pro-Syrian force and in a sense completed a circle, because it was working at the service of a force seeking hegemony in the area of Greater Syria and fighting for a transformation of the existing order in Lebanon.

Authoritative data concerning the communal composition of the PPS are not available, but certain general trends can be observed. The party still draws a large part of its membership from the Greek Orthodox community and is still seen to some extent as a representative and defender of that community's interest. But during the last decades the party has recruited heavily, or at least tried to recruit, among other communities—Shi'ites, Druze, and Sunnis. For them the PPS was one of the revisionist parties identified more closely with Syrian policy.

It is interesting that most of the party's achievements among the Shi'ites were erased by the rise and development of Al-Amal. Al-Amal was a genuine expression of the Shi'a community, and once it acquired legitimacy and effectiveness it could easily displace the PPS. But some of the party's losses among the Shi'ites were made up for by recruitment among Walid Junblat's Druze rivals in Southern Lebanon. In the absence of state authority, protection of party and militia became even more crucial. As opponents of the Junblats and their party, the PSP, these Druze have tended to join the PPS.

The Ba'th Party

The Ba'th Party was founded in the 1940s, but its origins can be traced to the 1930s—Michel Aflaq's and Salah al-Bitar's flirtation and subsequent conflict with communism, Akram Hourani's activity in Hama, Zaki al-

---

[5]For a description and analysis of the coup, see Y. Oron, ed., *Middle East Record, 1961* (Jerusalem, 1966), pp. 398–404.

Arsuzi's activity in Alexandretta and Damascus, and the short-lived career of an important but little-known party, the League of Nationalist Action.[6]

Like the PPS, the Ba'th attracted a generation that was dissatisfied with the social and political order, impatient with the traditional leadership and its style, and seeking a comprehensive ideology and all-embracing organizational framework. And also like the PPS, the doctrine and the party appealed to people from several countries—Syrians, Lebanese, Iraqis, and Palestinians. But while the PPS became a party of the Radical Right, the Ba'th placed itself on the leftist side of the Arab ideological spectrum.

The original doctrine of the Ba'th sought to combine a secular formulation of pan-Arab nationalism with a non-Marxist approach to socialism and social reform. These elements proved attractive to different groups. In Syria the party drew many Christians and heterodox Muslims who (like Michel Aflaq, one of the party's founders and the principal formulator of its ideology) saw a secular definition of Arabism as a solution to their problem. But though it had a disproportionately large number of members from the minority comunities, the Ba'th was not a minoritarian party; Sunni Muslim Syrians were attracted by the elaboration of a pan-Arab nationalist ideology, or in other cases by the vision of a humane Arab socialism that was different from the materialism and internationalism of the communist movement.

In other parts of the Fertile Crescent, the Arabism of the Ba'th proved to be more appealing than its socialism and secularism. In Lebanon the party attracted members from communities that were hostile to the Lebanese state, particularly Sunnis and Greek Orthodox. In Iraq it was a small party until the early 1960s, when it transpired that a powerful party organization had been developed clandestinely. The pre-1963 Iraq Ba'th did not have a particular appeal to either Sunni or Shi'ite Arabs and was indeed described as "a genuine partnership between Sunnis and Shi'a 'poor Arab' youth." They were attracted by the party's socialism and pan-Arabism—many of them saw Qassem's regime as a deviation from the Arab mainstream but were reluctant to join an outright Nasserite organization.[7]

The Ba'th's capture of power in Syria and Iraq, particularly in the former, and its success in building unusually durable regimes, turned it into a party identified with ethnic politics and minoritarian rule. To a large extent the Ba'th was a victim of its own success. During its first years in power the party was a complex entity, representing numerous social groups and ideas. Its regime consolidated the existence of an independent Syrian state and effected a social and economic revolution in Syria. But in later years, when these driving forces had been spent, the

---

[6]J. Devlin, *The Ba'th Party* (Stanford, Calif.: Hoover Institution Press, 1976), pp. 1–10.
[7]H. Batatu, *The Old Social Classes and the Revolutionary Movements in Iraq* (Princeton: Princeton University Press, 1979), pp. 1077–1093.

regime became preoccupied with power and survival. Because power was concentrated in the hands of one ethnic group, the Alawis, as we shall see below, Syrian politics since the late 1960s has been increasingly identified with the conflict between those seeking to preserve and those seeking to topple the power of the Alawis.[8]

When the Ba'th came to power in Syria in 1963, the ethnic or communal issue was but one of the dividing lines in Syrian politics. Alliances, rivalries, and factions were formed along personal, ideological, regional, and generational lines, along the line separating the military from the civilian and according to communal affiliation.

The increasing importance of the communal issue derived originally from the overrepresentation of the minorities (Christians and heterodox Muslims, Alawis, Druze, and Isma'ilis) in the ranks of the Ba'th, particularly its military wing. This contributed to the antagonism between the regime and the predominantly Sunni population of Syria's large cities. For the latter, the Ba'th was a radical and irreligious regime that stripped Syria's traditional elite of its political power and part of its social and economic power and planned to continue along the same lines. That Syria's new rulers were, or were perceived to be, largely or predominantly minoritarian added insult to injury.

In the internecine conflicts of the Ba'th regime, communal solidarity and communal suspicion and hostility proved more powerful than other factors. Furthermore, once this element was introduced it acquired a dynamic of its own. Alawi, Druze, and Isma'ili officers congregated against Sunnis in February 1966. Later, the Druze and the Isma'ilis were purged and the Alawis remained paramount. Within the regime other issues predominated, but in the relationship between regime and population the communal factor became overriding.

The establishment of Hafiz al-Asad's regime in November 1970 contributed both to an exacerbation of the problem and a temporary attenuation of it. Al-Asad's presidency aggravated the challenge to devout Muslims, who as we shall see do not view the Alawis as proper Muslims and who regard a regime headed by an Alawi as illegitimate. During his first six years in power, al-Asad pursued a successful strategy that sought to conceal the regime's Alawi inner core and to mitigate the conflict with the urban Sunni population.

This strategy collapsed in 1977. The regime quashed the challenge presented by the opposition in the years 1977–1980, but its continued existence has since depended on power and deterrence, rather than on the more

[8]N. Van Dam, *The Struggle for Power in Syria* (New York: St. Martin's Press; London: Croom-Helm, 1979), and H. Batatu, "Some Observations on the Social Roots of Syria's Ruling Military Group," *Middle East Journal* 35 (Summer 1981): 331–344.

subtle strategy of earlier years. Futhermore, al-Asad's illness and the beginning of a war of succession has underlined two interesting aspects of Syria's ethnopolitics.

One concerns the relations between Alawis and Sunnis in the regime, the party, and the army. Alawi predominance never meant exclusive rule and control. Alawis constitute some 12 percent of the population, and overrepresented as they might be, they could not hope—and indeed wisely never tried—to hold even a plurality of the political and military positions within the regime. Instead, Alawi predominance meant that Alawis had been nimbly placed in many key positions. The power struggle now adumbrated in Syria will not necessarily be conducted along communal lines, but it is possible that fear of their collective downfall and its consequences is already having a restraining effect on the Alawi officers.

The question has been raised in the past and is made all the more acute by the present circumstances with regard to the relationship between the members of the Alawi community who led the Ba'th regime and the Alawi community. Bits of reliable evidence point to a contemporary intra-Alawi power structure and to the influence it has on decisions made by Alawi leaders of the regime. How precisely the two groups function and interact remains a mystery. Little is known about the Alawi community and its structure since it was studied in the 1940s by the French social geographer Jacques Weulersse. Most of his findings must have been outdated by the community's modernization and politicization during the past few decades and by its spectacular rise from the fringes of Syrian public life to a position of power and dominance. This must therefore remain an area for further study, which current research and future developments are likely to illuminate.[9]

The political history of Iraq during the same twenty years can be described as, literally, a mirror image of the processes that took place in Syria. In Iraq the Sunni Arabs are a minority of some 20 percent that—as a result of four centuries of Ottoman rule and the policies of the British Mandatory— had enjoyed a lengthy preeminence in the country and the state. Such was the evolution of the Ba'th regime, particularly in its second (post-1968) phase, that power came to be monopolized by the Tikritis (natives of Tikrit) and their Sunni allies.

As in the case of the Syrian Alawis, the original choices were not confessional in nature. One joined a faction, made a commitment, and pledged allegiance on the basis of personal and family ties or common regional origins. These all implied affiliation with the same community, and so in time the regime found itself in the role of yet another upholder of the traditional Sunni hegemony. Until the late 1970s, the personal and regional

[9]Batatu, "Some Observations on the Social Roots of Syria's Ruling Military Group," *Middle East Journal* 35 (Spring 1981): 331–344.

factions within the regime tended to overshadow this fact. It was perceived in terms of primordial ties—the "regime of the Tikritis" rather than "the regime of the Sunnis." But the rise of Khomeini's regime in Iran shifted the emphasis, and the cleavage between the Sunnis and the Shi'ites became paramount.[10]

The Lebanese Kata'ib Party

The Lebanese Kata'ib Party, the other historical rival of the PPS, was founded in 1936 as a militant youth movement designed to protect the interests of the Maronite community and the Christian-dominated state of Greater Lebanon against the challenge of the PPS Arab nationalists and the Sunni community. To its adherents the organization offered more than the sense of fulfillment and gratification generated by participation in the defense of community and state. Like other radical parties and organizations of the period, it offered a charismatic leader, a demanding, all-encompassing framework, uniforms, discipline, dynamism, and a form of protest and rebellion against the traditional communal leadership.[11]

It was a distinctive characteristic of the Kata'ib that since its inception the organization had a dual character—a vigilante organization and a fairly pragmatic political party. Having contributed its share to the formation of an independent Greater Lebanese state, the Kata'ib attenuated its militia-like features and immersed itself as a political party in the Lebanese political system. But under the surface of a genuine and a very successful political party, the other face of the Kata'ib was retained—a militant militia ready to use its power to defend the state, the political system, and the Maronite-Christian community. This it did in 1958 and in the early 1970s.[12]

The interplay between these two aspects of the Kata'ib has been manifested by the three phases through which its ideology and orientation have gone since 1936. During its first years, the Kata'ib was a Maronite-Christian political organization seeking to protect and perpetuate a territorial and political status quo considered vital for the survival and well-being of the community. The very term Maronite-Christian reflects a deliberate ambiguity. The Maronite community clearly meets the criteria by which a national group is defined, but even the radical Maronites who demanded a state, and subsequently a Greater Lebanese state, spoke of a Christian rather than a Maronite entity. They must have felt that the Maronites were too few to sustain a state. Instead, Lebanon was seen and presented as a

[10]N. Van Dam, "Middle Eastern Political Clichés: 'Takriti,' and 'Sunni Rule' in Iraq; 'Alawi Rule' in Syria," *Orient* 21 (January 1980): 42–57.

[11]J. Entelis, *Pluralism and Party Transformation in Lebanon: Al-Kataib, 1936–1970* (Leiden: Brill, 1974).

[12]F. Stoakes, "The Supervigilantes: The Lebanese Kataeb Party as Builder Surrogate and Defender of the State," *Middle Eastern Studies* 11 (October, 1975): 215–236.

Christian homeland, fortress, and haven for the Christians of Lebanon and sometimes for the whole region. There had to be one state in the region in which Arabic-speaking Christians could live as free and full members of the body politic. Such were the arguments raised at the end of World War I by the spokespersons of the Maronite community—both clerics and political leaders—when they demanded a separate state with expanded borders under French protection.[13] In its early years the Kata'ib was a successor to this tradition and upheld it and lent it the support of its power. It was one among several Maronite groups belonging to this orientation, coupled by growing antagonism to the French authorities.

In the 1950s and 1960s, when the Kata'ib operated as a political party within Lebanon's pluralistic political system, it was no longer formally identified with a distinctively Christian, let alone Maronite, orientation. The party now became an advocate of Lebanonism, an ideology that argued that there had been and certainly was a Lebanese entity transcending the constituent communities. This notion had been put forth and elaborated in earlier decades by such people as Michel Chiha, Charles Corm, and Sa'id Aql, either to bind the Lebanese together or to present a counterpole to Arabism.[14]

The idea of a Lebanese entity, rooted in a historic tradition and serving as a bridge between East and West, though apparently secular, was perceived, certainly by its opponents, as Christian in orientation. Indeed, the Lebanonism of the Kata'ib, despite much elaboration and sophistication, was ultimately Maronite-Christian. This was clearly reflected in the party's communal makeup. Despite a serious effort to diversify it, the party's membership remained Christian and Maronite. Some members were recruited among the Druzes and the Shi'ites, but Sunni and Greek Orthodox Lebanese persisted in their reluctance and opposition.[15]

The party's ideological development during these years was not limited to its preoccupation with definition of the state and the political community. Much thought was given to social and economic reforms, which some of the leaders argued were necessary if the system was to be preserved. The internal debate on these issues resulted in crystallization of the conservative and radical wings in the party. The Kata'ib's distinctive ideology, large membership, and elaborate structure set it apart from the other Maronite

[13]The fullest and best-documented study of Maronite political attitudes in the late nineteenth and early twentieth centuries and the establishment of Greater Lebanon is Meir Zamir's *Formation of Modern Lebanon* (London: Croom-Helm, 1985). Part of Zamir's findings were published in his "Smaller and Greater Lebanon: The Squaring of a Circle," *Jerusalem Quarterly* no. 23 (Spring 1982): 215–236.

[14]Kamal Salibi, "The Lebanese Identity," *Journal of Contemporary History* 6, no. 1 (1971): 76–86.

[15]Entelis, *Pluralism*, pp. 101–124.

political parties and factions as well as from the community's religious establishment.[16]

These trends began to wane in the late 1960s as the domestic and external challenges to the status quo in Lebanon became more ominous. The Kata'ib became more distinctively Maronite. In 1968 the Kata'ib, together with Chamoun's National Liberals, and Raymond Eddé's National Bloc formed the essentially Maronite Tripartite Alliance. In the early 1970s, particularly after the Lebanese army's failure to check the PLO in May 1973, the original outlook of the vigilante organization was fully revived. The state occupied an important place in the party's thinking, but the community was more important than the state. If the Lebanese could not defend the community's existence and way of life, the party should undertake the task.

The trend was accelerated and accentuated by the civil war of 1975–1976 and by the continuing Lebanese crisis. The Phalangist militia was the single largest force fighting on behalf of the status quo coalition, and the Kata'ib was an important component of the Lebanese Front, an umbrella organization formed in 1976 to coordinate the policies of the Christian community. The Front's leadership included Camille Chamoun (as chairman), Pierre Jumayyil, Sharbal Qassis (head of the federation of Maronite orders), and other politicians and intellectuals (including the Greek Orthodox Charles Malik). The Front's outlook was expounded in a platform it published in 1980 under the title "The Lebanon We Want to Build." The platform demanded a special position for the Christians in Lebanon based not on their relative numerical strength, but on their role in the creation of Lebanon and on their objective needs.[17]

The civil war of 1975–1976 threatened the very existence of the Lebanese state and in any event signified the demise of the Lebanese political system as it had existed between 1943 and 1975. Several potential alternatives presented themselves—Syrian hegemony, partition and the establishment of a smaller Christian state, cantonization, preservation of Christian-Maronite hegemony over Greater Lebanon through an alliance with Israel, and a restructuring of the Lebanese political system through new communal alignments.

The Kata'ib were divided over these matters, and the division can be seen as a reincarnation of the party's original dualism. The party's leader, Pierre Jumayyil, and his elder son Amin, never quite relinquished the hope of reviving the traditional Lebanese system based on a slightly readjusted partnership with the other communities in Lebanon and on a modus vivendi with Lebanon's Arab environment. Jumayyil's younger son Bashir pursued a more militant line and developed an autonomous power base, affiliated

[16]Stoakes, "The Supervigilantes."
[17]"The Lebanon We Want to Build," December 1980.

with the Kata'ib but distinct from them. The Lebanese Forces developed as a militia organization based on a partnership between the militias of the Kata'ib, the National Liberals, and two smaller groups—the Tanzim and the Guardians of the Cedar. The Forces were affiliated with the Lebanese Front but were not its military arm. The Kata'ib militia provided the Forces, at least originally, with the bulk of its men, but the Forces should not be confused (as they often are) with the Kata'ib.[18]

Like the Kata'ib in their early days, the Lebanese Forces began as a militia and developed into a political movement, with its bureaucracy and an intellectual cadre and milieu. Until 1982 the tension between the new organization and the Kata'ib remained latent.

The Lebanese Forces began and developed as an uninhibited Maronite-Christian organization. Its first leader sought to impose for the first time a single effective leadership on the community and was willing to use force to achieve his purpose. He had partial success with the National Liberals and failed in North Lebanon. It is idle to speculate on the policy that Bashir Jumayyil would have pursued as president of Lebanon had he not been assassinated, but it is instructive to read the last speech he delivered a few hours before his death. It was the statement of a Christian leader about to become president of a state that he viewed as a Christian homeland.[19]

Bashir Jumayyil's assassination, Amin Jumayyil's election to the presidency, and the other developments of the years 1982–1984 further confounded the relationship between the Kata'ib, the Lebanese Forces, and the larger Maronite community. These developments cannot be analyzed here in detail, but the following statement made by Karim Pakradouni, now the political adviser to the Forces, in a press interview given in March 1984 reflects the Lebanese Forces' view of itself as a protector of the Lebanese Christians.

> The Lebanese Forces are drawing up a political program based on three main points:
>
> 1. The defense of Christian regions by establishing "red lines" around these areas. These "red lines" are both military and political—the military lines being mobilization of the Christian population to defend these regions, and the political ones being the contacts which the Lebanese Forces are undertaking at the regional and international levels. . . .
>
> 2. Proposing, at the national level, a plan for a federal republic with a view to achieving a comprehensive settlement of the Lebanese problem. . . . The Christians see reforms as forced concessions, while the Muslims consider them inadequate. This is why we believe the logic of reforms is not enough.

[18]L. W. Snider, "The Lebanese Forces: Their Origins and Role in Lebanon's Politics," *Middle East Journal* 38 (Winter 1984): 1–33.

[19]The text of this speech is included in a collection published on the first anniversary of Bashir Jumayyil's death.

3. Whereas the 1943 National Pact was based on an agreement between the Maronites and the Sunnites, we are becoming more and more convinced that the new National Pact will have to come about through an agreement between the Maronites and the Shi'ites.... [20]

Since the publication of this statement, the Lebanese Forces have been torn apart by internecine conflicts, and their posture and effectiveness as defenders of the Maronite-Christian cause have been seriously compromised.

The Muslim Brotherhood in Syria

In the span of some thirty years, the Syrian branch of the Muslim Brotherhood underwent a transformation from a movement reflecting the complacency of a confident majority to the militant representative of a beleaguered community. In the early years of Syrian independence, it would have seemed odd to examine the Muslim Brotherhood in the context of ethnic politics. The movement's leaders saw themselves as standing above such matters; they were spokesmen of the community and nation of Islam for Sunni universalism. Syria, to them, was an Islamic-Arab country inhabited by a large Sunni Muslim majority, and the Syrian state should have an Islamic government shaped by the Shari'a. Syria's non-Muslim citizens, be they Christian or heterodox Muslim Arabs, would have to adapt themselves to that projected reality.

The Brotherhood's position was articulated eloquently during the constitutional debate of 1950 by its leader, Mustafa al-Siba'i, who argued that Islam should be made the state religion in Syria. "In every state," wrote al-Siba'i, "there is a majority and a minority in religion." The minority, he implied, should resign itself to the supremacy of the majority, particularly because Islam recognized and respected the rights of the adherents of Christianity and Judaism.[21] The 1950 debate ended with a compromise: Islam was not declared the state religion, but it was specified that the president of the state must be a Muslim and that Islamic jurisprudence should be the major source of legislation. This became a standard formula in Syrian constitutions until the late 1960s.

The position taken by the Muslim Brotherhood in the 1950 debate mirrored a frame of mind current among Sunni Arabs, who tended to see themselves as the only full-blooded Arabs and who expected others to adjust to that state of affairs. Christian, Shi'ite, and heterodox-Muslim Arabs have responded to this attitude with varying degrees of resentment, envy, or

[20]*Monday Morning* (Beirut), March 5–11, 1984.
[21]R. B. Winder, "Islam as the State Religion: A Muslim Brotherhood View in Syria," *Muslim World* 49 (July and October 1954): 215–226.

resignation. Thus, one Arab student of Arab politics wrote bitterly about the Sunni Muslim leaders in the twentieth-century Arab world: "They came to the conclusion that they had a divine right, almost a God-given right, to lead the new community, now called a nation. . . . The implication of this was the Sunni community had a divine right to rule over Arabs. This right has now been enhanced by the fact that the new political elite was not only Muslim and Sunni Muslim but Arab too."[22]

During the first twenty years of Syrian independence, the Muslim Brotherhood was one of several parties and movements contending for power or influence in Syria. Its views on government and society likewise constituted one ideological current, with lesser impact than, say, Nasserism and Ba'thism. But Syria's ruling establishment, the traditional nationalists, and their immediate radical successors were Sunni Muslims. It was only in the 1960s that power shifted to an entirely different social group as the heterodox Muslims and Christians became preeminent in the upper echelons of the Ba'th regime.

The traditional roles were thus reversed. The Sunnis now felt dispossessed and humiliated. In the past they had not thought in ethnic terms, because their community's supremacy could be taken for granted; now they began to do so. In the circumstances obtaining in Syria, the Sunni religious establishment and the Muslim Brotherhood became the chief vehicles for transmitting the grievances of the large and diffuse Sunni community.[23] Social and political strife were blended with religious objection to domination by members of a sect (the Alawis) that strict Muslims regarded as lying beyond the pale. The Muslim fundamentalists came to represent a large group, many of whose members did not necessarily accept the movement's fundamentalism but saw it as the only authentic and effective defender of the Sunni majority.

For about a decade the Brotherhood and its allies conducted their struggle against the regime along conventional lines—trying to bring it down, to force it to change certain policies, or just expressing their frustration through strikes and demonstrations. In the mid–1970s it became clear that such traditional methods, while publicizing the opposition of a significant portion of the population to the regime, were futile as a strategy designed to bring it down. The stalemate was symbolized by the constitutional controversy of 1973. The devout Sunni demonstrators forced the regime to reinsert the compromise formula of 1950 it had tried to rescind. But an Alawi, Hafiz al-Asad, remained head of state.[24]

---

[22]A. R. Kelidar, "Religion and State in Syria," *Asian Affairs* 61 (February, 1974): 16–22. See also F. Ajami, *The Vanished Imam* (Ithaca, N.Y.: Cornell University Press, 1986).

[23]T. Mayer, "The Islamic Opposition in Syria, 1961–1982," *Orient* 24 (December 1983): 589–609, and E. Sivan, *Radical Islam* (New Haven: Yale University Press, 1985).

[24]Kelidar, "Religion and State," and I. Rabinovich, "The Islamic Wave," *Washington Quarterly* 2 (Autumn 1979): 139–143.

It was against this background that radical elements within the Muslim Brotherhood rejected the leadership of Isam al-Attar, whom they regarded as too timid. Organizationally, the movement lost its unity and coherence. In operative terms, its radical wing (or fringes) sought to bring the regime down through a strategy of terror and to exacerbate Sunni-Alawi tensions. During the 1973 constitutional controversy, the opposition's manifestos suggested cautiously that the regime was dominated by Alawis and that the Alawis were not proper Muslims. A few years later this was stated explicitly. Terrorist attacks were directed at Alawis as individuals and as a group. The massacre of some sixty Alawi artillery cadets in Aleppo in June 1979 was clearly intended to draw the Alawis to react and to bring about open warfare between Sunnis and Alawis. In the eyes of the radical Brotherhood this was preferable to the continued subjugation of the majority by the minority and to the rule of a secular and (in their view) a non-Muslim government.[25]

Politically, the radical wing of the Brotherhood succeeded in broadening its base by becoming the chief element in the Syrian Islamic Front in which its leaders were joined by well-known *ulama* (Muslim men of religion) who had not previously been affiliated or identified with the Brotherhood. The Front has devoted considerable effort to expounding its line in Syria and abroad. Its comprehensive program is an excellent guide to the movement's outlook and views. It includes a "call" and an "appeal" to the Alawis that seems to continue al-Siba'i's argument of 1950: "9 or 10 percent of the population cannot be allowed to dominate the majority, because it is against the logic of things. . . . In our case the sectarian war was not waged by the majority trying to protect itself against the domination of the minority. It is definitely the minority that forgot itself." Along with assurances for the Alawi community once it decided "to shake off the guardianship of the corrupt elements which drove them to this dangerous predicament," it included a vow: "We shall continue in our course, disregarding dangers and obstacles until this oppressive regime has fallen and gone for ever."[26]

The Brotherhood's offensive against the regime was broken, first in 1980 in Aleppo and then at a terrible price in Hama in February 1982. The brutal suppression of the opposition and the indiscriminate punishment of the environment in which it operated lent a new acuteness to the question of the Brotherhood's relationship with the larger Sunni community. Political attitudes could not, of course, be measured in Ba'thist Syria. It could be assumed that the Brotherhood had the sympathy and, to a lesser extent,

---

[25]Mayer, "Islamic Opposition."

[26]A translation of the program, appended with an elaborate introduction and apparatus, was published in book form by the sympathetic Mizan Press, as Dr. Umar F. Abdallah, *The Islamic Struggle in Syria* (Berkeley, Calif.: Mizan, 1983). Nothing is known about the author, but the book includes a foreword and a postscript by Professor Hamid Algar of the University of California at Berkeley.

the passive support of a considerable segment of the Sunni community. The latter, while not necessarily subscribing to the fundamentalists' views on Islamic government, would see them as the genuine expression of the majority's resentment against the regime. But the "environmental" punishment imposed by the authorities proved effective in forcing the Brotherhood's sympathizers to draw away from it in practice. Political conduct had to be divorced from political sentiment. It was a new reality that the Brotherhood had difficulty contending with.

The Communist Party

The record left by some sixty years of Communist activity in the Arab world bears ample testimony to the complex interplay between the party and the region's ethnic structure. It would be impossible within the scope of this chapter to examine the interplay as it had unfolded in several countries and branches, but its contours can be characterized in general terms.[27]

Communism was propagated in the post–World War I Middle East as a doctrine, as a disciplined and often secretive revolutionary organization, and as the arm of an international movement based in Moscow. Individuals were attracted to the party as leaders and members for a variety of reasons, but its main appeal in the 1920s and 1930s was to national and ethnic groups seeking a total transformation of their societies. This was true of Armenians in Syria and Lebanon, Kurds in Iraq and Syria, Greeks in Egypt, and Jews in Egypt, Iraq, and Mandatory Palestine.[28] Consequently, all Communist parties in the region had a disproportionate number of leaders and members from minority communities, particularly "harder" minorities that were not so easy to assimilate.

Herein lay an important difference between the Communists and parties like the PPS and the Ba'th. To the extent that they attracted members of minority communities, the latter two tended to appeal to "softer" groups, such as Greek Orthodox Christians or Alawis, who could hope to find an equal status in a redefined political community. The anticipated radical leveling consequences of a Communist revolution appealed to groups that were separated from the bulk of society by higher and thicker walls or placed across lines of national rather than ethnic or communal divisions.

Communism's appeal to groups preoccupied with national conflicts was

[27]For general studies and surveys of communism in the region, see W. Z. Laqueur, *Communism and Nationalism in the Middle East* (New York: Praeger, 1956), and E. Marqus, *Ta'rikh al-Ahzab al-Shiyu'iyya fi-l-watan al-Arabi* (History of the Communist parties in the Arab homeland) (Beirut, 1964).

[28]Batatu, *Old Social Classes*, and A. Flores, "The Early History of Lebanese Communism Reconsidered," *Khamsin* 7 (1981–1982): 7–19.

enhanced by the Soviet Union's attempt to cope with the national question within its own territory and by the fact that several national groups—Armenians, Jews, Kurds—were represented in both the Soviet Union and the Middle East. This pattern of recruitment provided Communist parties in the interwar Arab world with cadres of leadership and membership. But in later years the overrepresentation of the minorities, together with the internationalism and secularism of the party and the Soviet-Communist support for the establishment of Israel, militated against the party's spread among the Arab-Muslim majority.

Communists and Communist parties contributed their share to the revolutionary phase of Arab politics in the 1950s and 1960s. But as close as they seemed to be to seizing power on several occasions, they were ultimately defeated by nationalist elements. The ensuing disappointment (and Moscow's advice) led them to accept the suzerainty of the victorious nationalist elements, but it also led to heart-searching and schisms. The Syrian case is instructive and well documented. The brochure entitled "The Problems of the Conflict in the Syrian Communist Party" provides a detailed account of the rebellion against Khalid Bakdash, the party's historic leader and the best-known Communist in the Arab world (himself of Kurdish extraction). The rebels argued that the Syrian Communist Party must join the mainstream of Arab leftist politics and acquire a more nationalist coloring. In concrete terms the argument focused on the party's position in the Arab-Israeli conflict. The opposition to Bakdash believed that by endorsing Soviet acceptance of the legitimacy of Israel's existence the party was perpetuating its stigmatized position in Arab politics.

These reservations were stated explicitly and answered by a Soviet party delegation that tried to settle the controversy. But the text of the debate also reflects unstated tensions. The impatience of the opposition with the party's place in the periphery of Arab politics and its desire to join the "majority" was evident. Implied in this feeling was also the notion that the party should shed its minoritarian heritage and join the majority in that sense as well.[29] A similar trend in an entirely different context can be observed among Israel's Arab Communists. As Elie Rekhess' chapter in this volume shows, the history of Israel's Communist parties and of their predecessors in Mandatory Palestine has been shaped to a large extent by national as well as ethnic factors. Their efforts to transcend the Arab-Jewish conflict attracted some and repelled many in both communities. Among the Arabs, as in other parts of the region, it has attracted more Christians than Muslims.

Two interrelated trends recently became apparent. In the absence of a

---

[29]Extracts in English from this publication are published in the *Journal of Palestine Studies* 2 (October 1972): 187–212.

legal Arab national party in Israel, Rakah (the New Communist Party) became the principal outlet for expressing the political sentiments of Israel's Arab minority. And as the party became more nationalist in character, the discrepancy between a largely Christian-Arab leadership and Muslim-Arab voters became more pronounced and politically more significant. Ironically, then, it is a predominantly Arab Communist party in a Jewish state that has been the only effective communist party in the region in recent years. But effectiveness exacted an ideological price. In order to represent the nationalism of Israel's Arabs, the party had to shed most of its Marxist attributes.

This state of affairs raises two related questions. One concerns the Arab world's failure to produce a new ideological framework that would play a role similar to that played until the 1970s by pan-Arabism. The vacuum has been filled to some extent by the new salience and intensity of Islamic loyalties, but one still expects a fresh set of ideological formulations addressing the profound changes of the past fifteen years or so. The other draws on the crucial role played by ethnic and communal tensions in the interwar period in producing the ideologies that predominated in the 1950s and 1960s. During that phase, members of minority groups had sought to transform their status and predicament by transcending the political units created by the 1919–1921 peace settlement. These states have so far survived, but all are scenes of bitter intercommunal conflict. It is still an open question whether these conflicts will be conducted essentially as power struggles or whether some of them will give birth to new ideologies affecting the whole region.

10

Homo Oeconomicus—Homo Communitaris: Crosscutting Loyalties in a Deeply Divided Society: The Case of Trade Unions in Lebanon

Theodor Hanf

Do people act in accordance with economic laws, or is behavior primarily a product of culturally influenced values and norms? The dispute between economists and culturalists is as old as social science itself. What may be simply the subject of academic debate in culturally homogeneous societies is in plural societies a question of eminently political—indeed vital—importance. To whom does a person owe loyalty when the chips are down— the group of people pursuing similar interests, or the group to which one belongs on the basis of ethnic, religious, linguistic or other cultural characteristics? There is really no easy answer. Monocausal explanations are of little help in understanding complex, conditional interrelationships. The precise question is that of the relative weight of economic and cultural factors. It cannot be answered by a priori reasoning, but must be clarified by empirical investigation.

The case of the trade unions in Lebanon is appropriate for testing this approach.[1] Lebanon is an example of a country with extremely pronounced segmental cleavages. The conflicting groups coincide largely, if not completely, with religious communities. If cultural divisions ever do play an

[1]The descriptive parts and empirical material of this case study of trade unions in Lebanon are drawn from a detailed study by Theodor Hanf and Salim Nasr, *Gewerkschaftliche Konkordanz im Libanon. Bestimmungsfaktoren gewerkschaftlicher Einheit in einer kulturell und politisch fragmentierten Gesellschaft, eine empirische Untersuchung* (Consociational tradeunionism in Lebanon. Trade-union unity in a culturally and politically fragmented society, an empirical study) (Frankfurt am Main: German Institute for International Education Research, 1982). A French version will appear under the title *Syndicalisme consociatif et société segmentée: Une approche empirique du cas libanais*. The present interpretation is the sole responsibility of the author of this chapter.

173

important role in society, they certainly do so in present-day Lebanon. But in this deeply divided society there is a trade-union movement that is still active in most parts of the country and that draws its membership from all Lebanese communities. It has also remained unified at a time when numerous other organizations and institutions—from the state university to the army—have fallen apart.

How does one explain the relative cohesion of the trade-union movement in a society torn by deep cultural and political cleavages? In order to answer this question we shall examine four hypotheses:

1. *Class equals community*: Community and class membership largely over-lap. The trade-unionists belong for the most part to specific classes and communities and thus do not experience any conflict beween their iden-tification with the respective trade union and the class or community.

2. *Trade-unionists are progressive elements of traditional segments*: The trade-unionists are a particularly "modern" group in which individual economic interests and decisions carry more weight than traditional loyalties toward the respective communities.

3. *Behavior is determined by economic interests*: Trade-union activity is jux-taposed with communal and other divergent attitudes and behavior in other social subsystems.

4. *In a divided society there are still common labor interests*: The economic sphere is the only common ground between the different communities in a culturally and politically divided society. Hence, irrespective of com-munity membership, trade-unionists have a common perception of similar interests.

While the first of these hypotheses excludes the other three, the latter three are not mutually exclusive. They will be tested against the data from an empirical study conducted in 1982, which included structured interviews with a representative sample of trade-union members and with control groups of non-trade-unionists and self-employed (N = 500; 350 trade-union members, 50 non-unionized workers, and 100 self-employed).

A Consociational Trade-Union System

Formal trade-unionism has existed in Lebanon since 1946. The General Confederation of Lebanese Trade Unions assumed its present form in 1970.[2] The membership of the trade-union movement has grown continuously; in 1950 it had 14,000 members, in 1960 almost 26,000, in 1970 about 42,000,

[2]For a selected bibliography on the Lebanese trade-union system, see Hanf and Nasr, *Gewerk-schaftliche Konkordanz im Libanon*, appendix 3.

and in 1980 about 55,000—that is, in 1980 it comprised approximately 24 percent of the country's workforce, comparable to the level of organization in the United States of America or Mexico.

Organization is particularly strong in the tobacco and mineral oil industries, in banking, and the state water and electricity companies (80 to 90 percent) and above average in the textile industry as well as in the railroad and sea and air transport sectors (40 to 50 percent). It is low in the metal industries and parts of the service sector. There is a direct relationship between the level of organization and the size of companies. Whereas it has been relatively easy to organize labor in large concerns, it has proved difficult to do so in small businesses with few staff—for instance, in the service sector. The greatest weakness of the movement may well be the degree of organizational fragmentation: there are 165 separate trade unions and 18 trade-union federations. Some of them restrict their activities to specific industries and professions, others have a very diverse membership. Some are strongly politicized—be it Left or Right—others subscribe to a strictly apolitical concept of trade-unionism.

The 1960s were characterized by fierce political struggles, a sort of trade-union "cold war" in which, however, none of the opposing federations of trade unions was able to gain ascendancy. Eventually the opinion prevailed that ideological rivalry served only to weaken the labor movement as a whole. In 1970 there was an agreement that in many respects reflected the National Covenant of the political system, although it was more flexible.

The General Confederation of Lebanese Trade Unions (GCLTU) comprises all federations of trade unions—Left, Right, and apolitical, those restricted to specific industries and professions as well as the diverse, both the big and small. As soon as a new federation is formed, it receives automatic membership in the GCLTU. The principle of parity is paramount in the organization. In the General Assembly each federation—regardless of size—has four votes. In the executive committee, the most important decision-making organ, sit the president and general-secretary of every federation. The trade-union representatives in the state social security system, in the labor courts, in the wage negotiation commissions, and so on, are nominated in accordance with the principle of parity. The primacy of parity determines the organization's second principle—consensus in decision-making.

As a rule, the most important decisions are made unanimously. The principle of consensus forces a certain degree of depoliticization. The GCLTU does not take a political stand unless labor relations are involved (individual trade unions are permitted to express a political viewpoint, though never in the name of the whole trade-union movement). Since 1970, trade-union demands have concentrated on wages, working conditions, and matters concerning labor legislation.

Therefore, despite significant differences, the essential features of the Lebanese trade-union system function in terms of the consociational model. In contrast to the political system, change is possible through the co-optation of new federations, which is automatic. In contrast to the political system, the trade-union system is free of the strict proportionality between the religious communities. In the executive committee of the GCLTU, the Christians are a slight majority; at lower levels, Christians and Muslims have more-or-less equal representation. But whatever the majority or minority may be, this majority or minority is relativized first by the fact that religious affiliation and political orientation do not necessarily overlap (a number of "Christian" trade-union leaders are members of left-wing parties) and second by the principle of consensus, which in any case precludes the possibility of simple majority decisions. As in any consociational model, trade-union consociation also has its problems. Leading trade-union officials tend to remain, and age, in office. The executive committee is inclined to postpone making decisions when it is difficult to achieve consensus. From time to time the unity of the movement is preserved only by inactivity.

Nonetheless, the success of the consociational trade unions is impressive. Since 1970 they have forced the state to establish a national health service, improved protection against wrongful dismissal, and forced a dramatic increase in the minimum wage. Their policies during wage negotiations have been successful, even in wartime. Between 1977 and 1982, wage increases equal to at least the rate of inflation were pushed through in spite of the economic situation. In short, under difficult conditions the trade unions have preserved their unity—there is no other Lebanese institution in which Communists and Phalangists cooperate—and effectively defended the interests of the workers.

Class and Community

The hypothesis that there is a far-reaching coincidence between class and religious community is held by a section of the Lebanese Left and has gained popularity in international media in the form of the cliche "Poor Muslims—wealthy Christians." In the light of available data—for example, that on the composition of the Lebanese industrial workforce[3]—this has always seemed improbable. However, the possibility that Muslims might be strongly overrepresented in the trade unions, and/or that Christian trade-unionists had lost touch with their communities and adopted the class

[3]Salim Nasr and Marlene Nasr, "Remarques sur la composition structurelle du secteur industriel au Liban" (Remarks on the structural composition of the industrial sector in Lebanon) (mimeo., Beirut, 1971).

TABLE 1   Income Level (in 1982 Lebanese Pounds) by Religious Community in Lebanon, 1982

Income (in Lebanese Pounds)	Sunnites	Shi'ites	Druze	Maronites	Greek Orthodox	Greek Catholic
500–1,500	27*	46	47	42	37	33
1,500–2,000	35	27	24	23	40	29
2,000–10,000	39	28	29	35	23	38

*Figures in rounded percentages.
Source: T. Hanf and S. Nasr, *Gewerkschaftliche Kondordanz im Libanon*, p. 169.

position of the Muslim communities which according to this hypothesis represent the proletariat, cannot be excluded.

The data reveal a differentiated social reality far removed from that of the cliché.

Shi'ites, Druze, and Maronites are overrepresented in the lower income groups, Sunnites and Greek Catholics in the upper-income group (see Table 1). Moreover, there is considerable stratification within each community. There can be no question of overlapping between class and community. Levels of education by community also present a differentiated picture. Some 10 percent of all respondents had not completed primary school, but the figure for the Shi'ites was 17 percent. Twenty-six percent of Shi'ites have a university degree, but 38 percent of the Greek Catholics and 31 percent of the Greek Orthodox and Sunnites have university degrees. In employment by economic sector, there are no significant differences between the members of the different communities. In other words, in Lebanon, in contrast to many other plural societies, the employment structure of the workforce is not community-specific. Finally, there is no significant difference between the communities in terms of trade-union membership. The trade unions, with their Christian and Muslim membership, reflect Lebanese society.

What is the position with respect to class by itself—that is, class consciousness? Members of the Muslim communities have an above-average perception of themselves as members of the working class; Maronites, by contrast, regard themselvdes as middle-class. But almost one-fifth of the latter group see themselves as working class, and between one-fifth and one-quarter of the Muslim communities view themselves as middle-class (See Table 2). Thus, in terms of social consciousness or self-perception, it is difficult to give credence to the hypothesis of coincidence between class and community.

There is no difference between the members of the various communities in terms of the degree of satisfaction or dissatisfaction with job or place of work. There are some differences in attitudes toward the trade unions. The

Table 2   Perceptions of Class Affiliation by Religious Community in Lebanon, 1982

Percentage who regard themselves as:	Sunnites	Shi'ites	Druze	Maronites	Greek Orthodox	Greek Catholic
Middle class	18*	22	24	31	11	24
Office workers	5	4	12	6	8	5
Blue-collar workers	29	28	30	18	31	24
Employees	7	23	—	10	8	9
"Little men"	19	37	6	6	11	19
Civil servants	24	18	4	30	31	19

*Figures in rounded percentages.
Source: T. Hanf and S. Nasr, *Gewerkschaftliche Konkordanz im Libanon*, p. 203.

greatest enthusiasm is expressed by Shi'ites. The largest number of moderately positive people are among the Maronites; negative opinions are above average among the Greek Orthodox. However, these variances do not alter the main finding—that class cleavages and communal cleavages crosscut considerably.

Community and Political Orientation

There are considerable differences among the communities with respect to cultural and political orientations. Some of these can be illustrated by comparing the degree of religiousness (see Table 3).[4]

[4]The following items (statements) were chosen to determine "religiousness." Statistical factor analysis showed that the items, and hence the responses, are interdependent. The percentages below give the responses of the sample as a whole on a two-grade scale. The responses were then broken down by community and graded on a four-grade scale. This scale is presented in Table 3.

Statement	Percent Agreeing	Percent Disagreeing
I believe in life after death in which the good will be rewarded and the bad punished.	72	28
I try to live according to the teachings of my religion.	70	30
I often visit cult places.	46	54
I can be happy without God and enjoy life.	20	80
The believer must return to his spiritual and cultural roots and deepen his sense of religious belonging.	80	20

Source: T. Hanf and S. Nasr, *Gewerkschaftliche Konkordanz im Libanon*, p. 193.

Table 3   Self-reported Degree of Religiousness, by Religious Community, 1982

	Not Religious	Slightly Religious	Fairly Religious	Very Religious
Sunnites	20*	31	36	13
Shi'ites	16	18	24	41
Druze	18	35	29	18
Maronites	9	26	26	39
Greek Orthodox	6	44	25	25
Greek Catholic	19	29	24	29
Community not named	52	19	15	14

*Figures in rounded percentages.
Source: T. Hanf and S. Nasr, *Gewerkschaftliche Konkordanz im Libanon*, p. 195.

There is a direct relationship between the degree of religiousness and the degree of community identification. The Shi'ites and Maronites identify most strongly with their respective communities, the Greek Catholics least strongly.

As expected, the greatest divergence between the communities is in basic political orientation. The Left-leaning daily *al-Safir* is the preference of 55 to 60 percent of the Muslims and 28 percent of the Greek Orthodox, but of only 11 percent of the Maronites and 9 percent of the Greek Catholics. Conversely, 43 percent of both the Maronites and the Greek Catholics, as well as 19 percent of the Greek Orthodox, prefer the Phalangist daily *Al-Amal*, but only 6 to 8 percent of the Muslims do. This shows that to a large extent political polarization coincides with the basic orientation of the religious communities. However, one should beware of thinking that communal membership and political orientation overlap completely—there are also some crosscutting political cleavages.

Remarkably, there is no connection between the observed cultural, religious, and political cleavages and trade-union involvement. The degree of religiousness and irreligiousness among trade-unionists is average, as is identification with their respective communities, and there is no difference between their political orientation and those of non-trade-unionists.

Psychosocial Factors and Trade-Union Involvement

We have seen that neither economic nor politico-cultural factors provide much help in distinguishing between trade-unionists and non-trade-unionists. By contrast, some psychosocial factors are more explicit. Trade-unionists are less conservative and more open to social change than other respondents. They are far more likely to believe they have some scope for social action and are able to do something about "the condition of the people." Their attitude toward their social environment is far more positive than that of non-trade-unionists, and they believe in solidarity. Trade-unionists believe that above-average education and training and personal effort are the most important factors for success in life, whereas non-trade-unionists are more likely to believe in good luck or bad luck and independent "connections." In other words, trade-unionists are an achievement-oriented group.

Attitudes toward Trade Unions: Why Are Trade-Unionists Trade-Unionists?

By now it should be apparent that the attitudes toward trade unions vary according to numerous criteria and cannot be explained monocausally. We are able to recognize certain patterns of association by means of factor analysis.[5] To provide a basis for an examination of our initial assumptions and hypotheses, we distinguish five different factors that affect attitudes toward trade unions.

1. *Frustration.* Unsuccessful at work, dissatisfied, unsure in the social environment—for this type of person the trade union too is an object of his general dissatisfaction and criticism.
2. *Traditionalism and conservatism.* Tolerant and religious, not very educated, very conservative, most secure within the family and community circle—this type of person sees militancy and strikes as possible threats to his small, ordered world and therefore tends to reject trade-unionism.
3. *Business-oriented and achievement-oriented dynamism.* Desirous of personal success in business, open, dynamic, self-confident, and adaptable—this type of person favors the separation of religion and politics, because the connection is bad for business, and wants strong government, which is good for business. Because trade unions are not particularly good for business, he tends to be opposed to them, though neither strongly nor on principle.
4. *Militant dissatisfaction.* This type of person shares the frustrations of type 2, but becomes involved in the opposite direction— namely, active trade-unionism. For him there is a dichotomy in society. He rejects communities and decentralization and reads a progressive, left-wing paper. In his view the trade unions, as they are, are not militant enough.
5. *Reformism, populist-orientation.* This type of person has already done better than his parents, but feels that his future is threatened and wants to do something about it. He supports the Lebanese system of coexistence

---

[5]The results of the factor analysis are reported in the text. Statistical details will be supplied by the author on request.

among the communities and believes in middle-class society, but he is not blind to exploitation by a wealthy minority or to the social cleavages. He is optimistic about the economic situation but dissatisfied with working conditions. He hopes the new political leadership will be more efficient. In short, he is the type of person who is not unhappy with the existing economic, social, and political system, but feels that it can be improved. Hence, he is also for trade-unionism.

The investigation was based on the assumption that in Lebanon cultural factors are particularly apparent and that membership in a religious community is the most important distinguishing characteristic. The data support this assumption. The communities are clearly distinguishable and measurable "cultural variables." The individual communities—but not Muslims and Christians in their entireties—revealed significant differences in income and educational stratification as well as in reproductive behavior. In the attitudinal sphere the communities manifested differing degrees of conservatism, differing perceptions of the scope for social activity, and differing intensity of religiousness and of communal ties. But above all, they differ in political orientation. Incidentally, a large majority of the respondents are in favor of spiritual renewal and a strong religious influence on the life of the society. So there can be no doubt that the community is a major cultural factor and a useful indicator of diverging cultural factors.

What is the significance of this crucial cultural factor for trade-union involvement? On the basis of the data the answer is: very little. There is no significant relationship between trade-union membership and activity and community affiliation, or between trade-unionism and political orientation. There is a clear distinction between trade-unionists and nonorganized workers as well as the self-employed. These differences are, on the one hand, of a psychosocial nature—trade-unionists feel they can achieve more socially, are more positively disposed toward their social environment, and are more in favor of social change. On the other hand, they are of an economic nature—trade-unionists regard education, training, and personal effort as crucial factors in success; they are more achievement-oriented. There is no difference between trade-unionists and other workers with respect to religiousness, their ties to their respective communities, or even their view of society. Even their attitudes toward work as well as company loyalties are similar.

In short, as *homo communitaris, homo religiosus, and homo politicus*, the trade-unionist is an average Lebanese. He differs from the average *homo oeconomicus libanicus* only insofar as he is a relatively dynamic and achievement-oriented example of this species. Neither cultural factors specific to individual groups nor economic factors can account for his trade-unionism. Personal and social characteristics—confidence and the willingness to act, to achieve something, and to accept social change—are the determining factors.

Of the complex hypotheses set out at the beginning of this chapter, that of "class equals community" does not hold true, as might have been expected. There is no indication in our data on income and education or in terms of self-perception that communities even approximate classes. Trade-unionists are both Muslim and Christian, have rightist as well as leftist views on society, and have contrasting political opinions. There is some support for the hypothesis that trade-unionists are progressive elements of traditional social segments. The majority are able to adapt to and accept reforms. However, this by no means implies a weakening of communal loyalties. "Progressiveness" and strong communal ties are clearly not mutually exclusive. This means that the hypothesis of the juxtaposition of trade-unionist attitudes, on the one hand, and divergent attitudes in other social subsystems, on the other hand, is quite applicable. Among Lebanese trade-unionists, one will simultaneously find Communists and supporters of the Christian and Muslim militias, socialists and liberals, believers and non-believers—all of them active trade-unionists.

The fourth hypothesis is also confirmed by the data—regardless of cultural and political cleavages, trade-unionists have a common perception of similar interests. Does this common perception of interests explain the compatibility of otherwise apparently incompatible attitudes? There is some evidence that it does, but there is still the question of whether these common interests are perceived as exclusively economic.

Consociational Man

In 1982 the great majority of respondents, regardless of their differing ideological persuasions, expressed support for a political system based on the division of power between the communities (see Table 4). This indicates that over and above a common perception of economic interests there was— at least at that time—a common view of fundamental political interests. Almost 80 percent of all respondents supported the view that political decisions must be made only with the cooperation and agreement of all major religious communities. That is a huge vote for the essence of the "Lebanese Model," a form of consociational democracy. The supporters of the consociational model do not distinguish on the basis of religious community, income, or age. A majority would also like to see the consociational democracy as a strong state. Support for coexistence was greatest among those who identify most strongly with their respective communities. In other words, the most Sunnite Sunnites and the most Maronite Maronites are also the most convinced consociational men.

Table 4 Responses of Lebanese to Statements on Power-sharing, 1982

Statement	Percent Agreeing	Percent Disagreeing
In view of the nature of the Lebanese society, the most important political decisions must have the support of all large communities.	79	21
A strong and united Lebanese state is possible only if the communities, through their authentic representatives, are involved in the exercise of power.	68	32
In Lebanon the authority of the state can be strong and united only when the state has overcome the contrasts of the zu 'amā' and of the religious communities.	84	16

Source: T. Hanf and S. Nasr, *Gewerkschaftliche Konkordanz im Libanon*, p. 215.

Only a minority reject a political system based on the division of power between the communities and want only a strong state. This minority comprises mainly those with little religiousness; it also has an above-average proportion of graduates of foreign universities—political Jacobinism in Lebanon is an imported article.

Thus, in 1982, after seven years of war, after massacres and destruction, there was still a solid foundation for coexistence. Whether it has been shaken by the crises since then can be established only by further research. Nevertheless, the 1982 findings should make us cautious about prematurely burying the consociational system. As long as bullets count for more than ballots, events will be determined by the people who have a finger on the trigger. However, events in recent years have shown how brief trigger-happiness can be.

The will to coexist may prove to be stronger than many a warlord believes, and would like to believe, in his own interest—that is, the interest of those whose self-proclaimed leadership, power, money, and prestige is dependent on the continuation of the conflict. In the social institutions in which ballots still count, the will to coexist still has primacy. The trade-union leaders of the most varying political persuasions regard trade-unionist consociation as a model for improvements in political consociation and actively support both.[6] For example, the former president of the GCLTU says: "It was cer-

[6]A leader of the transport workers comes to the same conclusion on the basis of his professional experience: "All communities and all parties are represented on our committee. The president of the trade union is a Maronite, the general-secretary a Sunnite. All have an interest in the functioning of the firm. I believe that Lebanese national reconciliation should follow the example of our firm" (*Gewerkschaftliche Konkordanz im Libanon*, p. 107). The argument of a Socialist trade-union leader repeats this almost word for word: "In our branch there are thousands of workers from all communities, political persuasions, and parties. Hence, we are forced to pursue common interests and form a solid consensus. We, the workers, want national

tainly a most difficult task to preserve the unity of the trade unions during the crisis. We have been successful. I can only wish that the Lebanese politicians prove themselves just as capable of solving their task—namely, preserving the unity of the country."

Just as the old Lebanese political system differs from the systems in more homogeneous national states, so the Lebanese trade-union system has a specific structure and a specific politico-organizational culture that distinguishes it from both the ideologically characterized trade unions with a fixed line in the Latin countries of Europe and the all-embracing, uniform federation of trade unions in Scandinavia or Germany. Hence, the Lebanese trade-unionists' perception of interests is by no means purely economic. Historical experience in politics as well as in trade-unionism has led to consociation on both levels, though with different degrees of success. This historic experience could be the *tertium comparationis*: the will to exist despite all cleavages makes the coexistence of opposing attitudes in different spheres possible. Consociational man cannot be reduced to either his economic dimension or his ethnoreligious dimension. He is a contradictory person and acts in a contradictory manner, just as social reality is often contradictory.

---

reconciliation, the return of all displaced persons, the preservation of the unity of the state, peace and reconciliation—but not in the hypocritical manner of the politicians. If the politicians would reach agreement, as we trade-unionists do, then things would be far better in Lebanon" (loc. cit.). A Communist trade-union leader concludes: "A confederal structure is the only suitable one for the Lebanese political system" (loc. cit.). Naturally, liberal-conservative trade-union leaders take the same view: "Despite the ideologies and the communities, the workers are united by their mutual interests and their future. Our successes benefit all, regardless of differences between communities and political convictions. On the other hand, the trade-union leadership firmly believes in the unity of the people, the country, and its institutions. Its firm and unified action is an example and a testimony. Such is a healthy basis for the future reunification of the Lebanese people" (op. cit., p. 107). For the present, the principle of unity through consociation outweighs all reservations. Conservatives and Liberals are fairly happy with the status quo, Communists are in no hurry to change it.

11

The Druze in and between
Syria, Lebanon, and Israel

Kais Firro

Most studies of ethnic politics seem to be based on one of two approaches. The first approach traces the ethnic group's primordial givens from its present cultural features. Because these givens do not disappear with historical development, the group's identity and solidarity are regarded as stable and continuing realities. The second approach emphasizes the adaptive qualities of the ethnic group, whose identity and solidarity are modified by changes in its economic, social, and political environment. This case study of the Druze minority in the contemporary Middle East will not address the debate over the above-mentioned approaches, but a comparison of three Druze communities—in Syria, Lebanon, and Israel—will shed new light on the issues in that debate.

Most of the non-Druze scholars who dealt with the Druze adopt the primordial approach. They see the Druze sociopolitical situation as based on the *Taqiyya* principle.[1] According to them, *Taqiyya* is the practice of *pretending* to follow another religion and without this primordial principle, Druze history and politics cannot really be understood. "It is hard to distinguish between the practice of *Taqiyya* and everyday political opportunism."[2] In order to explain the political aspect of *Taqiyya*, most scholars quote from the *Ta'lim al-Diyana al-Durziyya* (The Teaching of the Druze

---

[1]Philip K. Hitti, *The Origins of the Druze People and Religion* (New York: AMS, 1982), pp. 40–48; H. Blanc, "Druze Particularism: Modern Aspects of an Old Problem," *Middle Eastern Affairs* 3 (November 1952): 315–321; G. Ben-Dor, *The Druze in Israel: A Political Study* (Jerusalem, 1979), pp. 37–51; A. Layish, "Taqiyya among the Druze," *Asian and African Studies* 19 (1985): 275–277; J. Teitelbaum, "Ideology and Conflict in the Middle Eastern Minority: The Case of the Druze Initiative Committee in Israel," *Orient* 26 (September 1985): 342–343.

[2]Teitelbaum, "Ideology and Conflict," p. 343.

Faith)[3] or from one another. They have recently begun to quote the new book *Bayna al-Aql wa al-Nabi* (Ratio and the Prophet),[4] which, while consulting additional sources on *Taqiyya*, continue to use al-Halabi's manuscript.[5] The quotations chosen tend to present *Taqiyya* as a tenet that encourages the Druze to follow the dominant religion of their environment—for example, "Our Lord has commanded us to hide in the dominant religion, be it what it may, with Christians, Christian, with Muslim, Muslim, and so on."[6]

But how can one accept a non-Druze source as the basis for a theory on the *Taqiyya* principle? Jubra'il al-Halabi was a Christian, as his first name testifies, and according to Druze shaykhs (religious leaders) his manuscript was written in the mid-nineteenth century, against the background of Druze-Maronite conflict. It represents no more than a subjective interpretation of the Druze faith, presented as a dialogue and framed in questions and answers. There are places where the text contradicts itself. For example, in reply to the question "Why do we deny all the [religious] books except the Qur'an?" we are told. "Because we hide in the Muslim religion."[7] Reliance solely on al-Halabi would lead to a confused interpretation of *Taqiyya*.

One must also approach the recently published *Bayna al-Aql wa al-Nabi* with caution, because in the chapter about *Taqiyya* the authors use al-Halabi's manuscript and other selected sources to prove the non-Islamism of the Druze and their "hatefulness" toward other religions.[8] The book was written in the shadow of the Lebanese civil war, at a time when the Druze were in the Muslim camp. The names of the authors are most certainly pseudonyms, and the book was published in Lebanon, not Paris. The book's conclusion reveals its authors' motivation. Under heading "At the Day of Baring the Secrets: The *Taqiyya*'s glory," they inform readers of the "secret contract" between Druze leaders and Israel that is aimed at establishing a Druze satellite state.[9] These sources give the impression that the political behavior of the Druze is always in accordance with *Taqiyya* practice, that is, going along with the dominant majority and joining the side that seems likely to win.[10]

This is not the place to discuss the *Taqiyya* principle in detail or to criticize

---

[3]Jubra'il al-Halabi, "Ta'lim al-Diyana al-Durziyya" (Principles of the Druze faith) (unpublished manuscript).

[4]A. Yasin, W. Al-Sayyid, and B. Sayf Allah, *Bayna al-Aql wa al-Nabi* (Ratio and prophet) (Paris, 1981).

[5]Ibid., pp. 279–298.

[6]See H. Blanc, *Hadruzim* (The Druze) (Jerusalem 1928), p. 137; Ben-Dor, *The Druze in Israel*, p. 41; Layish, "Taqiyya," p. 250.

[7]Al-Halabi, *Ta'lim al-Diyana al-Durziyya*.

[8]Yasin et al., *Bayna al-Alq wa al-Nabi*, p. 297.

[9]Ibid., p. 417–428.

[10]Ibid., p. 279.

studies dealing with the subject. And *Taqiyya* in itself is not sufficient explanation for the political behavior of the Druze. Various and complex factors determine such behavior—some peculiar to the Druze, others common to Middle Eastern ethnopolitics. In addition to *Taqiyya*, the Druze attitude to "strangers" was shaped by *taqammus* (transmigration of souls), *hifz al-ikhwan* (protecting fellow believers), *mihna* (persecution and experience that comes before the Last Judgment), and the tradition of settling in the mountains. Even today these factors continue to influence the political behavior of the Druze. But if one considers that the practice of *Taqiyya* makes the Druze "like lambs," forever joining the side that seems likely to win,[11] what explains their revolts against the Egyptians in 1838, the Ottomans in 1890, and the French in 1925? And what motivated the political crisis in the Golan Heights from 1978 to 1982 and the Shuf War in 1982?

There is no mention of the term *Taqiyya* in Druze religious books. The principle came from the Shi'ite sects and was used by heterodox communities to avoid persecution by the Sunni majority and Sunni rulers. As a traditional principle, it means the manifestation of Islam in preference to other religions.

During the Ottoman period, the Druze were treated as Muslims and officially incorporated in the Muslim *state* (or *umma*). However, the socioeconomic and political structure of the Ottoman Empire accentuated communal differences, and although each community declared its loyalty to the central government, each was allowed to preserve its particular identity. The Druze community isolated itself geographically in inaccessible mountainous areas and exhibited a certain degree of independence from the central administration. Until the end of the nineteenth century, the ethnic question was mainly a matter of community and religion. Even then the masses remained indifferent to the Western idea of nationhood and remained true to their communal and religious identity. Only the intellectuals reacted to outside influences.

Under the mandate regime—and later under the new states of Syria, Lebanon, and Israel—the Druze community was confronted with new religious and sociopolitical systems. The socioeconomic and political development within each of the three political units introduced, and continues to introduce, changes in Druze attitudes toward the states and their populations. But first we must deal with four complementary components that appear to determine the interrelationships between the Druze and their environment: (1) the new sociopolitical situation in Syria, Lebanon, and Israel and its impact on traditional Druze particularism; (2) the force of Islam as an ideological and political factor in the contemporary Middle East and its impact on the Druze community; (3) the concept of nationalism

[11]Ibid.

as expressed in several forms and versions and its impact on the Druze; and (4) the Middle Eastern state as a political institution, a social force, and an economic force, and its impact on the Druze.

French policy in Syria and Lebanon was based on the assumption that particularist feelings existed in the various communities. This, coupled with the tactic of divide and rule, induced the French to establish Alawi, Druze, and Lebanese states and grant each of them domestic autonomy. By creating such states, the French hoped to co-opt the Alawis and the Druze and thereby gain a weapon to do battle against the Syrian nationalist movement.

Druze autonomy in Hauran suited the community's particularism and isolation without jeopardizing its relationship with the Sunni majority, and the Druze avoided taking any step that would separate them from the Muslim environment. But Sunni mistrust was heightened when autonomy came to mean an autonomous state, and Druze loyalty to Islam and Arab-Syrian nationalism was put to the test. The problematic situation created by the establishment of the autonomous Druze state was reflected in the split between Druze leaders. The faction led by Salim al-Atrash in Hauran and some Lebanese notables accepted the new state, which was opposed by the other faction led by Sultan al-Altrash in Hauran and most of the Lebanese Druze leaders.

The Sunni Muslims, along with some of the Greek Orthodox, Shi'ite, and Druze leaders, were united in their distrust of the French administration. Harboring this feeling, they were strongly opposed to the French annexation of Southern Lebanon in 1920, the Bika valley, and the coast to Mount Lebanon in order to create Greater Lebanon (Le Grand Liban). They were in favor of Arab unity and the integration of Lebanon into Syria. In the 1940s they began to accept the notion of an independent Greater Lebanon stressing the country's Arab features, and they demanded close ties between Lebanon and the Arab world, particularly Syria.[12]

Although the new order established by the French separated the Druze of Lebanon from those of Syria, mutual communal interests continued to affect the relationship between the two communities. While confessional considerations prompted the Lebanese Druze to make an alliance with the Muslims, the Druze state in Hauran was a source of Muslim mistrust of the Druze in both Syria and Lebanon. Druze leaders and intellectuals were well aware of the problems inherent in the new situation imposed on them in 1920. While their attitude toward the French Mandate and Syria was linked to their own domestic politics and internal divisions, most Druze leaders did not accept full separation from Syria.

[12]K. Salibi, *Ta'rikh Lubnan al-Hadith* (The modern history of Lebanon) (Beirut, 1967), pp. 212–226.

In these circumstances Abdallah Najjar, a Lebanese Druze intellectual appointed to direct the Education Office in the Druze state, published his reflections on the problematic situation of the Druze in Syria and Lebanon. The main objective of his book was to prove the Islamism and Arabism of the Druze and to remove the suspicions of the Syrian and Lebanese Muslims. The first chapter deals with the differences between Muslims. The second deals with the differences between *madhhab* (school) and *din* (religion), and between *ta'ifa* (community) and *umma* (nation). Najjar defined the Druze as a school and a community rather than a religion and a nation.[13] His expositions concerning the Islamism and Arabism of the Druze were later accepted as the fundamental concepts of almost all the books written by Druze on these subjects.

In 1925, under the leadership of Sultan al-Atrash, who had good relations with the Arab nationalists, the Druze community in Syria revolted against the French. Al-Atrash mobilized the communities of Hauran, the Golan, Wadi al-Tim (in the Bika), and Mount Lebanon. Most of the Druze communities in Syria, Lebanon, and Palestine contributed something to the revolt. As mentioned earlier, this cannot be explained by *Taqiyya* in its sense of "following the stronger side." Only the obligation of *Hifz al-Ikhwan* in a time of *mihna* could mobilize such support and degree of solidarity. During the early stage, while it was still known as the Druze revolt (before it became the "Syrian Revolt"), most of the Druze leaders in Hauran emphasized the attachment of Hauran to Syria: "The Druze mountain is an integral part of Syria by common language, common nationality and economic interests."[14]

The political program of the Druze revolt was formulated in Syrian and Arab nationalist terms. Sultan al-Atrash, Adil Arsalan, and other Druze leaders of the revolt stressed its national dimension, not its communal dimension.[15] An alliance was created between Sultan al-Atrash and a group from the Syrian Arab national movement headed by Abd al-Rahman Shahbandar. Although Jabal al-Duruz (Druze Mountain) remained separated from the Syrian state until 1936, the revolt in 1925–1927 removed suspicion about the loyalty of the Druze community to the Syrian Arab national movement and people. Poets and writers in Syria, Lebanon, Egypt, and Iraq praised the Druze for their struggle against "French imperialism." Soon after the Druze revolt, the name of Jabal al-Duruz was changed to Jabal al-Arab (Arab Mountain) to emphasize Druze attachment to Syria

[13]A. Najjar, *Banu Ma'ruf fi Jabal Hawran* (The Druze in Hauran) (Damascus, 1924), pp. 14–32.

[14]"Petition against the Measures of Garbillet," in H. Abu Rashid, *Jabal al-Duruz* (The Druze mountain) (Cairo, 1925), p. 239.

[15]S. Ibeyd, *Al-Thawra al-Suriyya al-Kubra, 1926–1927; Watha'iq Lam Tunshar* (The History of the Great Revolt 1926–1927, unpublished documents) (Beirut, 1971), appendix.

and to weaken particularist tendencies in the Druze community. Until today, the Druze in Syria and Lebanon use their participation in the revolt against the French as proof of their loyalty to the Arab nation.

The traditional leaders of the Druze conducted their relationship with the central governments in Damascus and Beirut, with the French Mandate, and with the Arab nationalists and Sunni leaders until the independence of Syria and Lebanon. In both countries the paramount local force was located in the hands of the traditional leaders, who exercised the decisive influence over their community's external affairs. Although several new trends had emerged with regard to the French administrations, the old policy toward the Arab-Muslim environment was maintained, thereby avoiding separation and isolation from the Muslim and Arab worlds. Without exception, all the Druze leaders proclaimed their Islamism and Arabism—a significant indication of the trends that were to shape the Druze attitude after 1946.

After independence, Druze leaders, scholars, and writers again emphasized the Islamic character of the Druze faith, undoubtedly motivated by the traditional practice of *Taqiyya*. But the result of this practice in the modern period was different from that of the past, when *Taqiyya* had been an instrument for manifesting Islamism vis-à-vis the external world in order to maintain religious independence.

With the Druze community no longer isolated and the majority of the Druze able to get information about their religious faith from secondary sources, *Taqiyya* paradoxically resulted in dependence on, not independence from, Islam. The Druze doctrine becomes *madhhab* (school) and not *din* (religion). Although it is impossible to predict the future interrelationship between the Druze sect and Islam, the present tendencies are rooted in the period that saw Islam become an ideological force that affected politics.

Despite preservation of their heterodoxy, the Druze could have integrated into the social and political life of Lebanon and Syria had these been secular national states. It is therefore no wonder that many Druze joined secular political parties, such as the Syrian Nationalist Party (SNP), the Arab Ba'th Party, and the Socialist Progressive Party (SPP), which shared the common principles of secularization of public life and the building of national identity, even though they disagreed on the question of national territorial identity—the SNP espoused Greater Syria, but the SPP accepted the territorial state of Lebanon on the condition that it maintain its Arab features. Meanwhile, the SPP strove for Arab unity and the Ba'th Party called for pan-Arabism. It is worth noting that the new Syrian Nationalist Party in Lebanon has also adopted Arabism. In its Syrian and Lebanese versions, Arab nationalism fostered the Arabism of the Druze, whose acceptance has been facilitated by their claim to Arab racial origin.

Most Druze are considered to be descendants of the twelve Arab tribes that immigrated to Syria before the Islamic periods.[16] They reject Hitti's theory that their claim to Arab origin is related to *Taqiyya*[17] on the grounds that it had been pronounced as early as the Mamluk and Ottoman periods, when non-Arab dynasties ruled Greater Syria. Furthermore, because Muslim society is in itself multiracial, there was no need to invoke *Taqiyya* in that regard.[18] Islamization of their religious faith and the claim to Arab racial origin, together with the social-economic-political developments in Syria and Lebanon, contributed to the erosion of traditional Druze particularism. However, this took different forms in the two countries.

A major concern of the newly independent Syria in 1946 was the potential damage compact minorities could do to its sovereignty and statehood. To assimilate the Druze and the Alawi areas into the new state, the government had to control or even destroy the particularist tendencies that had been encouraged by the French Mandate. Under the banner of Arab nationalist ideology, and stressing "national unity," the Syrian government rejected the communal pluralism that would create internal division. Thus, the first step the Syrian government took as part of the trend toward national unity was to abolish the system of communal representation in parliament.[19] The Druze and the Alawis could not be permitted to continue dealing with the Syrian government through their traditional patterns, that is, showing their loyalty to the Syrian state and people while maintaining a certain degree of autonomy.

Syrian authorities made great efforts to destroy the military strength of the Druze and to impose the authority of the central government. One tool at their disposal was the internal division of the Druze clans of Hauran. Although almost all the Druze leaders in 1946–1947 expressed their loyalty to the Syrian state, there were two factions. The first was led by the Atrash family and accepted integration with Syria and the "Arab nation," but preferred to achieve it through the "historical leadership" of the community. The second, led by a coalition of families and called Al-Sha'biyya (Popular Families), was oriented toward a more active integration. Manipulation by the government led to internal dissension and feuding between the Druze factions in 1947. Although the Atrash family maintained its leadership, it

[16]Shakik Arsalan, "Al-Naqd al-Tarikhi wa-Urubut al-Ma'ruf" (The history, criticism, and Arab origin of the Druze), in *Al-Majma al-Ilmi al-Arabi bi Dimashq* (The Arab Scientific Academy in Damascus) (Damascus, 1931), p. 455; N. Abu Izzeddin, *The Druze: A New Study of Their History, Faith, and Society* (Leiden, 1984), pp. 1–14; A. Tali, *Asl al-Muwahhidin al-Duruz* (The origin of the Druze) (Beirut, n.d.), pp. 22–23; A. Abu Salih, *Ta'rikh al-Muwahhidin al-Duruz* (The history of the Unitarianists, the Druze) (Beirut, 1980), pp. 15–26.

[17]Hitti, *Origins*, p. 14.

[18]Izzeddin, *The Druze*, pp. 10–11.

[19]Moshe Ma'oz, "The Emergence of Modern Syria," in M. Ma'oz and A. Yaniv, *Syria under Assad* (London, 1986), pp. 18–22.

had to make concessions to the Al-Sha'biyya. These events signaled the beginning of the dissolution of the traditional leadership.

The role of Druz officers in the coups d'état that shook Syrian society between 1949 and 1967 made the struggle to survive even more difficult for the Druze community, and especially for its traditional leadership, during this crucial period of Syrian development. The military dictatorships of Husni al-Za'im and Adib Shishakli would not tolerate the central Druze minority. Za'im sent the army to the Hauran to disarm and subdue the inhabitants, and under Shishakli the new territorial state further endeavored to strengthen its power and control. Shishakli tried to impose modern Syria's first socioeconomic reforms by weakening the traditional Druze power base. In addition to the Arabization of public life, he fostered the Islamic character of the state and its public institutions.[20] The unrest created by the oppressive force of the state in 1954 sparked a Druze revolt led by the Atrash family against the Shishakli regime—the last communal uprising in modern Syria. This revolt is considered a turning point in the interrelationship between the central government and communal centrifugal forces. With the decline of the Atrash leadership and the rise of the Syrian State's power, the Druze minority in Syria lost the traditional means of bargaining in their name.

From 1954 to 1966 the integration of the Druze and Alawi communities in Syrian life could be achieved only through such institutions as the Ba'th Party and the Syrian army, not through the clans and communal leadership. The role of the army in the political life of the country made it possible for large numbers of Alawi and Druze officers to rise to positions of influence and authority. However, while the Alawi officers and politicians continued to amass power through the military coups d'état in the 1960s, the Druze ascendancy was held up after the aborted coup d'état of the Druze officer Salim Hatum in 1966. With both roads to power now blocked, the political influence of the community as an ethnic body seemed to be weakening daily. Integration of the Druze into the socioeconomic and political life of the country could be achieved only through the institutions of the Ba'th Party and through individual relations with the ruling elite and agents of the state.

In addition to Arab nationalism, which was used as an ideological instrument to overcome the ethnic or religious problems of the country, the economic development of Syria also changed the ancient demographic patterns that had been based on the full segregation of the Alawis and the Druze, who were concentrated in their mountain strongholds. Alawis migrated toward Hama, Latakia, Tartus, and Damascus; Druze of Hauran and other localities migrated toward Damascus and vicinity. These socio-

---

[20]Ibid., p. 21.

economic and political developments weakened the communal ties that had previously bonded the Druze community.

The establishment of Greater Lebanon (Le Grand Liban) in 1920 was achieved by annexing to Mount Lebanon areas in the north, south, and east that contained large numbers of Muslims who felt no attachment whatsoever to the new state. Like the Maronite leaders, the French assumed that the new political framework of "Le Grand Liban" would bring the heterogeneous populations together to build a "nation" and a "Lebanese identity." However, the Lebanese constitution of 1926 and the National Covenant of 1943 created the "political confessionalism" of Lebanon. The representation of the "recognized" communities in the state's institutions is proportional. Political life is at once both secular and confessional, and even religious.

The legitimacy of the state does not transcend the communities. Each community has remained an independent entity within the state. The leaders of the communities (*zu'ama*) accepted the political power of the state and its institutions as legitimate so long as the latter recognized the "legitimate rights" of each community. In addition to the weakness of the state, intercommunity relations and political representation in the organs of the state have since 1943 been predicated on the nation's only census, taken in 1933. This gave Christians the majority. Parliamentary representation is based on a ratio of 6 to 5 in favor of the Christians, 30 percent for the Maronites, 24 percent for other Christian communities, 39 percent for the Sunnis and Shi'ites, and 6 percent for the Druze. The National Covenant of 1943 makes a Maronite the president, a Sunni the prime minister, and a Shi'ite the speaker of parliament. The rest of the government's offices are distributed among the smaller communities. This system has failed to make Lebanon one nation.

Contrary to the Syrian experience, the political system of Lebanon did not result in any erosion in the traditional institutions and leaderships of the Druze community. The religious institutions of the Mashiakhat al-Aql increased its functions and became an intermediary between the state and the community.[21] Although this institution still relies on Druze leading families, it has gained some independence and autonomy. In Syria the Mashiakhat al-Aql lost its traditional functions and independence vis-à-vis the state, but in Lebanon it can bargain in the name of the Druze. In Syria the traditional Druze leading families have declined in power but have new avenues for participating in politics, but in Lebanon the Druze participate through the "intermediate families." The leading families—Junblat, Arsalan, and others—represent the Druze in the Lebanese parliament and gov-

[21]For details on the origin and development of this institution, see Amin Tali, *Mashiakhat al-Aql* (The spiritual leadership of the Druze) (Beirut, 1971).

ernment. In Lebanon, unlike Syria, Arab nationalism and even Islam have been introduced to the Druze community through the leading families without eroding its particularism.

Socioeconomic and cultural developments in Lebanon have exacerbated the above problems, widening the gap between the rich and the poor, between the educated and the less educated. The interaction between the political system and socioeconomic and cultural developments caused the socioeconomic struggle to become confessional. This situation created dual patterns of politics, mixing modern—or Western—and traditional elements.

While the Arsalan faction continued to deal with Lebanese politics through traditional means, the Junblats, under the leadership of Kamal Junblat, began to adopt Western means in the political struggle in 1946. The Socialist Progressive Party (SPP) was established in 1948 by Junblat in response to Druze political needs. The modern ideologies of the party—for example, socialism, democracy, secularization, and Arab nationalism—attracted many Druze, even from the Arsalan faction. The SPP reflects the aspiration of a minority—abolition of political confessionalism, not "replacement of one confessional domination by another."[22] The party has given the Druze an important role in Lebanese politics since 1952. Kamal Junblat led the "progressive movement" coalition that was established during the civil wars of 1958 and of 1976–1977, and his son and successor, Walid, continues to lead the party and the community in the same way. The civil war (1976–1982) and the Shuf War (1982–1983) reinforced Junblat's party. Its emergence as an armed force in 1976 brought the Druze to the forefront in Lebanon's conflicts. The impact of the SPP reinforced the political role of the community. The direct correlation between the party and the community created a neo-particularism that is a synthesis of both traditional and modern elements.

The permanent crisis in Lebanon continues to erode the power of its central institutions. The direct intervention of Israel in 1982, the clashes between the Druze and the "Lebanese Forces" during the Israeli occupation, and the Shuf War after the Israeli withdrawal completed the rupture between the Druze and the state. The aftermath saw neo-particularism translated into Druze de facto autonomy. But this does not mean isolation. The autonomy itself has reinforced the Druze position in the struggle over the future structure of the Lebanese state.

The Druze of Galilee and Carmel constituted a small minority of the population of Palestine during the Ottoman and mandate periods. They never enjoyed political importance, and there were no leading families on

---

[22]Al-Hizb al-Taqaddumi al-Ishtiraki, *Rub Qarn min al-Nidal* (The Progressive Socialist Party, quarter-century of struggle) (Beirut, n.d.), 1:25.

the model of the Atrashes, Junblats, or Arsalans who represented the community. Although the Khayr family from Abu Sinan village, the Tarif family from Julis, and the Ma'di family from Yarka had political positions, they never became intermediaries between the authorities and the community.

Before 1948 the political behavior of the Druze in Palestine was typical of a minority settled in a peripheral area. Like the Jabal al-Sumaq near Aleppo and the Ghuta near Damascus, the Druze settlements in Palestine were more vulnerable than such centers as Hauran and Mount Lebanon, and the Druze in Palestine depended on these centers in religious and political matters.

In the absence of traditional leading families and intellectuals, Palestinian Druze remained indifferent to Arab and Palestinian nationalism. Their particularism prevented them from adopting any national loyalties beyond their communal identity during a period of confusion between nationalism and religion. Thus, for the Druze of Palestine the Zionist-Palestinian conflict was no more than a Jewish-Islamic conflict. However, both interested parties had their suspicions and hopes regarding the Druze. The Palestinians saw any individual cooperation between the Druze and Jews as treachery by the community as a whole; the Zionists perceived individual Druze cooperation as an opening for them in the Druze community.

The cooperation of a few Druze with the Zionists during the upheavals of 1936–1938 created a confessional reaction among Muslim Palestinians. In Usfiyya, Shafar Amr, and Daliyat al-Karmel, the Palestinian fighters executed "collective punishment," murdering Druze civilians just because they were Druze,[23] pushing these villages further toward cooperation with the Jews. Thus, unlike the experience in Syria and Lebanon, where Druze integration in national movements was facilitated during the mandate period, the Zionist-Palestinian conflict created friction between the Palestinian movement and Druze from Usfiyya, Shafar Amr, and Daliyat al-Karmel. Although other villages did not face the same situation, the events of 1936–1938 reinforced Druze particularism and communal identity. Thus, while the national idea in Syria and Lebanon began to shake the traditional particularism, in Palestine it created a certain antagonism within the Druze community. As the political development in Mandatory Syria and Lebanon shaped the general lines of future Druze political behavior in the independent states, the events of 1936–1938 and onward facilitated the association between the Druze and Jews and shaped its political features in the State of Israel.

The Israeli authorities dealt with the community through the family leaders who had cooperated with the Zionist movement in 1936–1938. In

[23]Most of the Druze killed during these events were peasants who had no interest in the conflict.

order to maintain their political position in the new state, the other family leaders had to follow suit. The Israeli authorities made an immense effort to develop loyalty to the Israeli state and at the same time to obtain the support of the Druze sector of the country's non-Jewish population. To do so, they emphasized the uniqueness of the Druze community and religion. Immediately after the establishment of Israel, and with the support of some family leaders, the "Unit of the Minorities in the Israeli Army" was established. In 1956 the Law of Security Service was extended to include the Druze at the request of or with the concurrence of those family leaders. These events characterize the interrelationship between the Druze and the state. The family leaders were the communal representatives of the Druze in their relations with the authorities, so it is no wonder that the Druze spiritual leader, Shaykh Amin Tarif, became the intermediary through whom the authorities bargained.

Although the non-Jewish population of Israel was made up of several "minorities," in the 1950s the government created an "Arab Department" through which the authorities dealt with the minorities. However, conscription into the armed forces gave the Druze a different status from that of other Arab communities, and it was unreasonable to expect them to remain on the same footing as those who did not take on that obligation. Therefore the application of conscription to the Druze was followed in 1957 by recognition of the Druze as an autonomous religious community. In 1961 the authorities decided to enter "Druze" as a classification of nationality in identity cards, instead of only "Arab." Thus in 1967 the Druze were removed from the jurisdiction of the Arab Departments, and in 1976 the government created a Druze Section for Education separate from the Arab section. Although certain groups within the community opposed these steps, the majority of the Druze did not reject them, hoping that they would lead to equal rights for the Druze.

Although there are several factors that determine the attitude of the Druze minority toward the majority, the modern state remains the major force. In Israel the policy of separating the Arab minorities and granting the Druze a special status reinforced the community's particularist political behavior. Their military service marks the Druze as a minority with the majority's feelings, more confident than ever before—more than just a minority within minorities. Israeli policy, coupled with the traditional particularism, reinforced the Druze identity and separated it from Arabism and Islam. While the Palestinian Druze had no national leadership, an intermediate leadership arose under Israeli sovereignty and used the Druze identity and solidarity in its interaction with the state institutions.

In Lebanon the confessional political system, coupled with the ethnopolitics of the Middle East, created a measure of neo-particularism. Despite the adaptation to such new ideologies as nationalism, socialism, and secularism, the Druze community in Lebanon maintains its traditional leadership and its communal institutions. In Syria, however, the Druze traditional leadership has ceased to exist. Adaptation to the Syrian political system and state ideology is now made individually. Clan leaders no longer bargain in the name of the community. The process of integration in the sociopolitical system may lead the Syrian Druze to become fully assimilated within Syrian society.

PART V

THE IRANIAN SCENE

12

Ethnicity and the Iranian Peasantry

Farhad Kazemi

Differentiation based on ethnic, religious, or linguistic criteria has been a constant feature of Middle Eastern societies. Iran is no exception to this general pattern. In its cities, towns, and villages, groups of people have been classified and set apart by themselves and by others according to a set of fluid characteristics that mark the differences among these groups in the social order. The relative importance attached to this compartmentalization of groups has varied over time. Depending on the force of a given political, economic, or social issue, the significance of group differentiation has fluctuated. However, primordial sentiments have continued to remain a basic force that helps, under favorable conditions, to organize and mobilize the discontented groups and direct their grievances. This chapter will look at the ethnic factor of the Iranian peasantry from the second half of the nineteenth century and analyze the impact of ethnic diversity on peasant political behavior.

Rural Society: Ethnicity and Diversity

Iranian society, whether rural or urban, has always been characterized by significant ethnic diversity. Several observers have likened this diversity to a "colorful mosaic" or "complex kaleidoscope."[1] During the period under investigation, differences along linguistic and religious lines were common

---

[1]Ervand Abrahamian, *Iran between Two Revolutions* (Princeton: Princeton University Press, 1982), p. 11, and James Bill and Carl Leiden, *The Middle East: Politics and Power* (Boston: Allyn & Bacon, 1974), pp. 11, 255.

in the rural areas of Iran. Important groupings of Shi'is, Sunnis, Christians, Baha'is, and Jews, as well as various subgroups of Shi'is and Christians, were present in rural locations throughout the country. Further divisions into linguistic categories of Persian, Turkish, Kurdish, Baluchi, Gilaki, Arabic, and others added to the overall complexity of rural society.

Aside from these diverse features, the villages exhibited other character-istics that set them apart from the urban centers. These included, among others, the following: (1) Apart from villages that were located near major cities and were part of the agro-city complex,[2] most villages were scattered over a vast country far from city centers. Some 40,000 to 50,000 such villages dotted the rugged terrain and the complex physical geography of rural lands. (2) Owing to a variety of factors, including difficult terrain and a poor or nonexistent system of infrastructure, these villages remained largely isolated from one another. (3) Village self-sufficiency and a modified form of autarky was the normal form of economic activity. (4) Religious, lin-guistic, and other differences among the villages made horizontal contact and communication among rural inhabitants difficult and unrewarding. (5) Some villages were composed totally or primarily of tribal settlements. This in turn resulted in maintenance of ties with the tribes, reinforced particularism, and furthered isolation of one village from another.

A typical Iranian village was small and rarely consisted of more than a few hundred inhabitants. Although the village economy tended toward self-sufficiency and was made up essentially of individuals of similar ethnic background, significant differences of another kind were apparent within each village. These differences derived from the basic Iranian agrarian structure that remained relatively unchanged until the land reform program of the 1960s was implemented. The hierarchical divisions of the agrarian structure encompassed, on one end, the powerful broad category of large absentee landlords and, on the other end, the poor, landless peasants who had no cultivation rights and privileges. In between the two poles were small landowners, peasant proprietors, and sharecroppers. The ethnic unity and the generally self-contained economy of the village was crisscrossed by a clear hierarchical order of political, social, and economic power. This order was enforced by the perpetuation of extensive economic and social dependency of the poor peasants—whether sharecroppers or those without any cultivation rights—on the absentee landlords or their village agents.[3]

Two observations about this system are relevant to this chapter. First, the villages exhibited, to use Barrington Moore's words, basic conservative

[2]See the description of the agro-city in Albert Hourani, "The Islamic City in the Light of Recent Research," in *The Islamic City*, ed. A. Hourani and S. Stern (Philadelphia: University of Pennsylvania Press, 1970), pp. 16–17.

[3]See Ann K. S. Lambton, *The Persian Land Reform, 1962–1966* (London: Clarendon, 1969), pp. 25–26.

solidarity. Complaints and grievances were tied in with the system.[4] The "inward-looking" peasants needed the landlords both for protection from the outside world and in order to ensure subsistence and survival of their marginal economic lives.[5] Perhaps Tawney's apt metaphor about the conditions of a Chinese peasant is equally applicable to the Iranian counterpart. Tawney described the position of the peasant as "that of a man standing permanently up to the neck in water, so that even a ripple might drown him."[6] In such a system, conflict resolution was an integral part of the village organization. Justice was meted out by the village system through its controlling voices and instruments.

Second, the ethnic unity of the villages also extended to the absentee landlords. The common pattern of rural holding in Iran was generally to invest in areas where the peasants were of the same ethnic background as the landlords. Exceptions, of course, could be found. For the most part, however, the element of ethnic unity transcended economic, social, and political differences between landlord and peasant.

Rural Change and Ethnicity

From the second half of the nineteenth century, several significant developments slowly changed the rural society and its traditional system. Perhaps the most profound of these was the beginning of commercialization of agriculture in Iran.[7] The impact of commercialization varied from one area of the country to another, but on the whole it eroded some of the villages' traditional self-sufficiency as the raising of cash crops and integration into the larger market economy began in earnest. Village, town, city, and even international markets developed ties and commercial relations. Although this process did not necessarily supplant the pre-commercial economy, it supplemented its traditional operation. The process of transforming the peasants from "inward looking" to "outward looking" had set in, even though it remained incomplete in many areas. The resultant village-town contacts—an important long-range by-product of agricultural com-

[4]Barrington Moore, Jr., *Social Origins of Dictatorship and Democracy: Lord and Peasant in the Making of the Modern World* (Boston: Beacon, 1967), pp. 475–79.

[5]For a fuller discussion of "inward-looking" peasantry, see Joel Midgal, *Peasants, Politics, and Revolution* (Princeton: Princeton University Press, 1974), p. 26.

[6]R. H. Tawney, *Land and Labor in China* (Boston: Beacon, 1966), p. 77, quoted in James Scott, *The Moral Economy of the Peasant: Rebellion and Subsistence in Southeast Asia* (New Haven: Yale University Press, 1967), p. 1.

[7]Vahid Nowshirvani, "The Beginning of Commercialized Agriculture in Iran," in *The Islamic Middle East*, ed. A. L. Udovitch (Princeton: Darwin, 1981), pp. 547–592; Charles Issawi, ed., *The Economic History of Iran, 1800–1914* (Chicago: University of Chicago Press, 1971); and Ahmad Seyf, "Commercialization of Agriculture: Production and Trade of Opium in Persia," *International Journal of Middle Eastern Studies* 16 (May 1984): 233–250.

mercialization—brought about greater ethnic interactions and relation-ships. As villages came in contact with urban-dwellers and commercial middlemen, the number and range of interethnic relations increased con-siderably. This process was further augmented with the government-spon-sored program of land reform of the 1960s and later.

The impact of land reform on rural society was profound. It dramatically altered the pattern of landholding by breaking up large estates and redis-tributing them among some of the peasants. As the land reform program moved through the various stages of implementation, it soon became ap-parent that the face of rural society would no longer be the same. It is not my purpose here to discuss the merits or shortcomings of the land reform program.[8] It suffices to point out that it adversely affected the landless peasants, agricultural laborers, and village proletariat, who had enjoyed no previous rights of cultivation. Land was redistributed only to peasants who had established rights of cultivation (*nasaq*) on landowners' property. Con-sequently, a substantial number of poor peasants were pushed off the land and migrated to major urban centers in search of employment. For similar or different reasons, other rural residents also were part of the cityward migration of the 1960s or 1970s.[9]

The high rate of migration from rural to urban areas affected ethnicity in an important way. The urban centers, particularly Tehran, emerged as major melting pots where different ethnic groups were regularly found in interaction with one another. Not only were both the rural and the urban societies brought into closer contacts, but a new and more sustained min-gling of ethnic groups was in evidence. Nevertheless, the poor peasant migrants in shantytowns or low-income communities tended to reside in residential clusters with people of similar ethnic backgrounds. In other words, amid a multiethnic urban society some semblance of ethnic unity was preserved in the residential patterns of poor migrants. This situation did not generally extend to the economically better-off migrants who se-lected their homes irrespective of the ethnic element.

Another process that began about the same time as agricultural com-mercialization was the effort toward centralization of the state. This de-velopment was initiated by the Qajars, but it saw its fullest progress under the Pahlavis, especially the latter part of reign of Mohammad Reza Shah (1941–1979). Centralization of the state had important consequences for the ethnic composition of both rural and urban areas. The impact can be seen in at least three distinct but related areas.

In the first place, centralization of state power brought the government

[8]For a full discussion, see Eric Hooglund, *Land and Revolution in Iran, 1960–1980* (Austin: University of Texas Press, 1982), pp. 36–122.

[9]For more details, see Farhad Kazemi, *Poverty and Revolution in Iran: The Migrant Poor, Urban Marginality, and Politics* (New York: New York University Press, 1980), pp. 32–45.

into far greater contact than ever before with the ethnically controlled regions. This further increased possibilities for conflicts and dissension between distinct ethnic groups and the central government. For example, the Pahlavis on different occasions found themselves in conflict with the Arabic-speaking population of Khuzestan, the Bakhtiaris in Isfahan region, and the Kurds in Kurdistan. The first Pahlavi monarch, Reza Shah, ensured control over ethnically distinct provinces by appointing governors with an ethnic identification that was different from that of the region's dominant population. This was used as a device to watch over and report potentially seditious developments in these regions.

Second, establishment of a national standing army by Reza Shah in 1925 provided a regular military force to support the state's activities. The standing army was based on a program of universal male conscription and extensive reserve units. Service in the armed forces affected peasants and other conscripts in several ways. The training program regularly exposed ethnic groups and individuals to one another under a united national banner. The literacy program taught conscripts reading and writing in the dominant language, Persian, reducing linguistic differentiation. On the whole, then, service in the armed forces had an important and incremental impact on the ethnic identity of the rural conscripts. The extent to which military service muted ethnic differentiation is a matter of conjecture. Similar situations have sometimes resulted in a heightening of ethnic consciousness, not its reduction. As some observers point out, "Increasing ethnic *political* consciousness frequently occurs at the same time that 'objective' differences among ethnic groups are declining."[10] There are clearly other factors that are relevant and may intervene in this relationship. It is apparent, however, that military service raised ethnic interactions of the peasant conscripts to a new and higher level. This is another instance where state decisions and actions have a direct bearing on ethnic relations.

The impact of centralization of the state's power can especially be seen in the attempts at economic integration of a region, where a certain ethnic group predominates, into the national economic system. The war-torn province of Khuzestan is an example. With the discovery of oil in Khuzestan in the early twentieth century and the increasing importance of the oil industry in the nation's economy, ethnic unity of the province slowly eroded. The Arab-speaking population working in the oil fields or related industry were for the most part integrated into the dominant Persian ethnic groups. Furthermore, the requirements of operating the vast petroleum operation necessitated migration of Persian-speaking managers and skilled workers

---

[10]James Scarrit and William Safran, "The Relationship of Ethnicity to Modernization and Democracy: A Reassessment of of the Issues," *International Studies Notes* 10 (Summer 1983): 17, and Cynthia Enloe, *Police, Military, and Ethnicity: Foundations of State Power* (New Brunswick, N.J.: Transaction Books, 1980), pp. 1–27.

from other parts of the country to Khuzestan. The fact that the substantial majority of the Arabic-speaking population of the province were Shi'ites facilitated the integration process.[11]

To some extent, this Shi'ite factor and the national economic integration of the region were the reasons that no fifth column emerged in Khuzestan after the Iraqi invasion of Iran in September 1980. The invasion and the subsequent destruction of much of the province's industry created a huge number of refugees who were settled to the north. The war may have inadvertently facilitated further integration of the Arabic-speaking people with the Persian-speaking population. This process will probably continue and in two or more generations will result in even further integration into the dominant ethnic group.

Expressions of Dissent

Peasants and villagers in Iran have generally been relatively quiescent in the past century. During this period, peasant uprisings and collective violence have been the exception rather than the norm.[12] Nevertheless, there have been expressions of peasant discontent in response to political pressures, economic inequality, and perceived injustices. My concern here is restricted to expressions of dissent in which the ethnic factor has played some role. Four types of dissent are worth examining in more detail.

Social Banditry

Peasant protests in the form of feeding, hiding, and protecting local outlaws took place on several occasions. In the words of Eric Hobsbawm, these "bandits" are "peasant outlaws whom the lord and state regard as criminals, but who remain within peasant society, and are considered by their people as heroes, as champions, avengers, fighters for justice, perhaps even leaders of liberation, and in any case as men to be admired, helped and supported."[13] They are usually found in rural precapitalist agricultural societies "before the poor have reached political consciousness or acquired more effective methods of social agitation."[14] Social banditry is important

[11]It is important to stress the Shi'ite factor in Khuzestan. Unfortunately several academic and journalistic accounts have incorrectly identified the Arabic-speaking population of Khuzestan as Sunni Muslims (e.g., Akbar Aghajanian, "Ethnic Inequality in Iran: An Overview," *International Journal of Middle Eastern Studies* 15 [May 1983]: 212).

[12]Farhad Kazemi and Ervand Abrahamian, "The Nonrevolutionary Peasantry of Modern Iran," *Iranian Studies* 11 (1978): 259–303.

[13]Eric Hobsbawm, *Bandits* (New York: Dell, 1969), p. 13.

[14]Ibid., p. 23.

in raising peasant consciousness and the desire for a more just and egalitarian social system, but this form of protest is limited because "it protests not against the fact that peasants are poor and oppressed, but against the fact that they are sometimes excessively poor and oppressed."[15]

During the period under discussion, there emerged in Iran a few social bandits of note who attempted to redress perceived wrongs to peasants and rural inhabitants. As expected, the bandits received their primary, if not only, support from among the peasants who had the same ethnic identification they did. The enemy was almost invariably the state or its agents. In the end, the bandits were defeated by state forces through a number of planned and concerted efforts.

Two acts of banditry in which the leaders gained special notoriety require brief examinations. One took place in the 1920s in the Kurdish region, the other in 1957 in the Baluchistan province. In the Kurdish area, the banditry was led for several years by Isma'il Aqa Simtqu (Simko) in the region of Lake Urumiyeh. Simtqu had many active and passive supporters among the impoverished rural inhabitants and had successfully expanded the geographic area of his activity. The government's effort to curb Simtqu through local Kurdish chiefs was unsuccessful. Simtqu inflicted heavy casualties on the forces of the local chiefs and found refuge among his supporters. Regular rampages by Simtqu continued until he was eventually defeated by the central government's forces in 1922. Simtqu fled to Turkey but returned intermittently to resume his activities. These came to an end with Simtqu's murder in 1930.[16]

The Simtqu affair raises an interesting issue concerning ethnic support for social banditry. It is clear that Simtqu's support came from Kurdish peasants and tribesmen who saw him as a liberator from their misery and an avenger of their rights. This support was deep enough to allow Simtqu to operate against active resistance for so many years. However, he was simultaneously attacked by Kurdish tribal chiefs and others of the same ethnic background. Some of the bloodiest encounters Simtqu had involved battles with fellow Kurds. The obvious conclusion is that universal ethnic support cannot necessarily be expected for social bandits. In social banditry, as in other acts of protest, one can expect both support and resistance from the same ethnic group. Ethnicity alone is not a sufficient explanation for peasant support of social banditry.

The banditry in Baluchistan, led by the notorious brigand Dad Shah, reveals a similar division among the local Baluchi population. Dad Shah

---

[15]Ibid., p. 24.

[16]For various accounts of Simtqu's activities, see Donald Wilber, *Riza Shah Pahlavi: The Resurrection and Reconstruction of Iran, 1878–1944* (Hicksville, N.Y.: Exposition, 1975), pp. 59, 61, 66, 100, and A. R. Ghassemlou, "Kurdistan in Iran," in *People without a Country: The Kurds and Kurdistan*, ed. G. Chaliand (London: Zed, 1980), p. 117.

and his twenty or thirty followers attacked and killed a small group of American and Iranian employees of the Point Four program in the remote Baluchistan province in March 1957. The bandits found refuge and hid among the Baluchi peasants near the Iran-Pakistan border. For several months the Iranian government tried unsuccessfully to capture the brigands. It eventually enlisted the support of local Baluchi tribes and distributed arms to them. On January 1958, after a long and bloody confrontation, Dad Shah and his brother were killed and the episode came to a formal end. It is clear that in the Baluchi banditry, as in the Kurdish case, both support and opposition were advanced from the same ethnic unit.[17]

Conversion and Messianism

Expressions of dissent, couched in vague or explicit religious terms and confined to one group or category of population, have sometimes existed in the rural areas. Their significance lies both in their persistence over time and in their attraction to some groups. One must be cautious, however, in attributing greater importance to them as an ethnic phenomenon than the available evidence warrants.

Two examples are worth noting. One is the conversion of segments of Iranian Jews to Babism and later Baha'ism in the nineteenth and twentieth centuries. The reasons and underlying conditions for this conversion from one religious minority to another have not been fully explored. There is, however, evidence to support the occurrence of this conversion phenomenon among both rural and urban Jews of Iran at certain periods. Because persecution of Babis and Baha'is in Iran has been severe on many occasions, the conversion raises important issues and questions for further study.[18]

The other example concerns the appearance of millennial and apocalyptic movements in the countryside and the emergence of the messiah figure, the Mahdi. The widespread belief of Shi'ites in the return of the Mahdi to prepare the world for the Day of Judgment has occasionally led to strong mass views that the world will come to an end at a designated predeter-

---

[17]Details of the Dad Shah episode can be found in *Ettela'at*, March 26–31, 1957; April 1, 1957; and January 9–11, 1958.

[18]Walter Fischel, "The Bahai Movement and Persian Jewry," *Jewish Review* 1 (March 1943): 47–55, and Hayyim Cohen, *The Jews of the Middle East, 1860–1972* (New York: Wiley, 1973), pp. 162–63.

mined time and prompted large mass gatherings awaiting the signs of the Mahdi's arrival.[19] These feelings have often been expressed in times of severe economic, political, or natural disasters, when conditions of life have visibly worsened.

A corollary development of this broader issue has been the intermittent appearance in the villages of Iran of a phenomenon referred to popularly as the "thirteenth Imam." Although the idea of a "thirteenth Imam" is anathema in official and mainstream Twelver Shi'ism, it has nevertheless persisted among some of the illiterate villagers in various parts of the country. A typical "thirteenth Imam" pretender goes from one village to another performing "miracles" and attracting followers. Feeding local superstitious beliefs and legitimizing his role by vague appeals to popular Shi'ite notions, the "thirteenth Imam" could gather a nucleus of antiestablishment supporters. Whenever the followers have expanded beyond a certain size, the government and organized clerical establishments have joined hands to put the potential threat down and to dismember the group.

Membership in Radical Organizations

Radical organizations and parties that espouse dramatic change and restructuring of the social order appeal to ethnic and minority groups. The social base of these organizations has traditionally centered in the urban areas, but there have been occasional inroads into the rural sector among the peasants. Abrahamian points out that the Tudeh (Communist) Party "made persistent efforts to attract rural masses. Party branches, journals, and newspapers frequently discussed agricultural programs. City cadres went into the countryside to recruit villagers and agitate against landlords."[20] The Tudeh ultimately failed to organize the countryside, but it did attract some peasant members, especially in the Gilan and Mazandaran provinces.[21]

The Tudeh's relative success among the peasants of the Caspian littoral underlines the broader appeal of this radical organization to certain ethnic

---

[19]For a good discussion of Shi'ite messianism, see Abdulaziz Sachedina, *Islamic Messianism: The Idea of the Mahdi in Twelver Shi'ism* (Albany: State University of New York Press, 1981), pp. 150–78. See also Vladimir Minorsky, "Iran: Opposition, Martyrdom, and Revolt," in *Unity and Variety in Muslim Civilization*, ed. von Grunebaum (Chicago: University of Chicago Press, 1955), pp. 183–206. Note also that the Akhbari tradition of Shi'ism persisted among some of the Arabic-speaking population of Khuzestan, while the Persian-speaking groups adhered to the Usuli tradition.

[20]Abrahamian, *Iran between Two Revolutions*, p. 375.

[21]Ibid., p. 382.

groups. Although the party espoused a class-based movement and had a diverse ethnic membership, it nevertheless held special appeal for groups of linguistic or religious minorities. The Azeri-speaking population and the Christian communities of Armenians and Assyrians played significant roles in the Tudeh Party and its activities.[22] Much of the minority membership of the Tudeh was concentrated in towns and cities, but Azeri-speaking peasants and Assyrian and Armenian villagers supported the party too.

On several occasions in the Tudeh congresses and conferences, minority members expressed ethnic sentiments, highlighting their sense of discrimination and oppression in Iranian society. In fact, some Azeri activists formed a separate communist organization in 1945, Ferqeh-e Demokrat, and specifically appealed to the Azeri ethnic sentiments in their plans and programs.[23] The ethnic factor, then, was an issue that could not be so easily dismissed among the Communists in Iran. The historical irony of this situation underlines the persistent role of the ethnic/minority issue among individuals who belonged to a radical organization that at least in theory transcended the ethnic factor and couched its principles in universalistic terms.

Autonomous Drives and Rebellion

Uprisings and rebellions by peasants and rural-dwellers are among the most obvious expressions of dissent. On some occasions and under certain conditions in the period under investigation, Iranian peasants participated in rebellions. For example, the drives for autonomy in the two adjacent northwest provinces of Azerbaijan and Kurdistan betwen 1945 and 1946 enjoyed Azeri and Kurdish peasant support. In both cases a superior external power and the weakness of the central state were important to the initial success of the movements. These drives based their forces on the ethnic support of the Azeri- and Kurdish-speaking population. Much of the movements' propaganda was directed to the grievances and real or perceived ethnic discrimination. Ethnic appeal was used, then, as a means of mobilizing support for the movements' demands and goals.[24]

The rebellion in the Gilan province led by the Jangali movement in 1915–1921 was a significant peasant uprising of the modern period. The specifics

[22]Ibid., p. 385.
[23]Ibid., pp. 398–415.
[24]George Lenczowski, *Russia and the West in Iran, 1918–1948* (Ithaca, N.Y.: Cornell University Press, 1949), and William Eagleton, Jr., *The Kurdish Republic of 1946* (London: Oxford University Press, 1963).

of the Jangali rebellion are beyond the scope of this paper,[25] but we should point out here that the peasants of Gilan, who spoke primarily the Gilaki dialect of Iranian, responded favorably to the Jangalis and provided the rank-and-file support for the movement. When the Jangalis' circle of supporters increased substantially, the government sent troops to the area to quell the uprising. The rebellion was eventually crushed in 1921, and its leader, Kuchak Khan, who had fled the onslaught, froze to death in the mountains of Gilan.

In the drives for autonomy of Kurdistan and Azerbaijan and in the peasant rebellion of Gilan, the ethnic element was a present and conscious force. The three movements appealed to primordial sentiments and were able to successfully recruit peasants into their ranks. The ethnic factor facilitated popular mobilization and provided additional direction and focus to the movements.

Concluding Remarks

It is clear that it is difficult to pinpoint the ethnic factor as an independent force above and beyond the larger environment within which it functions. The single conclusion the author can make unhesitatingly is that ethnicity, or broader group differentiation, is only one of several factors that affects the life of the Iranian peasantry. Ethnicity can be a source of conflict as well as of accommodation. Many other variables in the social system operate side by side in conjunction with the ethnic factor. Beyond this, several concluding remarks and general statements not raised fully in this chapter warrant brief discussion.

Social Class and Urban Settlement Patterns

Low-income rural migrants to urban centers tend to reside in ethnic clusters in shantytowns and low-income communities. This is in contrast to the economically well-off migrants, who reside in various parts of the city with no special regard for the ethnic composition of the quarter. There are occasional exceptions to this pattern, but on the whole it appears that economic and social class positions have priority over ethnicity in this group's decision about where to live in the urban centers. Economic and

[25]The specifics are available in Kazemi and Abrahamian, "Nonrevolutionary Peasantry," pp. 284–293, and Ibrahim Fakhra'i, *Sardar-e Jangal Mirza Kuchak Khan* (Tehran, 1969).

class positions are also operative forces in intermarriage and in interethnic integration. The closer the members of two ethnic groups are in economic and class position, the greater the possibility of intermarriage among their members. This relationship holds particularly among the higher-income-bracket ethnic groups.

Fluidity of Valued Ethnic Background

The relative value of a given ethnicity in the society is subject to change. An ethnic identity may be valued higher at one point in time than in another.[26] Emphasis on a certain ethnic background as a significant form of identification changes in accordance with both the individual and the societal view of its value and importance. Similarly, when a person can claim two or more ethnic descent lines, he may use exclusively the particular descent that is more highly esteemed in the social order. Or the person may opt to use different ethnic identifications according to changing social circumstances.

This use of "situational" ethnicity, as described by Fredrik Barth and others, has to do with how an individual adapts his ethnicity to changing situations. Emphasizing the criterion of boundary and its maintenance in defining ethnic groups, Barth maintains correctly that critical elements in the definition of ethnicity are "not the overt, 'objective' differences" that distinguish one group from another, but rather the "socially relevant factors" that are "diagnostic for membership" and allow for "continuing dichotomization between members and outsiders."[27] Situational ethnicity, then, entails the individual's use of tactical, strategic, or rational calculations in ethnic identification. Some maintain, however, that situational ethnicity "remains limited by the reality of objective ethnic identification."[28] Although this may have some relevance, John Armstrong is fundamentally correct when he says, "the primary characteristics of ethnic boundaries is attitudinal. In their origins and in their most fundamental effects, ethnic bound-

---

[26]E.g., Arab ethnic descent used to have a position in Iran that was valued more greatly than in the past few decades.

[27]Fredrik Barth, "Introduction," in *Ethnic Groups and Boundaries: The Social Organization of Culture Difference*, ed. F. Barth (Boston: Little, Brown, 1969), pp. 14–15. Barth points out: "The critical focus of investigation from this point of view becomes the ethnic *boundary* that defines the group, not the cultural stuff that it encloses" (p. 15). See also two outstanding recent works on the subject: Donald L. Horowitz, *Ethnic Groups in Conflict* (Berkeley: University of California Press, 1985), and Ali Banuazizi and Myron Weiner, eds., *The State, Religion, and Ethnic Politics: Afghanistan, Iran, and Pakistan* (Syracuse, N.Y.: Syracuse University Press, 1986).

[28]See Scarrit and Safran, "Relationship of Ethnicity to Modernization and Democracy," p. 17, discussing the revisionist school of ethnicity and modernization.

ary mechanisms exist in the minds of their subjects rather than as lines on a map or norms in a rule book."[29]

Ethnic Integration and Boundary Maintenance

The maintenance of boundaries is an important feature in the interaction of the Azeri- and Persian-speaking groups. The Turkish-speaking Azerbaijanis are "a well-integrated linguistic minority" in Iran.[30] The Azerbaijanis make up close to one-third of the country's population and are located not only in the northwest region but also in other major towns and cities. Through a long process of interaction, the Azerbaijanis (especially those residing in Tehran and other major cities) have assimilated with the Persian-speaking population. Intermarriage and other forms of contacts between the groups have been frequent.[31] The common Shi'a religious background has served as a significant facilitator in the assimilation of the two separate linguistic groups. The sectarian identity is an important factor because similar assimilation has not developed between the Persian-speaking Shi'ites and Turkish (non-Azeri)-speaking Sunnis.

In spite of this integration of the two groups, the Azerbaijanis tenaciously preserve and adhere to their linguistic distinctiveness. In a gathering of Azerbaijanis, when non-Turkish speaking countrymen are not present, Turkish is almost invariably used as the language of communication. This phenomenon supports Barth's observation that the persistence of boundaries and the "continuing dichotomization between members and outsiders" are critical factors in an analysis of ethnic identity.[32]

State Persecution and Persistence of Ethnic Identity

The state's role in the politics of ethnicity has generally been viewed in the literature from two different perspectives: the state as the manager in society or as the controller in society. According to the first perspective, the state is viewed as the mediator of intergroup conflicts and as the neutral

---

[29]John Armstrong, *Nations before Nationalism* (Chapel Hill: University of North Carolina Press, 1982), p. 7. Barth's discussion of the change of identity of Southern Pathan to Baluch in the Afghanistan-Pakistan border area is relevant to the above discussion. See Fredrik Barth, "Pathan Identity and Its Maintenance," in *Ethnic Groups*, pp. 117–134.

[30]Patricia Higgins, "Minority-State Relations in Contemporary Iran," *Iranian Studies* 17 (Winter 1984): 59.

[31]The Turkish-speaking dynasties that ruled Iran for many generations contributed to the integration process.

[32]Barth, "Introduction," p. 14.

manager of ethnic-group differences. The second perspective views the state and its institutions as being utilized by a dominant section of the population "to coerce compliance on the part of the community at large."[33] The second perspective—the state as controller—is a closer approximation of the Iranian state's role in the politics of ethnicity. In the more extreme cases, formalized state persecutions of ethnic groups usually occurred on religious grounds. These persecutions have not succeeded in destroying the intragroup solidarity and ethnic identity.[34]

Multiethnic Participation in Iranian Nationalist Causes

This discussion of ethnicity would not be complete without mentioning the regular pattern of multiethnic participation in major Iranian national events and causes. The various linguistic, religious, or other groups that make up the Iranian nation-state have contributed significantly to promotion of common goals and aspirations. Whenever there has been a consensus on ultimate goals, the ethnic groups have taken joint action to bring about the collective good.[35] This has been demonstrated repeatedly in the events of the Tobacco Regie of 1891–1892, the Constitutional Revolution of 1905–1911, the oil nationalization of 1951–1953, and the revolution of 1978–1979.

Ethnicity, therefore, must be viewed in the broader context of a nation's history and culture. The basically unchanged territorial state of Iran over the past two centuries and its long history and influential culture have affected and molded the country's inhabitants. Consequently, attitudes and sentiments that transcend ethnic diversity and group differentiation have also developed and been nourished in this environment. These attitudes exist side by side with those that emphasize ethnic particularism and differences. The appearance of one or the other of these twin forces depends on political and economic realities of the period and other relevant domestic and international factors.

[33]Donald Rothchild and Victor Olorunsola, "Managing Competing State and Ethnic Claims," in *State Versus Ethnic Claims: African Policy Dilemmas*, ed. D. Rothchild and V. Olorunsola (Boulder, Colo.: Westview, 1983), p. 5.

[34]As Enloe points out, "if one group is systematically excluded from avenues of mobility, its members will come together out of a sense of common deprivation" (see Cynthia Enloe, *Ethnic Conflict and Political Development* [Boston: Little, Brown, 1973], p. 179).

[35]See Enloe's similar observation in ibid., p. 183.

13

Khomeini's Policy toward Ethnic and Religious Minorities

David Menashri

In the years that have elapsed since the revolution of 1979, followers of Ayatollah Ruhollah Khomeini's doctrine have been steadily reinforcing their control, to become the exclusive rulers of the Islamic Republic of Iran. Under their rule, Khomeini's doctrine is considered the sole legitimate interpretation of the Prophet Muhammad's legacy. Accordingly, it is seen as the only appropriate basis for policy-making in foreign and domestic matters, including issues relating to ethnic and religious minorities. In practice, however, the conduct of the Islamic republic's policies has been significantly influenced by political and pragmatic considerations. This chapter focuses on the ideological foundations of the regime's attitude toward minorities and on its policies toward them during its first eight years in power—specifically the Kurds, the ethnic minority that has been waging the most active, continuous, and violent struggle against the regime, and the Jews, a tolerated minority that has been seeking to find ways to live in peace alongside the revolution.

Ethnic Minorities

Although the myth of Iran as a unified entity with a political history of twenty-five centuries is commonly accepted, the reality is quite different. Iran has always been a multicultural society divided into a number of socioeconomic units—sedentary agricultural and urban units in the central plateau, surrounded by nomadic and seminomadic units inhabiting the peripheral areas. These units include the largest—though in many ways unique—minority of Azeri Turks in the northwest, the Kurds in the west,

215

the Arabs of Khuzistan in the southwest, the Baluchs in the southeast, and the Turkomans in the northeast. Almost half the population of Iran is made up of minority groups.[1] Despite extensive internal migration, the great majority of Kurds still live in Kurdistan, Baluchs in Baluchistan, and so on. This is also true of the tribal groups of the Qashqa'i, the Bakhtiari, the Luri, and others. The modernization process of the last century has accomplished no more than a surface integration of minority groups and has not prevented continued backwardness in the periphery.[2]

The ethnic minorities differ from one another in their historical developments, in the history of their efforts to achieve autonomy, in their religious affiliation (to the Sunni or Shi'ite sects of Islam), in their political strength, and in their active struggles against the Khomeini regime, but several common denominators make them a serious problem for the regime. The minority groups are concentrated mainly in border areas and have ties with parallel ethnic groups across the border. (The Arabs are also located in an economically sensitive region.) All have fostered separatist movements, some of which led to the establishment of independent states for short periods of time (such as the Kurdish republic of Mahabad and the Turkish republic of Azerbaijan). In all these groups the subnational local-ethnic loyalty overshadows the national, let alone supranational, loyalty that Khomeini preaches. All feel social and economic deprivation and are indignant because the process of development has bypassed their areas. No less serious is the fact that these groups are largely Sunni (including most of the Kurds, the Baluchs, and the Turkomen), which clearly complicates the interrelationship between them and the Shi'ite regime.

After the fall of the Shah, all the ethnic minority groups (except for the Turkish Azeris) demanded autonomy, as they have always done whenever the central government seemed too weak to keep a firm grip on their regions. Khomeini's response was decisive and unequivocal. He vigorously denied the existence of ethnic or Muslim-religious minority groups within the Islamic community and consequently refused to guarantee them any specific rights. He regarded the very raising of such demands as an "imperialist plot" aimed at dividing and weakening the Muslim world in order to exploit it. His statement of December 1979, following approval of the new constitution, which disregarded the existence of such minority groups, is typical:

Sometimes the word minorities is used to refer to people such as the Kurds, Lurs, Turks, Persians, Baluchis, and such. These people should not be called

---

[1]Different and often contradictory statistics on ethnic minority groups are found in the literature. For a rough estimate of numbers in 1977, see Patricia J. Higgins, "Minority-State Relations in Contemporary Iran," *Iranian Studies* 17 (Winter 1984):48.

[2]For a historical review of the monarchy's failure to integrate minority groups into the state, see Leonard M. Helfgott, "The Structural Foundations of the National Minority Problem in Revolutionary Iran," *Iranian Studies* 13, nos. 1–4 (1980):195–214.

minorities, because this term assumes that there is a difference between these brothers. In Islam, such a difference has no place at all. There is no difference between Muslims who speak different languages, for instance, the Arabs or the Persians. It is very probable that such problems have been created by those who do not wish the Muslim countries to be united. . . . They create the issues of nationalism, of pan-Iranism, pan-Turkism, and such isms, which are contrary to Islamic doctrines. Their plan is to destroy Islam and the Islamic philosophy.[3]

Before Khomeini came to power, he ignored the existence of ethnic minority groups. In his books *Kashf al-Asrar* (Revealing of the secrets), *Touzih al-Masa'el* (Clarification of the questions), and *Hukumate Islami* (The Islamic government), in which he discusses the complexity of sociological, theological, economic, and political problems, there is no mention of the ethnic minority groups. There has also been a consistent refusal to acknowledge their existence since the rise of the new regime.

If the regime ever refers to the problems of ethnic minorities, it is in terms of their religious affiliation—as Sunnis. But this distinction still puts these groups at a disadvantage, as Sunnis can only enjoy an inferior position in a Shi'ite society. Shi'ites regard Sunnis as only one level above heretics (kafirun) and far below the level of the "true believers" (mu'minun). They are generally regarded as the *amma* (common people), while the Shi'ites are the *khassa* (people of distinction). A careful study of Khomeini's early writings reveals the profound hatred the Shi'ites have for Sunnis and their feeling of superiority toward them. In his *Kashf al-Asrar*, Khomeini claims that by mounting the *"fitna* of Karbala" (which resulted in the massacre of the sons of Ali in A.D. 680), the Sunnis caused "the greatest disaster" of Islam and changed the course of Islamic history.[4] He not only condemns the first caliphs for usurping the rule that rightly belonged to Ali, but also accuses them of conspiring to annihilate Ali's dynasty.[5] One chapter in the book is devoted to Abu Bakr's opposition to the Qur'an ("Mokhalefate Abu-Bakr Ba Nasse Qur'an"), another attributes a similar sin to Umar.[6] He also attacks the Umayyad and Abbasid dynasties as "the worst [*badtarin*] and most usurpatory (*zalemanetarin*) regime" in history.[7] Sunni clerics in the Arab world also receive their share of criticism today.

Since the revolution, Khomeini and his associates have changed their tone. Adhering to pan-Islamic ideology, they are now more inclined to point

---

[3]Radio Tehran, December 17, 1979—British Broadcasting Corporation (BBC), Summary of World Broadcasts, Middle East and Africa, December 19.

[4]Ruhollah al-Musavi al-Khomeini, *Kashf al-Asrar* (Tehran, 1979), p. 109 (first published in the early 1960s).

[5]Ibid., pp. 285–286.

[6]Ibid., pp. 144–147 and 147–150, respectively.

[7]Ibid., pp. 285–286.

out the common ground between Sunnis and Shi'ites than the differences between them. President Muhammad Ali Khameneh'i's message to Sunni clerics from Khorasan in October 1983 demonstrates this change in attitude: "We have the same Qur'an, the same Ka'ba, the same [religious] obligations and the same prayers. . . . Despite the marginal differences between us, that which unifies us is great."[8] One cannot ignore, however, the large number of anti-Sunni sentiments that still pervade Shi'ite Iran. This was manifested, for example, in one of the president's speeches in December 1983. He intended to explain to Sunni clerics that there are no differences between Sunnis and Shi'ites, but in the process he gave way to a fierce attack on the Umayyad and Abbasid dynasties for initiating the schism. In so doing, he exposed the yawning chasm between these two Muslim sects.[9] Anyone who witnessed the mourning procession of the Ashura, accompanied by acts of self-flagellation and a display of intense religious feeling, will find it easy to understand the hatred the Shi'ites have toward their Sunni brothers.

Since the revolution, these factors have undoubtedly retained their importance. Yet the primary factor shaping the regime's attitude toward Sunnis has not been their ethnic identity or their religious affiliation, but rather the inherent danger they presented to the stability and territorial integrity of the Islamic republic. Their activities against the revolutionary regime, their ties with internal opposition movements, their connections with the opposition in exile, and foreign influences in their areas have made them, in the eyes of the regime, a threat to the revolution. Just as the regime regarded the political opposition as an enemy of Islam (because it regarded itself as being "the Islam"), it viewed minority opponents of the regime as "enemies of Allah" and not as seekers of autonomy. This attitude is illustrated by the fact that propagandists of the regime refer to the Kurdish (Sunni) religious leader Izz al-Din (Glory of Religion) as Zed al-Din (Anti-Religion). When he outlawed the Kurdish Democratic Party (KDP) in August 1979, Khomeini labeled it "a party of Satan" and an "enemy of Islam."[10]

In the first eight years of the Islamic republic, the Kurdish struggle against the regime was the most violent and comprehensive. The Kurds wanted to achieve their goal of autonomy before the regime was able to stabilize itself; the government wanted not only to suppress their struggle but also to discourage other minority groups from following suit.

During the first two years of the Islamic republic, relations between the Kurds and the regime alternated between periods of negotiations and periods of violence. In each round of talks, initial hopes of settling the dispute invariably faded when just before the concluding stage of negotiations the

[8]*Ettela'at*, October 8, 1983.

[9]*Kayhan*, December 31, 1983.

[10]*International Herald Tribune*, August 20 and 23, 1979; *Daily Telegraph*, August 20, 1979; *The Guardian*, August 20, 23, and 25, 1979.

Kurds realized that the regime had no intention of honoring its promises. This realization led time and again to new waves of violence. The Kurds declared that they would not give up their fundamental claims for full autonomy and self-rule in all Kurdish territories, while the regime refused to go beyond a strictly limited and mainly cultural autonomy. Moreover, the government regarded the total disarmament of the Kurds as a sine qua non to any agreement. Fearing the loss of the only effective leverage they had against the regime, the Kurds not only refused to disarm, but also demanded total withdrawal of the Revolutionary Guards from all Kurdish regions and a promise that the army would not enter Kurdish towns.[11]

Whatever hopes the Kurds and the Islamic regime may have had initially for a mutual accommodation, such hopes completely faded by the time the new regime was in its second or third year. Periods of violence now alternated with periods of uneasy tranquillity during which both sides prepared for yet another confrontation. The government was mainly concerned with postponing any dialogue on autonomy until after the war with Iraq was over and the revolution was stabilized, and in the meantime it refused to grant any concessions. The Kurds, for their part, persisted in their demands. Late in 1980 the KDP, the most active Kurdish faction, lost faith in the government's willingness "to negotiate seriously." Its leader, Abdul Rahman Qasemlou, stated that the Kurds "no longer have any illusions about Khomeini."[12] Consequently, in 1980 and 1981 the KDP strengthened its ties with the regime's most violent opponents, Mujahidine Khalq, with the declared aim of forming a united front.[13] Even more critical was the KDP's decision in the autumn of 1980 to intensify its guerrilla warfare against the regime and its categorical refusal to join the "national liberation war" against Iraq. In a statement published on October 1, 1980, Qasemlou urged Tehran to "recognize the principle of autonomy for Kurdistan and withdraw its troops from the province," before it asked "Kurdish guerrillas to turn their weapons against the Iraqi invaders."[14]

After two years of often violent confrontation, however, the balance in all ethnic fronts shifted in the government's favor. Tension had considerably abated since the outbreak of the Gulf war, but both the regime and the ethnic minorities remained consistent in their opposing stands.

Strong motivation and intimate knowledge of the terrain gave the Kurds an advantage in their military operations against the regime, but the passage

---

[11]For such contradictory positions at that phase, see, e.g., *Kayhan*, April 16, 17, and 20, 1980.

[12]See interviews with Qasemlou in *Le Monde*, December 13, 1980; *Al-Hawadith*, April 3, 1981.

[13]According to Qasemlou, ties between the two movements had already grown closer since the approval of the constitution in December 1979 (see *Al-Hawadith*, April 3, 1981).

[14]*Le Monde*, December 13, 1980.

of time also exposed their weaknesses, the greatest of which was their internal divisiveness.[15] And there was no way to hide their great inferiority in number of troops and the fact that they did not have control over their supply lines. The defeat of the Kurds in the big cities during the first two years of the republic dictated the nature of the future struggle: Kurdish strategy sought to control the mountain passes and strategic routes, while the strategy of the government was to wipe out one Kurdish stronghold after another. The struggle became less spectacular, but it was nonetheless hard fought, violent, and costly to both sides.

Spokesmen for Kurdish groups presented a gloomy picture of their situation. In November 1980, Qasemlou stated that Kurdistan was worse off under Khomeini than it had been under the Shah. The Revolutionary Guards were killing children and old people and had burned women alive; they were, he said, "even worse" than the Tartars and Mongols.[16] In October 1981 Qasemlou said his people were "experiencing difficult and trying times."[17] The Kurdish religious leader, Izz al-Din Husayni, asserted in January 1982 that the economic sanctions of the government had left the children short of milk, the sick and wounded short of medical supplies, and the peasants without fuel. The Kurds, he added, were going "through a very difficult moment in their history."[18] A similar description was given by Ja'far Shafi, one of the leaders of the Komaleh faction.[19] Nevertheless, all Kurdish groups vowed to continue their struggle.

The regime appeared keen to reduce tension over the Kurdish question both because of the Kurds' presence close to the Iraqi front and because of the cooperation of some Kurdish factions with Iraq. At the same time, the regime sought to delay dealing with the root of the issues until after the war. Using the carrot-and-stick method, it tried to convince antiregime Kurdish groups to lay down their arms. To achieve this goal it also labored to enlist the help of Kurdish *ulama* to bring the Kurds over to the side of the revolution. Government spokesmen repeatedly stressed that those refusing to lay down their arms would be fought to the end, while those who dissociated themselves from the opposition leaders would be treated with the forgiveness and mercy "characteristic of the Islamic regime."[20] Partly

---

[15]For the main Kurdish factions and their different policies, see David Menashri, "Iran," in *Middle East Contemporary Survey*, ed. Colin Legum, Haim Shaked, and Daniel Dishon vol. 4, 1979–1980 (New York: Holmes & Meier, 1981), p. 467.

[16]Radio Voice of Iranian Kurdistan, November 16, 1980, Daily Report, Middle East and North Africa Daily Report, November 19. Similarly in interview with *Svenska Dagbladet*, February 25, 1981—Daily Report, March 3.

[17]Radio Voice of Iranian Kurdistan, October 9, 1981—BBC, October 10.

[18]*Le Monde*, January 14, 1982.

[19]Ibid., February 21–22, 1982.

[20]See a typical appeasing statement by *Majlis* speaker Ali Akbar Hashemi Rafsanjani in *Kayhan*, August 28, 1983. A typical threat, voiced by Sayyad Shirazi, commander of the ground forces, is quoted in *Ettela'at*, July 77, 1983. Both "carrot" and "stick" were presented by Sanjaki,

out of tactical considerations aimed at bringing the Kurds closer to the revolution and partly as a demonstration of their concern for Muslim unity, the government sought closer ties with Kurdish Sunni religious leaders. Delegations of Sunni clerics were frequently received by the top leaders of Tehran, where they were assured that their beliefs would be respected and that development projects would be started in their regions. At the same time, they were called on to ensure their people's loyalty to the revolution.[21] Typical of this approach was a speech made by Shaykh Attar, governor of West Azerbaijan, at a seminar of Kurdish Sunni clerics in May 1983: "With your help, we will turn Kurdistan [literally, the land of the Kurds] into a Golestan [a rose garden]...but into a Gurestan [a cemetery] for the messengers of Imperialism."[22]

Expressions of support by Sunni clerics were given prominent media coverage. In a different vein, the regime promised that minority regions would be given priority in its overall development plans.[23]

The minority groups felt the stick, but did not see any significant signs of the carrot. During the first eight years of the regime they were shown no benevolence whatsoever. The constitution stipulates personal equality "regardless of ethnic and tribal origin" but ignores the demands of the ethnic minorities for a recognized autonomous status. It states that only a Shi'ite may be president and that obviously only a Shi'ite may succeed Khomeini as a "leader" (rahbar). And again, when Qasemlou was elected to the Council of Experts formed to finalize the constitution, Khomeini rejected him, saying he was corrupt and "an enemy of Islam."[24] The failure of the regime to take any concrete steps to alleviate poverty in the areas inhabited by minority groups was attributed to its preoccupation with the war and the revolution.

Compared with the Kurds, other ethnic groups continued their struggle only sporadically and on a limited scale, though none abandoned their original goals. The government was successful in keeping ethnic trouble within bounds, but it failed to provide definitive solutions to the ethnic

---

commander of Hamza Seyyed al-Shohada base, *Kayhan*, March 7, 1983, by Sayyad Shirazi, ibid., June 21, 1983, and by Shaykh Attar, governor of West Azerbaijan, as quoted below.

[21]E.g., Prime Minister Mir-Husayn Musavi met with Sunni clerics from Marivan in February 1983 (*Kayhan*, February 16); Rafsanjani met clerics from Kurdistan in June 1983 (ibid., June 11); President Muhammad Ali Khameneh'i met Kurdish clerics in September 1983 (ibid., September 7); Ayatollah Uzma Husayn ali Montazeri and Musavi met Sunni clerics from Baluchistan also in September 1983 (*Kayhan*, September 10 and 11), and both also received Turkoman Sunni clerics in October 1983 (*Ettela'at*, October 3).

[22]*Jumhuriyye Islami*, May 8, 1983.

[23]E.g., Khomeini's speech over Radio Tehran, November 11,—BBC, November 11, 1982; Rafsanjani's speech to Baluchi clerics cited by Radio Tehran, December 6, 1982—BBC, December 8, 1982; and his speech to Kurdish clerics quoted by *Kayhan*, August 28, 1983.

[24]*International Herald Tribune*, August 20 and 23, 1979; *The Guardian*, August 20, 23, and 25, 1979.

problems. While consolidation of the regime enabled it to tighten its control in the peripheral regions and thus to shift the balance in its favor, most of the minority groups managed to establish a degree of de facto autonomy. Large areas of minority regions became "free zones" in which the army and the Revolutionary Guards had no foothold.[25] All in all, the minority groups continued to pose a threat to the authority of the central government.

Religious Minorities

Unlike the ethnic minority groups, who perceived the revolution as an opportunity for self-rule, the religious minority groups were quick to see the need to gain Khomeini's protection and consequently expressed their support for the Islamic regime. Generally speaking, these religious minorities—mainly Jews, Armenians, and Zoroastrians—came to rely on a measure of tolerance and protection extended by Khomeini, in keeping with the traditional attitude of Islam to the *dhimmis*, the non-Muslim protected minorities. They received official recognition as "religious minorities" and were given a place in the *Majlis* (Parliament). Their freedom of worship was not substantially restricted, and their religious holidays were given wide coverage on radio and television. There was no government campaign of incitement or any systematic harassment. This tolerant attitude did not apply to the Baha'is, who were not recognized as a religious minority.

The official tolerance did not preclude individual acts of persecution and even the execution of some of the most prominent minority leaders—among them Habib Alqanayan, head of the Jewish community. However, given the high total of executions of men of the old regime, minority groups were not singled out for death sentences beyond their share in the Shah's establishment. The regime stressed that no one was executed because of religious belief; Alqanayan's execution did not mean that the regime was against Judaism, just as the execution of many Muslim supporters of the former regime did not express antipathy to Islam.[26]

---

[25]The deputy commander of Hamza Seyyed al-Shohada base conceded that in many cases, at least until late in 1982, the Kurdish city of Sardasht could be supplied only by air (*Kayhan*, March 7, 1983). The local gendarmerie commander said in summer 1983 that (only) 80 percent of the routes in the Kurdish zones were controlled by government forces (*Ettela'at*, June 8, 1983).

[26]*Ettela'at*, May 10, 1979; Radio Tehran, May 11, 1979—Daily Report, May 16. Radio Tehran added that religious minorities in Iran "enjoy the highest degree of security" and that there is "no room for worry for our religious compatriots" following Alqanayan's execution. It added that "Alqanayan's sin had nothing to do with the fact that he was a Jew. . . . He was an individual who wished to equate Jewry with Zionism" (Radio Tehran, May 11, 1979—DR, May 16). Meeting with the heads of the Jewish community following the execution, Khomeini stated, "Islam does not differentiate between . . . those who hold different faiths" and added, "We distinguish between the Jewish community and Zionists. Zionism has nothing to do with

At the same time, there was an attempt to make the minority groups conform to norms of personal conduct that the regime thought appropriate for the Islamic republic. On September 29, 1982, in a meeting between the heads of the Revolutionary Courts and minority spiritual leaders, the religious judge Husayni asked the minority groups to respect these norms. Demanding that minority members refrain from consuming alcoholic drinks in public, he described the regime's expectations as follows: "At home the minorities can act according to their customs, but . . . in public places they must conform to norms of the Islamic republic."[27] This advice was carefully adhered to by the minorities, more so than by some of their Muslim compatriots. In the existing revolutionary atmosphere they found it wise not to give the authorities any pretext for harassing them.

While on the surface the relations between the regime and the religious minority groups seem relatively good, at a deeper level relations are much more complex. There is a palpable conflict between the basic Islamic approach of tolerance toward monotheistic faiths and the many passages of invective against Jews, Christians, and Zoroastrians (let alone the Baha'is). In the view of this writer, such speeches and writings reveal the true attitude of the regime toward the minority groups and are therefore indicative of the probable future behavior of the regime and even more so of the masses. The Jewish minority is likely to be the most vulnerable. (On the eve of the revolution there were more than 80,000 Jews in Iran. By the end of 1984, according to most estimations, more than half of them had left the country.)

A careful study of Khomeini's writings before his coming to power reveals an extremist anti-Jewish stand. On the very first page of his *Hukumate Islami* he points out: "Since its inception, the Islamic movement has been afflicted with the Jews, for it was they who first established anti-Islamic propaganda and joined in various stratagems, and as you can see, this activity continues down to our present day."[28] Referring to Muhammad's dealings with the Jews of Medina, Khomeini claims that the Prophet "eliminated" the Jews of Bani Qurayza because they were a "troublesome group, causing corruption in Muslim society and damaging Islam and the Islamic state."[29] In another place he adds: "We see today that the Jews (may God

---

religion" (Radio Tehran, May 15, 1979—DR, May 16). At the same time, the media went on describing Alqanayan as "a Jewish billionaire" and emphasized his being a Jew. See, e.g., *Ettela'at*, May 10, 1979.

[27]*Kayhan*, September 30, 1982; *Ettela'at*, October 23, 1982. See also an interview by the minister of Islamic guidance, Abdul Majid Ma'adikhwa, to the Islamic Republic News Agency, May 29, 1982—BBC, June 1.

[28]Ruhollah Khomeini, *Al-Hukuma al-Islamiyya* (n.p., 1970), p. 7. This and the following quotations are generally based on Hamid Algar's translation, *Islam and Revolution* (Berkeley, Calif.: Mizan, 1981). However, the author of this article preferred translating the *ubtuliyat bi-al-yahud* (in the Arabic version) or *gereitare yahud* (in the Persian version) as "afflicted with the Jews" and not "to contend with them," as Algar did.

[29]Khomeini, *Al-Hukuma al-Islamiyya*, 83.

curse them) have meddled with the text of the Qur'an and have made certain changes in the Qur'an they have printed in the occupied territories [the West Bank and the Gaza Strip]. . . . We must protest and make the people aware that the Jews and their foreign backers are opposed to the very foundations of Islam and wish to establish Jewish domination throughout the world."[30]

An inkling of Khomeini's attitude toward non-Muslims is also revealed in his earlier book, *Touzih al-Masa'el*, which serves as a guide to Muslims in their daily life. In this book he emphasizes the characteristic Shi'a distinction between Muslims who are pure and non-Muslims who are infidels and therefore ritually unclean. According to Khomeini, "an infidel is one who denies Allah. . . . The Infidel's entire body, even his hair and fingernails and [body] secretions, are impure." The child of an infidel parent or grandparent is "impure."[31] It is forbidden to buy products that cannot be purified, such as meat and vegetables, from infidels.[32] Khomeini singles out the prohibition against working for Jews and says that it "is a disgrace" to work under a Jewish foreman, even though it is permissible.[33] Many other invectives are interwoven in his speeches delivered before the revolution, among them criticisms not only of Jews and Judaism as a whole, but also of Iranian Jewry specifically. In a speech in 1973, for example, he blamed Iranian Jews for "actively supporting Israel" and called on the Iranian people to prevent such initiatives "with all their means."[34]

Since the revolution, however, there has been a radical change in Khomeini's pronouncements regarding the Jews. The venomous attacks have given way to more balanced and tolerant statements. Khomeini has repeatedly declared, "We make a distinction between Judaism on the one hand, and Israel and Zionism on the other." Nevertheless, there still are abundant manifestations of anti-Jewish sentiment, not only among the masses but even in the pronouncements of higher government officials. As is the case in the Arab world, the distinction between Jews on the one hand and Israel and Zionism on the other is often blurred. There are many references to Israel as "a handful of Jews" or of its government as "a government of unbelievers, of Jews." For example, Israel's national airline, El Al, is called "a Jewish company." In the same vein, American Jewry is referred to as "Zionists." The confusion can also be retrospective, as evidenced by the expression "the Zionist of Muhammad's time," which is occasionally used.

---

[30]Ibid., p. 121.
[31]Khomeini, *Touzih al-Masa'el* (Clarification of the questions) (Tehran, 1962), p. 18.
[32]Ibid., pp. 324–325.
[33]Ibid., p. 509.
[34]For some of many examples of anti-Jewish expressions in Khomeini's speeches, declarations, and interviews prior to the revolution, see Algar, *Islam and Revolution*, pp. 180, 196.

Examples of this confusion between Jews and Zionists abound. Ayatollah Uzma Husayn Ali Montazeri said in one of his Friday sermons in Qum in December 1979 that Judaism had been racist from its inception and that Zionism is a continuation of "the same Judaism." He concluded that the Zionists of today are equivalent to the Jews of the past, and vice versa.[35] Khomeini himself made a revealing slip in a speech in September 1982. He began by expressing amazement at those who follow in the path of Jesus and saying that they were even worse than the Jews. He then remarked that it was perhaps "impossible to say that there is something worse than the Jews," whereupon he retracted his statement, saying, "I mean the Jews of Israel."[36]

More-direct attacks on Judaism and Iranian Jewry have become commonplace. For example, the *Kayhan* reported that an Israeli battalion bore the brunt of overpowering the anti-Shah mass demonstrations on the bloody Black Friday of September 8, 1978; it added that the "many Iranian Jews" that fought in the ranks of this battalion were members of "the secret defense organization of Iranian Jewry."[37] Or Hujjat al-Islam Muhammad Ali Allahi, writing in the *Ettela'at*, stated that Israel's hostility to Islam is nothing new: "According to the Qur'an testimony, ever since the birth of Islam . . . the corrupt [Jewish] culture . . . a culture of covetousness, a life of usury and interest, treachery, aggression, murder, and sowing divisiveness . . . developed a front against the culture of Islam." He quoted Qur'anic verses to prove that the Jews are the greatest enemies of Islam—for example, "Cursed were the unbelievers of the Children of Israel by the tongue of David, and Jesus, Mary's son; that, for their rebelling and their transgression. They forbade not one another any dishonor that they committed, surely evil were the things they did" (the Sura of the Table, N.82).[38] An example of another sort had to do with an operation mounted in February 1984 during the Gulf war that was given the code name Khaybar, after the Jewish oasis that Muhammad besieged and conquered in A.D. 628. Every Muslim knows the significance of this name and its historical connection with the Jews. To leave no doubts, the president explained in a Friday sermon that "Khaybar" was "in memory of the glorious victories of the warriors of Islam in the days of the Prophet in their struggle against the Jews of that time. . . . [Because] the front opposing us today is a Zionist front, this will serve as a reminder for us of the struggle of Islam against the Jews of Khaybar."[39] Hujjat al-Islam Ali Akbar Hashemi Rafsanjani pointed out a similar con-

[35]*Ettela'at*, December 29, 1979.
[36]*Jumhuriyye Islami*, September 20, 1982.
[37]*Kayhan*, June 12, 1979.
[38]*Ettela'at*, February 28, 1984.
[39]*Kayhan*, February 25, 1984.

nection in a speech in the *Majlis*.[40] In addition, since the revolution, perhaps a dozen Jews have been executed, among them prominent members of the community. Although the regime insisted that they were not sentenced because of their Judaism, the nature of the charges brought against them have been extremely disturbing. Verdicts made public in Iran (and one that was smuggled out of Iran and that reached this writer) reveal that, alongside other charges (mainly of economic offenses), some of them were sentenced for their links with the Zionist movement and Israel. Accusations in such general terms could easily be leveled against many Jews in Iran. Also since the revolution, the Protocols of the Elders of Zion with venomous anti-Semitic caricatures have often been published in Iranian newspapers.[41] A final example of the direct attacks on Judaism and Iranian Jewry is a warning sent to many Jews in Tehran in June 1978, which added greatly to their anxiety. One of them, signed by a group calling itself the National Front of Iran's Young Muslims, read:

> O bloodthirsty people, who suck the blood of each one of us Muslims. You have gathered in our Islamic state, taken away the money from us Muslims by means of interest, theft, and fraud, and send it to the Zionist state of Israel.
>
> You have seized houses, land, stores, and gardens belonging to us Muslims.
>
> Now your golden dreams have come to an end.
>
> You are hereby warned that you must leave this country as soon as possible, otherwise we shall massacre all the Jews from the youngest to the oldest.
>
> Every age needs its Hitler to take care of the people of deceit and eradicate the offspring of the Jews from the earth, so that our brothers in religion in the Arab countries will live in peace.

What emerges is a picture of ideologically and religiously motivated rejection of Jews and Judaism, combined with a measure of tolerance—precarious, to be sure, but so far mostly predominant in practical matters. Practical moderation is reinforced by two further factors. First, by the government, which is fully aware that the Jews do not pose any political threat, that on the contrary, they have proved loyal to the regime. Like the other religious minorities, they publicly supported Khomeini when he was in Paris; they have strictly complied with the regime's instructions and have observed Muslim behavioral norms; they have "contributed" to the finances of the regime, including the war effort; and they have at regular intervals issued statements identifying themselves with the regime and denouncing its opponents. Thus, leaders of the Jewish community have harshly criticized

[40] Ibid., February 26, 1984.

[41] See, e.g., *Imam* (London) 4 (February 1984): 14–15, the article headlined "The Protocols of the Meetings of the Learned Elders of Zion."

Israel and Zionism[42] and even pressured Israel not to publicize the problems of Iranian Jewry.

Second, in keeping with the characteristics of revolutionary movements in transition from opposition to power, Khomeini's ideology changed once he was confronted with the harsh realities of running a state. While in exile he expressed anti-Jewish views, which in the view of this author represented his true feelings and were reinforced by the identification of the Jews with the Shah's regime. But once in power, he could not totally ignore the loyalty of the Jewish minority, and he has also felt a certain obligation to them as part of his responsibilities as a Muslim ruler. Khomeini was trained as a jurist and is juridically minded. Consequently, he has endeavored to base all his policies on Islamic law. His relationship with the religious minorities was also undoubtedly shaped by the Islamic code of law, which prescribes tolerance toward monotheistic religious minority groups.

Thus, in its first years in power, the policy of the Islamic regime toward the Jews of Iran was one of generating hatred against them yet preventing it from being translated into violence, and one of making a distinction between Judaism and Zionism but at the same time systematically blurring the two terms—in short, a combination of instigation and restraint. This was best illustrated by the following. *Jumhuriyye Islami* (the official organ of the Islamic Republican Party) and *Kayhan* both published a lecture in 1986 given in 1971 by the late purported professor Amir Tavakol Kambuziya. It appeared under the title (presumably provided by the editors) "The Art of the Zionists." The whole lecture is a piece of wild agitation against the Jews, from the inception of their history up to the present. It defines them as "a dirty people" and "enemies of mankind" and goes on: "If we really want to visualize all that has been said about Ahriman [the devil in Zoroastrian mythology] we must envision the Jews." By fraud and trickery, according to Kambuziya, they betrayed the peoples among whom they had resided throughout their history. They do not hesitate to destroy mankind (which was the intention of the theories of Freud, for instance) as long as they advance their own targets. From the inception of Islam, the author continues, they have "worked against the Prophet, the Caliphs, and the [Muslim] people." Quoting anti-Jewish verses from the Qur'an and referring to their "recent crimes" in the Middle East, he advises the Iranian people

---

[42] E.g., when the credentials of the Jewish *Majlis* deputy, Khosrow Naqi, were being discussed in the House on February 21, 1982, Naqi declared that he rejected "Israel's right to exist" and regarded it as an "appendage of imperialism" (*Ettela'at*, February 22, 1982). Rabbi Uriel Davoudi, head of the Jewish court, stated at the end of September 1982 that Iranian Jews condemned Israel and that "Israel is not part of us." Referring to the Sabra and Shatila massacre of September 1982, he noted, "The Jewish community [of Iran] condemns all of Israel's actions" (*Kayhan*, September 30, 1982; *Ettela'at*, October 3, 1982). Similar views expressed by Davoud were cited in *Ettela'at*, September 25, 1982, and in the statement by the Jewish students' organization in *Kayhan*, September 19, 1982.

"to recognize their real enemy." Mentioning Hitler's massacre of 6 million Jews, he denounces that action as contradictory to the principles of Islam yet claims that "execution" is the only way to stop these people.

After quoting the lecture in detail, however, the following editorial note is added: "It may be needless to say so, but in fact it is clear from the context, that the professor in using the term Jews . . . is not speaking of the pious followers of this religion. The professor explicitly and frankly distinguishes between Zionists and Jews." In fact, the editors advise the readers to understand the accusations against the Jews as referring to the Zionists only. Nevertheless, whoever reads the lecture is left with no doubt that the author did indeed mean Jews whenever he used that term. Could he have referred to Zionists when writing of the stubborn Jews who made life so hard for Abraham or fought the Prophet Muhammad? From his few references to Zionists it is also clear that Kambuziya was aware of the distinction between the two terms and that therefore when he wrote Jews he meant Jews. Moreover, can the editors really have expected readers to replace the term Jews with Zionists every time the former appears in the text? The very publication of the lecture, fifteen years after it was delivered, and the inclusion of the editorial note, attest to our conclusions stated above.[43]

The dangers to which religious minorities, particularly the Jews, are potentially exposed should therefore not be ignored. A regime that has systematically inflamed mob passions and revolutionary fervor to keep itself alive (as in the case of persecution of the Shah's loyalists, the taking of the American hostages, and the Gulf war) is likely to turn popular wrath against the Jews. At such a time the masses are unlikely to distinguish between Judaism and Zionism. Economic difficulties (aggravated first by the revolution itself, then by the war, and next by the recent decline in oil prices) are likely to incense people against the Jews. Jewish history is rife with anti-Semitic resentment at times of economic distress. The persecution of the Baha'is has set an alarming precedent. After Khomeini's death, the situation is likely to deteriorate. In the meantime, the precarious combination of instigation and restraint continues to mark government policy.

Conclusion

The regime's policy toward ethnic and religious minority groups cannot be divorced from the principles of Khomeini's general policy on internal

[43] The lecture was first published in the literary supplement of *Jumhuriyye Islami*, the official organ of the Islamic Republican Party (*Sahife*, no. 31), and was reprinted in the weekly *Kayhan* (*Kayhan Hava'i*, March 12, 1986).

and external problems. Both manifest not only radical ideology and a revolutionary modus operandi, but also tactical and pragmatic considerations. With regard to both religious minorities and ethnic groups, the regime has appropriated the right to decide who constitutes a minority and who does not. Accordingly, it alone has the prerogative to determine the nature of its relationship with each religious or ethnic group. For those declared "enemies of Allah" (such as the Baha'is and elements of the Kurds) there is no mercy. Ideology legitimizes all forms of violence against them.

If the regime's treatment of ethnic minorities has differed from its treatment of religious minorities, this can be partly attributed to the behavior of the minorities themselves. It has been common practice in modern Iran that in times of crisis, when the central government seems weak, the ethnic minority groups are the first to contest it. Living on the periphery and possessing independent military strength, they regard such times as opportunities to change their status. On the other hand, the largely urban and virtually defenseless religious minority groups have always been dependent on the regime and sought its protection in order to maintain their status. This explains why in the Islamic republic ethnic minorities, who are Muslim, are oppressed, while the religious minorities (except for the Baha'is) enjoy relative tolerance.

PART VI

IRAQ AND
THE SUDAN

14

The Kurdish Question
in the 1980s

Charles G. MacDonald

The present level of violence and armed conflict in the Middle East involving ethnic and religious minorities indicates that the current state system is not responsive to minority demands for autonomy and increased freedom of action. In some cases, governments not only fail to protect minority groups adequately but also systematically seek to destroy cultural values, deny ethnic identity, and even adopt policies that border on genocide. The major prevailing conflicts within the region were in part caused by or have exacerbated ethnic and religious rivalries. The ongoing internecine violence in Lebanon, Syria, Iraq, Iran, and Turkey, among other Middle Eastern states, demonstrates the inability of the "territorial state" to deal effectively with the upsurge of ethnic and religious nationalism as it is wedded to forces of national liberation. Moreover, new shocks to the status quo, and perhaps to the state system itself, are emanating from militant Islamic fundamentalism and its pan-Islamic advocates. Islamic Iran's export of revolution is undermining the power and legitimacy of many Middle Eastern governments and creating serious doubts about the efficacy and acceptability of the contemporary state system. Both traditional monarchs and more-progressive secular republics are under attack.

The emergence of militant Islamic fundamentalism is having an uncertain impact on ethnic and religious minorities throughout the Middle East. On the one hand, it has sometimes loosened the bonds of state authority and has given minorities a greater freedom of action with weakened governments more amenable to minority demands. On the other hand, militant Islamic fundamentalism as spread by the Ayatollah Khomeini's Islamic revolution, has failed to recognize ethnic rights or calls for greater ethnic autonomy. In fact, Islamic Iran has moved to crush ethnic nationalists, suggesting they are only agents of imperialism and Zionism. Pan-Islam today, as fostered and directed by Islamic Iran, not only threatens to force minority groups to submit to the control of the Islamic Republic, but also raises the specter of genocide for those who refuse to submit.

The Kurds, the largest single ethnic group in the Middle East that does not have its own state, are at the conjuncture of these two broad historical developments. The stateless Kurds are experiencing new levels of organization. They also stand, for the most part, in open opposition to Khomeini's Islamic fundamentalist policies. As the Kurds become increasingly important not only within Iran in their defiance of Khomeini, but also within Iraq and in the Gulf war between Iraq and Iran, the traditional "Kurdish question" is taking on a new light. The Kurds promise to be crucial actors in any redrawing of the maps of the Middle East in the aftermath of the Gulf war or following the possible fragmentation of post-Ba'thist Iraq or of a post-Khomeini Iran. In particular, the Kurds in Iran initially emerged as Khomeini's most formidable opposition. The Kurds in Iraq, despite being promised a new degree of autonomy, continue to fight to defend Kurdistan in Iraq from both Iraqi troops and Iran's Islamic soldiers. The presence of Kurds in Turkey remain a silent but critical factor in determining the degree of self-rule that Turkey and certain external powers might tolerate for the Iraqi and Iranian Kurds. The transborder Kurdish existence, increasing activities of Kurdish political groups, and designs on Kurdish areas by outside powers place the Kurds at the nexus of the Machiavellian politics of the day in the Middle East and make them a target for political machinations and intrigue. The Kurdish experience, however nebulous and politically complex, points to a new and important role for nonstate actors in the Middle East. The refocusing of the Kurdish question in the 1980s reflects certain trends we can use to consider and better understand the emerging roles of ethnic minorities in the Middle East in general.

Kurdish Identity in the 1980s

The Kurds are an Indo-European people who claim to be descendants of the Medes.[1] The name "Kurds" historically was a generic term that was used to denote nomads—non-Arab nomads in particular.[2] But some Kurds contend that the name "Kurd," which stood for a people, resembled a

---

[1] In Northern Kurdish areas, Kurds often have blond characteristics, with blue or green eyes. For a description of their general physical appearance, see Great Britain, Naval Intelligence Division, *Persia*, BR 525 (Restricted) Geographical Handbook Series, September 1945, pp. 323–326.

[2] See Richard N. Frye, *The Golden Age of Persia* (London: Weidenfeld & Nicolson, 1975), pp. 111–113.

similar-sounding word in Kurdish that meant "warrior" or "ferocious fighter."[3] Today's usage of "Kurd" has apparently combined the two concepts and to a degree has stereotyped Kurds as ferocious and warlike.[4]

Today Kurds are commonly known by several names. Kurds in Iran primarily refer to themselves as "Kordes" and to their region as "Kordestan." "Kurdistan" is also commonly used to refer to Kurdish areas in Iraq, but it is also used to refer to Kurdish areas in Iran. Turkey refers to its Kurdish inhabitants as only "Mountain Turks who have forgotten their native tongue."[5] Turkey chooses to ignore the national and cultural sentiments of Kurds, insisting that Kurds are nonexistent in Turkey, despite the presence of possibly as many as 8 to 10 million within Turkish borders.[6]

Kurdish fighters or guerrillas are usually referred to as "Pesh Merga," which literally means "those who face death." All Kurdish guerrillas, regardless of their political association, are commonly known as Pesh Merga. Khomeini has sought to capitalize on the name Pesh Merga and claims the support of the "Islamic Pesh Merga." Kurdish nationalists assert that such alleged pro-Khomeini Kurds are really only agents of the central government and thus are *josh*, or Kurdish traitors. (Some Kurds, espcecially some Shi'a Kurds in Iran, do appear to support Khomeini, but they remain a small minority.)

Iranian Kurds are traditionally viewed as an Iranian people with long-standing historical ties. Also, the Kurdish language is closely related to Persian. Iran has attempted to assimilate the Kurds and other minority groups into Iranian society, but with no special nationality status or privileges. Some invidivual Kurds have been quite successful in Iranian society, but Kurds as a group remain separate.[7] Iraqi Kurds are also, to a degree, individually integrated into Iraqi society, even though the "autonomous region" per se is a separate and distinct entity with some limited group rights and privileges.

Kurdish areas often include smaller minorities, such as Assyrians, Ar-

---

[3] In considering the derivation of the word *Kurd*, John Limbert notes a possible "connection with the Semitic root QRD, meaning brave or strong" and suggests that "the name *Kurd* probably comes from the Persian *Gord*, meaning 'hero.' " See his exceptional scholarly study of the origin of the Kurds in "The Origins and Appearance of the Kurds in Pre-Islamic Iran," *Iranian Studies* 1 (Spring 1968): 41–51.

[4] Vera Saeedpour, director of Cultural Survival's Kurdish Program, has worked diligently to remove this unfortunate stereotype from leading dictionaries in the United States.

[5] See Vera Saeedpour, "A Decent Respect to the Opinions," *Cultural Survival Quarterly* 7 (Summer 1983): 39–41.

[6] Ibid.

[7] Nader Entessar suggests, "In both Iraq and Iran the integration of Kurds seems to have taken place at the individual rather than group level," and draws attention to Karim Sanjabi and Dariush Foruhar, two Kurds who served as foreign minister and labor minister respectively in Iran's first post-Shah cabinet. See Nader Entessar, "Kurdish Ethnic Nationalism in Iran and Iraq" (paper presented at the 25th Annual Meeting of the International Studies Association, Atlanta, Georgia, March 31, 1984), p. 7.

menians, and Jews, who speak Kurdish as well as an Aramaic dialect. It is not uncommon to hear the expression "Kurdish Jews."[8] The population of non-Kurdish minorities within Kurdish regions is sometimes included in Kurdish population figures. Kurdish nationalists, for example, have sometimes included Lurs and Bakhtiari as Kurds.

Population

Kurds are the largest ethnic group in the Middle East denied a state. With a population perhaps as high as 19 million, the Kurds might represent the third largest national entity in the Middle East (behind both the Arabs and the Turks and probably ahead of the Persians).[9] Some, however, place the Kurds as the fourth largest people behind the Arabs, Turks, and Iranians. If one considers the Kurds to be "Iranian," such a designation would be problematic.

Kurdish population estimates vary considerably. Some scholars suggest that variations have resulted from "deliberate underestimates of governments hostile to Kurdish nationalism, and the exaggerations of some Kurdish nationalists."[10] Citing infrequency, inadequate censuses, and deliberate understatements by central governments, Richard Sim estimated Kurdish populations in 1980 to be as follows: Iran, 4.5 million out of 38.146 million; Iraq, 3 million out of 13.134 million; Turkey, 8.7 million out of 45.182 million; Syria, 0.6 million out of 8.534 million, Lebanon, 0.1 million out of 2.981 million; and the Soviet Union (Armenia, Georgia, Azerbaijan), 0.2 million out of 14.031 million—or a total of 17.2 million.[11]

Territoriality

The difficulty of determining Kurdish population figures is also closely linked to the Kurdish geopolitical settings in each of the Kurds' host countries. Greater Kurdistan is in effect divided among five states—Iran, Iraq, Turkey, Syria, and the Soviet Union. In each the Kurdish communities have

---

[8]See Shiftan Epstein, "The Jews of Kurdistan," *Ariel* (Jerusalem) 51 (1982): 65–78.

[9]See M. Charles, "The Middle East and the Kurds: Presentation of an Emerging Nation" (Russian Research Center, Harvard University, n.d., Mimeographed), pp. 1–6.

[10]Martin Short's estimated Kurdish minimum and maximum populations in the mid–1970s were: Turkey, 3,200,000–8,000,000; Iran, 1,800,000–5,000,000; Iraq, 1,550,000–2,500,000; Syria, 320,000–600,000; USSR, 80,000–300,000; Lebanon, 40,000–70,000. See Martin Short and Anthony McDermott, *The Kurds* (London: Minority Rights Group, 1975), pp. 5–6.

[11]Richard Sim, "Kurdistan: The Search for Recognition," *Conflict Studies*, no. 124 (November 1980): 3.

followed separate and distinct historical developments and have to a degree been incorporated differently into their host societies. The imposition of the European state system, with its emphasis on sovereignty and rigid national boundaries, has effectively divided or fragmented the Kurdish community. The historical separation within the borders of disparate territorial states accentuated regional differences and promoted discontinuities in the Kurdish language, culture, and political aspirations. Many Kurds have become difficult to distinguish from their fellow Muslims, as they have adopted the host-state language and share religious practices.

Also, the major areas of Kurdish population are sometimes misunderstood in host countries or even puposely misrepresented by central governments to downplay the importance or influence of Kurds. For example, in Iran the province known as Kordestan represents only a small part of "Kurdistan in Iran." Kordestan Province lies in the heart of Kurdistan in Iran, which stretches northward through Western Azerbaijan and southward in Ilam and Kermanshah. Parts of Zanjan and Hamadan have sizable Kurdish communities east of Kordestan Province, as do Luristan and Charhar Mahall Va Bakhtiari. In addition, Kurdish communities exist outside of Kurdistan in Iran, such as in Khorasan Province, where the Kurdish presence dates back to the seventeenth century. Kurdish communities can also be found in Gilan and Mazandaran provinces. Similarly, the Kurdish "autonomous region" as set apart in the Autonomy Law of 1974 does not contain all Kurdish areas in Iraq. The autonomous region is limited to the provinces of Sulaymaniyya, Irbil, and Dohuk, but it does not include all the territory within them. Other Kurdish communities in Iraq, especially Kirkuk, are not included in the autonomous region.

The artificial division of geographical Kurdistan, an area of 500,000—520,000 square kilometers, among five states, and the further subdivision of the Kurdish communities within the states, has contributed in large part to a lack of cooperation and common goals among the various Kurdish communities. Moreover, the Kurds commonly refer to the idea of Greater Kurdistan as "the five parts" or "the five sections," not with an expression of single "whole."

Language

The Kurdish language is an Indo-European language that to a degree parallels Persian. Kurdish and Persian are both Iranian languages and distinct from one another, despite their many common words and phrases. Linguistic approaches to the Kurdish dialects and subdialects vary and are beyond the scope of this paper, but it is important to note that Sorani has emerged as the predominant dialect.[12] Technically, Sorani is a single dialect, but it is also used to refer to all southern dialects. Sorani is used primarily in radio broadcasts and in Kurdish publications. It is important to note that the Kurdish dialects are not mutually intelligible. In fact, Kurds from different regions often cannot readily communicate in Kurdish.

The alphabets used by host states represent another major obstacle to Kurdish communications. In Turkey and Syria, Kurdish communities commonly use the Latin alphabet. Some Kurdish intellectuals in Iran also support the use of the Latin alphabet, but most literate Kurds in Iran use the Arabic alphabet. In the Soviet Union, Kurds use the Cyrillic alphabet. The different dialects and scripts represent major barriers to Kurdish unity.

Religion

The Kurds are predominantly Sunni Muslim in the northern and central areas of Kurdistan, with some minor exceptions. Bijar, for example, in Iran's Kurdistan Province, is Shi'ite. Kurds in southern Kurdistan are often Shi'ite. Abdul Rahman Qasemlou, leader of the Kurdistan Democratic Party of Iran (KDPI) asserts that Iranian Kurds are 75 percent Sunni and only 25 percent Shi'ite.[13]

The split between Shi'ite and Sunni Kurds is not as significant as one might imagine. The Kurds as a whole are not nearly as zealous as others in Iran, such as the Azeris. Although the Shi'ite Kurds in the southern reaches of Iranian Kurdistan are more likely to support the Khomeini government, this is not simply because they are Shi'ite, but rather probably because of the lack of communication and transportation links between the south and central or northern Kurdistan. In addition, the particular school of Islam followed by the Kurds is also significant in setting Kurds apart from their neighbors. In southern Kurdistan a number of Kurdish tribes belong to the "twelver" form of shi'ism, but others are Ali Ilahis, who are more closely associated with the Isma'ili "sevener" Shi'ism.[14] Still another group, the Yezidis, whose syncretistic religion has "sevener" influ-

[12] For a more comprehensive examination of Kurdish dialects, see Martin Van Bruinessen, *Agha, Shaikh, and State: On the Social and Political Organization of Kurdistan* (London: Luzoc, 1978), pp. 20–22. See also Great Britain, Naval Intelligence Division, *Persia*, pp. 324–326; and Limbert, "Origins of Kurds in Iran," p. 41.

[13] See Abdul Rahman Qasemlou, "Kurdistan in Iran," in *People without a Country*, ed. G. Chaliand (London: Zed, 1980), p. 110. Some observers suggest the percentage of Kurdish Shi'ites in Iran is much higher. See Yosef Gotlieb, *Self-determination in the Middle East* (New York: Praeger, 1982), p. 73.

[14] Van Bruinessen, *Agha, Shaikh, and State*, pp. 31–33.

ences, have often been persecuted by Muslims.[15] Similarly, the Sunni Kurds who follow the shafi'ite school are often religiously distinct from their non-Kurdish neighbors (Turks and Arabs), who tend to follow the hanafite school.[16] The secret tribal practices of some Kurdish mystical orders also represent major obstacles to Kurdish unification efforts and at the same time present problems for any close cooperation with the central government.

The various parts of the Kurdish identity combine to form a basis for a Kurdish ethnic group consciousness, but this group consciousness is fragmented and does not yet approach a coherent Kurdish national consciousness that seeks a "Greater Kurdistan." It is true that the Kurds have a population. They are concentrated in a given territory, they have a Kurdish language, and to a degree they are mostly Islamic. However, the historical legacy arising from the arbitrary division of Kurdistan into "the five parts" following World War I, and the impact of the separate development under modern territorial states based on the European state system, have effectively divided the national energies of the Kurds and directed them to seek narrow goals based on the Kurdish experience in each national setting, within each host state.

The complex political setting of the Kurds has created an interesting situation in which the Kurdish communities as groups are not integrated into their host countries but still view their goals primarily with respect to their host country. This is especially true in the case of the relative influence exercised by Kurds in Iraq and Iran. A separate Kurdish influence is yet to make its numbers felt in Turkey, and the Kurdish communities in Syria, the Soviet Union, and Lebanon are relatively small and not influential in their host states. In other words, Kurdish communities are effectively fragmented into five (six, counting Lebanon) states. The Kurds have become an integral part of the host countries, even though they have not been assimilated into the modern societies. This becomes apparent as one examines some of the political goals espoused by Kurdish groups and political organizations that have developed in the separate states. The political goals sought are primarily limited to the Kurdish experience within their respective host states. The impact of the Iranian revolution and the effort to export the revolution by the Gulf war might, however, serve to merge political interests of Iraq and Iranian Kurds, as they attempt to defend themselves from the advance of Khomeini's Islamic legions.

---

[15]Yezidis are sometimes associated with the Zoroastrian religion. For a discussion of the Association Zoroastrienne Kurde de France, see Remi Haaz, "Ex Orient Lux," in *Lettre Persane*, March–April 1983, p. 17.

[16]Van Bruinessen, *Agha, Shaikh, and State*, pp. 31–33.

The Search for Kurdish Autonomy

The Kurds remain the largest ethnic group in the Middle East denied statehood. A scheme of local Kurdish autonomy that could have led to an independent Kurdish state was proffered in the Treaty of Sèvres following World War I.[17] The Treaty of Sèvres, in overseeing the breakup of the Ottoman Empire, recognized, inter alia, Armenia as a free and independent state (article 88). It granted Kurdistan "local autonomy" (article 62) with the prospects of independence within one year if a majority of the Kurdish population desired independence and if the League Council considered Kurds capable of independence and recommended such (article 64). The treaty, however, was never ratified by the Turkish Grand National Assembly. Turkish nationalists led by Mustafa Kemal forced the Allies to renegotiate. The resulting Lausanne Treaty of July 24, 1923, failed to mention Kurdistan.[18] The subsequent national boundaries resulted in Greater Kurdistan being divided among five states—Iran, Iraq, Syria, Turkey, and the Soviet Union.

After World War II the Kurds had another opportunity to establish their own state. The Iranian portion of Greater Kurdistan generally fell under Soviet occupation. Qazi Mohammed, a respected political and religious leader in the Kurdish community, came to rule a small Kurdish enclave within the Soviet-controlled portion of Iran. Qazi Mohammed was active politically and founded the Kurdish Democratic Party in 1945, which put forth an eight-point program.[19] Included in the program was a call for "autonomy" within Iran's frontiers, the study of official use of the Kurdish language in Kurdish areas, a legal basis for peasant-landowner relation-

---

[17]See Ottoman Peace Treaty at Sèvres, August 10, 1920, in *Diplomacy in the Near and Middle East*, ed. J. C. Hurewitz, vol. 2: *A Documentary Record, 1914–1956* (Princeton: Van Nostrand, 1956). pp. 81–89. See also Great Britain, *Parliamentary Papers, 1920*, Treaty Series No. 11, Cmdr. 964, pp. 16–32.

[18]For text, see *Diplomacy in the Near and Middle East*, 2:119–127. See also Great Britain, *Parliamentary Papers, 1923*, Treaty Series no. 16, Cmdr. 1929.

[19]The eight points were as follows: (1) The Kurdish people in Iran must manage their own local affairs and be granted autonomy within Iran's frontiers. (2) Kurds must be allowed to study their mother tongue; the official administrative language in the Kurdish territories must be Kurdish. (3) The country's constitution should guarantee that district councilors for Kurdistan be elected to take charge of all social and administrative matters. (4) State officials must be chosen from the local population. (5) A general law should provide the basis for agreements between peasants and landowners, so as to safeguard the future of both sides. (6) The KDP struggles for complete fraternity and unity with the Azerbaijani people and with the minorities resident in Azerbaijan (Assyrians, Armenians, etc.). (7) The KDP is committed to progress in agriculture and trade, to developing education and sanitation and to furthering the spiritual and material well-being of the Kurdish people and the best use of natural resources of Kurdistan. (8) The KDP demands freedom of political action for all the people of Iran so that the whole country may rejoice in progress. See Qasemlou, "Kurdistan in Iran," p. 118.

ships, and an improvement of the material well-being of the Kurdish people, among other things.

Qazi Mohammed declared the establishment of the "State of the Kurdish Republic"on January 22, 1946, but whether his Mahabad republic would be an "autonomous regional government" or a "fully independent republic" was never resolved.[20] (The Soviets also reportedly suggested incorporation of both the Kurdish republic and Azerbaijan into the Soviet Union.)[21] The Mahabad republic lasted less than a year and included only about 30 percent of Kurdistan in Iran. Following the withdrawal of Soviet forces from Iran, Iran's central government, with the backing of the United States and Great Britain, crushed the Kurdish republic militarily and executed its leaders.

Iranian Revolution and Kurdish Aspirations

The Kurdistan Democratic Party in Iran maintained the stated goal of autonomy, as put forth in 1945, but did not have another good opportunity to realize its goal until the Iranian revolution. In 1973 a new KDPI program did call for armed struggle to achieve autonomy.[22] When the Shah's authority began to crumble in 1978, the Kurds moved to take greater control of their own affairs. Qasemlou returned from his exile in Paris and worked with Shaykh Ezzedin Husayni, a leftist Sunni cleric, to gain de facto control of Kurdistan in Iran. In January 1979, military garrisons and gendarmerie outposts were taken by Kurds, and stockpiles of weapons were seized. Efforts were made to set up peasant councils and establish some semblance of direct Kurdish control, but the Kurds could not agree on what was to be done.

On March 2, 1979, after more than thirty years of clandestine activity, the KDPI held a public press conference and put forth their goals for an autonomous Kurdistan within Iran. The party asserted:

1. The boundaries of Kurdistan would be determined by the Kurdish people and would take into consideration historical, economic, and geographical conditions.
2. On matters of defense, foreign affairs, and long-term economic planning, Kurdistan would abide by the central government's decisions. The Central Bank of Iran would control the currency.

[20] Ibid., p. 119. See also William Eagleton, Jr., *The Kurdish Republic of 1946* (London: Oxford University Press, 1963), and Archie Roosevelt, Jr., "The Kurdish Republic of Mahabad," in *People without a Country*, ed. Chaliand.

[21] Gotlieb, *Self-determination*, p. 87.

[22] Sim, "Kurdistan," p. 5.

3. There would be a Kurdish parliament, whose members would be popularly elected. It would be the highest legislative power in the province.
4. All government departments in the province would be run locally instead
of from the capital.
5. There would be a people's army, but the police and gendarmerie would
be abolished and replaced by a national guard.
6. The Kurdish language would be the official language of the provincial
government and would be taught in all schools. Persian would also continue to be an official language.
7. All ethnic minorities in Kurdistan would enjoy equal rights and would
be allowed to use their own language and traditions.
8. Freedom of speech and press, rights of association, and trade-union activities would be guaranteed. The Kurdish people would have the right
to travel freely and choose their own occupation.[23]

The KDPI leader, Qasemlou, denied that Kurdistan was seeking independence, asserting "charges of secessionism are levelled against us by reactionary forces."[24] Qasemlou stated: "Let the central government have control
over the army, defense matters, foreign policy and finance, [but] let us have
authority over local administration and domestic policies."[25] Ezzedin Husayni similarly maintained, "We are Iranians. We want a federal republic."[26]
Qasemlou suggested the Yugoslav federated model for Iran.

On March 28, 1979, a Kurdish document formulating the Kurdish position
was submitted to Khomeini. It indicated the following:

> Our people have fought for two major goals: the overthrow of the dictatorship
> and its replacement by a humane regime which would respect political free-
> doms and rights throughout Iran, and the realization of national rights for all
> nations in the form of autonomy or a federation in free Iran. As there are
> several oppressed groups in Iran, the most suitable formula would be a federal
> system.... Autonomy, or a federal structure, are in no way a contradiction
> with the unity and territorial integrity of Iran.[27]

On August 6, 1979, *Ayandegan* (Tehran) published an open letter from
the KDPI Central Committee to Khomeini that reiterated the KDPI's two
fundamental goals—"To overthrow the monarchy regime and establish a
democratic regime in Iran in the framework of which the national rights
of the Kurdish people would be provided in the form of self-autonomy or

[23]*Times* (London), March 4, 1979.
[24]*Kayhan International*, March 4, 1979.
[25]See David Menashri, "Iran," *Middle East Contemporary Survey*, 3: 1978–79, p. 527.
[26]Ibid.
[27]For quote from *Le Monde diplomatique*, see Franjo Butorac, "Iran's Revolution and the
Kurds," *Review of International Affairs* (Belgrade), April 20, 1980, p. 17.

federation."[28] The letter charged that the Iranian media were "broadcasting false news" and "misrepresenting the people of Kurdistan."[29] In apparent response to the letter, the *Ayandegan* was banned. Soon thereafter, on August 19, 1979, Khomeini identified Kurdish leaders Qasemlou and Husayni as enemies of the revolution. He also outlawed the KDPI, banned all Kurdish political organizations, and barred Qasemlou from participating in the Assembly of Experts. Khomeini ordered the Iranian military to crush the Kurdish rebels. After bitter fighting between Kurdish forces and government troops, Khomeini ordered a cease-fire and sent a negotiating team to Mahabad on November 2, 1979. The KDPI responded positively, and Husayni presented a plan for Kurdish autonomy. However, Islamic Iran was unwilling to accept Kurdish demands and again moved to destroy Kurdish resistance.

Once again, in January 1980, Khomeini made overtures to the Kurds by promising to amend the constitution to guarantee Sunni religious practices in areas of Sunni predominance.[30] No such amendment was forthcoming. His promise came to be viewed as a tactical measure to encourage minorities to vote in the presidential election. Since August 1979, Iranian Kurds have faced repeated attacks by government forces. Their slogan remains "Autonomy for Kurdistan and democracy for Iran," but now they seek to overthrow Khomeini instead of the Shah.

Islamic World Order and the Kurds

If one would have focused on Khomeini's concept of an Islamic republic and his concept of world order, it should have been apparent early in the Islamic revolution that the Kurdish goals of autonomy and democracy did not fit into Khomeini's concept of an Islamic World Order. A close look at the revision of the Islamic constitution points to trouble ahead for the Kurds and other Iranian minorities.

Iran's Islamic constitution, as approved in November 1979, was markedly different from the original draft put before the Assembly of Experts.[31] Not only did the new constitution fail to provide for Kurdish autonomy, but it limited still further certain cultural and religious rights. In the draft constitution, article 5 provided "All peoples in the Islamic Republic of Iran,

---

[28]*Ayandegan* (Tehran), August 6, 1979—Joint Publications Research Service, Near East and North African Report, October 9, 1979, p. 33.

[29]Ibid., p. 34.

[30]*New York Times*, January 21, 1980.

[31]For an English translation of the draft constitution of the Islamic Republic of Iran, as translated by Hamid Algar and published in *Iran Voice*, July 2, 1979, see "Documents: Draft Constitution of the Islamic Republic of Iran," *Ripeh* 3 (Fall 1979): 20–51.

such as Persians, Turks, Kurds, Arabs, Baluchis, Turkomans, and others, will enjoy completely equal rights." Concerning religion, the draft constitution in article 13 provided:

> The official religion of the country is Islam and the Ja'fari school of thought, which is the school of thought followed by the majority of Muslims of Iran. Other Islamic schools of thought, including the Zaydi, the Hanafi, the Maliki, the Shafi'i, and Hanbali, are valid and are to be respected, and in areas of the country where Muslims following these schools of thought constitute the majority, local regulations, within the bounds of the competence of (local) councils, are to be in accordance with the respective schools of thought. With respect to matters of personal status and religious education, every Muslim acts in accordance with *his* own school of thought, in whatever area of the country he may be.

Draft article 21 guaranteed the use of local languages in schools but not in official correspondence: "The common language and script of Iran is Persian. All official texts and correspondence must be in this language and script. However, the use of local languages in local schools and press is permitted."

When the draft constitution became public, great concern and fear were registered among minority communities, especially because article 5 failed to grant the autonomy and democratic freedom of action they sought. When the constitution was finalized by Khomeini's Assembly of Experts, the fears of the ethnic minorities were realized.[32] Reference to equal rights of all people, with specific identification of the major groups, such as the Kurds, was deleted. No reference was made to ethnic nationalities that were Muslim. Concerning religious tribunals and courts, the new constitution failed to provide for religious rights of the Sunnis in areas where they were the majority. In January 1980, Khomeini subsequently promised to amend the constitution to guarantee Sunni practices in Sunni areas, but such an amendment was not forthcoming.

Concerning language, article 15 of the Islamic constitution provided for the use of local minority languages in the press, the mass media, and the schools. However, the local languages were to be used only alongside Persian, and textbooks had to be in Persian. Under the Shah the Kurdish language had been officially banned and no Kurdish schools were allowed. Radio stations did broadcast in Kurdish, however, as in Kermanshah, but apart from music the Kurdish broadcasts sought to support the Shah's policies and tended to suggest that Kurdish was a dialect of Persian.[33] Under

---

[32] For an English translation, see *Constitution of the Islamic Republic of Iran*, trans. Hamid Algar (Berkeley, Calif.: Mizan, 1989).

[33] Qasemlou, "Kurdistan in Iran," p. 111. See also Eden Naby, "Rebellion in Kurdistan," *Harvard International Review* 2 (November 1979): 29.

the Khomeini regime the apparent promise of bilingual schools in the constitution has not been realized. In January 1984, National Voice of Iran's clandestine radio charged that the Islamic government had made the study of English, Arabic, and other foreign languages "compulsory for the peoples of Kurdistan" and had "simultaneously banned or made impossible education in the mother tongue."[34]

The revision of the draft constitution and subsequent policies by the Islamic government toward ethnic minorities points to Khomeini's approach toward ethnic minorities and ethnic nationalism. In December 1979, Khomeini explained his views toward Kurds and other ethnic minorities. He stated:

> Sometimes the word minorities is used to refer to people such as the Kurds, Lurs, Turks, Persians, Baluchis, and such. These people should not be called minorities, because this term assumes that there is a difference between these brothers. In Islam, such a difference has no place at all. There is no difference between Muslims who speak different languages, for instance, the Arabs or the Persians. It is very probable that such problems have been created by those who do not wish the Muslim countries to be united. . . . They create the issues of nationalism, of pan-Iranism, pan-Turkism, and such isms, which are contrary to Islamic doctrines. Their plan is to destroy Islam and the Islamic philosophy.[35]

In other words, Khomeini views the breakdown of peoples into states and into substate ethnic groups espousing nationalism, as a divide-and-conquer technique of imperialist powers. Accordingly, he asserts that national or state boundaries are nothing more than an imperialist conspiracy. In Iraq's case he has called for its Islamic peoples to overthrow Saddam Husayn and join the Islamic republic.[36] Khomeini's conception of the Islamic republic has no provision for nationalism or national self-determination and suggests the merging of Islamic areas into the Islamic republic. As one scholar notes, Khomeini viewed nationalism a "a great trick of the West to undermine Islam."[37]

In considering Khomeini's concept of an Islamic republic linking all Muslims under a single theocratic rule, the Kurdish goals of autonomy and democracy have no place. Khomeini's centralized clerical control is in direct

---

[34] National Voice of Iran (Clandestine), January 31, 1984—Daily Report, VIII, February 3.

[35] Radio Tehran, December 17, 1979—British Broadcasting Corporation, Summary of World Broadcasts, December 19.

[36] For Khomeini's comments, see Tehran Domestic Service, June 21, 1982, Daily Report, VIII, June 22, 1982.

[37] See Farhang Rajaee, *Islamic Values and World View: Khomeini on Man, the State, and International Politics*, vol. 13 (Lanham, Md.: University Press of America, 1983), p. 72. For Khomeini's views on Iranian nationalism versus pan-Islam, see David Menashri, "Shi'ite Leadership: In the Shadow of Conflicting Ideologies," *Iranian Studies* 13 (1980): 129–132.

conflict with a democratic, decentralized Iran that the Kurds seek. Moreover, the expansion of Islamic Iran would directly threaten the rights and privileges of Iraqi Kurds in the "autonomous region" of Iraq.

Kurdish Reaction to the Islamic Republic

The Kurdistan Democratic Party of Iran (KDPI) and the Revolutionary Organization of the Toilers of Kurdistan, commonly called Komaleh,[38] represent Iran's two most important Kurdish political organizations. The KDPI is predominant and is led by Qasemlou. It should not be confused with the Iraqi Kurdistan Democratic Party (KDP) headed by the Barazani brothers or the several pro-Ba'th KDPs. The KDPI claims support from 80 percent of Iran's 4 million Iranian Kurds,"[39] including the pro-monarchist Rizkari.[40] The KDPI reportedly controls some 12,000 Kurdish Pesh Merga and an additional 60,000 armed peasants.[41] There have been rivalries among Kurdish groups in Iran, but general agreement on the common goals of autonomy and democracy prevails.

After the failure of the Kurds to maintain control of cities and fixed territory against the advance of government forces, Kurds have resorted to guerrilla warfare and have resigned themselves to controlling rural areas. The Kurds could not defend themselves against Khomeini's technologically superior forces. The Kurds have worked together with other leftist forces, in particular the Mujahidine Khalq and the Fida'iyyine Khalq (minority), but have been opposed by the pro-government Tudeh. After Saddam Husayn's forces were forced to assume the defensive in the Gulf war, the Iraqi Patriotic Union of Kurdistan (PUK) under Jalal Talabani increased its cooperation with the KDPI. The Iraqi Kurdistan Democratic Party (Iraqi KDP) under Idris and Mas'ud Barazani openly assisted Khomeini against the KDPI and Komaleh.

In October 1981, Qasemlou announced that the KDPI had agreed to join the National Resistance Council of Mas'ud Rajavi in its effort to bring down the Islamic republic.[42] Komaleh, under the leadership of Abdullah Mohtadi, refused to cooperate with the National Resistance Council, criticizing its approach to social revolution and the presence of Bani-Sadr (however, Bani-Sadr was ousted from the council in early 1984, possibly because of KDPI

---

[38]After late 1983, Komaleh became known as the Organization of Kurdistan—Communist Party of Iran.

[39]*Le Monde*, November 3, 1982—Daily Report, VIII, November 9.

[40]See Qasemlou interview in *Liberation Today*, Free Voice of Iran, April 8, 1982—Joint Publications Research Service, April 29.

[41]Agence France Presse (Paris), November 9, 1983—Daily Report, VIII, November 10.

[42]Abdul Rahman Qasemlou, "Report of the Central Committee to the Fifth Congress of the Kurdistan Democratic Party of Iran," December 1981, p. 65.

influence). Komaleh still worked with the KDPI toward a common goal of democracy and autonomy.[43]

In late 1983 the KDPI announced that it had reached an agreement on an "autonomy formula" with the National Resistance Council.[44] Presumably "Kurds would be allowed to elect a legislative council to establish territorial laws. The Kurds would also be in charge of maintaining territorial security," but the central government would be responsible for defense, foreign policy and trade, financial affairs, planning, and natural resources.[45] All members of the National Resistance Council reportedly supported the "autonomy plan," but Komaleh openly challenged the plan.[46] The KDPI sought to guarantee its future autonomy in Iran after Khomeini by achieving prior approval of their desired autonomy as well as by implementing "autonomy" in areas under Kurdish control. The KDPI affiliation with the National Resistance Council did not last, but KDPI cooperation with Mujahidine fighters continues. The goal of the KDPI remains, at present, "autonomy for Kurdistan and democracy for Iran."

The Gulf War and Kurdish Autonomy in Iraq

The goal of the Iraqi Kurds, as advocated by Talabani's PUK, is "democracy for Iraq, autonomy for Kurdistan" or "recognition of the right of the Kurdish people to a real and genuine autonomy within an Independent Iraqi Republic."[47] The goal reflects the struggle of the Iraqi Kurds since World War I for self-determination and for the establishment of their own government.[48] The Kurds did reach agreement with Baghdad on March 11, 1970, following a prolonged insurrection, but the subsequent Autonomy Law of 1974 fell short of Kurdish expectations. The Kurdish opposition to the plan was repressed in 1975 following Iraq's agreement with Iran and the cutoff of Iranian and American assistance to the Iraqi Kurds. The Iranian revolution brought new security concerns for Iraq, as Iran ended its effort to control transborder Kurdish activities. Iraq increased its security measures along the border areas of Iraqi Kurdistan and resettled many Kurds

---

[43]*Le Monde*, February 21–22, 1982—Daily Report, VIII, March 2.

[44]Iraqi News Agency (Baghdad), November 7, 1983—Daily Report, VIII, November 9.

[45]Agence France Presse (Paris), November 9, 1983—Daily Report, VIII, November 10.

[46]See Abdullah Mohtadi, *The Bourgeois Opposition Are Afraid of Kurdistan Revolutionary Movement: A Look at NRC's Plan for Kurdish Autonomy* (n.p.: Communist Party of Iran, December 1983).

[47]See "Revolution in Kurdistan: The Essential Documents of Patriotic Union of Kurdistan," PUK Publications No. 1 (1976).

[48]For an excellent overview of the Iraqi Kurdish situation, see Ismet Sheriff Vanly, "Kurdistan in Iraq," in *People without a Country*, pp. 153–210. See also Edmund Ghareeb, *The Kurdish Question in Iraq* (Syracuse, N.Y.: Syracuse University Press, 1981).

to the south. Some Kurdish political organizations, the Iraqi KDP in particular, took advantage of the sanctuary offered by the revolution to renew its anti-Ba'th efforts. Not until the Gulf war, however, did Iraqi Kurds really have the opportunity to take up arms again to seek their desired autonomy.

The Iraqi Kurds have been divided between the Kurds willing to cooperate with the Iraqi government in order to enjoy whatever limited rights and privileges are offered in the "Kurdish" autonomous region, and the forces of Kurdish nationalism that seek to overthrow the Ba'th regime and achieve a more just autonomy. In this regard, the Iraqi Kurdish nationalists are quite similar to Kurdish nationalists in Iran; they seek to overthrow the central government and establish autonomy within the borders of the state.

Two major Kurdish political organizations exist in Iraq—the Iraqi KDP and the PUK. Although they have shared the common goals of overthrowing the Ba'th regime and establishing a democratic state with an autonomous Kurdistan, they have a history of mutual distrust and at times open conflict. Each has worked to establish unified fronts against the Ba'th regime, but their differences have prevailed and cooperation has been short-lived. On November 12, 1980, the Democratic National and Patriotic Front (DNPF) was formed in Damascus and included the PUK but excluded the Iraqi KDP. The Iraqi KDP responded by joining with two members of the DNPF, the Iraqi Communist Party (ICP) and the Kurdish Socialist Party (KSP), to form the Democratic National Front (DNF).[49] Another united front was the Islamic National Liberation Front of Revolutionary, Islamic, and National Forces, under the leadership of General Hasan Mustafa al-Naqib. Although the fronts were not significant in terms of joint antigovernment operations, Kurdish participation did underscore the Kurdish goal of autonomy within Iraq as opposed to secession.

The increasing unrest among the Kurds, and major setbacks at the front by Husayn's forces in 1982, led President Husayn to adopt a more conciliatory approach to Kurdish nationalists. Baghdad pardoned Kurds accused of anti-government activities,[50] and Husayn put new emphasis on the rights and privileges enjoyed by Iraqi Kurds and the threat to the Kurds represented by the Islamic forces of Khomeini. Baghdad's appeals for Kurdish support continued through 1983. On August 5, 1983, elections were held for the Legislative Council of the Kurdish Autonomous Region.[51] In December 1983, finally bowing to Kurdish demands, Husayn signed a far-reaching "political and security agreement" with PUK leader Jalal Talabani.[52] The Iraqi gov-

---

[49] Voice of the Iraqi People, June, 15, 1982—Joint Publications Research Service, June 25.

[50] See Iraqi News Agency (Baghdad), July 12, 1982—Daily Report, v, July 13; and Radio Baghdad Voice of the Masses, July 8, 1982— Daily Report, v, July 9.

[51] See Times (London), August 6, 1983; and Radio Baghdad Voice of the Masses, August 5, 1983—Daily Report, v, August 9.

[52] For details, see Paris Radio Monte Carlo, January 3, 1984—Daily Report, v, January 4.

ernment had agreed to "free and democratic elections for the legislative and executive councils" of the Kurdish autonomous regions; to form and equip a "Kurdish army comprising roughly 40,000 men to defend Kurdistan from foreign enemies"; to "allocate 30 percent of the state budget to the reconstruction of Kurdish areas damaged by the war"; "to establish new development projects in the area"; and "to expand the Kurdish autonomous zone" to include oil producing areas in Kirkuk and Khanaqin—adjacent to the Iranian border—and in Sulaymaniyya, Dohuk, and Irbil."[53] The agreement provided only for Kurdish forces to protect Kurdish areas, not be sent to other parts of Iraq to combat Iran's invading forces.

The PUK received harsh criticism from the DNPF and DNF members for dealing with Baghdad, but it asserted that, following the Turkish invasion of Iraq in May 1983 and the Iranian move into the Haj Umran area in July 1983, PUK forces were forced to fight on four fronts—against the Turks and Iranians as well as against the Iraqi KDP and central government forces.[54]

The threat of Islamic Iran's pan-Islamic expansion clearly led to a major rapprochement between the PUK and the Iraqi government. Khomeini's approach to Iran's Kurdish question, his use of military force to deny Kurdish autonomy, probably signaled to the Iraqi Kurds, with the possible exception of the Iraqi KDP, that Khomeini's militant pan-Islamic expansion represented a greater danger than Husayn's Ba'th regime.

PUK cooperation with the Husayn regime proved to be short-lived, but conflict among Iraqi Kurdish groups continued. In 1987 Kurdish successes in northwestern Iraq put increased pressure on the Husayn regime. Despite Kurdish assistance from Iranian commandos in Iraq, Kurdish fears of an expansionist Iran remain.

Geopolitical Realities and Other Considerations

Kurdish efforts to achieve autonomy and freedom of action have been repeatedly thwarted by central government action and by outside interference. Charges of imperialism and exploitation have been made repeatedly by Kurdish nationalists. The geopolitical realities concerning Kurdish areas, superimposed on the numerous schisms and divisions among Kurds, make the establishment of an independent Greater Kurdistan virtually impossible and Kurdish autonomy in any of the "five parts" limited. Kurdish autonomy in one state could represent a threat to the stability of neighboring states with a Kurdish population. Kurdish autonomy would also represent a threat

---

[53] Ibid.
[54] *Middle East* (London), February 1984, p. 9.

to stability of the host state if other minorities sought to emulate the Kurdish achievements.

Iran, Iraq, and Turkey, the three states with the largest number of Kurds, have traditionally cooperated to keep the Kurds under control. The Sa'dabad Pact of July 8, 1937,[55] represented an instrument that could control transborder Kurdish activities. Each member of the Sa'dabad Pact agreed "to prevent within his respective frontier, the formation of activities of armed bands, associations, or organizations to subvert the established institutions, or disturb the order or security of any part."[56]

Turkish Incursion into Iraqi Kurdistan

The Iranian revolution and the Gulf war led to increased transborder Kurdish activities. Following the 1975 withdrawal of Iranian support for Iraqi Kurds, many refugees remained in border areas. Also, Kurds traditionally took advantage of the borders for sanctuary from antigovernment activities. In August 1981 an Iraqi-Turkish agreement that would enable Iraq or Turkey "to penetrate 9 km into each other's territory to pursue opposition forces" was reported.[57] The purpose of the agreement was probably twofold—to control efforts to export the Iranian revolution and to control Kurdish antigovernment activities.

In May 1983, Turkish forces invaded parts of Iraqi Kurdistan, attacking Kurdish camps along the border.[58] Turkey explained that its action was aimed at "aggressors who posed a threat to security and peace in the area."[59] The Iraqi ambassador to Ankara acknowledged that Iraqi permission had been granted for the Turkish incursion and thanked Turkey for its operation against "separatist adventurers."[60] Numerous Kurdish organizations, the Iraqi KDP in particular, and the Armenian Secret Army for the Liberation of Armenia (ASALA) claimed to be victims of the Turkish move.[61]

The Turkish move was shrouded in secrecy and raised many questions.[62] Was the Turkish incursion aimed at stemming anti-Turkish activities emanating from Iraq? Was it primarily to assist a weakened Iraqi government

[55] For text, see *Diplomacy in the Near and Middle East*, 2:90–91.
[56] Ibid.
[57] Voice of Iraqi Kurdistan, August 12, 1981—Daily Report, v, August 14.
[58] See Rasit Gurdilek, "Turks Crossed Border into Iraq to Hit Kurdish Separatists," *Times* (London), May 28, 1983; Sam Cohen, "Turkey's Mysterious Strike into Iraq Underlines Ongoing Effort to Uproot Kurdish Nationalism," *Christian Science Monitor*, July 14, 1983; and *New York Times*, May 31, 1983.
[59] *New York Times*, May 28, 1983.
[60] Ambassador Taha Mahmud al-Qaysi, interview, *Istanbul Gunes*, May 30, 1983—Daily Report, v, June 1983.
[61] *Armenian Reporter*, June 16, 1983; *Sunday Times* (London), July 24, 1983.
[62] See *Middle East* (London), August 1983, pp. 24–25.

against its own rebellious Kurds? Considering Iranian support of the Iraqi KDP, and possible Iranian links to Armenian terrorists, could it have been to counteract possible Iranian efforts to export its Islamic revolution into Turkey?[63]

Another scenario could also be considered, one dating from Turkey's claim to some Kurdish areas of the Ottoman Empire after World War I. A magazine article in the *New Statesman* brought widespread Arab concern over possible American-Turkish conspiracy to reclaim Iraqi Kurdish provinces.[64] Moreover, with a lingering threat that Islamic Iran might promote its pan-Islamism in Turkey, Turkey would be reluctant to accept an Iranian takeover of Iraqi Kurdistan as a spoil of the Gulf war. Similarly, Turkey would be concerned about any formation of a Kurdish state in a fragmented Iraq because of the destabilizing effect that might have on Kurdish nationalists in Turkey. Kurdish nationalism in Turkey has not developed to the degree that it has in Iraq and Iran, but presumably it could develop into a major force in Turkey under certain conditions, conditions that Turkey would like to avoid.

Kurdish Nationalism and the West

Kurds have traditionally been used by outside powers to destabilize host states. After World War II it appears that despite the Kurdish stated desire for autonomy within Iran and clear distinction between Azerbaijan and the Kurdish Mahabad Republic, Kurds were considered guilty by association. In the American view, the Kurdish aspirations for democracy and autonomy were overshadowed by the Soviet Union's active manipulation of the Kurdish movement. Previously classified documents show that the U.S. Joint Chiefs of Staff believed that autonomy for the Iranian Kurds would result in their merging with Iraqi Kurds to become "a willing instrument of the USSR for the creation of discord, dissent, and revolt in the Near and Middle East."[65]

The socioeconomic realities of Kurdish areas with lingering tribal and neofeudal relationships[66] have driven most of the Kurdish political orga-

[63] In December 1979 Khomeini had stated: "The regimes in Egypt, Iraq, and Turkey are standing up thanks to the bayonets. Once these are removed, those people will follow our way." See Sam Cohen, "Turkey's Relations with Iran Strained after Khomeini Slur," *Christian Science Monitor*, December 27, 1979.

[64] See Claudia Wright, "Young Turks Manoeuver to Invade Iraq," *New Statesman*, May 14, 1982, pp. 13–14. See also *Times* (London), May 28, 1983.

[65] See *Foreign Relations of the United States, 1946*, 7:531.

[66] Although the impact of tribalism on Kurdish nationalism is an integral part of the Kurdish question, a major contributing factor in the lack of Kurdish unity, and a topic worthy of study, it is beyond the scope of this paper. For some contemporary studies on tribalism, see Van Bruinessen, *Agha, Shaikh, and State*; James Reid, "Comments on Tribalism as a Socioeconomic Formation," *Iranian Studies* 12 (Summer–Autumn 1979): 275–281; Lois Beck, "The Tribe and

nizations to the left of the political spectrum. A great majority of the Kurds are poor and landless as a result of feudal ownership patterns that developed in the second quarter of the twentieth century.[67] Iran's central government has applied land reform measures unevenly in Kurdistan to gain the support of tribal leaders. Modernization has begun to break down tribalism and the feudal control of the *aghas*, but even the Islamic republic has continued to seek support from the landowners. Awareness of the economic and social inequalities, and efforts to correct the inequities, have often placed the Kurdish political organizations in opposition to the large landowners and brought accusations that the Kurds were Communists and agents of the Soviets. These accusations rang loud and clear in August 1979, when Khomeini decided to move militarily against Iranian Kurdistan.

While the Kurds are not agents of the Soviet Union, though they have received some assistance from the Soviets, the major Kurdish political organizations in Iran and Iraq take pride in being "part of the world liberation movement" and staunch enemies of "American imperialism, Zionism, and reactionary regimes."[68] Such anti-imperialist positions have made it difficult for the West to view the Kurdish struggle dispassionately and fairly. As the Gulf war continues, it remains to be seen whether the new hopes of Kurdish autonomy in the autonomous region of Iraq will be realized. The pan-Islamic expansion and threats from Islamic Iran have led to increased cooperation among Iranian and Iraqi Kurds, but as yet Iraqi and Irani Kurds have not espoused any goals to unite their respective areas. They continue to seek autonomy in their respective states. Security interests of Turkey, Iran, and Iraq suggest that too much autonomy for any Kurdish area would be unwelcome. It appears that the Kurdish question in the 1980s will result in only limited Kurdish self-determination in host states, at best. If Islamic Iran is successful in redrawing the map of the Middle East, Kurdish self-determination may again be sacrificed to Great Power geopolitical considerations. What is certain is that the Kurdish struggle and Kurdish suffering will continue.

---

the State in Revolutionary Iran," *Iranian Studies* 13 (1980): 215–255; and Leonard M. Helfgott, "Tribe and Uymaq in Iran: A Reply," *Iranian Studies* 16 (Winter–Spring 1983): 73–78.

[67]Qasemlou, "Kurdistan in Iran," p. 115. For a study showing the many inequalities and poverty that exist in Kurdistan, see Akbar Aghajanian, "Ethnic Inequality in Iran: An Overview," *International Journal of Middle East Studies* 15 (May 1983): 211–224.

[68]Voice of Iraqi Kurdistan, August 17, 1981—Daily Report, v, August 18; see also Voice of the Iraqi Revolution, July 7, 1982—Daily Report, v, July 28.

15

The Ethnic Factor in Sudanese
Politics: South vs. North

Haim Shaked and Yehudit Ronen

Fourteen years after the end of the bloody war between the Sudanese central government and the South, which began some thirty years ago with the military insurrection in Equatoria, the situation has again deteriorated into a civil war. After a protracted internecine war, the 1972 Addis Ababa peace agreement ushered in a relatively long period of conciliation and cooperation between the Muslim-Arab north and the Christian-animistic south.[1] However, in the late 1970s this gave way to a deepening crisis that in 1986 reached the level of the violent and bloody conflict which had marred Sudanese life between 1956 and 1972.

The deterioration of relations that led to the civil war had been brewing for a long time. The first signs indicating the growing tide of armed rebelliousness in the south against Khartoum had appeared during 1983. In the beginning of 1984, Muhamed Omer Bashir, a leading academician in Khartoum and a proliferate author on the North-South issue in Sudanese politics, summarized the situation by stating, "We have now war."[2] During 1985 and, much more significant, in the course of 1986, the armed conflict escalated further, assuming new and alarming proportions. The renewal of the war reopens the serious and complicated question of North-South relations and, perhaps more generally, the whole question of the identity of the Sudan.

This chapter deals with two interrelated issues: the Sudanese identity

---

[1] The latest official Sudanese estimate available (1983) puts the Southern population at 23 percent of the 22 million inhabitants of the Sudan.

[2] *International Herald Tribune*, March 16, 1984.

and the evolution of Southern Sudanese autonomy. Both will be discussed in the context of pluralism, ethnicity, and minority-majority issues.

The Identity of the Sudan

In the case of the Sudan, the question of the country's identity is of great significance on the national level and is germane to the political history of the Sudan. It is therefore not surprising that there is much literature attempting to analyze and explain what Sudanese identity is all about. Prevailing definitions in the existing literature provide four basic statements about the Sudan.

The first definition, proposed in 1968 at a conference in Khartoum by a well-known specialist in African politics, 'Ali A. Mazrui, refers to the Sudan as an area of multiple marginality. According to Mazrui, the Sudan lies on the fringe of many cultural and political zones but is central to none. It is a bridge between Arabic-speaking Africa and English-speaking Africa, between Christian Africa and Muslim Africa, between the Africa of the homogenized mass nation-states of the future and the Africa of deep ethnic cleavages of the present, and finally between West Africa as a cultural unit and Eastern Africa.[3] A second definition, which is prevalent in many nuances and forms in the literature, regards the Sudan as a crossroads for influences and counterinfluences that have produced a great deal of turbulence in the past.[4] A third formula was proposed by an exponent of Sudanese academic-political, or political-academic, thinking—Muddathir Abd al-Rahim. Al-Rahim suggested that, in order to understand the nature of the country and its identity, one should consider it a microcosm of the whole of Africa, a country in which, despite physical, ethnic, and cultural diversity, strands of Arabism and Africanism have been so interwoven that it is difficult to tell them apart.[5] This point of view would not be at great odds with the prevailing view of the Sudanese government. The fourth definition—which surfaces in the literature produced by secessionists—

---

[3]'Ali A. Mazrui, "The Multiple Marginality of the Sudan," in *Sudan in Africa: Studies Presented to the First International Conference Sponsored by the Sudan Research Unit, 7–12 February 1968*, ed. Y. F. Hasan (Khartoum, 1971), pp. 240–255.

[4]R. C. Stevenson, "The Significance of the Sudan in Linguistic Research: Past, Present, and Future," in ibid., pp. 11–25.

[5]Muddathir 'Abd al-Rahim, "Arabism, Africanism, and Self-identification in the Sudan," in ibid., pp. 228–239.

regards the Sudan as an artificial amalgamation of two distinct and divergent units: the North and the South.

All four definitions share an obvious common denominator: the Sudan is a country of great pluralism as far as race, language, culture, religion, political structure, tradition, and, one should add, expectations are concerned. This pluralism is anchored in a number of basic facts. The Sudan has boundaries with eight other states: Egypt, Libya, Chad, the Central African Republic, Zaire, Uganda, Kenya, and Ethiopia. Like many other countries that came into being during the colonial and imperial period, the boundaries of the Sudan are artificial. They were not determined by ethnic, linguistic, cultural, or traditional considerations, but rather by the conveniences and compromises that were shared outside the country, or even outside the continent. Several basic topographical and geographical factors, primarily the famous Sudd swamps, have created a barrier between North and South. On the other hand, a number of migration waves that rolled over this vast country of 967,500 square miles have created remnants of different groups of people, or a number of pockets of "minorities." In the geographical boundaries of what constitutes the modern state of the Sudan, there are important minorities, such as the Nubians in the North, the Fur in the West, the Beja in the East and the significant but diversified group of African Negroid tribes in the South. With all this pluralism and diversity, the borders of the country called the Sudan probably should have been drawn in a different way. Perhaps it should not have been one country, but more than that, or perhaps it should have been set up completely differently.

In historical perspective, however, certain facts pertaining to the country called "the Sudan" cannot be overlooked. First, for the last 150 years or so, without any significant interruption, the Sudan has been governed by one central government, more or less with the boundaries that exist today. Second, this government was located in the North, and it was Northern on two counts: the "Turk" or Egyptians, and then the British, came from the North. Third, within the Sudan, it was the North that provided the center of gravity. This is true for a succession of four administrations: the Turko-Egyptian occupation (1821–1881), the Mahdist state (1881–1898), the Anglo-Egyptian Condominium (1899–1955), and the Sudanese administration, which was created before and after independence (January 1, 1956). Over the years, the Sudan has become an Arab-Muslim country that functions in two worlds—the predominant one is the Muslim and the Arab world, the subordinate one is the African world. The Sudan functions within the African circle, but has not been assimilated into it. The best illustration of this is a provision of the Sudanese Permanent Constitution, promulgated in May 1973. Article 1 of the constitution states: "The Democratic Republic of the Sudan is a unitary, democratic, socialist and sovereign republic, and is part of both the Arab and African entities."[6] It is as true to say that the Sudan is an African entity as it is right to argue that it is democratic and socialist. The same constitution contains a number of other elements that are more operational and more important. Thus, article 9 states explicitly, "The Islamic Law and custom shall be the main source of legislation," with the added lip service that "personal matters of non-Muslims shall be governed by their personal laws." Furthermore, article 10 states: "The Arabic language shall be the official language of the Democratic Republic of Sudan."[7]

Even though the Sudan is a heterogeneous society, with several centrifugal forces operating from within, the historical axis of unrest has been the North-South one. This axis is much more important in Sudanese affairs than the East-West axis, or any of the localized problems that have arisen in the West, in the East or in Kordofan. The historical development of the North-South problem has already been overresearched and documented and is not in need of further elaboration. We need only mention that the roots of the North-South trouble in the Sudan go back to the pressure toward the South of the Turko-Egyptian administration, which created a dual process of enslavement and Islamization-Arabization. The Mahdist raids into the South did not alleviate the pressure. Then, under the Condominium, the existing differences between North and South were accentuated by a deliberate British policy that aimed, until as late as 1947, to separate the South from the North and even to join the latter with one of the Sudan's African neighbors. Just before the Sudan was granted independence, the inherent differences and accumulated tensions between the North and the South exploded into open warfare. The North regarded the war as illegitimate violence. The South sought self-determination. Both parties drained one another's energies and resources until the Addis Ababa agreement was reached in 1972.

In the course of seventeen years of bloodshed, a number of solutions to the problems of this axis were proposed. One was total independence for the South. Even names for the independent state were invented or proposed—for example, Azania[8] or the Nile Republic. Another proposal for resolving the North-South conflict was to attach the South to one of its neighboring African countries. A third arrangement was federation with the North. A fourth was total integration, otherwise known as Sudanization,

---

[6]See C. Legum, ed., *Africa Contemporary Record (ACR)*, 1973–1974, pp. C107–120.

[7]Another interesting feature of the 1973 Permanent Constitution is its opening phrase—using the Islamic *basmala* formula. In the summer of 1984, when the Shari'a was being applied in the Sudan, Numayri ordered that a committee to review the constitution in order to introduce the changes necessitated by the Islamization process be set up.

[8]Azania is the name of an ancient East African kingdom.

which is a euphemism for Islamization and Arabization. In reality, however, it was a fifth idea that was actually experimented with: regional autonomy.

The Regional Autonomy Experiment

Autonomy has been experimented with in only three places in the Middle East. In one case it was the Kurds in Iraq, in another it was the Sudan, and in the third case it was the West Bank and Gaza, where autonomy is still very much a proposed arrangement rather than an implemented solution to a situation of national conflict. In the case of Iraq, there are no independent Kurdish states around the area where the Iraqi Kurds concentrate, but in the Palestinian and Sudanese cases there are several Arab and African states in the vicinity of the areas where the Palestinian and Negroid populations reside.

"Regional Self-Government," which was negotiated and agreed on in Addis Ababa in 1972, is the official name of the autonomy arrangement for the southern part of the Sudan.[9] The agreement provided the three provinces of the South (Bahr al-Ghazal, Equatoria, and the Upper Nile) with self-governing authorities and self-governing institutions. It also arranged for economic rehabilitation, the return of refugees, military incorporation of the Southern, or Anyanya, fighters into the regular Sudanese military, and so on. The Addis Ababa agreement was a major breakthrough when it was negotiated and signed.

Two important but contradictory facts must be noted with regard to this agreement. First, despite the skepticism expressed by many pundits in 1972, the agreement held. For a relatively long time it provided the basis for peace and quiet and, more important, for trust and cooperation between the government in the North and the South as well as among the various Southern groups. Second, and no less important, the beginnings of distrust and hostilities were the result of an accumulation of problems emanating from a gradual erosion of the very foundation of the Addis Ababa agreement. Some of these problems were inherent in the texture of ethnic divisions, political differences, and economic difficulties in the South. Others were an outcome of the Khartoum government's policy on a number of issues that related to the well-being of the South. The chronological watershed was around 1975–1976. The year 1976 is significant because during the July coup d'état the most dangerous coup the Numayri regime had faced until its overthrow in 1985, the radio station located in the South became the mouthpiece for the beleaguered Numayri government and helped it

---

[9] For the full English text of the agreement, see *Arab Report and Record* (ARR), March 1972, Supplement, pp. 161–168.

fend off the pressure of the insurgents. That year was the high point of cooperation between North and South. A year later the situation began to deteriorate.

What were the causes of the cooperation between Khartoum and the South? How was it undermined? Several factors supported the Addis Ababa arrangement and helped the parties to the agreement develop and maintain a measure of cooperation between them. Of great importance was the right atmosphere. By the early 1970s the North was weary from the constant bleeding of lives and resources caused by the protracted rebellion in the South. Moreover, the war in the South and its cumulative effects had a negative impact on the very stability of the central government in Khartoum manifested during General Ibrahim 'Abbud's reign (1958–1964). Numayri, who until the mid-1970s devoted a major effort to the consolidation of his power base in the North, realized that the price for compromise with the South was far lower than the damage caused by an ongoing war within the country. The South too was exhausted by the attrition caused by the war and the "scorched earth" tactics the Sudanese army used. No less exhausting were the hunger and malnutrition, the plagues, and other disasters that descended on the area.[10] The emergence in 1970–1971 of a strong military-political leadership in the South headed by Joseph Lagu was also significant, because for the first time there was a strong Southern partner to negotiate with the central government.

Shifting political alliances in the region were instrumental in reaching and maintaining an agreement between the North and the South. To begin with, Uganda stopped its support of the South in keeping with Idi Amin's change of heart and policy toward the end of 1971. Realizing that in retaliation for Amin's support of the Southern secessionists the Khartoum government might unleash Milton Obote's supporters who found refuge in the Sudan (after Amin toppled him in January 1971), Amin felt that it would be wiser to cut Uganda's help to the South. Amin's political rapprochement with the Arab world in general, and Libya in particular, also affected his decision to turn away from the Southern rebels' military organization, the Anyanya (who were then being helped by Israel). Primarily due to the Eritrean situation, but also in order to alleviate the heavy burden of Southern refugees who concentrated near the border with the Sudan, Ethiopia was also willing to stop its support of the Southerners. Once these two main bases were denied to the Anyanya, its ties with the outside world were severed, and its base of power had been weakened accordingly. On the other hand, a number of countries immediately rallied to support the

[10]Estimates of Southerners killed during the war vary from 500,000 to 1,000,000 or more. See R. Simon, "Yahasey Memshelet al-Sudan 'Im Hadarom Be'idan Ha'azmaut" (The relations between the government of Sudan and the South during the era of independence), *Hamizrah Hehadash* 27, no. 4–3 (1978): 225.

Khartoum government when the latter expressed willingness to negotiate an agreement, and they pledged the provisions of the means necessary to rehabilitate the South. Among these were, primarily, the United States, Saudi Arabia, the Persian Gulf countries, and the Vatican.

Other factors that contributed to the agreement were the severe fragmentation in the South, the competition between tribes and political groups, and the general backwardness of the South, pitted against the technological and military supremacy of the North. A less-tangible but significant factor was the mood of the African continent in the 1960s and 1970s. There was a great reluctance to endorse the redivision of countries in order to accommodate the mounting pressures of domestic forces unleashed by the processes of decolonization and independence (as the case of Biafra demonstrates). Finally, during the first years of their autonomy, the Southerners did not feel threatened by their cooperation with the North because Khartoum was concentrating on implementing socialism and secularism. In this context the good personal relationship between Numayri and the Southern leadership headed by Abel Alier and Joseph Lagu was a great help. Alier represented the "insiders"—Southerners who had collaborated with the central government during the war. Lagu represented the "outsiders"— those who had fought the government. Between them, however, they covered the majority of relevant Southern politicians. Numayri's positive relations with both these leaders gave him the leverage necessary to deescalate the tension in the South. Their divisiveness[11] also guaranteed that the South would not unite to become a threatening challenge.

Around the mid–1970s all this began to change. The change was brought about by a combination of factors having to do with domestic politics in both the North and the South, the economic hardship of the country, Khartoum's change of attitude toward the South, and the realignment of Sudan with Egypt, which was perceived as a traditional threat by the South. The signing of the Sudanese-Egyptian economic agreement at the beginning of 1974[12] and the decision by both countries to implement jointly the digging of the Jonglei Canal (designed to create large areas of arable land in the South), ignited old Southern suspicions. Anonymous publications circulated in the South declared that the North was about to embark yet again on a project whose hidden intention was to exploit the South. The reaction—a wave of violent demonstrations and disturbances in the South against the project—was fueled by rumors that the Khartoum government intended to settle 2.5 million Arabs from the North and from Egypt on lands reclaimed by the Jonglei project.

[11]For the conflict between these two camps and their impact on politics in the South, see Nelson Kasfir, "Southern Sudanese Politics since the Addis Ababa Agreement," *African Affairs* 76 (April 1977): 143–166.

[12]For the full text of the agreement, see *ACR*, pp. C87–90.

The joint military agreement signed by Sudan and Egypt in July 1976 following an abortive coup in the Sudan,[13] further aggravated the apprehensions of the South by enhancing the suspicion that the Sudanese-Egyptian ties would strengthen the Arab-Islamic nature of the North and weaken the political, economic, and religious status of the South. The process of "national reconciliation" (as it was referred to by the Sudanese government) between the Sudanese government and the National Front (or the traditionalist, Islamic-oriented opposition), which formally began in the autumn of 1977, added an extra dimension to the grievances of the South. The Muslim Brotherhood, who were co-opted by the government, soon assumed a political influence they had hitherto been lacking. By joining the ruling political establishment and working with Numayri instead of against him, they created a degree of dependence on his part. Before long, they began to demand greater Islamization in the country. In September 1977 a special committee headed by Hasan 'Abdallah al-Turabi, leader of the Muslim Brotherhood and well known for his antagonism toward the South, was set up. The committee was charged with examining the laws of the Sudan and revising them in conformity with the Shari'a law. The very chairmanship of al-Turabi and the charge of the commission marked the beginning of a major process of Islamization in the Sudan, which culminated in enforcement of the Shari'a in September 1983. This fueled suspicion in the South.[14] The simultaneous strengthening of Sudan's political ties with Egypt, manifested by Sudan's support of Anwar al-Sadat's trip to Jerusalem in November 1977 and by the Egyptian-Israeli peace process that ensued, was interpreted in the South as yet another indicator of new circumstances that the South perceived as movement away from the spirit that had produced the Addis Ababa agreement.

Other factors directly contributing to the problematic side of this ledger were inherent in the conditions that prevailed in the South. To begin with, the autonomy arrangement did not really eliminate the situations that had in the first place created and then nourished the North-South tension. It subdued the symptoms, but it did not eradicate the ailment. Nelson Kasfir, who studied the autonomy in practice in 1977, aptly said, "In the Sudan they came to recognize that civil wars, unlike Gordian knots, cannot be entirely resolved by a single dramatic gesture."[15] This became more and more obvious toward the late 1970s. The struggle in the South raged over the political control of the region and was aggravated by the rifts between the "insiders," led by Abel Alier and based primarily on the strong Dinka group of tribes, and the "outsiders," led by Joseph Lagu (of the Madi tribe).

---

[13]For the full text, see ARR, July 16–31, 1976, p. 472.

[14]See, e.g., an article by the Southern senior politician Bona Malwal, in Sudanow, October 1977.

[15]Kasfir, in ibid.

The central government, perhaps left without a choice, interfered in this power struggle in a tough and manipulative manner. The result was twofold. The political system in the entire South was adversely affected, and relations between the South and the North deteriorated. The contacts of the various political factions with Khartoum became exacerbated because they were so competitive, and the traditional economic backwardness of the South did not help. The response to Southern demands for resources for development was so much lower than expected that many Southerners took this to be a deliberate policy of discrimination by Khartoum. They refused to accept Khartoum's real economic shortages as mitigating circumstances.[16] A severe drought at the end of 1980 and a new wave of approximately 170,000 refugees from Uganda, in addition to the many Eritreans who were inundating the South,[17] added to the long list of grievances in the South. It was just a matter of time before a spark would set this situation aflame.

The spark was soon provided by Numayri's announcement at the end of 1980 of his decision to build a refinery in the North for oil, which had been discovered in the South a few months earlier. The Southerners reacted with unprecedented vehemence to what they perceived as yet another discriminating attempt to perpetuate the economic disparity between the two parts of the country. Khartoum's attempts, made at the same time, to alter the provincial demarcation lines in a manner detrimental to Southern interests[18] instigated a wave of protest against the government and President Numayri. He canceled the plan to change the provincial boundaries, but the damage had been done. The decision to transfer the oil from the South to the North, in particular, raised tempers in the South against the Khartoum government's robbing the region of "its oil."

The next controversy erupted around the question of the redivision of the Southern region into subregions, each having its own independent leadership. In 1979 Joseph Lagu, while in the leadership seat in the South, was opposed to Numayri's ideas for a redivision of the region. Early in 1980, however, he changed his mind after he was forced to resign from the presidency of the Southern Higher Executive Council (the regional government).[19] "Exiled" in Khartoum after his resignation, he came to realize in 1981 that only a redivision of the South would break the grip Alier's Dinka coalition had on Southern politics. Numayri, who in 1980 had introduced

---

[16]For a detailed review of North-South relations from 1976, see C. Legum, H. Shaked, and D. Dishon, eds., *Middle East Contemporary Survey (MECS)*, all volumes, chapters on Sudan, by Haim Shaked and Yehudit Ronen.

[17]According to the *International Herald Tribune*, April 5–6, 1980, the total number of refugees in the Sudan reached nearly 500,000 in 1980.

[18]See *MECS* 1980–1981, pp. 764–765.

[19]See ibid., 1979–1980, p. 730.

a decentralization plan into the North by redividing it into five subregions,[20] greeted Lagu's endorsement of the plan to redivide the South with enthusiasm, emphasizing its advantages for the administrative and economic systems in the South. Numayri's underlying motive was probably the age-old dictum of "divide and rule." This is precisely why the plan was greeted with great opposition by the South.

Southern politicians regarded the plan as a flagrant breach of the Addis Ababa agreement. The Khartoum government was not impressed, and it took a number of unilateral steps aimed at making progress with the redivision plan. These in turn brought about a strong reaction in the South and a resurrection of the insurrectional spirit that had been in abeyance since 1972. On June 5, 1983, Numayri formally announced the redivision of the Southern region into three subregions: Bahr al-Ghazal, Equatoria, and the Upper Nile. The maneuvering that preceded Numayri's decision, and its implementation, aggravated the disagreement between the Khartoum government and the Southern camp, which supported Abel Alier. It also deepened the tension between the latter and Lagu's camp. The deterioration in law and order in the South, including demonstrations and counterdemonstrations as well as street violence, compelled Numayri to take several strong steps. These included dissolution of the Southern Higher Executive Council, headed by Alier, and the appointment in October 1981 of a new regional government headed by Qismallah 'Abdallah Rasas. This appointment generated protest in the South, which claimed that it represented an unwarranted interference in the local affairs of the South and constituted yet another breach of the Addis Ababa agreement. When Numayri reshuffled the central government in Khartoum in November 1981, without including even one Southern minister in his new government, frustrations in the South reached a new high, and the political leadership in the South was increasingly motivated to act against Numayri.

The seriousness of the evolving crisis was evident when, in January 1982, Sudanese authorities revealed that an organization called the Council for the Unity of Southern Sudan (CUSS) had been formed. It was composed of the local Southern political elite and chaired by Clement Mboro, an elder Southern statesman. The Numayri government claimed that the CUSS received financial aid from abroad and was in collusion with the Organization for African Unity (OAU), the World Council of Churches, and heads of some neighboring states (alluding to Libya and perhaps also to Ethiopia). Numbering between twenty-one and thirty-one, the CUSS members were arrested at the end of December and the beginning of January 1982.

Numayri proceeded with his tough policy toward the South. In June 1982 he appointed a new Southern government, headed by Joseph James Tum-

---

[20]See ibid., pp. 726–728, and 1980–1981, pp. 766, 768–769.

bura, a supporter of the redivision plan. Abel Alier was deposed from the post of vice-president of the republic, and Joseph Lagu was appointed in his stead. The Charter of Integration, signed by the Sudan and Egypt in October 1982, again raised the temper of the South to a dangerous level. When Numayri visited Rumbek in Bahr al-Ghazal in December 1982, the accumulated tension erupted in the form of angry demonstrations directed against the president in person. A wave of arrests of senior Southern politicians followed on the heels of his visit, indicating that Numayri had taken the expressions of resentment seriously.

Before long it became clear that the Rumbek incident was only the tip of the iceberg. A wave of violent attacks throughout 1983 against "Northern" objectives in the South reflected the depth of the resentment that developed into open rebellion. On January 18, 1983, a railroad station in Bahr al-Ghazal was attacked, leaving eighteen dead and wounded. An organization that called itself Anyanya No. 2 and was equipped with sophisticated weapons and supported by the local population, took credit for the attack.

Arrests of senior Southern politicians, including a major figure, Bona Malwal, who had cooperated with the Khartoum government and was therefore considered an "insider," were symbolic of the deterioration of North-South trust and confidence. In the spring of 1983 a Southern military unit refused orders to move northward, probably fearing not only separation from families and the natural environment but also that they might be included in the units being dispatched by Numayri to the Iraqi front against Iran. The Southern soldiers deserted and escaped into the bush with their weapons. Before long, attacks were launched against Sudanese military targets, [21] under circumstances reminiscent of the civil war that had raged at the end of the 1960s. In mid-May 1983 the 105th Battalion of the First Division in the Southern Command, which was stationed in Bor, rose in rebellion against orders to transfer the battalion away from the Southern region. Several hundred civilian locals joined the rebels. In the end there were approximately one hundred dead on both sides, and about eight hundred rebels arrested.[22] These statistics, and the decision by Sudanese authorities to use Egyptian airplanes for bombing rebel strongholds, indicated that the situation was serious.

The political tremors in the South, and the renewal of the fighting against the North on a scale that was unprecedented since the Addis Ababa agreement, brought concern in Khartoum. Even without all the trouble in the South, Numayri's regime was under tremendous pressure, which threatened

[21]*Jerusalem Post*, April 5, 1983, a report from Juba; Gulf News Agency (Manama), April 7—DR, April 7, 1983; *Newsweek*, May 16, 1983; *New African*, June 1983.

[22]Sudanese News Agency (SUNA, Khartoum), May 19—Daily Report (DR), May 20, 1983. *Economist Intelligence Digest*, June 15, 1983; *May*, June 6, 1983 (an interview with Lagu); *Africa Confidential*, June 22, 1983.

to undermine its very existence. Numayri was forced to take action, and toward the middle of 1983 he embarked on new tactics. His first move, in May 1983, was the appointment of two senior Southern politicians, Abel Alier and Mary Basyuni, to the central government in Khartoum, hoping that they would help him implement the redivision of the South, which he formally announced a short while later.

But Numayri's announcement did not cause open turbulence, perhaps because of his clever tactics in appointing the chief opponents of redivision to key positions in the South. As soon as they were appointed, the new functionaries were integrated into the new administration. It may have been the instinct for political survival that allowed them to overcome their opposition to redivision of the South. Thus, in the Bahr al-Ghazal area, 100 percent of the members of the new government were former opponents, while in the Upper Nile government they constituted more than 70 percent. Clement Mboro, who had been chairman of the Council for the Unity of Southern Sudan was appointed Minister without Portfolio and charged with implementing decentralization in the South. This was a policy he had vehemently opposed at the time he went into exile in Kenya in protest. Mboro returned from his self-imposed exile at the beginning of 1984 and received his appointment in early 1984. This was the greatest irony of all.

The calm that followed Numayri's redivision of the South did not last long. When Numayri dramatically announced the decision to impose the law of Shari'a on the country in September 1983, the South could not but interpret this move as a flagrant violation of the Addis Ababa agreement, with far-reaching consequences. Khartoum's ambivalent reactions to expressions of Southern concern and anxiety further aggravated the situation. Throughout 1984, amid a growing number of rumors, there was some hard evidence indicating that the war in the South had been resumed.[23] It was not clear at that time whether the hostilities were of an order or magnitude that might engulf the whole region, as had been the case before 1972, but it was obvious that the incidents could no longer be dismissed as minor and unrelated. As the trickle of information about the situation in the South grew stronger and steadier, a new rebel organization came into being: the Sudanese People's Liberation Movement (SPLM) and its military wing, the Sudanese People's Liberation Army (SPLA). During 1984 the SPLM-SPLA became the major Southern entity to act against the Khartoum government. They raised the banner of toppling the Numayri regime rather than "merely" attaining independence for the South, as had been the case in the past. What is more, Libya and Ethiopia joined the melee and were supporting and equipping the opposition to Numayri. Egypt allied

---

[23] See *MECS*, 1983–1984.

itself with Khartoum, helping Numayri in his attempts to subdue the warfare.

By the beginning of 1985 it was clear that the war had been rekindled in the South. The potential for joint action between subversive elements internally and at least two neighboring states externally, Libya and Ethiopia (the latter contiguous with the most frustrated of the Southern Sudan areas, the Upper Nile), was reminiscent of the circumstances that had produced the previous war between the North and the South. Under the dominant leadership of Colonel John Garang, the SPLA intensified its fighting against the government army and its propaganda war against the Numayri regime, vowing to bring about the regime's downfall. Indeed, the war in the South acted as a catalyst in Numayri's overthrow on April 6, 1985.

The very short period of euphoria prevailing both in Khartoum and among the SPLM-SPLA in the immediate aftermath of Numayri's demise was not exploited by the SPLM-SPLA or by the new regime to bring about a breakthrough toward a settlement of their violent conflict. During the second half of 1985 the new government, led by General 'Abd al-Rahman Muhammad Hasan Siwar al-Dahab, made some conciliatory gestures to the SPLM-SPLA. Among them were the revoking of Numayri's 1983 division of the South into three regions and the validating of the articles of the 1972 Addis Ababa agreement "as a general framework for regional rule in the South."[24] The SPLM-SPLA, however, was not impressed. It continued to adhere to its categorical rejection of any contact with the new regime, which Garang referred to as "Numayri's May 11 regime."[25] The SPLM-SPLA reiterated its commitment to fight the new regime until the "reactionary structure" in Khartoum was "completely removed and the edifice of socialism [was] constructed on the ruins of the ancient regime."[26] The SPLM-SPLA's consistent rejection of Khartoum, and actual fighting against it, was made possible mainly by the consistent support of Ethiopia. Libya stopped its support of the SPLM-SPLA after its rapprochement with the new regime in Khartoum.

The war continued to escalate during the second half of 1985. The call of Khartoum's transitional government to Garang to open a dialogue went unheard because of the SPLA's preconditions: that there be reference to the "problem of Sudan" instead of "the so-called problem of southern Sudan"; that the state of emergency imposed in late September in Khartoum be lifted; that the Transitional Military Council (the governing body of Sudan after Numayri's overthrow) and the cabinet be dissolved; that the appli-

---

[24]SUNA, April 18—DR, April 19, 1985.

[25]R. SPLA, May 27—British Broadcasting Corporation, Summary of World Broadcasts (BBC), May 29, 1985.

[26]R. SPLA, April 11 and 19—monitored by the American Daily Report, Middle East and Africa (DR), April 19 and 22, 1985.

cation of the Shari'a law be canceled; and that "personal agreements with foreign countries" (apparently a reference to Egypt, but mainly to Libya) be abolished. Fierce fighting continued. Even after the formation in mid-May 1986 of an elected government in Khartoum, the SPLA continued to adhere to its declared preconditions, which Khartoum continued to reject. The latter did not make an attractive offer that might draw the SPLA to the negotiating table. The summer of 1986 witnessed more intense and bloody fighting between the SPLM-SPLA and the government troops. Neither side was able to win the war.

At the time of writing—the end of the summer of 1986—it is impossible to predict the precise direction for further developments in the South-North conflict. It is clear, however, that the autonomy formula of the 1972 Addis Ababa agreement had not fulfilled the expectations of either side. Therefore, any future arrangement between the central government and the South will encounter difficulties if there is an attempt to base it on the autonomy principle.

When it was devised, the formula was considered a breakthrough almost too good to be true. It aroused hopes for a new, constructive era of mutual trust and cooperation. Indeed, in its first years the autonomy arrangement worked in a relatively satisfactory manner. The impact of the long internecine war was fresh, and both parties needed time to heal their wounds and to recover. Consequently, they engaged in special efforts designed to make the autonomy formula work as smoothly as possible, and the prevailing sense of goodwill and optimism made up for the deficiencies. Khartoum's careful and sensitive handling of its relations with the South contributed to reduction of the tensions that had built up over the long years of warfare. As the years passed, however, the autonomy arrangement became routinized, and both sides devoted less attention to its consolidation. The initial euphoria was reduced by the harshness of day-to-day realities, and this led to the reawakening of many original causes of the North-South rift.

Domestic politics in the North and the South, severe economic problems, inefficiency and corruption, as well as conflicting personal ambitions—all continued to undermine the sensitive relationship between North and South. On balance it was the Numayri government that made the decisive contribution to the deterioration of North-South relations. With the passage of time the basis of the autonomy arrangement was undercut by Numayri's increasingly arbitrary and heavy-handed measures. The Numayri regime acted with considerable misjudgment and poor management. Numayri's systematic violation of the basic premises of the autonomy framework in religion, politics, and economics eventually reignited the North-South war. While Khartoum was unwilling to leave the South to its own destiny, it was not able to fulfill its basic promises to the South to provide its vital needs.

Most probably, the lesson is that—until the new outbreak of the war in 1983—deterioration of the North-South relationship was more a case of mismanagement than the result of an inevitable process. The more general conclusion may be that autonomy, when actually implemented, is very different from autonomy as a conceptual abstraction.

PART VII

CONCLUSION

16

Ethnic Politics:
How Unique Is the Middle East?

Milton J. Esman

I am the only contributor to this volume who is neither a specialist on the Middle East nor a resident of that region. My field is comparative politics. From a social science perspective, area specialists are vulnerable to an occupational hazard—the tendency to overestimate the distinctiveness, even the uniqueness, of the systems they describe and analyze. Their great strength is their knowledge in depth and in detail of the particular societies with which they work. Comparativists, on the other hand, tend to look for similarities across time, across cultures, and across world areas, to propose and to test general hypotheses about these apparent similarities, and to find explanations for the differences they observe. Their strengths are in the broad base of data they bring to their enterprises and their efforts to achieve general explanations. Their vulnerabilities are their tendency to generalize too hastily, and especially—as area specialists never tire of re-minding them—their limited knowledge of specific societies.

To complement the impressive array of Middle East specialization represented in this volume, my intent here is to present a comparative perspective, to compare ethnic politics in the Middle East with similar experiences in other world areas, and to arrive at some judgments about the relevance of the Middle East experience to some of the general ideas that have evolved in the study of ethnic politics in recent years.[1] In order to relieve the reader's suspense, let me at this point state my major conclusion: The manifestations and expressions of ethnic politics in the Middle East are in most respects similar to those that have been observed through-

[1]For a good summary of major concepts and propositions, see Joseph Rothschild, *Ethnopolitics: A Conceptual Framework* (New York: Columbia University Press, 1981).

out the Third World. The principal exception is the greater prominence and salience of the religious definition of communal solidarity in the Middle East. This can be traced to the Islamic and Ottoman legacies that defined communities and peoples primarily in religious terms. Despite secularization, religiously defined solidarities have not been depoliticized; instead, they have become important actors on the political scene. This accounts for the tight boundaries, the persistent distrust and the harsh, uncompromising expression of so much of the ethnic pluralism and conflict in the contemporary Middle East.

Territorial States and Third World Comparisons

The relevant point of departure for the analysis and appreciation of ethnic politics in the contemporary Middle East is the territorial state. The main political legacy of European colonialism and of Western intellectual hegemony has been the emergence of the territorial state as the universally recognized macro-political structure. This structure of political authority claims exclusive control (sovereignty) over the territory it occupies and the allegiance of all communities and people residing in that territory. Any competing loyalty is looked on as threatening, illegitimate, and likely to be temporary. The state is presumed to be the political expression of a single people acting in its name and on its behalf—hence the concept of the "nation-state."[2]

Where the state's territory contains ethnic minorities, it is considered to be the responsibility of the state's elites to reduce and if possible to eliminate such divisive and potentially dangerous pluralism, preferably by the process of "nation-building."[3] Nation-building is to be achieved by the transfer of allegiance from ethnic groups to the symbols and institutions of the state, or by encouraging assimilation of minorities into the dominant ethnic community, eventually achieving the union of nation and state. The majority of territorial states in the modern world have not achieved this degree of homogenization and have been forced to come to terms with the realities of social pluralism. Exacerbated by modernization and by the expanding activities of the state, this pluralism tends to become politicized. Yet the model of the nation-state continues to appeal to political elites, especially in Third World societies, as the goal toward which they should strive.

It is the Third World states, especially those of Asia and Africa, that

---

[2] See Elie Kedourie's chapter in this volume. See also Paul Brass, ed., *Ethnic Groups and the State* (New York: Barnes & Noble, 1985), and Donald Rothchild and Victor A. Olorunsola, *State vs. Ethnic Claims: African Policy Dilemmas* (Boulder, Col., Westview, 1983).

[3] Karl W. Deutsch and William Foltz, eds., *Nation Building* (New York: Atherton, 1966).

provide the proper basis for comparison with the Middle East.[4] Unlike European states, which have developed over many generations and even centuries, the Middle Eastern polities are, with few exceptions, recent creations dating from the withdrawal of European hegemony and colonial control. Neither the states of the Middle East nor their constituent ethnic communities have had time to absorb the shocks of modernization and the learning experiences needed to arrive at acceptable patterns of coexistence. Nor have these states accrued sufficient administrative resources or moral legitimacy to earn the willing compliance of minorities.

I am not suggesting that ethnic pluralism has disappeared in Western or in Eastern Europe. Indeed, it has enjoyed a considerable resurgence in recent years, and the reawakening of geographically concentrated homeland peoples—Basques, Croats, Scots, Flemings, Bretons—has been matched by the growing assertiveness of large communities of immigrant laborers who will have to be accommodated permanently in the countries of Western Europe.[5] My point is that these long-established political systems command moral and material resources and experience that give them considerable advantages in coping with ethnic pluralism—advantages that are not available in similar degree to most Third World states. Among these advantages have been the depoliticization of religion and the reduction in its salience as the basis for communal solidarity. For such reasons as these, the appropriate comparison for the Middle East is not the older states of Europe but the newer postcolonial political structures of Africa and Asia.

Despite the differences among them, the polities of the Third World share a number of properties that affect their ability to cope with ethnic politics. All of them are variable factors occurring with greater or lesser frequency and intensity in individual states. I shall set forth four of these factors that are common to Third World states, and after discussing each in general terms I shall suggest how they apply to the Middle East.

Proliferation of Ethnic Communities

The first of these factors is the proliferation of ethnic communities, ranging from two major groups in Sri Lanka, to nearby India, with its sharp Hindu-Muslim cleavage, complicated by the presence of thirteen major

[4]There is a large literature on ethnic pluralism in the Third World. One of the most useful works is by Crawford Young, *The Politics of Cultural Pluralism* (Madison: University of Wisconsin Press, 1976).

[5]On homeland peoples, see Milton J. Esman, ed., *Ethnic Conflict in the Western World* (Ithaca, N.Y.: Cornell University Press, 1977). On migrants, see Stephen Castles (with Heather Booth and Tina Wallace), *Here for Good: Western Europe's New Ethnic Minorities* (London: Pluto, 1984).

ethnic and linguistic nations, of which seven have populations of more than twenty million. African states are even more heterogeneous, along both religious and linguistic lines, ranging from Nigeria with its three highly mobilized major "tribes," one Muslim and two Christian, to Zaire with its dozen or more ethnic communities at various stages of political mobilization.

This demographic pluralism is partly the consequence of imperial politics, borders having been drawn to suit the convenience of colonial powers and to avoid conflict among them, with little or no regard for historic or demographic boundaries. These colonial boundaries have, however, enjoyed remarkable stability in the wake of political independence. The inheritors of the colonial states have shown little inclination to revise boundaries to make them more compatible with demographic realities. In their commitment to the territorial state and to the exigencies of nation-building, they have been supported by the prevailing international consensus concerning the inviolability of state borders and the fear of chaos if border changes should be considered legitimate. Except for the dismemberment of Pakistan in 1971 and the subsequent creation of the new ethnic state of Bangladesh, colonial boundaries have survived.

But even if boundaries had been redrawn in efforts better to equate nations and states, such are settlement patterns in most of the Third World that the outcome would have been myriads of mini-states or, more likely, new states with patterns of ethnic pluralism that differ little from those that exist today, except that a few of today's minorities might dominate the new states, and vice versa. The failure of the post–World War I efforts to create genuine nation-states in eastern Europe based on the doctrine of self-determination of peoples, and the irredentism and oppression of minorities that followed in its wake, suggests what would probably result from similar efforts in the postcolonial Third World.[6]

The states of the contemporary Middle East are pluralistic in various degrees, but no more so than the Burmas, Ethiopias, Zaires, and Malaysias of this world. Turkey, with one major minority, the Kurds ("Mountain Turks"), and Egypt, with one important religious minority, the Copts, are more homogenous ethnically than the Third World norm. At the other extreme is Lebanon, in whose small territory the state has disintegrated under the pressure of its Muslim-Christian cleavage, complicated by three antagonistic sects within each religious group, and combined with the invasion and occupation of parts of its territory by Palestinians after 1970 and the military interventions of neighboring Israel and Syria. All the states of the Middle East are pluralistic, but no more so than most Third World

[6]Alfred Cobban, *The Nation-State and National Self-Determination* (New York: Crowell, 1969).

countries. The tensions are not any more severe than in Uganda and Vietnam, where ethnic minorities have been summarily and brutally despoiled and expelled, or in Burundi and East Timor (now annexed to Indonesia), which have witnessed genocide on a terrifying scale, or in Burma and Ethiopia, where costly but indecisive ethnic insurrections have been waged for more than a generation. Few instances of ethnic conflict in the states of the Middle East cannot be matched by similar or more intense confrontations elsewhere in the Third World. In the degree of pluralism and in the scope and violence of its expression, there is nothing unique about the Middle East.

Modernization

The second factor common to Third World states is their rapid but uneven rate of economic development and modernization. Increasing literacy, the spread of mass communications, improved public health and life expectancy with rapid population growth and massive migration to cities, rising standards of consumption, especially in urban areas, the secularization of aspirations and life-styles—these trends are evidenced in varying degrees throughout the Third World. They are facilitated by the global spread of capitalist enterprise, foreign economic and military assistance, and the Western mass media. By most indicators of economic development and modernization, the Middle East is further along than most of Asia and all of Africa.[7] Much of the Middle East, which is geographically closer to Europe, was penetrated by Western education and commerce earlier and more intensively than other regions of the Third World. Since World War II, and especially since 1973, oil revenues have brought to much of the region fabulous wealth that has facilitated economic and social modernization. But once again one must generalize only cautiously. While the Fertile Crescent and urban Egypt experienced early Western penetration, while the Persian Gulf states and Libya have prospered from oil, other areas, such as Yemen and the Sudan, remain backward even by Third World standards.

At this point it might be useful to confront two propositions that occur prominently in the literature and to examine their validity in the light of Middle East experience. The first of these is the idea that modernization

[7]By the rough indicator of gross national product per capita, no Middle Eastern country is found among the thirty-four "lower income economies"—the poorest Third World countries. Among the thirty-seven "lower middle income" countries, there were only five from the Middle East (Sudan, the two Yemens, Egypt, and Turkey). All other Middle Eastern countries are found among the "upper middle income" and "high income oil exporters." Similar rankings are found in statistics on health, education, value added per worker, and so on. Middle Eastern economies are far above the norm for Third World countries (World Bank, *World Development Report, 1984* [London: Oxford University Press, 1984]).

attenuates ethnic pluralism and eventually eliminates ethnic conflict. According to the conventional wisdom of functionalist sociology, of classical liberalism, and of Marxism as well, modernization breaks down parochial solidarities, transfers allegiances to modern structures such as the nation-state or occupational classes, and eliminates the utility of traditional ties in the economic marketplace, where success depends on individual performance rather than on ascriptive membership. Nothing in the Middle East lends credence to this proposition. Instead, modernization and economic development appear to have enhanced ethnic solidarity and exacerbated ethnic conflict. Economic development has converted ethnic groups into competitors for economic resources and contestants for political advantage. As the role of government expands with modernization, ethnic structures become the most available instruments of collective mobilization. Through these structures, competitive claims for resource allocation can be promoted and communities can resist unwanted interference by the expanding agencies of the state, especially when it is controlled by ethnic competitors. In the Middle East, as elsewhere in the Third World, modernization has activated ethnic solidarity and infused it with fresh and vital functions.[8]

Nor does Middle East experience lend support to the Marxist expectation that class consciousness will supplant ethnic solidarity in the wake of modernization.[9] Every ethnic group is stratified to some degree by economic and social class. In the absence of ethnic pluralism, class factors can and do emerge as politically significant differentiators, but nowhere in the Middle East has class solidarity across communal boundaries been able to survive the brutal pressures of ethnic conflict. Theodor Hanf's account in this volume of the brave struggle of trade-unionists in Lebanon to protect their interethnic institutions in the vortex of ethnic civil war is the poignant tale of a local effort that was overwhelmed by forces beyond their control. People can compartmentalize ethnic and class loyalties, and both can coexist, but only under conditions of relative peace and order. When ethnic tensions threaten polarization and violence, class solidarities dissolve and yield to the exigencies of ethnic conflict. Nowhere in the Middle East, nor indeed in the Third World, have cross-ethnic class structures displaced ethnic solidarity when the two have come into conflict.

Limited Resources and Capabilities

The third factor common to Third World states is that they tend to claim vast powers in relation to the societies under their territorial jurisdiction,

[8]On this theme, see Robert Melson and Harold Wolpe, "Modernization and the Politics of Communalism," *American Political Science Review* 64 (December 1970): 1112–1130.

[9]On Marxist perspectives, see Walker Connor, *The National Question in Marxist-Leninist Theory and Strategy* (Princeton: Princeton University Press, 1984).

yet lack the skills and the resources to exercise many of those powers. Because of limited financial resources and feeble administrative and military capabilities, they are unable to penetrate their societies with the services they promise. Their writ cannot be routinely enforced beyond the large urban settlements, and their officials can often be suborned or ignored at the local level.

As postcolonial states improve their bureaucratic capabilities and accumulate financial resources, their policy and resource-allocating decisions become increasingly significant to constituent interest groups. Those that can be most readily mobilized for political combat are ethnic communities. Speaking in their name, political entrepreneurs battle to achieve "fair shares" for their communities under conditions in which political power, economic resources, and cultural privileges are unlikely to be distributed to the satisfaction of competing groups.[10] Members of the ethnic group or ethnic coalitions that control the state are, of course, likely to be at a great advantage. Others who feel victimized, deprived, or unable to aspire to fair shares demand territorial or cultural autonomy that governments are reluctant to concede. Governments are besieged by demands that exceed their capacity to manage at a time when their ability to deliver benefits and to enforce their will is severely limited. For such reasons, most Third World polities are considered "weak states."[11]

As elsewhere in the Third World, the contemporary states of the Middle East vary in their capacities to regulate and to serve the societies under their territorial jurisdiction. Yet despite some assertions in this volume, not all Middle Eastern states can correctly be designated as "weak," if by "weak" is meant limited capacity to govern and to exercise authority. Such governments as Turkey, Egypt, and Israel mobilize a substantial proportion of their gross domestic product through taxes and borrowing, provide a wide range of public services, protect their borders effectively, and have impressive capacity to extract compliance with their policies and regulations even from dissident ethnic communities. Compared with most of the states of Africa and Asia, their capacity to govern is quite convincing.

On the other hand, the majority of polities in the Middle East do suffer from the malintegration of state and society, and consequently from limited legitimacy among ethnic groups that are excluded from political power or consider themselves the victims of discriminatory treatment. This same sense of collective grievance impairs the legitimacy of the state in many of the plural societies of the Third World. It is particularly prominent in the Middle East, where politicians who control the state apparatus on behalf

---

[10]On ethnic conflict, see Donald Horowitz, *Ethnic Groups in Conflict* (Berkeley: University of California Press, 1985).

[11]This concept was originally popularized by Gunnar Myrdal in *Asian Drama: An Enquiry into the Poverty of Nations* (New York: Pantheon, 1968).

of their own ethnic community have demonstrated little skill and often less inclination to accommodate the interests of others. Outsiders who feel excluded, deprived, insecure, and aggrieved are often equally intransigent and unwilling to compromise, and so they deny these regimes the allegiance and the legitimacy that enable effective government. In the sense that large sections of their populations, often majorities, feel alienated from government on grounds of ethnic discrimination, some Middle Eastern states can be considered weak, even when, as in Syria and Iraq, the minority regimes have accumulated impressive coercive resources. In this sense, however, Middle Eastern regimes are no weaker than many Asian or African states that have experienced ethnic-based violence and even insurrections during the past decade because of serious cleavages between the state and important ethnic minorities.

A special set of problems has compromised and weakened several of the Arab states in the Middle East. In addition to the unresolved claims of internally based ethnic communities, these states have been forced to cope with important trans-state ideologies, especially pan-Arabism and more recently pan-Islamism. These movements challenge the legitimacy of the territorial state and drain away potential support even from members of the dominant Arab and Muslim majorities who might otherwise be expected to extend their loyalty to territorial states under their control.[12] These competing pressures on Arab states from above and from below weaken them in ways that are unique in the Third World. We shall return to this problem.

Susceptibility to External Influence

The fourth factor common to Third World states is that they tend to be exposed to many forms of external intervention. As a corollary to military weakness, economic dependency, and technological backwardness, they are forced to rely and even seek out economic investments, commercial penetration, and foreign assistance—technical, economic, military—on terms that are often in the long run disadvantageous and allow foreigners significant influence in shaping public policies. When threatened by unfriendly neighbors or by internal dissidents from regional or ethnic opposition

[12] Neither pan-Africanism, pan-Turanism, pan-Malayanism, or any other "pan" movement has represented such a challenge to the territorial state in other regions of the world. John Armstrong argues that Islam has never accepted territoriality as the basis for political authority. Because Islam originated in nomadic societies, extended kinship, not territoriality as among sedentary societies, constitutes the legitimate unit for governance. This has been expanded to include the entire nation of believers by the constitutive Islamic myth. See John A. Armstrong, *Nations before Nationalism* (Chapel Hill: University of North Carolina Press, 1982).

groups, Third World countries may call on friendly powers, including those outside their region, for assistance, especially if they can claim that their enemies are being sponsored or abetted by other outside powers. In this way the superpowers are invited to participate in local conflicts. Such participation inexorably entails some external influence in the internal affairs of indigenous governments. Some leaders of Third World countries develop considerable skill in managing their dependency in efforts to protect their autonomy while extracting maximum benefits from external intervention. Diversifying sources of assistance is one such strategy, but this only demonstrates dependency and exposure to outside pressures. The source of external intervention is usually other states, but it may come from transnational enterprises or political movements, international agencies, or diaspora organizations.[13]

External intervention has been a prominent feature of Middle Eastern politics during the past century and especially since World War II. The Arab-Israeli conflict, the global strategic importance of Middle Eastern oil, and competing Western and Soviet objectives have ensured that internal ethnic conflicts would draw the interest of outsiders by the latters' initiative or by the invitation of local parties. The Jewish community in the United States has contributed mightily to the support of Israel and to large-scale military, economic, and diplomatic support from the U.S. government. Some Arab states have responded by inviting military and diplomatic assistance from the Soviet Union. Others, fearful of the link between the Palestine Liberation Organization (PLO) and the Soviet Union, have sought military assistance from the United States and its European allies while buying protection from the threat of PLO terrorism and insurgency with lavish subsidies. The ethnic civil war in Lebanon, beginning with the PLO's occupation, led to significant military and political intervention by regional powers (Syria, Israel, Saudi Arabia) and by European states (France and Greece) as well as by the superpowers.

This is not the place to detail the incidence of external influences on Middle East politics except to note that it has been a prominent and persistent factor. With the possible exception of racial conflict in southern Africa, no ethnic conflicts have drawn such a plethora of external interventions across state boundaries as those in the Middle East. In this respect the Middle East may be distinctive. Ethnic conflicts elsewhere in the Third World are prone to draw some external interest, but seldom to the degree and with the intensity that the Middle East has witnessed since World War II.

[13]For an analysis and evaluation of the diaspora phenomenon, see Milton J. Esman, "Diasporas and International Relations," in *Modern Diasporas in International Politics*, ed. G. Sheffer (London: Croom-Helm, 1985).

Ethnic Strategies and Tactics

We turn now to a brief discusson of the goals and strategies of ethnic groups in the Middle East and to a more extended treatment of the conflict-management practices employed by regimes in the region. Ethnic groups in the Middle East tend to be internally divided along the dimensions of class, ideology, region, and extended kinship, like ethnic groups in other parts of the world. For example, from its beginning the Jewish community in Palestine was split between the religious and the secular, and among the latter between socialists, liberals, and extreme nationalists. Their common enemy, the Palestinians, have been similarly divided, and these divisions have led (as in Northern Lebanon in 1983) to bloody internecine warfare promoted in large measure by the sponsors of different factions among competing Arab states. Internal divisions influence both the goals and the tactics of ethnic communities. The stakes in these internal rivalries are the power to control the resources available to the ethnic group and the right of opposing claimants for leadership to represent the group in its intercourse with outsiders.

Generally, however, there are common patterns in the goals and tactics of ethnic groups.[14] Recent immigrants tend to demand equal inclusion in the polity and the economy and official recognition and respect for cultural differences. The Sephardim in Israel are an example. Geographically compact groups in their ancestral homelands, if they cannot aspire to control of the state, desire independence or at least some measure of officially recognized territorial autonomy within their homeland. Examples are the Kurds and the peoples of southern Sudan. This usually conjures up fear of secession among the state elites. Confessional or sectarian minorities desire cultural autonomy, including control of their own educational institutions and of tribunals that apply their own religiously sanctioned legal codes. Because of the heritage of the Ottoman *millet* system, which institutionalized this practice, the states of the Middle East have been more willing to concede such limited autonomy to sectarian groups than have regimes elsewhere in the Third World. Similar claims for autonomy outside the Middle East are often seen as unacceptable threats to the sovereignty of the state and, especially in the field of education, as impediments to the process of nation-building.

The tactics of struggle by ethnic communities in the Middle East are no different from those employed outside the region by similar groups seeking to impress their demands on the public agendas and to promote and protect

---

[14] For a brief outline of these patterns, see Milton J. Esman, "Two Dimensions of Ethnic Politics: Defense of Homelands, Immigrant Rights," *Ethnic and Racial Studies* (July 1985): 438–440.

their group interests. Where nonviolent political means are available— from quiet persuasion, to formal petitioning, to voting and lobbying—such methods are employed. Where these are unavailable or unavailing, mobilized ethnic groups may resort to civil obedience and violence ranging from terrorism to insurgency. As their aspirations grow and as these aspirations are frustrated, militant factions tend to gain ascendancy within the ethnic community and to use confrontational and violent tactics. Because opportunities to pursue their interests within the system are not available to opposition groups, including ethnic minorities in most of the Middle East, and because the sources of cleavages so often contain a religious element, the propensity for ethnic violence may be higher in the Middle East than elsewhere.

Conflict Regulation by Governments

One of the main functions of governments is to manage the disputes that occur among groups within their territorial jurisdiction and between such groups and the state. Conceptually there are two kinds of strategies that regimes can employ to regulate ethnic conflict. The first is to eliminate or reduce pluralism, the second is to legitimize and manage it. Most of the conflict-management practices used elsewhere in the Third World are evident also in the Middle East.[15]

Apart from genocide and from expelling unwanted minorities, the most common regime strategy for reducing pluralism is to encourage and reward acculturation and the eventual assimilation of individuals into the dominant community and thus to build a more homogeneous nation. I know of no recent instances of attempted genocide in the Middle East since the massacres of Armenians in Turkey during World War I. The events surrounding the flight of 75 percent of the Arabs who lived in areas controlled by Israel during its war of independence in 1948 remain in dispute. There is convincing evidence, however, that at least some of this flight was prompted by elements of the Israeli military. After the armistice only a handful were permitted to return. The independence of Israel triggered serious outbreaks against Jews in most Arab countries, which their governments made little effort to control. These were followed by mass migrations of Middle Eastern Jews to Israel. The virtual elimination of long-standing Jewish communities in most of the Arab world exacerbated, in turn, the ethnic pluralism within Jewish society in Israel.

[15]On the management of ethnic conflict, see Horowitz, *Ethnic Groups*, pp. 563–680. See also Milton J. Esman, "The Management of Communal Conflict," *Public Policy* 21 (Winter 1973): 49–78, and Eric Nordlinger, *Conflict Regulation in Divided Societies*, Occasional Papers No. 29 (Cambridge: Harvard University Center for International Affairs, 1972).

In the Middle East the policy of assimilation is actively pursued where religious differences do not constitute a barrier to crossing ethnic boundaries. The Turkish regime attempts to assimilate its large Kurdish minority by proscribing the expression of Kurdish nationalism and by rewarding, through co-optation and economic benefits, use of the Turkish language and participation of ethnic Kurds as individuals in Turkish cultural and political institutions. Morocco and Algeria attempt actively to Arabize their Berber majorities. The dominant Ashkenazim (Jews of European origin) in Israel have followed the policy of "absorbing" and assimilating more recent immigrants from the Middle East and North Africa, who now comprise the majority of Israelis, by actively promoting and rewarding modernization (Europeanization) and by discouraging ethnic political movements. The effects of these strategies of assimilation need not detain us here. What is significant is that in the Middle East assimilation is perceived by regimes to be a feasible strategy for dealing with ethnic pluralism only where religious boundaries present no barrier. Arab regimes can attempt to assimilate Berbers, but the Sunni government in Iraq cannot employ this strategy toward the Shi'ites, nor can Muslims in Egypt employ it toward the Coptic minority. Because of the prevalence of sectarian solidarities and boundaries, however, assimilationist strategies aimed at the gradual reduction and eventual elimination of pluralism are available in only a few situations in the Middle East.

The alternative to eliminating pluralism is to manage it. There are four methods of managing pluralism, only three of which are evident in the Middle East. By the first of these methods, the regime—which is not controlled by any of the ethnic communities within its boundaries—attempts to develop allegiance to the nonethnic symbols and institutions of the state and to reduce the political salience of ethnicity. In no polity in this region does the state enjoy sufficient autonomy from its ethnic communities that it can claim to be a neutral arbiter among them, building loyalty to political institutions that respect cultural pluralism while transcending particularistic solidarities. Ethnic solidarities are too prominent in the Middle East to permit this strategy of state-building.

Consociational politics—the practice of including component ethnic organizations within the structures of the state itself—have been attempted, notably in Lebanon.[16] There the National Pact of 1942 legitimated ethnic pluralism by including every sect within the legislative and executive institutions of the state according to a meticulously devised formula of proportional representation. Politics within consociational Lebanon involved a process of continuous diplomacy among the elites of the three major Chris-

[16]For an authoritative exposition of the consociational idea, see Arend Lijphart, *Democracy in Plural Societies: A Comparative Exploration* (New Haven: Yale University Press, 1977).

tian and the three major Muslim communities. Though biased to favor the Christians, and among the Christians the Maronites, though subjected to frequent strain, and despite its inability to build a strong state, Lebanon's consociational arrangements succeeded in governing this highly segmented polity and providing relative peace and prosperity for three decades until the system was overwhelmed by the invasion of the PLO after its expulsion from Jordan in 1971.

The concession of autonomy to ethnic minorities is another method of consensual conflict management. Territorial autonomy for geographically concentrated ethnic communities is a common practice in federal states, but there are no federal states in the Middle East. A federal-like arrangement was implemented in the Sudan in 1972, successfully terminating a bloody and destructive seventeen-year civil war in which the black-Christian communities in the peripheral south resisted the domination of the Arab-Muslim regime at the center of the polity in Khartoum. Regional autonomy for the south brought peace to the Sudan for more than a decade. The transformation of that country into an Islamic state, beginning in 1983, reignited the southern insurgency.

Religious and cultural autonomy is a long-standing practice in the Middle East based on the Qur'anic principle of protection for "peoples of the book" as implemented in the Ottoman institution of *millets*. This form of autonomy in matters relating to religious practice and personal status remains in effect in much of the Middle East. The autonomy proposed in the Camp David negotiations by former Prime Minister Menachem Begin for the Palestinians in the West Bank and Gaza is a contemporary expression of the *millet* idea—cultural autonomy without political power. In an era dominated by notions of ethnic nationalism, self-determination of peoples, and the illegitimacy of rule by foreigners, Begin's proposals are unacceptable even to the most compliant Palestinians. They regard it as a travesty of real autonomy, a method of domination by which the regime that controls the state apparatus attempts to purchase the compliance of a subordinate ethnic community at a very low price.

The principal process of conflict management in the Middle East, as elsewhere in the Third World, is the fourth method—coercive domination by the ethnic elites that control the apparatus of the territorial state. Where ethnic cleavages are looked on as permanent by all parties, there can be no expectation that they will be reduced through gradual acculturation and assimilation. Control of the state machinery is maintained by domination of its coercive instruments, including the military, the police, and the judiciary, from which subordinated groups are effectively excluded. Political power may be an end in itself, but it often guarantees members of the dominant group both cultural hegemony and economic privileges. The dominant group may be a majority—Jews over Arabs in Israel, Muslims over Copts in Egypt—or a minority. In Iraq the Sunni Arabs dominate the Shi'ite majority and the Kurds; in Syria the small, heretical Alawite sect has dominated the Sunni majority for more than a decade; in Jordan, Bedouins underpinning the Hashemite regime continue to rule over a Palestinian majority. Because of the authoritarian style of politics in the Middle East, dominant ethnic elites can be replaced only by violent revolution or by external intervention.[17]

There are several explanations for the determination of Middle East ethnic elites to maintain their dominance by permanently subordinating other groups instead of attempting to weaken them gradually through co-optation and absorbing them through assimilation. The dominant Alawite minority of 12 percent in Syria cannot hope to absorb the Sunni majority of 70 percent. The wealthy but numerically and politically weak Sunni Arab autocrats in the Persian Gulf states have no interest in according any permanent status to their numerous Asian immigrant guest workers and are even more fearful of resident Palestinians with their revolutionary ideology. The main reason, however, is the religious definition of so much of the pluralism and group solidarity in the Middle East. Internal social controls and mutual suspicion prevent any significant passing across sectarian boundaries. Despite rapid secularization, there is little evidence that group solidarities defined in religious terms are losing their salience for individuals so that religion might eventually be depoliticized. Religiously defined groups in the Middle East expect their boundaries to be respected and insist on exercising the internal autonomy to which they became accustomed during centuries of Ottoman rule. Dominant groups see no possibility that assimilationist policies could do more than inflame their religious minorities. Power-sharing is deemed to be antithetical to the constitutive basis of the state—for example, the concept of Israel as a Jewish state—or threatening to the continued hegemony of dominant groups, such as the Alawite minority in Syria and the Sunni minority in Iraq.

Ethnic conflict without a religious base can be bitter and bloody, an example in the Middle East being the long struggle between the Kurds and the Iraqi state. But religious solidarity among groups claiming exclusive access to ultimate truth, regarding outsiders as violators of God's will yet accustomed to a large measure of internal self-governance, guarantees the persistence and salience of pluralism. Very limited intergroup trust makes compromise an unacceptable style of negotiation for the spokesmen of either dominant or subordinate groups. Leaders inclined to compromise risk the loss of their mandate to more militant and intransigent competitors. Elites and their constituents prefer to enjoy full control of the state rather than

---

[17] Victory by Iran in the current war with Iraq would probably lead to the ascendancy of the Shi'a majority in Iraq.

entertain the risks of power-sharing or the implausible notion of assimilation. Thus the religious definition of much of the pluralism in the Middle East lends an especially intractable character and harsh tone to the expression of ethnic politics.

What Is Distinctive about the Middle East?

To a student of comparative ethnic politics, it is no surprise that the dimensions and expression of ethnic pluralism in the Middle East can be understood and analyzed within the same conceptual frameworks that have evolved from the recent experiences of other postcolonial states in Asia and Africa. The postcolonial territorial state, now the universal macro-structure for political authority, faces the problem of coming to terms with preexistent ethnic communities activated politically in the increasingly competitive environment of social and economic modernization. Modernization and the growing salience of the territorial state create the arenas and the conditions for the contemporary flourishing of ethnic politics. There is as much variability in the Middle East as in other world regions. Yet its geopolitical situation, its Islamic and Ottoman institutional heritage, and over a large area of the Middle East the presence of cultural, religious, and even national affinities that transcend state boundaries have exerted important common influences on ethnic politics in this region. These have, in turn, contributed distinctive elements, which I shall attempt to summarize and evaluate in this concluding section.

Limited Legitimacy of Regimes

The Arab states, except for Egypt, remain relatively weak. Like most Third World states these regimes must cope with considerable ethnic pluralism within their borders, and their legitimacy is often compromised by the hegemony of minorities (Alawites in Syria, Sunni in Iraq, Bedouin in Jordan). Added to these burdens has been the siren song of pan-Arabism that compromises the legitimacy of the territorial state in the name of a transcendent loyalty to the Arab nation. And as the promise of pan-Arabism fades, it is succeeded by the emotionally more powerful appeal of pan-Islamism and Islamic fundamentalism which the secular rulers of Arab states must attempt to appease. Thus the territorial basis of political authority is challenged by powerful transnational myths that, combined with internal pluralism and minority domination, undermine the legitimacy of territorial states and the capacity of Arab political elites to govern except through coercion.

External Intervention

In the ethnic politics of the Middle East there is a larger measure of external interference than in other Third World areas. During the final half-century of Ottoman rule, the European powers capitalized on sectarian rivalries to penetrate the region commercially and culturally. These patterns of intervention laid the basis for the latter-day colonialism that succeeded the Ottoman Empire after World War I; they also survived the formal demise of the colonial era. Zionist immigration, which precipitated the Arab-Israeli conflict, made the Jewish diaspora an active party in Middle Eastern politics. Combined with the importance of Middle Eastern oil, this conflict drew the attention of the global superpowers, whose interventions affected the course of local ethnic competition.

Meanwhile, regional states pursued their own interests independently and sometimes in tacit league with external powers. So salient is ethnic pluralism to the politics of most Middle Eastern states that foreign involvement, regardless of the motives of external actors, is perceived by the internal parties as a continuing reality providing opportunities to enhance their own interests. When the Soviets arm Syria to counter the pressure of U.S.-supported Israel, they are perforce strengthening the Alawite minority domination of that state and helping Syria to promote the interests of its Druze and Shi'ite allies in Lebanon against the Israeli-supported Maronites. When the French sell weapons to Iraq, they strengthen the minority Sunni regime at the expense of the Shi'ite majority and the Kurdish minority—the latter aided in minor ways by Israel. Though the external powers may sometimes be innocent of the effects of these interventions on internal ethnic conflict, the ethnic groups themselves are quite sophisticated on this subject.

The geopolitical importance of the Middle East and the Arab-Israel conflict have attracted the competitive interests of outside powers. The persistence and intensity of external intervention continues to affect the course and the outcomes of ethnic conflict in the Middle East far more than in other Third World regions.

The Salience of Religious Solidarities

The parties to conflict in the Middle East have shown little tendency to accommodate their differences. This, I believe, can be attributed to the religious definition of communal solidarity, which ensures that boundaries will be tight, compromise difficult to achieve, and accommodation unstable and short-lived. The heritage of centuries of experience with the Ottoman *millets* has endowed religious communities with a proto-national character that reenforces religious solidarity and undermines other claimants to political authority, especially the secular territorial state. Even within Jewish society in Israel, which is united by the Zionist appeal of territorial nationalism in a state beset by implacable external enemies, the cleavage between the orthodox and secular communities is a continuing source of severe tension. Religious communities in the Middle East offer their members not only a belief system but also codes of laws and institutions that regulate their lives, provide security, and alienate them from outsiders, even outsiders with whom they share the same language. Nationalism, the normal doctrine of the territorial state, has had only a limited capacity to transcend these more primordial solidarities. Political authority exercised by those who represent another religious community is ipso facto suspect and often illegitimate, even within societies that have experienced a high degree of secularization. Power-sharing with heretics or infidels can be considered only as a last resort. Assimilation may be a conceivable strategy only when differences are not defined in religious terms.

Religious solidarities impart a particularly rigid character to communal boundaries and are prone to delegitimize any political authority that can be suspected as the instrument of outsiders. The competition between Jewish and Palestinian nationalism for control of the same territory would be difficult enough to compromise, but when each party claims religious sanction for its demands, mutual accommodation becomes virtually impossible. As Rabinovich indicates in this volume, many have attempted it, but it has not yet been possible for Middle Eastern regimes to depoliticize religious definitions of group solidarity so that national loyalties could supplant them or coexist comfortably with them as the basis of common citizenship in a territorial state. The persistence of religiously defined boundaries and solidarities, though not unique to this region, is a more important source of conflict and a greater barrier to state-building than in any other region of the contemporary world.

This is the most conspicuous aspect of Middle Eastern ethnic pluralism that emerges from this volume. It reminds comparativists that while the intensity of ethnic conflicts depends on their concrete context, religiously defined solidarities, when politically mobilized, can produce rigid boundaries, persistent and bitter hostility, and maximal claims that are especially resistant to the normal arts of political diplomacy or to erosion by social change. They are more intractable than divisions based on language or common origin. The most distinctive contribution of the study of pluralism in the Middle East is the recognition that unless religiously based pluralism can be successfully depoliticized, it will continue to generate more intense, persistent, and violent conflict than pluralism based on other lines of cleavage.

Contributors

Gabriel Ben-Dor is Rector and a Professor of Political Science at Haifa University. He is the author of *Druses in Israel: A Political Study* and *State and Conflict in the Middle East*, among other works.

Milton J. Esman is Professor of Government at Cornell University and formerly Director of the Center for International Studies at the same university. He has written extensively on the politics of ethnic pluralism. His works include *Administration and Development in Malaysia: Institution Building and Reform in a Plural Society* and an edited volume entitled *Ethnic Conflict in the Western World*.

Kais Firro is a Lecturer in the Department of History of the Middle East at Haifa University. He specializes in the History and Politics of the Druze Community.

Aziz Haidar is on the faculty of Bir Zeit University and the Hebrew University of Jerusalem. He has been a Visiting Professor at the Center for Contemporary Arab Studies at Georgetown University.

Theodor Hanf is with the Arnold Bergsträsser Institut in Freiburg, West Germany. He is an authority on ethnopolitics with a particular emphasis on Lebanon and southern Africa. He is co-author of *South Africa: The Prospects of Peaceful Change*.

Hanna Herzog is a Senior Lecturer in the Department of Sociology and Anthropology at Tel Aviv University. She is the author of *Political Ethnicity: The Image and the Reality* and *Contest of Symbols: The Sociology of Election Campaigns through Israeli Ephemera*.

Farhad Kazemi is Professor of Politics at New York University and former Director of the Hagop Kevorkian Center for Near Eastern Studies.

Kemal Karpat is Professor of Ottoman History at the University of Wisconsin at Madison and author of *Ottoman Population, 1830–1914: Demographic and Social Characteristics* and *The Gecekondu: Rural Migration and Urbanization*.

Elie Kedourie is a Professor at the London School of Economics and Political Science. Among his books are *Nationalism*; *The Chatham House Version and Other Middle Eastern Studies*; and *Islam and the Modern World*.

Charles G. MacDonald is Professor and Chairman of the Department of International Relations at Florida International University. He is the author of *Iran, Saudi Arabia, and the Law of the Sea: Political Interaction and Legal Development in the Persian Gulf*.

David Menashri is a Research Fellow at the Dayan Center for Middle Eastern and African Studies at Tel Aviv University. He is the author of *Iran: The Islamic Revolution and Beyond* and *Iran in Revolution*.

Itamar Rabinovich is the Head of the Dayan Center and the Ettinger Professor of Contemporary Middle Eastern History at Tel Aviv University. His previous book, *The War for Lebanon*, was published by Cornell University Press.

Elie Rekhess is a Research Fellow at the Dayan Center for Middle Eastern and African Studies at Tel Aviv University. He is the author of numerous studies of the society and politics of the Palestinian Arabs.

Yehudith Ronen is a Researcher at the Dayan Center for Middle Eastern and African Studies at Tel Aviv University and a regular contributor to the Center's *Middle East Contemporary Survey*. She specializes in Libyan and Sudanese politics.

Haim Shaked is Professor in Middle Eastern History at Tel Aviv University and a Senior Research Fellow at the Dayan Center for Middle Eastern and African Studies at Tel Aviv University. He is author of *The Life of the Sudanese Mahdi* and co-editor of *From June to October* and *The Middle East and the United States*.

P. J. Vatikiotis is Professor of Arab Politics at the School of Oriental and African Studies at London University. His many books include *The Modern History of Egypt*; *Politics and the Military in Jordan: A Study of the Arab Legion, 1921–1957*; and *Arab and Regional Politics in the Middle East*.

Index

Library of Congress Cataloging-in-Publication Data

Ethnicity, pluralism, and the state in the Middle East.

"Published in cooperation with the Dayan Center
for Middle Eastern and African Studies, at Tel Aviv
University."
  Contributions from a conference held May 1984 at
Tel Aviv University.
  Includes bibliographies and index.
  1. Minorities—Middle East—Congresses. 2. Middle
East—Ethnic relations—Congresses. 3. Middle East—
Politics and government—Congresses. I. Esman,
Milton J. (Milton Jacob), 1918–   . II. Rabinovich,
Itamar, 1942–   . III. Merkaz Dayan le-ḥeker ha-Mizra
h ha-tikhon ve-Afri kah (Universiṭat Tel-Aviv)
DS62.4.E86   1988   305.8'00956   87-47866
ISBN 0-8014-2001-6
ISBN 0-8014-9502-4 (pbk.)